ONE-PARTY GOVERNMENT IN THE IVORY COAST

ONE-PARTY GOVERNMENT IN THE IVORY COAST

BY ARISTIDE R. ZOLBERG

REVISED EDITION

PRINCETON, NEW JERSEY
PRINCETON UNIVERSITY PRESS
1969

L.C. Card 63-12673

Printed in the United States of America
by Princeton University Press, Princeton, New Jersey

Revised Edition, 1969

First Princeton Paperback Printing, 1969

TO *Fred*

IN MEMORIAM

INTRODUCTION TO REVISED EDITION

✧ LIKE many others of my generation, I was initially drawn to the study of non-Western politics, and particularly to Africa, by a desire to participate in two processes of revolutionary change: The emancipation of nonwhite colonial peoples and the emancipation of the study of politics in American Universities. Africa was both a political cause and a social science laboratory. The cause of African freedom could be served by recording in an earnest and sympathetic manner the achievements of African nationalist movements; the laboratory enabled young scholars to experiment with new theories and new methods while minimizing the risk of interference from established academic authorities who were often indifferent to and almost always ignorant of political life in the Third World. The re-publication of this book provides an opportunity to reflect on the aftermath of both revolutions.

As the original introduction and concluding chapter to this study suggest, by the time I conducted field work in the Ivory Coast in 1959 it had become obvious that the achievement of freedom from colonial rule did not necessarily coincide with the establishment of political liberty. The most striking feature of Ivory Coast politics, as well as of West African politics more generally, was the emergence of authoritarian tendencies, especially in the form of a one-party state. This phenomenon captivated my attention and overshadowed what had originally been a more sociological interest in the relationships between society and politics during periods of rapid historical change. Many other observers shared a concern with the quality of political life in the new African states, and the ensuing debate over democracy and one-party systems dominated the activities of political scientists interested in Africa at the beginning of the 1960's.

That debate has since been superseded, but some of its implications remain interesting because they provide a link between the study of politics in Africa and the study of political modernization more generally. For many of us who identified with various shades of the liberal left in the United States, the deplorable authoritarian features of some African regimes were redeemed by their commitment to racial equality, populism, and economic justice. Some went so far as to argue that authoritarian rule was even necessary and hence justified in order to maintain freedom, to achieve equality, and to promote economic development. It did not matter if governments were not democratic, since democracy was inherent in the characteristics of mass parties and since the policies carried out by some regimes would have eventual democratic consequences.

The Ivory Coast occupied a special place in this debate. Since its spokesmen initially rejected independence and later eschewed Socialism, *Négritude*, Pan-Africanism, and Neutralism, they could not earn the label "democratic" on the basis of their policy orientation; furthermore, since the party had been dismantled after the period of militancy and later transformed into a political machine, it was no longer a "mass party," hence the regime could not be dubbed "democratic" on that ground. On the basis of this study, the Ivory Coast was eventually categorized by others as an important example of the "pragmatic" as against the "revolutionary" version of the one-party state in Africa. But this provided little comfort. To study the Ivory Coast entailed removing oneself from the mainstream of what had initially been most attractive about studying Africa; the student who did not denounce the regime even risked facing the uncomfortable silent charge of being a conservative-by-association. The only compensation was that to study the Ivory Coast helped overcome at an early time the temptations of romanticism which lay in wait for all of us who had participated vicariously in the African emancipation movement. In the light of later events, this was no mean advantage.

It was thus partly a concern with self-defense, but much more a general skepticism about the terms of the debate over the qualities of African one-party states, which led me to investigate both the terms of the debate and the data on which the debate was based. One step was to examine in detail the case of Mali, an almost unknown country whose regime had earned a reputation as perhaps the purest case of mass party democracy in West Africa.[1] This was followed by an attempt to clarify our general understanding of the culture, institutions, and processes of the "West African party-state" by comparing patterns of political life in the Ivory Coast, Mali, Ghana, Guinea, and Senegal from the perspective of the creation of political order.[2]

From this point of view, I suggested that variations in the content of explicit ideologies, as well as in the prominence of these ideologies in the system as a whole, were less significant than the similarities that could be detected in what might be called the "cost-benefit analysis" applied by African rulers to institution-building. This hypothesis led me to assert that as the result of systemic constraints on their choices, African rulers tended to behave more uniformly than they initially appeared to do and than they said they did in relation to political investment. Variations could be accounted for in

[1] The announcement that Mali had experienced a military coup, which reached me as this preface went to press, prompted a friend to ask whether the Ivory Coast would be next. I was reminded that another friend warned when I first went there in 1958 that a study of the Houphouet-Boigny regime was a bad investment of effort since that regime would obviously not last. Ten years later, in spite of the regime's survival, I would maintain that the likelihood of a successful coup is indeed the best bet one can make for any African country, including the Ivory Coast, for reasons which I hope this study and the others cited in notes 2 and 4 make clear. But while the making of social science books requires us to make some bets, it is not the same thing as bookmaking. We should be more concerned with studying the overall behavior of horses and jockeys and with the culture and structure of tracks than with merely predicting which horse will be first past the post.

[2] Published as *Creating Political Order: The Party-States of West Africa* (Chicago: Rand McNally & Co., 1966).

small part as a function of leadership style but much more significantly as a function of available economic and organizational resources. Thus, one country might invest more heavily in building up a state bureaucracy while another might invest preferentially in a party bureaucracy, depending on the particular circumstances which prevailed at the time these decisions had to be made; but they would differ more significantly in the extent of their total investment in both activities combined. Ultimately, it is the extent of the total investment that matters from the point of view of an understanding of this early stage of political modernization.

The approach leads to an alternative view of authority in the new African states: the major problem is not too much authority, but too little. Although there are some variations in the degree of political institutionalization achieved by African regimes, the total range of variation is narrow and this group of countries as a whole must be placed very low on a universal scale.

What are the consequences of this alternative vantage point for an evaluation of the quality of African regimes? An examination of evaluative terms such as "democracy" and "totalitarianism" in political science suggests that they refer implicitly to the evaluation of political structures and processes which have achieved a much higher level of institutionalization than is the case for the African group under consideration. In other words, African regimes are much more like one another than any of them is like the relatively modernized countries from which available qualitative labels derived their contemporary meaning.[3] If we wish to evaluate African and other Third World regimes from a normative point of view—as I believe Western intellectuals have an obligation to do—we must devise appropriate criteria and labels in order to avoid utter confusion. That is one of the tasks political philos-

[3] Samuel P. Huntington stresses a similar view in the opening paragraph of *Political Order in Changing Societies* (New Haven: Yale University Press, 1968), p. 1.

ophers must undertake if they wish their work to be relevant in the contemporary world.

Overshadowed by my discussion of the one-party state and by the title of this book is an attempt to approach the study of political modernization in a specific manner. In my first undertaking, I was interested in examining the consequences of modernizing stimuli of a certain type on a set of traditional societies with particular characteristics; in the identification of ensuing social relationships as patterns of cleavages which are likely to produce specific types of conflict; in the consequences of these "givens" upon the structure and outlook of an emerging political elite; in the organizations this elite might create; in the manner in which this elite would define and approach its major tasks; and finally, in the consequences of its actions upon the society as a whole. These interests would have been communicated more clearly if I had called the book *Integration and Conflict in a Modernizing Polity: A Study of the Ivory Coast.* Since I have had opportunities to discuss these interests further in other publications, I shall limit myself here to a brief discussion of the underlying approach.[4]

In the process of transforming the study of politics into a more scientific undertaking, there has been a recurrent tendency to abstract politics from its societal and historical context. The early literature dealing with political development often extrapolated from research monographs in which good insights were imbedded to generalizations formulated at a level from where the past, the present, and the future appear to be clearly visible. The study of how a specific traditional system was transformed into a relatively modern one in a particular place at a particular time was taken to be a para-

[4] For a more explicit discussion of these concerns in relation to Africa, see my two articles, "Patterns of National Integration," *The Journal of Modern African Studies*, v, No. 4 (1967), 449-67; and "The Structure of Political Conflict in the New States of Tropical Africa," *American Political Science Review*, LXII, No. 1 (March 1968), 70-87.

digm of how *the* traditional system is transformed into *the* modern system. Yet we know on the basis of common sense observation that political development, modernization, or nation-building can entail very different processes. There is a great contrast, for example, between a pattern in which national communities are being carved out of a more universal one based on religion, and the stratification system is characterized by a sharp distinction between urban elites and peasant masses; and another in which many small societies devoid of this sharp differentiation are being amalgamated into arbitrarily defined larger wholes under the leadership of a group of recently educated men drawn more or less evenly from the societies that constitute the country. There are equally great contrasts between the modernization of a society which numbers several hundred million human beings and one which numbers only a few million, or between efforts to modernize before and after the invention of transistor radios.

The analysis of nation-building in a particular setting therefore requires us to pay attention first to the available building materials, then to the characteristics of the architects, contractors, and crews, as well as to the blueprints they are utilizing. It then becomes possible to discuss what sort of obstacles they are likely to encounter in pursuing their goals and finally to evaluate the chances of completing their tasks. This approach seeks to attain a knowledge of political life which entails some intimacy of the kind we commonly call "understanding." It seeks to achieve this understanding by analyzing important variations in the patterns of social and political life which result from man's peculiar interaction with his environment through the medium of culture. One of its requirements is a willingness on the part of the inquirer to subject his theoretical concerns to frequent confrontations with political reality as concerned actors, *including himself*, experience it. This requirement is in no sense incompatible with the requirements which link political inquiry with other scientific undertakings; but it does subject the search for precision to the additional discipline of political relevance.

This approach to the study of political modernization has in recent years influenced the field of "comparative politics" more generally. But it is possible to detect some links between it and similar trends in other fields of political science. They point to the emergence of a new field which transcends the old distinctions between the study of American and foreign, developed and underdeveloped, democratic and authoritarian systems, as well as between the study of domestic and international politics. That field might be called "macro-analytical political sociology" if that term were not somewhat pompous. Its abbreviation into MAPS might be better because it inadvertently points both to its origins and to the particularly useful contributions its approach can make to the exploration of any political *terra incognita.*

ARISTIDE R. ZOLBERG

Chicago, 1968

ACKNOWLEDGMENTS

THIS study was first planned in 1957, shortly after the Ivory Coast obtained a limited measure of self-government as a member of the French Union. Most of the information reported and analyzed was gathered in 1959, when the country had rejected the opportunity of becoming fully independent and had chosen to be a member of the French Community. By the time writing was completed in mid-1962, the Republic of the Ivory Coast had become a sovereign state, one of many new nations in Africa. Because of rapid change, any attempt to record patterns of political development can be no more than tentative.

Although I have used both published and unpublished documents whenever available, the interpretation presented owes much to personal observation and interviews with politicians and officials, as well as to innumerable informal conversations with Ivoiriens. Throughout, the Ivory Coast Government showed a great deal of patience and understanding, putting at my disposal official archives and precious time. Without the cooperation and the hospitality of leaders and members of the *Parti Démocratique de Côte d'Ivoire* and the *Jeunesse R.D.A. de Côte d'Ivoire*, in Abidjan and in many parts of the hinterland, I could not have even begun to understand the politics of their country. I am grateful to all, but since all cannot be named here, I should like to acknowledge my indebtedness and gratitude to President Félix Houphouet-Boigny; M. Philippe Yacé, President of the National Assembly; M. Ernest Boka, President of the Supreme Court; Messrs. Coffi Gadeau, Auguste Denise, Mathieu Ekra, and Charles Donwahi, members of the Ivory Coast Government; Messrs. Jean-Baptiste Mockey, Amadou Bocoum, Usher Assouan, Camille Alliali, and Koreki Mian, Ambassadors of the Ivory Coast. The following officials and friends also deserve to be cited: Nanlo Bamba, Pierre Huberson,

Joseph Amichia, Joseph Coffie, Jerome Achy, Yapo Komet, Gon Coulibaly, Mamadou Coulibaly, Amon d'Aby, and Mrs. Marie Dosso. I am deeply grateful to Bernard Dadié, whose wisdom, warmth, and wit, contributed much more than what is contained here. Among Europeans working in the country at the time this study was conducted, I owe special thanks to Messrs. Toulouse, Tournier, Holas, Blanchard, Dorthan, and Clignet.

A number of scholars have bestowed their advice, encouragement, and criticism. At the very beginning, I was privileged to benefit from the generosity of Dr. Ruth Schachter, who pioneered in the field of the study of politics in French-speaking Africa. French social scientists who were kind enough to share their experience include Professor Georges Balandier and Messrs. Raulin, Tardits, Meyassoux, and Mercier, as well as Mrs. Chiva. Dr. Jean Rouch helped me face the *rite de passage* of African field work. I should like to thank also E. Milcent, Ph. Decraene, and A. Blanchet, whose long experience as reporters of French African politics was very helpful. During a short stay in England, I was privileged to discuss this study with two outstanding British scholars, Professor Kenneth Robinson and Mr. Thomas Hodgkin.

But for the inspiration, guidance, and encouragement of Professor David Apter, teacher and friend, this work would not have been undertaken or completed. It was a privilege to benefit from his scientific imagination and keen political sense during all stages of this study. In addition, I should like to thank also Professor L. Gray Cowan, who first launched me on the study of Africa, and Professor William O. Brown, who sustained my interest. I am grateful to the Ford Foundation, which made this study possible through an Area Training Fellowship from 1958 to 1960. During the following year, I benefited from contact with the members of the Committee for the Comparative Study of New Nations at the University of Chicago, as the holder of a fellowship sustained by the Carnegie Corporation. I should like to thank Professor E. Shils, Chairman, and the members of the Committee, for their kindness and stimulation. For the three excellent maps of the Ivory Coast I am indebted to the Cartographic Laboratory of the University of Wisconsin. Although these individuals and institutions made this study possible, they are by no means responsible for the facts and interpretations, the burden of which is my own.

Finally, I am happy to be able to thank three gracious and helpful ladies. Mrs. Doreen Herlihy and Mrs. Shirley Clarkson, at the University of Chicago, helped expedite this enterprise when speed was of the essence. My wife, Vera L. Zolberg, deserves a special tribute for the outstanding performance of a bewildering multiplicity of roles from beginning to end of my task.

Throughout this study I have translated all quotes from published and unpublished documents, as well as from interviews conducted in French. Whenever possible, appropriate references have been supplied for interview materials. At times, however, it was necessary to respect the anonymity of informants. In order to facilitate the task of later research, I have followed French practice whenever citing African tribes and names of places and of individuals.

CONTENTS

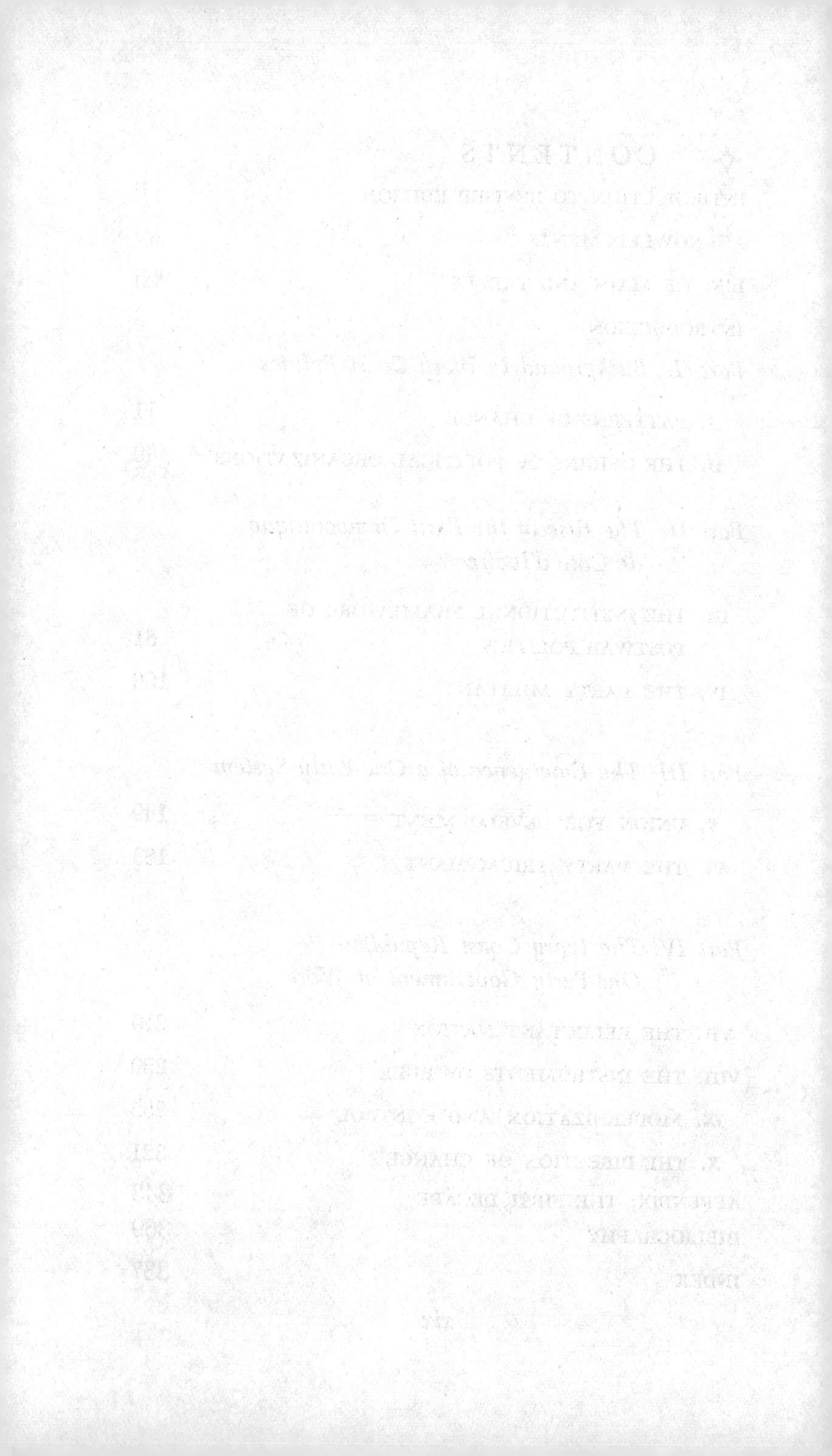

✧ MAPS AND TABLES

Maps

Tables

FIGURE

ONE-PARTY GOVERNMENT IN THE IVORY COAST

INTRODUCTION

POLITICAL life in the Ivory Coast has been centered in recent years around the activities of one man, Félix Houphouet-Boigny, and of one organization, the *Parti Démocratique de Côte d'Ivoire.* By 1957, three years before the country became independent, they had gained a virtual monopoly over access to public office at all levels. Having acquired power and authority, the new rulers of the Ivory Coast created instruments of government in their own image. They defined the rules of the game, recruited the players, and chose the goals to be pursued. The purpose of this study is to explore the origins of this regime, its present characteristics, and its possible future.

The Ivory Coast illustrates a commonly found, but hitherto relatively unexplored political phenomenon. As Professor Coleman has observed: "*Personalismo* (the tendency for political groups to be organized in support of particularly strong personal leaders) is common not only in Latin America, where it has flourished for generations, but also in many countries of Africa, the Near East and South and Southeast Asia. One-party systems tend to predominate, although there are important differences in this type. . . ."[1] The category that concerns us here includes many former African dependencies where one-party government is the legacy of the recent nationalist past. The P.D.C.I., like the Convention People's Party of Ghana, the *Parti Démocratique de Guinée*, and many others, developed as a comprehensive movement which transmuted discontent among many sectors of the African population into demands for greater participation in public life, and eventually for self-government.

Previous political studies have been concerned mainly with the origins of such movements and with the nationalist

[1] Gabriel A. Almond and James S. Coleman (eds.), *The Politics of the Developing Areas* (Princeton: Princeton University Press, 1960), p. 551.

phase proper.[2] The transformation of these movements into parties concerned mainly with the management of their country's government is so recent that the consequences of this major turning point are not well known. This study, therefore, is less concerned with the phenomenon of nationalism than with the period that follows logically and chronologically—the birth of a new nation, when the dominant organization becomes a political demiurge.

Because the traditions and structures derived from previous periods constitute the Ivory Coast's political inheritance, earlier phases of development are reviewed. Part One examines the origins of political organization to 1945. The development of the P.D.C.I. as an all-encompassing movement involved in agitational politics after World War II is discussed in Part Two. Although this is not primarily an institutional history, the framework provided by the changing colonial system conditioned political development and will be summarized at appropriate points in this study. Beginning in 1952, but especially from 1956 onward, reforms in this framework enabled Africans to participate more effectively in government. During this period of diarchy, analyzed in Part Three, the character of Ivory Coast politics underwent a major transformation. The P.D.C.I. became a political machine, similar in some respects to those with which students of American politics are familiar, and eliminated most other actors from the political stage. Part Four examines the organization at work in the Ivory Coast Republic from 1958 on.

[2] The outstanding general study of nationalism in the area is Thomas Hodgkin, *Nationalism in Colonial Africa* ("Man and Society Series"; London: Frederick Muller, Ltd., 1956). Valuable case studies on particular countries in West Africa are David Apter, *The Gold Coast in Transition* (Princeton: Princeton University Press, 1955), and James S. Coleman, *Nigeria: Background to Nationalism* (Los Angeles: University of California Press, 1958). There are few studies on French-speaking Africa, with the outstanding exception of the work by Ruth Schachter, "Political Parties in French West Africa" (unpublished Ph.D. dissertation, Oxford, 1958).

While no attempt is made to survey the many aspects of social, economic, and cultural change that have transformed Ivory Coast society in recent years, one consequence of these processes, which seems particularly relevant to political growth, the development of social cleavages, is examined in Chapter II.

The Ivory Coast derives no unity from its own traditions. Although the country is the confluence of four African civilizations, it is the center of gravity of none. Ethnic groups have greater cultural and social affinities with tribes living outside the country than with one another. One of the major tasks of political leaders has been to divert the traditional patterns of social communication, which created a centrifugal tendency, into a new pattern in which these groups interact with one another within the boundaries of a modern political community. Their task has been complicated by the consequences of the processes of change launched by Western impact. Although some of these changes have created conditions favorable to the development of a national society, not all have pointed in this direction. Many have reinforced old differentiations between tribes by adding to them new ones based on modern attributes, such as wealth and education. In short, "in a country where no natural factor was able to provide unity, the complexity of the human factor is extraordinary. It might be said, in addition, that throughout the centuries, men have used their ingenuity to multiply these divisions."[3] The result is that cleavages tend to be consistent.

The characteristics of cleavages found in a society have an important bearing on national integration. In a restatement of Simmel's theory of conflict, Lewis Coser has suggested: "The multiple group affiliations of individuals make for a multiplicity of conflicts criss-crossing society. Such segmental

[3] *Présentation de la Côte d'Ivoire* (Abidjan: Editions du Centre IFAN, 1953), p. 36.

participation . . . can result in a kind of balancing mechanism, preventing deep cleavages along one axis. The interdependence of conflicting groups and the multiplicity of noncumulative conflicts provide one, though not, of course, the only check against basic consensual breakdown in an open society." He goes on to state that "pluralistic societies . . . which are built on multiple group affiliations tend to be 'sewn together' by multiple and multiform conflicts between groups in which the members' personalities are involved only segmentally."[4] In societies of this type, conflict can be viewed as an index of the stability of relationships.[5] In other cases, affiliations are confined mostly within ethnic groups, or economic strata, or religious groups, and fail to bind these groups. There, "the lines of cleavage are already set."[6] Controversy rapidly turns into conflict; the latter may have adverse consequences for the society. Where this exists, in the words of James Coleman, "two consequences for community conflict are the greater difficulty of reaching consensus from such an extended spread of opinion, and the inability of opposing groups to 'understand' each other. Thus, there is a greater likelihood of imputing evil motives to the others, and directing antagonism against them." Furthermore, "in the community which does not create in its members the potential for cross-pressures, individuals are consistent; groups of friends are of one mind; and organizations are unified—all the conflict is shifted to the level of the community itself."[7]

The same variable is a determinant of the consequences of outside conflict for the group under consideration. Where the web of group affiliations has provided some cohesion in the community, outside conflict tends to heighten inner co-

[4] Lewis Coser, *The Functions of Social Conflict* (Glencoe: The Free Press, 1956), pp. 79-80.

[5] Georg Simmel, *Conflict*, trans. Kurt H. Wolff (Glencoe: The Free Press, 1955), pp. 46-47.

[6] James S. Coleman, *Community Conflict* (Glencoe: The Free Press, 1957), p. 22.

[7] *Ibid.*

hesion. Where it is lacking, as in the case of communities where cleavages are consistent, "disintegration of the group, rather than increase in cohesion, will be the result of outside conflict," although some unity may be despotically enforced.[8]

The pattern of cleavages has had different consequences for Ivory Coast politics during the various phases discussed in this study. On the whole, political activity has mirrored ethnic antagonisms that continue to prevail between groups. This fact makes the growth and the persistence of a single party the more remarkable, but it suggests also that this must have been achieved at the cost of very great effort. Most important, the experience of past conflict has led many Ivoiriens to seek unity at any price. P.D.C.I. leaders, as will be shown, have used it to justify their efforts to eliminate all political competition and the memory of the consequences of conflict has made many others tolerant of these efforts.

Students of contemporary politics have sometimes taken the number of parties in a political system as a sufficient clue to the understanding of the character of a polity. It has been suggested, for example, that "one might recognize in the opposition of the one party versus the two and multiparties the fundamental cleavage of our time: *dictatorship versus democracy*."[9] This view is anchored in a political theory which states that "the democratic method is that institutional arrangement for arriving at political decisions in which individuals acquire the power to decide by means of a competitive struggle for the people's vote."[10] From the point of view of this definition, it is clear that recent events in many newly sovereign states, including the Ivory Coast, indicate that the demise of colonial rule will not be followed

[8] Coser, pp. 92-95.

[9] Sigmund Neumann (ed.), *Modern Political Parties* (Chicago: The University of Chicago Press, 1956), p. 403.

[10] Joseph A. Schumpeter, *Capitalism, Socialism and Democracy* (3d ed.; New York: Harper and Brothers, 1950), p. 269.

by the birth of a democratic era. One-party systems are by definition beyond the pale of democracy.

From another point of view, however, the new regimes can be evaluated in the light of their consequences rather than according to their form. Non-totalitarian, monopolistic parties, based on mass popular support, concerned with modernization and with the dissemination of equality in their societies, ultimately may have democratic consequences. Indeed, almost all claim that they intend to use their control to promote the material and cultural transformations necessary to institutionalize democratic forms in the future. Maurice Duverger, viewing the People's Republican Party of Turkey in this light, asks: "Is it possible to generalize and to hold that the single party might . . . serve as a temporary guardian, making it possible for the fragile plant of democracy to grow in soil that is not prepared for its reception?"[11] In order to answer Duverger's question it is necessary to compare statements of intention with political accomplishment. Is the Ivory Coast a tutelary democracy?[12] During the brief period they have been in power, the leaders have made many decisions to implement their political preferences. They have also reacted to problems arising from the particular nature of Ivory Coast society. By analyzing some of these activities, we attempt to discern the direction of political evolution, agreeing with Duverger that "scientifically speaking, we can draw no conclusions from a single example that is still provisional. The question is however worth asking."[13]

[11] Maurice Duverger, *Political Parties* (New York: John Wiley and Sons, Inc., 1955), p. 280.

[12] For a discussion of this type, see Edward Shils, "Political Development in the New States," *Comparative Studies in History and Society*, II (1960), 389-93.

[13] Duverger, p. 280.

PART I

BACKGROUND TO IVORY COAST POLITICS

CHAPTER I

PATTERNS OF CHANGE

✧ ALTHOUGH the lack of unity in the Ivory Coast has long been apparent to many observers, it is necessary to organize empirical data that bear upon this generalization into a conceptual form useful for the present analysis. After a brief examination of the heterogeneity of traditional societies and a summary of the history of Western impact, the consequences of change upon the network of relationships will therefore be analyzed in terms of the types of social cleavages that characterized Ivory Coast society during its political formative years.

Traditional Societies

Located between the fifth and the tenth parallels north of the equator, the Ivory Coast is a square-shaped area with sides of 350 miles each, half the size of France and about equal to that of Italy. In 1960 its total population was estimated to be 3,200,000 and growing at an approximate rate of 2 per cent a year.

Ever since an early student of African languages reported that he found there at least 60 variations of the spoken word, this number has been used to denote the great variety of tribes in the country.[1] Prime Minister Denise stated during the debates on the constitution of 1959: "We are not a territory fortunate enough to have but a limited number of ethnic groups. . . . We have more than sixty-two tribes."[2] In an interview President Houphouet-Boigny himself suggested that before the French occupied the country, the Ivory Coast was nothing but an agglomerate of 60 disparate ethnic groups.

[1] Maurice Delafosse, *Vocabulaire comparatif de soixante langues ou dialectes parlés en Côte d'Ivoire* (Paris: Leroux, 1904). The word, "tribe," is used here to denote a group, not necessarily a political entity.

[2] Ivory Coast, "Avant-Projet Constitutionnel. Procès-Verbaux des Débats" (Abidjan, 1959), p. 23.

These many groups have been classified into four culture circles or civilizations, differentiated in terms of social structure, language, and economic activity. Physical environment adds to the contrast. Two of them are located in the southern part of the country, an area of tropical rain forest and coastal lagoons. The other two are in the north, a dramatically different physical setting of savanna and Sudanese grasslands.[3] Within each of the culture circles there are numerous differentiated groups and subgroups, as Table 1 indicates. These classifications are by no means the result of ethnographic imagination alone but correspond to widely shared perceptions among the population.

Southern Peoples

The southern part of the country is the meeting point of the Atlantic East circle, which extends to western Nigeria, and the Atlantic West circle, which reaches as far as Senegal. They are physically separated by the Bandama River and are sharply differentiated in terms of culture and social organization. Together, they make up approximately 60 per cent of the population.

The easterners are mostly Twi-speaking Akan who migrated to the Ivory Coast from the seventeenth century on from Ashanti and points north.[4] More important population movements occurred as the result of dissensions within the Ashanti Confederation after the death of Osei Tutu around 1750. At that time the contemporary Agni states were established and the Baoulé crossed the Comoe River into the region they

[3] The classification followed is the one contained in H. Baumann and D. Westermann, *Les peuples et les civilisations de l'Afrique*, trans. L. Homburger (Paris: Payot, 1957), pp. 340-424. A similar one is found in George Murdock, *Africa: Its People and Their Culture History* (New York: McGraw-Hill Book Company, Inc., 1959), pp. 64-88, 252-64.

[4] Gabriel Rougerie, *Les pays agni du Sud-Est de la Côte d'Ivoire forestière* ("Etudes Eburnéennes," VI; Abidjan: Centre IFAN, 1957), pp. 51-59.

Major Ethnic Groups in the Ivory Coast[a]

Ethnographic Circle	*Major Group*	*Ethnic Groups*	*Location*	*Percentage of Population*
Atlantic East (Twi)	Akan	Agni, Nzima, Ehotilé, Abouré, Abron	Abengourou, Bondoukou, Bassam, Aboisso	5.6
		Baoulé	Bouaké, Dimbokro	19.0
	Lagoon Cluster	Abidji, Adjukru, Ebrié Attié, Abbey, Alladian, Avikam	Aboisso, Abidjan, Bassam, Agboville	7.3
Atlantic West	Kru	Bété	Gagnoa, Daloa, Sassandra	9.3
		Kru, Dida, Guéré, Wobé, Godié, Neyho	Grand-Lahou, Man, Tabou, Sassandra	9.0
	Peripheral Mandé	Dan, Yacouba,	Man	5.7
		Gouro, Gagou	Bouaflé, Séguéla	5.5
Upper Niger	Mandé	Malinké, Bambara, Dioula, Mahou	Odiénné, Séguéla, Korhogo, Bondoukou	15.2
Volta	Sénoufo	Sénoufo, Minianka	Korhogo	13.1
	Lobi	Djimini, Tagouana, Lobi, Kulango	Katiola, Bondoukou	5.9
Others				6.8
Total				100.0

[a] Population figures are drawn from Ivory Coast, Ministère du Plan, *Inventaire économique de la Côte d'Ivoire 1947-1956* (Abidjan, 1958), p. 26.

now occupy.[5] Both the Baoulé, the largest ethnic group in the Ivory Coast, and the Agni are farmers and artisans who had mastered the arts of raffia weaving and gold and bronze working before European penetration. Their family structure is based on matrilineal descent. Their political organization is a centralized chiefdom system with a differentiated political structure. Political power is concentrated in a hereditary chiefly lineage, with a ranking of other lineages in order of precedence depending upon their relationship to the uppermost one. There are countervailing forces institutionalized within the system to which the rulers are somewhat accountable.[6] This pattern is better preserved among the Agni than among the Baoulé. Unlike the Ashanti, however, the Akan of the Ivory Coast were never unified into an empire.

Besides the Agni and the Baoulé, there are many smaller Akan groups living around the lagoon areas of the south who probably mingled with earlier inhabitants and who traditionally engaged in fishing rather than in farming. Their family structure is similar to that of the other Akan, but they appear to have little or no political organization above the village level.[7]

On the other side of the Bandama River dwell the members of the Kru family, who are thought to be the oldest inhabitants of the Ivory Coast. According to some anthropologists, they represent the original form of culture and social organization in the Guinea Coast forest, before the invasions of Sudanese from the north.[8] All the Kru are hunters and gatherers and rely on rice as a basic staple rather than on the banana and yam of their eastern neighbors. The subgroups include a

[5] Jacques Bertho, "La Légende de la reine qui sacrifie son fils unique," *Notes Africaines de l'IFAN*, XXXI (July 1946), 432.

[6] For a thorough analysis of the Akan political system, see Apter, pp. 99-118.

[7] Few of these groups have been studied. The Attié are discussed in M. J. Vincenti, *Coutumes attié* (Paris: Editions Larose, 1914), p. 26.

[8] B. Holas calls them "archaic forest cultures" in B. Holas, "Les peuplements de la Côte d'Ivoire," *Cahiers Charles de Foucauld*, VI (June 1954), 218.

variety of tribes that had almost no contact with one another in the past. Generally, they have a patrilineal family structure. A typical form of political organization, exemplified by the Bété, is a village gerontocracy based on segments within lineages.[9]

Northern Peoples

Above the seventh parallel, the forest gradually gives way to the park savanna which marks the beginning of the western Sudan, toward which the northern peoples of the Ivory Coast were traditionally oriented. The Upper Niger circle (also called the Mandé civilization), which includes northern Guinea and the entire contemporary state of Mali, named after the historical Mandingo Empire, is represented in the Ivory Coast by the Malinké, the Bambara, and the Dioula. The other northern circle contains the Voltaic peoples, whose Ivory Coast representatives include the Sénoufo, the Djimini, and the Tagouana.

The Sénoufo are the second largest ethnic group. They migrated to their present location in two major waves in the sixteenth and nineteenth centuries.[10] The later migration was probably the result of pressures exerted by the Malinké conqueror, Samory. These two waves have resulted in the superimposition among the Sénoufo of two types of cultural and social organization, a more archaic form, based on paternal lineage groups within the villages, and a more complex form, similar to that of the Mandé, based on widely disseminated clans. All are farmers who live in fairly large villages scattered throughout the plain, strikingly similar in appearance to the walled-in towns of Medieval Europe.

The Malinké are unique among the Ivory Coast peoples

[9] E. Dunglas, "Coutumes et moeurs des Bété," *Coutumiers juridiques de l'Afrique Occidentale Française* (Paris: Editions Larose, 1939), III, 361-454.

[10] B. Holas, *Les Sénoufo y compris les Minianka* ("Monographies Ethnologiques Africaines de l'Institut International Africain"; Paris: Presses Universitaires de France, 1957), p. 13.

in that they came under the influence of Islam at a fairly early date, thus making this religion a part of their tradition. Although they were originally farmers, many of them have specialized in trade and are known throughout the country as Dioulas, the word for trader in their own tongue. During the eighteenth century, they founded the city of Kong, which for many years was a major center of radiation for Islam. From Kong caravans traveled down to the coast through Bondoukou, another important Moslem center.[11] At the close of the nineteenth century, the Malinké were associated with Samory and temporarily established their dominance over many of the other peoples of the north, including some Sénoufo tribes. Today they continue to play an important role in the economic life of the country.

Traditional relationships and communications among the tribes of the Ivory Coast, before the country had contact with the West, ranged from hierarchical relationships between conquerors and conquered peoples, as between the Agni and the Ehotilé around Aboisso, to regular commercial exchange between the forest and the savanna regions.[12] Large states, such as the Hausa-Fulani emirates in northern Nigeria, or confederations, such as in Ghana, did not exist. In the final analysis, Africans in the Ivory Coast have not found within their past a source of myth for contemporary unity. Amon d'Aby, the country's historian, has written: "Before the arrival of the French, the country was parcelled into an infinite number of principalities, where anarchy, internecine wars, and human sacrifices reigned supreme, in almost every case. Sometimes, very rare businesslike relationships united

[11] Louis Tauxier, *Le noir du Soudan* (Paris: E. Larose, Libraire-Editeur, 1912), p. 393. For an interesting account of the city of Kong as viewed by a contemporary European observer, see in particular Book III, Chapter I, "Les Mandé-Dyoulas," pp. 379-401.

[12] The Sudanese regions provided gold and slaves, as well as cotton cloth, in exchange for salt and cola-nut, a stimulant, from the south. (Jean Tricart, "Les échanges entre la zone forestière de la Côte d'Ivoire et les savanes soudaniennes," *Cahiers d'Outre-Mer*, IX [July-September 1956], 209-38.)

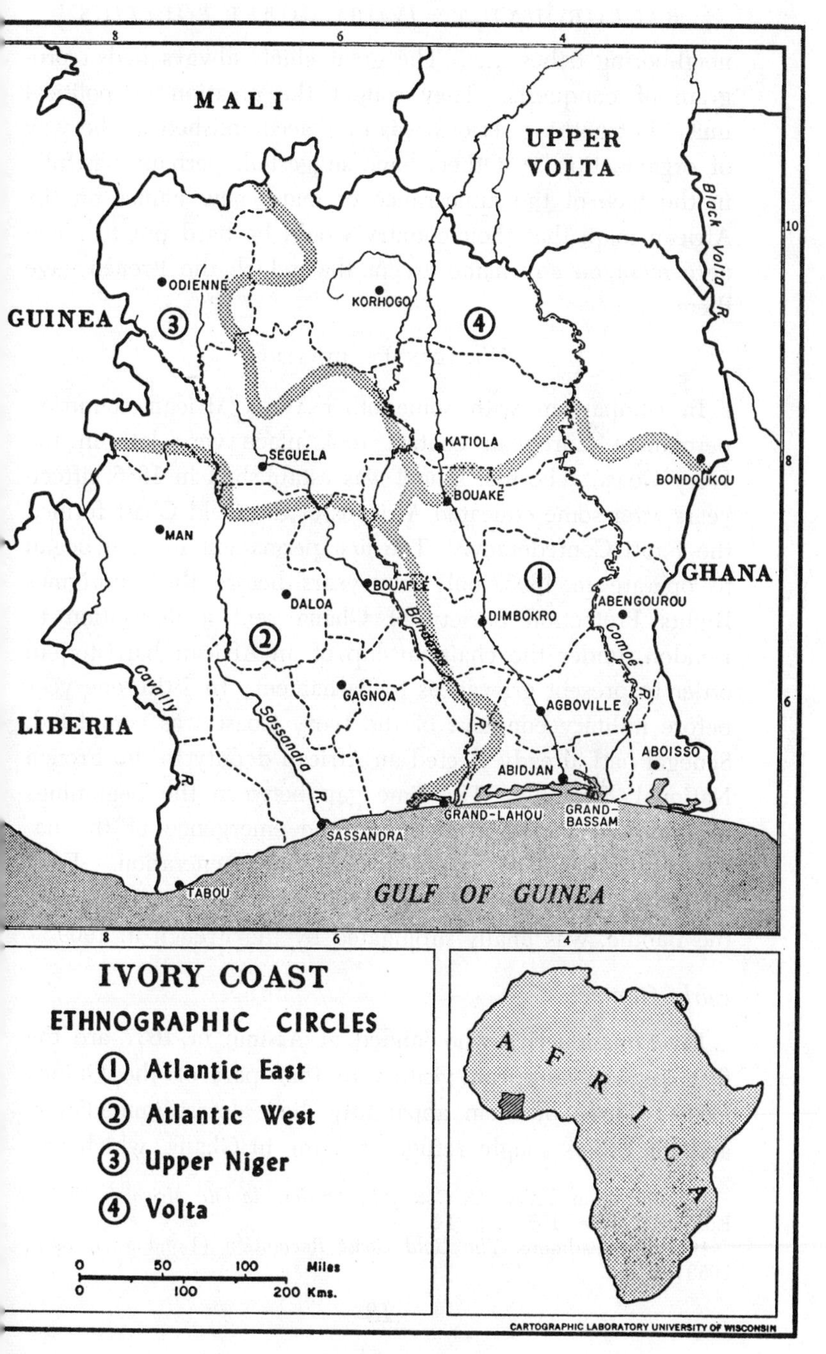
MALI
UPPER
VOLTA
GUINEA
GHANA
LIBERIA
Black Volta R.
ODIENNE
KORHOGO
KATIOLA
SEGUELA
BOUAKE
BONDOUKOU
MAN
BOUAFLE
DALOA
DIMBOKRO
ABENGOUROU
GAGNOA
AGBOVILLE
ABOISSO
ABIDJAN
GRAND-LAHOU
GRAND-BASSAM
SASSANDRA
TABOU
Cavally R.
Sassandra R.
Bandama R.
Comoe R.
GULF OF GUINEA
IVORY COAST
ETHNOGRAPHIC CIRCLES
① Atlantic East
② Atlantic West
③ Upper Niger
④ Volta
0 50 100 Miles
0 100 200 Kms.
AFRICA
CARTOGRAPHIC LABORATORY UNIVERSITY OF WISCONSIN

Map 1

neighboring tribes. . . . The great chiefs always had a program of conquests. They sought the creation of political unity, but nothing serious was ever accomplished in the way of organization."[13] Others have suggested, perhaps wistfully in the face of the appearance of many new names on the African map, that their country would be hard put to reach agreement on any name except that which the French gave them.

Western Penetration

In comparison with some other West African countries, permanent European contact took place very late in the Ivory Coast. The first school was established in 1886, fifteen years after some educated Africans of the Gold Coast formed the Fanti Confederacy.[14] The first permanent mission began to operate in 1895, only two years before the Aborigines Rights Protection Society of Ghana sent a delegation to London, under the chairmanship of an African barrister, in order to present grievances to Parliament. In 1916, one year before military conquest of the Ivory Coast was completed, Senegal had already elected an African deputy to the French National Assembly. The time gap between the beginnings of intensive Westernization and the emergence of the nationalist movement spanned but one generation. Félix Houphouet-Boigny was four years old when his own tribe, the Baoulé, was finally subjugated by the French in 1909.

Early Contact

Five missionaries who landed at Assinie in 1637 are the first known European visitcrs to that part of the Guinea Coast. Three of them apparently died almost immediately and the others sought refuge at Axim, in Ghana, which was

[13] F. J. Amon d'Aby, *La Côte d'Ivoire dans la cité africaine* (Paris: Editions Larose, 1951), p. 14.

[14] George Padmore, *The Gold Coast Revolution* (London: Dobson, 1953), p. 34.

then a Portuguese settlement.[15] No further attempts were made to evangelize the coast because of its oppressive climate, endemic fevers, and the dangers to navigation created by the powerful surf. To these factors, common to the entire Gulf of Guinea, may be added the bad reputation of the local region. For many years, the area was designated on maps as the "*Côte des Malgens.*" A new effort was launched at the end of the seventeenth century by Louis XIV, who organized a *Compagnie de Guinée* to establish a French sphere of influence to offset the British and the Dutch. Another French post established in Assinie in 1687 was destroyed by the Dutch the following year.[16] The search for empire began with renewed vigor under Louis-Philippe. In 1842 the Minister of the Navy gave an officer the task of exploring the coast and of establishing friendly relations with local rulers. These efforts, concentrated again on the eastern part of the coast, led to the negotiation of a series of treaties with African chiefs at Bassam, Assinie, and other places. According to these documents, the French undertook to protect the local populations against their enemies, to refrain from interfering with their sovereignty, and to pay an annual tribute to their rulers. The Africans agreed in return to transact business with the French alone, to afford them free navigation along inland waterways, and to grant them some land for the establishment of a fort.[17] Similar treaties were negotiated with western coastal tribes during the remainder of the nineteenth century, but nothing was done to occupy these regions.[18] Until 1900, "the Kings retained all their

[15] Paul Roussier, *L'établissement d'Issiny, 1687-1702* ("Publications du Comité d'Etudes Historiques et Scientifiques de l'Afrique Occidentale Française"; Paris: Librairie Larose, 1935), p. xxiii.

[16] Henry Mouezy, *Assinie et le royaume de Krinjabo* (Paris: Larose, 1954), p. 22.

[17] Amon d'Aby, *La Côte d'Ivoire . . .*, pp. 167-200, has the text of the treaties.

[18] *Ibid.*, p. 34.

prerogatives and continued in effect to rule their own country."[19]

The few trading posts created during the 1850's failed to prosper. All French establishments were abandoned once again at the time of the Franco-Prussian War. Afterwards, Arthur Verdier, a French businessman, was appointed Resident, with the assignment of checking the extension of British influence westward after the defeat of the Ashanti made this possible in 1874. He sponsored expeditions to the hinterland, especially among the Agni and the Abron peoples, in order to secure their allegiance before they pledged support to the British. Treaties were negotiated in 1887 and 1888 along the main eastern caravan route from the Coast to Bondoukou and Kong;[20] the western border between the Ivory Coast and Liberia was defined in 1892 through diplomatic negotiations. At about the same time, military expeditions were undertaken to check the expansion of Samory in the north. Although the French and the British came to an agreement over the Ivory Coast-Gold Coast border at the time of Samory's defeat in 1898, the definition was not complete. (In recent years some areas have been contested by the Ivory Coast and Ghana.) From 1893 on, the Ivory Coast was administered as an autonomous colony, with a governor accountable directly to the Minister of Colonies in Paris. Between 1895 and 1904, however, a series of French decrees resulted in its inclusion, along with other colonies, in a larger unit, French West Africa.

Military Pacification

At the beginning of the twentieth century, the interior of the country remained uncontrolled. Governor Gabriel Angoulvant wrote that when he began his tenure of office in 1908, there was little commerce and no security. Verdier had developed an experimental coffee plantation at Elima,

[19] *Ibid.*, p. 25.
[20] Mouezy, p. 150.

and there he also built the first school in 1886. Other attempts to diversify crops for export were not successful. Altogether, production amounted to only 29 tons of coffee in 1905 and 6 tons of cocoa in 1910.[21] The drop in the world market prices for palm oil discouraged many Africans from processing it for export. The governor therefore introduced coercive methods to induce Africans to engage in commercial agriculture.[22] Furthermore, he undertook military pacification often with the aid of coastal tribes, to overcome what he considered to be the mistaken policy of peaceful penetration followed by his predecessors.[23]

Since traditional rulers often led their peoples in the struggle against the French, a system of direct administration was imposed upon the newly conquered regions. During this period, which lasted until after World War I, "chiefs who had fomented revolt were deported; the natives were disarmed; others were interned; war fines were imposed on various tribes amounting to more than 700,000 francs between 1910 and 1912. In order to keep the natives under control the government regrouped native villages."[24] To facilitate administration, the government had unified its methods and instituted direct rule, even in the areas where protectorates had been negotiated during the nineteenth century. From 1900 on, the payment of tribute to African chiefs was eliminated. Instead, chiefs were granted a rebate on the taxes which they were ordered to collect from their tribesmen. This led to further revolts and to ever greater control. After 1910 new African auxiliaries were appointed on the basis of their loyalty to France rather than because of any traditional

[21] Amon d'Aby, *La Côte d'Ivoire . . .*, p. 76.

[22] Henri Labouret, *Paysans d'Afrique Occidentale* (Paris: Gallimard, 1941), p. 243.

[23] Gabriel Angoulvant, *Guide du commerce et de la colonisation à la Côte d'Ivoire* (Paris: Office Colonial, 1912), p. 23.

[24] Raymond L. Buell, *The Native Problem in Africa* (New York: The Macmillan Co., 1928), I, 918.

qualifications. The individuals appointed to rule over the *canton* (county) were interpreters, war veterans, or junior clerks, often not even members of the ethnic group which they were appointed to control; in some cases they were not even Ivoiriens, but Africans from more advanced colonies such as Senegal.[25]

By the time military pacification was completed in 1917, differences in the timing of contact had already begun to take effect. Some Ivoiriens were already attending a secondary school in Dakar at a time when others were still engaged in a last-ditch defense against foreign domination. The peoples of the southeast had already begun to gain access to positions in the European-imposed bureaucratic structures. The method of Western contact had also left important traces. Although the French unilaterally terminated all treaties, they continued to consider those tribes which had welcomed French penetration as being naturally more civilized than those which had not. The stereotypes that Europeans developed during this period were used to guide the training of the African population for various tasks, a practice which has resulted in widely different degrees of Westernization.[26]

Intensive Colonization

France has neglected her colonies. This was the theme in the years following World War I. If these colonies were properly developed, the Minister of Colonies wrote, there would be less need to depend on foreign countries for raw materials and a new market would be created for French goods. The franc would be steady. At the same time, French

[25] Georges Hardy, *Histoire sociale de la colonisation française* (Paris: Larose, 1953), p. 179.

[26] Stereotypes are found in such works of semi-official character as: Roger Villamur et Leon Richard, *Notre colonie de Côte d'Ivoire* (Paris: A. Challamel, 1903); Gaston Joseph, *La Côte d'Ivoire: Le pays, les habitants* (Paris: Larose, 1917); and even have persisted to the present, as shown in *Afrique Occidentale Française* (Paris: Encylopédie Coloniale et Maritime, 1949), II, 8-9.

civilization would be brought to the natives. The moral force of this civilization, dispensed through education, would have more authority in the long run than military force. Therefore, a serious effort should be undertaken to educate Africans and to transform them into the auxiliaries of colonization. The educational system, he continued, should be adapted to local needs; it should have a practical bent to compensate for the lack of Europeans in supervisory positions, without creating, however, a stratum of dissatisfied native literati. Furthermore, he stated, native civil servants and employees would be less costly than Frenchmen.[27]

These thoughts guided policies in the Ivory Coast during the next two decades and the implementation of various programs brought about rapid change in all sectors of society. Moreover, the Ivory Coast became more closely attuned to the evolution of French politics in the metropole. The alternation of a liberal period, such as the Popular Front, and a period of reaction, such as existed under the Vichy government, as well as specific administrative and economic features of the colonial system provided the sources of grievances that gave direct impetus to the organization of African protest groups and defense associations, themselves the building blocks of postwar political organizations.

Patterns of Change

Economics

Until about 1925, the Ivory Coast's main contributions to the French economy continued to be timber and palm oil. But as the result of Governor Angoulvant's efforts, cocoa soon was added to this list. European *colons*, who had been encouraged to settle after World War I,[28] and Africans, especially those living in the southeast, produced about

[27] Albert Sarraut, *La mise en valeur des colonies françaises* (Paris: Payot et Cie., 1923).

[28] The *colons* will be discussed in the following chapter in relation to African grievances.

1,000 tons of this commodity in 1920. During the next decade, as Table 2 indicates, production of cocoa was much more substantial. By 1930, however, the Ivory Coast and other colonies produced more cocoa than France could absorb.

TABLE 2

Exports of Major Commodities
(in metric tons)[a]

Commodity	*1928*	*1938*	*1948*	*1958*
Coffee	248	14,076	55,391	113,500
Cocoa	14,493	52,714	41,220	46,300
Timber	([b])	42,887	73,101	415,600
Bananas	1	12,271	13,447	46,000

[a] Figures for 1928 and for 1938 are from: Ivory Coast, *Service de l'Agriculture, Rapport Annuel: Année 1938*, pp. 14-20. Data for 1948: Ivory Coast, Ministère du Plan, *Inventaire* . . ., pp. 34-90. For 1958: Ivory Coast, Ministère du Plan, *Supplément trimestriel au bulletin mensuel de statistique* (ler trimestre, 1959), p. 24.

[b] Quantity unknown.

On the other hand, because France imported most of its coffee from other monetary zones, coffee growing was encouraged by means of premiums and preferential prices.[29] At the close of World War II, it had bypassed cocoa and has continued to expand greatly.

The further growth of commercial agriculture after World War II was reflected in the increase of the total area of land devoted to this purpose from 337,000 hectares in 1950 to 588,700 in 1956.[30] During the same period, European production of coffee and cocoa decreased from 11 and 12 per cent of the total to 3 and 2 per cent respectively.[31] This was therefore essentially an African phenomenon, the result of the entrance of many new farmers into the commercial circuit rather than of the expansion of existing holdings. There were

[29] Ivory Coast, *Programme d'action économique et sociale* (Abidjan: Imprimerie du Gouvernement, 1933), pp. 25, 30-31.

[30] Ivory Coast, Ministère du Plan, *Inventaire* . . ., pp. 35-37.

[31] *Ibid.*

about 40,000 cocoa and coffee farms in 1944, 120,000 in 1956, and an estimated 200,000 in 1959.[32] Before the war, most of them had been concentrated in the southeast, but in recent decades, as Table 3 shows, commercial agriculture has spread throughout the southern half of the country and penetrated even into the marginally suited districts of the center. By 1957, each of the three geographical areas produced approximately one-third of the total.

TABLE 3

Decentralization of Cocoa and Coffee Production

Region	1942[a]		1951[a]		1957[b]	
	Tons	*Per Cent*	*Tons*	*Per Cent*	*Tons*	*Per Cent*
Southwest	21,920	25	30,610	27	43,825	35
Center	19,600	22	42,500	36	38,709	31
Southeast	46,100	53	43,500	37	41,749	34
Total	87,620	100	116,610	100	124,283	100

[a] Computed from data obtained from: Ivory Coast, *Rapport présenté à la session budgétaire de l'Assemblée Territoriale* (Abidjan: Imprimerie du Gouvernement, 1952), pp. 22, 31, 32. The 1942 figure for the southwest includes a large proportion of European production.

[b] Data obtained from: Ivory Coast, *Rapport sur l'activité générale pour l'année 1957* (Abidjan: Imprimerie du Gouvernement, 1958), p. 273. These figures include African production only. The total differs from exports for that year because of unsold stocks.

This growth was accompanied by the development of transportation, communications, and electrical energy. Between 1947 and 1956, the total network of roads increased by 54 per cent; the number of vehicles in circulation grew from 2,097 to 19,064; and the consumption of electrical energy rose from 1.7 million kilowatt-hours to 19.9 million.[33] But

[32] The figure for 1956 was issued by the government and reported in Agence France-Presse, *Bulletin quotidien d'information*, January 7, 1956. Estimates for 1944 and for 1959 were obtained from officials of the Chamber of Agriculture of the Ivory Coast.

[33] Ivory Coast, Ministère du Plan, *Inventaire* . . ., pp. 68, 147, 155.

the Ivory Coast was still essentially an agricultural country. Industries remained rare and were entirely in the hands of European concerns.[34] In 1959 there were only 85,000 non-agricultural wage earners, of whom 25,000 were employed by various government agencies. Of those in the private sector of the economy, the bulk were in commerce or in transportation, activities related to the import and export of commodities.[35] However, these figures do not show that a large number of Africans were involved in trading. The dividing line between farming and trading is an easy one to cross; during a good year, a successful farmer may buy a truck and become a businessman; during a bad year, he may return to his farm when he loses his truck by defaulting on time-payments.[36]

Commercial agriculture fostered the growth of a stratum of Africans who shared similar concerns and who were affected in the same way by colonial policies, competition with European *colons*, and cyclical fluctuations in the world market for primary commodities. Commercial communications among them channeled a greater awareness of their common situation and fostered the organization of economic defense associations among cocoa and coffee growers. This was the beginning of African political participation in the Ivory Coast.

It is more difficult to determine to what extent agricultural change has resulted in a new pattern of social stratification. It is sometimes suggested, in order to explain the relatively conservative politics of the Ivory Coast regime in recent years, that the P.D.C.I. based its strength on a sort of planter *bourgeoisie*, and that this new class now dominates Ivory Coast

[34] André Hauser, "Les industries de transformation de la Côte d'Ivoire," *Etudes Eburnéennes*, IV (1955), 108-13.

[35] M. Leblan, "Les salaires dans l'industrie, le commerce, et les services en 1957," Ivory Coast, Service de la Statistique, *Supplément Trimestriel*, I (ler trimestre, 1959), 57-83.

[36] The consequences of increasing African sensitivity to the fluctuations of the world market as the result of commercial agriculture will be discussed later on.

society. Many of the founders of the party, including Houphouet-Boigny and Auguste Denise, do control sizable landholdings. Nevertheless, it seems an exaggeration to speak of a landed class in the Ivory Coast. For the country as a whole, it has been estimated that of those who exploit commercial farms, 74 per cent have less than 5 hectares; only 10 per cent have over 10.[37] In the southeast, farms tend to be larger, and farmers tend to hire more manpower outside their own family than in the southwest and the center.[38] But within any given region, age is the most important determinant of the size of an agricultural holding. This can be explained by the inheritance system, which works in chain-letter fashion, with an accumulation in the hands of the oldest survivor in a given lineage and a further redistribution after his own death. There is no evidence of intergenerational transmission of concentrated landholdings, except in a few rare cases where the land has been registered under the French civil-code system.[39] Furthermore, there is no agricultural proletariat to speak of in the Ivory Coast proper. In Bongouanou, for example, 35 per cent of the farmers had hired help; of a total of 100 workers, only 18 were from the Ivory Coast; the remainder came from neighboring territories, especially from Upper Volta.[40] Finally, since land continues to be held mostly by extended families, wage earners outside agriculture are not cut off from revenue from the land.

The most significant economic differentiation is the one which has developed between regions. The south is much

[37] Agence France-Presse, *Bulletin quotidien d'information*, January 4, 1956, p. 1. Detailed studies of particular regions have shown a range of 60 to 70 per cent in the less-than-5 ha. category, and of 6 to 12 per cent above 10 ha. Ivory Coast, *Enquête agricole à Bongouanou* (Abidjan-Imprimerie du Gouvernement, 1956), p. 51.

[38] André Kobben, "Le Planteur Noir," *Etudes Eburnéennes*, v (1956), 59.

[39] Ivory Coast, *Enquête Bongouanou*, pp. 51, 56. *Enquête Premier secteur*, pp. 29, 35.

[40] Ivory Coast, *Enquête Bongouanou*, p. 51.

richer than the north, and the gap between them has grown; in the south, easterners are richer than westerners; the center is somewhere between the two extremes. These differences between regions correspond generally to the culture circles discussed earlier and are summarized in Table 4. Traditionally, the several regions were economically self-sufficient, although as we have seen, there was some exchange between them. Per capita revenue in agriculture, which includes the sub-

TABLE 4

Income Differentiations in the Ivory Coast by Regions[a]

Region	*Estimated Population*	*Per Capita Revenue in Agriculture*[b]	*Per Capita Cash Income in Agriculture*	*Per Cent Sub-sistence*
Forest East	905,000	31,750	11,800	63
Forest West	980,000	15,750	7,400	56
Center	360,000	27,600	5,900	82
North	995,000	21,350	2,000	91
Country	3,220,000	22,750	6,500	78

[a] Computed from data contained in: S.E.R.E.S.A., "Rapport d'enquête dans le secteur agricole" (Abidjan, 1959), pp. 22-28. The figures are for 1957 and are expressed in C.F.A. francs. One dollar equaled about 245 frs. C.F.A. in 1959.

[b] The report computed these figures on the basis of the value of subsistence crops when marketed locally; per cent subsistence equaled per capita revenue in agriculture minus per capita cash income in agriculture.

sistence sector, shows a range of 2 to 1 for the entire country. But per capita cash income varies in the ratio of 6 in the richest region to 1 in the poorest. According to another estimate, income in the southeast, for a family of 8, is 100,000 C.F.A. fr. per year, but only 15,000 C.F.A. fr. in the north.[41] Because the largest part of this cash income is spent on consumption goods, variations in income are clearly visible in the daily lives of the inhabitants of the regions.

[41] Ivory Coast, Ministère du Plan, *Troisième plan quadriennal 1958-1962* (Abidjan: Imprimerie du Gouvernement, 1958), 83-95. Figures are for 1956.

Nowhere in the Ivory Coast is there great misery. In the north, Sénoufo farmers meet their basic needs in food, shelter, and clothing from traditional economic activities. But the implements of modern living are rare; the arrival of an automobile in a village is an unusual event; many Sénoufo wear imported cotton cloth only as their shroud; few can afford to send their children to school. In the southeast, among the Agni or the Abouré, for example, many individual farmers live in houses built of permanent construction materials; modern means of transportation, including bicycles, motor bikes, or even automobiles, are common; children who do not earn government scholarships can be sent to school at their family's expense. Although it is incorrect to speak of economic classes, economic differentiations coincide with traditional cleavages; there are now rich and poor tribes in the Ivory Coast.

Western Education

Before World War II, the educational system of the Ivory Coast was underdeveloped even by the low standards of French West Africa. Within this group of territories, it ranked below Senegal and Dahomey. In 1922, 1 out of every 100 children of school age attended school; in 1935, 1 out of 50; by 1948, the proportion was still only 1 out of 20.[42] Opportunities to go beyond this level were extremely limited. In 1940 the entire post-primary school population totaled about 200, most of them attending the Ecole Primaire Supérieure at Bingerville.[43] The apex of the prewar system was the Ecole Normale William Ponty established in Senegal

[42] Information for the prewar system is based on various issues of *L'Education africaine*, a periodical published irregularly by the government of French West Africa from 1922 on, and from another periodical from the same source, *Bulletin de l'enseignement en A.O.F.* For additional information, see Vera L. and Aristide R. Zolberg, "The Ivory Coast" in Helen Kitchen (ed.), *The Educated African* (New York: Frederick A. Praeger, 1962), pp. 453-73.

[43] I.F.A.N., *Livret-Guide*, Appendix, Table XXVIII.

to service the entire federation. Its graduates, who had a total of thirteen years of formal education, were recruited as clerks or teachers in the colonial service. Some went on to a three-year training course in medicine or in pharmacy and became *médecins africains* (A. Denise or Houphouet-Boigny), or *pharmaciens africains* (Jean-Baptiste Mockey). The first Ivoirien graduated from Ponty in 1921. About 4 students a year obtained their diplomas during the remainder of the decade. During the 1930's, the Ivory Coast (which then included most of Upper Volta) produced about 20 graduates a year. In 1945 there were about 200 or 300 for the entire country. This was normally the highest level of education to which an African could aspire. At the end of World War II, the Ivory Coast had only 4 university graduates and 3 or 4 students in French universities.[44]

The most dramatic rate of increase occurred during the 1950's. Between 1948 and 1957, the proportion of children of school age attending school rose from about 5 per cent to nearly 20 per cent, bypassing all other French West African territories except Dahomey.[45] As the number of children with an elementary school education increased, secondary schools were created as well. Scholarships were also granted to enable students to obtain a secondary education in France or to attend French universities. The economic boom also enabled some families to send students to school abroad at their own expense. By 1959, it was estimated that about 1,000 Ivory Coast students were in France;[46] in addition, there were about 200 at the University of Dakar.[47]

It is often assumed that the French colonial educational system reflected until recently the "assimilationist" character

[44] Cited by Houphouet-Boigny in *Afrique Nouvelle*, December 4, 1959.
[45] French West Africa, *A.O.F. 1957* (Dakar: Imprimerie du Gouvernement, 1957), pp. 115-18.
[46] *Afrique Nouvelle*, December 4, 1959.
[47] *Le Monde*, December 9, 1959.

of French colonial policy. Important political conclusions have been drawn from this alleged fact: "The assimilationist character of the educational system in French Africa was a crucial factor in creating an African political elite which identified itself with France and French culture, and insofar as the present generation has been concerned, it has been an elite willing, until recently, to seek political self-realization within the framework of some form of permanent Euro-African relationship."[48] This statement refers essentially to the generation educated at William Ponty. In a discussion of the education dispensed there, a former director of the school wrote that "we avoid everything that reeks of scholarship, of books, of laboratories."[49] If students were tempted, nevertheless, to live on an intellectual cloud, they would be brought back to reality by regularly performing manual labor. He concluded as follows: "Our motto is: 'Let us be modest, let us go slowly in order to go far, let us maintain a healthy suspicion of words, those perfidious friends, and of formulae, which contain a dangerous poison.' One day, perhaps, the great light that shines from the North will provide illumination that does not blind; for the time being, let us remain in the cave of which Plato speaks so beautifully, and let us look at the overly bright sun only through its reflection in the muddy waters of African streams."[50]

An Ivoirien alumnus of Ponty indicates that the system was neither "assimilationist," for it did not attempt to transform Africans into educated Frenchmen, nor was it "obscurantist." It was an "adapted" system: "The colonial system could certainly not do without education altogether, but it

[48] James S. Coleman, "The Politics of Sub-Saharan Africa" in Gabriel A. Almond and James S. Coleman, *The Politics of the Developing Areas* (Princeton: Princeton University Press, 1960), p. 281.

[49] Georges Hardy, *Une conquête morale: L'enseignement en A.O.F.* (Paris: Librairie Armand Colin, 1917), p. 172.

[50] *Ibid.*, p. 167. Hardy also explains that the school was built to a large extent through pupil labor and adds that this would make Jean-Jacques Rousseau cry with joy.

was a matter of dispensing a well-balanced education, well proportioned, barely sufficient to allow Africans to become useful to the colonial system, but insufficient to transform them into 'pedants' and into 'rebels.' "[51] The French system in practice was less assimilationist than the British system, which allowed more Africans to obtain a university education and to acquire a familiarity with and respect for British values and ways of life. Only one item in the French system fits the "assimilationist" designation, the use of the French language as a medium of instruction from the lowest levels on up. Spoken French has become a sort of *lingua franca.* But since school attendance was extremely restricted, literacy remained low and there was no mass exposure to French culture. An explanation for the desire of political leaders such as Houphouet-Boigny to remain closely associated with France must be sought elsewhere than in the educational system.

The prewar educational system did perhaps contribute to postwar political orientations, but in a different way. The Ponty-educated elite had no contact with French culture and society in the metropole itself. During their formative years, they were effectively insulated from currents of world thought. In the Ivory Coast, after they were graduated, they were subjected to the indignities of racial segregation in various aspects of public life. But metropolitan France, which they did not know, could stand as an idealized society. Perceived disparities between the theory of equality preached at school and the practice of inequality could be dismissed as the aberrations of local *colons* and officials. This partly explains why, around 1945, there was a great deal of bitterness against local Europeans but little desire to sever relationships with France. Great differences of opinion within the metropole also made it possible to differentiate between the true French, those of the left, and the reactionaries of

[51] Amon d'Aby, *La Côte d'Ivoire* . . ., p. 142.

the right. The desire to be closely related to France meant for a long time to participate in a political system of the Popular Democracy type, a likely outcome of the French convulsions after the war.

For the postwar generation of educated Africans, assimilation through education was much more of a reality than it had been for their seniors. Because of demands for equality, all schools were patterned after those of the metropole. In the Lycée of Abidjan, Africans and Europeans studied side by side. Practical features of the educational system were considered to be degrading and were eliminated altogether. Furthermore, many more students could go to France. But it is precisely from the ranks of the younger elite that dissatisfaction with the policy of close association with France began to grow. Increased contact with the realities of French life, exposure to new currents of thought, and perhaps more important, the social situation of African expatriates in Paris or in the provinces, led to the development of such concepts as *négritude* which, when translated into political ideology, led to demands for independence. Reference-group theory provides a clue to the understanding of this reaction. African students may have compared themselves with their more fortunate French fellows rather than with their less fortunate countrymen. Although they had greater opportunities than the older elite, they were *relatively* more deprived.[52]

Western education has resulted in additional differentiations between ethnic groups. In 1957, when the national average proportion of children of school age actually attending was reported to be 30 per cent, variations ranged from 87 per cent scolarity in Abengourou, a *cercle* inhabited mostly by Agni, to less than 10 per cent in the Sénoufo-

[52] For a discussion of the concept, see Robert K. Merton and Alice S. Kitt, "Contributions to the Theory of Reference Group Behavior," *Studies in the Scope and Method of the American Soldier* (eds.) R. K. Merton and P. Lazarsfeld (Glencoe: The Free Press, 1950), pp. 16-39.

dominant *cercle* of Korhogo. Generally, the areas in which commercial agriculture was highly developed, mostly in the eastern part of the south, also had the most developed educational facilities.[53] These differences were important because they were eventually reflected in differential recruitment in the civil service as well, since some areas had a larger pool of educated individuals than others.

At the same time, education has fostered the development of a small but growing group of individuals who have shared a common educational and occupational experience. At the end of World War II, this community included the few hundred individuals who had attended William Ponty or the Ecole Primaire Supérieure in Bingerville. Almost every tribe could boast at least some *intellectuels*, as those who have had enough education to hold down white-collar jobs are called. Most of them became civil servants, because of their obligation for a free education, or employees of European commercial firms. They were assigned to various parts of the country and even to other territories. In every town, whether in Abidjan or in the hinterland, these *commis* usually live in housing provided by the government or by European enterprises. This section, located somewhere between the European and the popular African sector of town, was often called *Komikro*—the village of the clerks. Within the *Komikro*, throughout the country, a new community has grown, in which traditional ties are often transcended. During the late 1930's and after the war, when Africans were allowed to organize voluntary associations, this "leading social group"[54]

[53] Ernest Boka, "L'éducation en Côte d'Ivoire," *Marchés Tropicaux et Méditerranéens*, April 18, 1959, p. 1026. Mr. Boka, then Minister of Education, based these figures on a population size about 30 per cent below the best available estimate; hence the difference between this figure for the national average and the one cited above. Nevertheless, the range remains probably of the same order of size.

[54] Karl Deutsch, *Nationalism and Social Communication* (New York: John Wiley and Sons, Inc., 1953), p. 75. This term seems more appropriate than the word "elite" in this context.

provided leadership for them. Each ethnic group appealed to its *intellectuels* to act as the spokesmen for their grievances, and thus these men became a tie between the old and the new society. When political movements were launched, the network of communications which existed between the *intellectuels* as well as between each of them and the traditional society from which they stemmed greatly facilitated organizational tasks.

Religion

Christianity is of recent origin in the Ivory Coast. Aside from the intermittent contacts noted in an earlier section, the first permanent Catholic mission was not established until 1895.[55] Protestant proselytizing and educational activities were discouraged because of French xenophobia. Later, activities were hampered by the struggle between Church and State in France. The colonial administration, long dominated by anticlerical, radical-socialist officials, showed little sympathy for priests and nuns. Between 1920 and 1940 there were about 60 missionaries at work in the country and approximately as many nuns.[56] Although missions received some subsidies from local funds to carry out their educational activities, these remained limited. In 1934 only 1 out of 5 pupils was in a religious school.[57] After World War II, the Church's activities expanded. There were about 200 missionaries in 1950, and in 1957 1 out of 3 pupils was in a Church school.[58] Throughout most of this period, since missions supplemented their meager resources by engaging in economic undertakings for which their flocks were made to labor, Africans remained suspicious of these establish-

[55] *Abidjan-Matin*, June 28, 1960. The issue contains a summary of the development of missions.

[56] R. Pottier, "Les oeuvres missionaires," *Marchés Coloniaux*, April 28, 1951, p. 1273.

[57] *L'Education africaine*, No. 93 (January-March 1936), p. 5.

[58] E. Boka, p. 1028.

ments.[59] Christianity has made little quantitative inroads; the Church claimed only 5 per cent of the population among its flock in 1951.[60] Christian influence was almost entirely limited to the coastal area. In recent years the Church has attempted to expand its membership through the medium of an African clergy. Although the first Ivory Coast priest was ordained in 1934 and the second one thirteen years later, by 1960 their number had reached 32. There were then also 18 African nuns.[61] Three weeks before the Ivory Coast became independent, one of the priests was elevated to the rank of archbishop.[62]

Islam reached the northern part of the country in the wake of Samory's conquests, not long before European penetration began in earnest. By the time its expansion was checked by French military action, the northwestern corner of the Ivory Coast—the entire Upper Niger culture circle area—had become almost entirely Moslem. Elsewhere in the north, approximately one-fourth of the population now follows the religion of the prophet, but this fourth includes the upper strata of Sénoufo society.[63] Islam continued to grow under French rule, carried by the Dioulas from north to south. Its appeal is very strong because it requires of converts few changes in social habits and little knowledge of theology and liturgy; it is viewed by Africans as a non-white religion; and it is particularly useful at a time when Africans seek to derive status from identification with a "superior faith."[64]

[59] For African attitudes toward missionaries, see in particular the novel by Mongo Beti, *Le pauvre Christ de Bomba* (Paris: Robert Laffont, 1956). This reflects attitudes shared by many in the Ivory Coast.

[60] Pottier, *Marchés Coloniaux*, p. 1273.

[61] *Abidjan-Matin*, issues of December 11, 1959, March 8, 1960, April 25, 1960.

[62] *Ibid.*, June 28, 1960. On this occasion, A. Denise congratulated the Church for having "won the race."

[63] Holas, *Les Sénoufo*, p. 161.

[64] *Ibid.*

French policy was originally anti-Moslem because Islam was an important source of resistance to European penetration and of cultural competition afterwards. Later, however, colonial administrators viewed with interest the more orthodox Tidiana and Kadria brotherhoods which prevail throughout the area and which preach obedience to constituted authority. Many French administrators had received their field training in Moslem countries of North Africa before moving south of the Sahara. Koranic law, included in the curriculum of the Ecole Coloniale, was a more convenient instrument for the administration of local justice than were the incomplete compendia of local customs. The administrators also considered Islam more *évolué* than animism. In response to this attitude, many Africans professed to be Moslems in the hope of better treatment at the hand of the *commandant*.[65] The Moslem population is now estimated at about 10 per cent of the total.[66]

Both Christianity and Islam have, in addition, given rise to syncretist offshoots, in which self-appointed African religious leaders have sought to adapt imported religions to local conditions. Messianic movements have appeared here as they have elsewhere in Africa as a response to tension, deprivation, and frustration produced by culture contact when no institutional outlets were available for the expression of discontent.[67] The Ivory Coast has been the main area of development for Harrism, named after a Liberian-born prophet who preached during World War I. Harris, a Methodist, tolerated traditional customs and preached obedience

[65] Alphonse Gouilly, *L'Islam dans l'Afrique Occidentale Française* (Paris: Editions Larose, 1952), especially "L'Islam et nous," pp. 245-75.

[66] *Abidjan-Matin*, January 10, 1957. This may be an underestimate because it was furnished in order to demonstrate that the population of Moslems was too small to warrant a Moslem tribunal.

[67] For a general discussion of this topic, see particularly the chapter "Priests and Prophets," in Thomas Hodgkin, *Nationalism in Colonial Africa*, pp. 95-114, and James S. Coleman, "Nationalism in Tropical Africa," reprinted in Lyle W. Shannon (ed.), *Underdeveloped Areas* (New York: Harper and Brothers, 1957), pp. 37-52.

to the colonial administration. However, because rumors of the imminent departure of the whites sprang up in his wake, he was forced to leave the country. Nevertheless, the movement he founded survived, especially in the *cercle* of Grand Lahou.[68] There is no evidence that it has had any contemporary political significance.[69]

Hamallism, which began as a Tidianist reform movement in French Sudan at the beginning of the twentieth century, has been more clearly a substitute for other expressions of discontent. It was carried to the Ivory Coast by the founder, Cheick Hamallah, who was exiled there during the 1930's. One of his most important followers, Yacouba Sylla, later became an important R.D.A. leader in the Gagnoa region.[70] The movement placed less emphasis on ritual and theology than did the orthodox sects; it tolerated magic ornaments and traditional African statuary. As with Harrism, there was no evidence of subversive activity on the part of Hamallah, but the orthodox brotherhoods convinced the French that the movement was responsible for the disturbances in the Sudan between 1923 and 1940 and obtained its suppression.

The consequences of Christianity, as distinct from French culture generally, are difficult to assess. It is perhaps more important to note that Christianity has *not*, as may perhaps have been expected, done much to create patterns of social relationships that transcend traditional ones. Where they have the most followers, in Abidjan proper, Catholic and Protestant churches have become acculturated to local conditions. In religious processions, Catholic women, grouped

[68] Information on Harrism and other cults is contained in B. Holas, "Bref aperçu sur les principaux cultes syncrétiques de la Basse Côte d'Ivoire," *Africa*, xxiv (January 1954), 55-61; Gaston Joseph, *La Côte d'Ivoire* (Paris: E. Larose, 1917), p. 178; Grivot, *Le Cercle de Lahou*, pp. 84-86.

[69] A similar conclusion was reached by Mme. Denise Paulme, of the Musée de l'Homme, Paris, who conducted an investigation of religious movements in the Ivory Coast in 1958.

[70] Gouilly, p. 134.

by tribe, carry banners in the name of the tribal saint whom they have chosen in accord with the Church hierarchy. The Adioukrou are proud of their patron, Saint Theresa; the Church has done very little to bring them into contact with the Attié, who are particularly fervent admirers of Saint George. The Protestant church in Treichville was happy to report recently that a sufficient number of Attié had been baptized to warrant the creation of an Attié section in the congregation.[71]

To a limited extent, the localization of Christianity in the south and Islam in the north has reinforced cultural distinctions between these areas. Whether they are practising Moslems or not, northerners have adopted Moslem clothing and other outward signs of that religion. Holas has suggested that although the impact of Islam is very superficial, this does not prevent it from creating a feeling of unity among northerners, who can use it as a political stepping stone.[72] This has been reinforced by the attitudes of the southerners, who often generalize all northerners into Dioulas and "Marabouts." In the towns, where Islam is carried by the Dioula traders, these distinctions reinforce ethnic and economic differences.

Population Movements and Urbanization

Urbanization, internal migrations, and immigration have transformed the Ivory Coast into a complex human mosaic made up of the many ethnic groups that remained in their own region, as well as the Africans who moved to other areas and to the new cities, and the immigrants from other parts of the continent.[73] With the exception of the city of Kong, which had a population of nearly 20,000 before it

[71] *Abidjan-Matin*, May 13, 1960.

[72] Holas, *Les Sénoufo*, p. 161.

[73] European and Levantine immigration will not be discussed here, since the main concern of this study is to consider transformation of African society. References to these two groups will be made whenever relevant.

was razed by the French during the Samory campaigns, the Ivory Coast did not have traditional urban centers comparable to those found in some other African countries. In 1920 only 2 per cent of the population lived in villages and towns with a population of 2,000 or more; and of this 2 per cent half were concentrated in Abidjan and in Grand Bassam, which had already become French administrative and commercial centers.[74]

Towns and cities have grown rapidly in recent years. By 1948, 7 per cent of the population lived in centers of 2,000 or more inhabitants. In 1955 there were 10 towns of 10,000 or more located throughout the country;[75] at this time nearly half of the 12 per cent who were urbanized lived in Abidjan and in Bouaké, the second largest city, located at the meeting point of the forest and the savanna. The largest city is Abidjan, which grew from a small Ebrié fishing village, with a population of 720 in 1910, to a town of 5,371 in 1921. In 1945 it had become a city of 46,000, and ten years later its population was 127,585.[76] Recent estimates are as high as 200,000. In 1935 the Ebrié were relocated on the nearby island of Petit Bassam to make room for Frenchmen on the Plateau, as the original location of Abidjan has come to be called. On this island is found the most populous area of the city, the borough of Treichville, with a population of nearly 100,000 in 1959. On the other side of the Plateau is the second major African borough, Adjamé, originally a cluster of villages which were incorporated into the city as it grew.

Because the pool of educated Ivoiriens was too small to meet the demands of private and public bureaucracies, the French recruited personnel from other colonies. *Commis*,

[74] French West Africa, Gouvernement-Général, *Annuaire 1922* (Dakar: Imprimerie du Gouvernement, 1922), p. 694.

[75] These figures are based on unpublished census.

[76] For a study of the origins of the city and its later character, see Jean Dresch, "Villes d'A.O.F.," *Cahiers d'Outre-Mer*, III (July-September 1950), 200-30.

schoolteachers, and shopkeepers, came from Senegal and from Dahomey. Fanti fishermen from Ghana came to supply the needs of the population of the growing coastal cities. Yorubas—called *Nagos* in the Ivory Coast—and other Nigerians came to trade; Upper Volta supplied a continuous stream of agricultural workers. In recent years it has been estimated that about one-fourth of the population of the Ivory Coast is made up of foreigners, including at least 300,000 workers from Upper Volta.[77] Internal migrations also occurred because of the scarcity of labor in the most developed regions of the country. Workers imported to these areas often settled there afterwards, obtained land, and became farmers. Enterprising Africans from regions unsuitable for commercial agriculture colonized other parts of the country, sometimes with the encouragement of the colonial administration.[78]

These population movements have given the urban centers a heterogeneous character. (See Table 5.) Everywhere, except in Man, located outside the mainstream of commercial activity, the cities have a majority of immigrants from foreign countries or from other regions of the Ivory Coast. Foreign Africans make up nearly half of the total population of Abidjan. The original inhabitants, the Ebrié, constitute less than 7 per cent of the total in the city. Similarly, in some rural districts there are more foreigners than natives. In a county of the *cercle* of Bouaflé, originally inhabited by the Gouro, two-thirds of the population is now made up of Baoulé and

[77] Ivory Coast, Ministère du Plan, *Troisième plan quadriennal* (Abidjan: Imprimerie du Gouvernement, 1958), p. 80. A study of migrations to the Ivory Coast is currently being completed by Dr. Jean Rouch.

[78] In 1933, for example, the government encouraged the creation of colonization villages in the west by Baoulé and Malinké from savanna areas. These pioneer farmers were given tax exemptions, free building materials for houses, free seeds or shoots, priorities in medical care, and most important of all, were exempt from forced labor. In addition, the government granted them the usufruct of surrounding lands regardless of the wishes of the local inhabitants. Ivory Coast, *Programme d'action . . .*, pp. 215-16.

TABLE 5

Geographical Origins of Africans in Selected Cities[a]
(in per cent of total)

Town	*Born in Foreign Countries*	*Born in the Ivory Coast*[b]			*Total*
		Far	*Near*	*Native*	
Abidjan	46	36	11	7	117,892
Agboville	30	33	27	10	12,292
Dimbokro	17	34	19	29	9,336
Abengourou	32	24	16	27	15,757
Man	8	18	32	42	18,208
Daloa	13	50	2	35	10,618

[a] The data for this table were computed from the following sources: Ivory Coast, "Recensement d'Abidjan" (1955), pp. 13-16 (mimeographed); for Daloa, Henri Raulin, *Problémes fonciers dans les régions de Gagnoa et Daloa* ("Missions d'Etude des groupements Immigrés en Côte d'Ivoire," Fascicule 3; Paris: O.R.S.T.O.M., 1957), p. 123. For all others, information was transcribed from unpublished results of a census conducted in 1958.

[b] "Far" signifies born outside the *cercle* in which the town is located; "near" is within the *cercle*, but not a member of the tribe that originally inhabited the city; "native" is a member of the tribe on whose territory the city is located.

Malinké immigrants.[79] This phenomenon is generally found throughout the southwest, where the local populations did not respond to appeals to grow coffee and cocoa. But a similar pattern has been found even in the southeast. In 1953, out of a settled population of 32,000 in the central subdivision of Aboisso *cercle*, which corresponds to the traditional territory of the Agni State of Sanwi, one-third were strangers. In addition, there were about 20,000 temporary immigrants working on local farms, many of whom later settled in the region.[80]

We shall not dwell here on the important role of new towns in Africa and in the transformation of societies in

[79] Raulin, p. 125.

[80] This information is based on an unpublished manuscript by Miss Dupire of O.R.S.T.O.M. on population and land problems in Aboisso.

general. As Louis Wirth has suggested, "the influence which cities exert upon the social life of man are greater than the ratio of the urban population would indicate, for the city is not only in ever larger degrees the dwelling-place and the workshop of modern man, but it is the initiating and controlling center of economic, political and cultural life that has drawn the most remote parts of the world into its orbit and woven diverse areas, peoples, and activities into a cosmos."[81] Everywhere in Africa, the new towns have become not only the disseminators of Westernization but also the centers for the radiation of the activities of political movements.[82] The Ivory Coast is no exception to this general process. Most of the crucial events that occurred during the period of anticolonial agitation occurred in Abidjan and in the urban centers of the interior, such as Abengourou, Dimbokro, or Séguéla. Although political organizations reach down to the village level, the head town of each administrative *subdivision* is also the most important rung in the ladder of organization within the P.D.C.I.

Social Relationships

African towns have been viewed as the "crucible" in which nations are formed and universalistic relationships prevail.[83] While it is undoubtedly true, as Table 5 indicates, that Ivory Coast urban centers provide a meeting place for many different ethnic groups, it is necessary to ask to what extent have these towns also become catalysts that precipitate the formation of new social relationships? More generally, if new networks of communication, providing multiple group affiliations and crisscrossing cleavages, have appeared, it is

[81] Louis Wirth, "Urbanism as a Way of Life," reprinted in *Reader in Urban Sociology* (eds.) Paul K. Hatt and Albert J. Reiss, Jr. (Glencoe: The Free Press, 1951), p. 32.

[82] Thomas Hodgkin, *Nationalism in Colonial Africa*, pp. 63-83.

[83] Daniel F. McCall, "Dynamics of Urbanization in Africa," *The Annals of the American Academy of Political and Social Science*, CCXCVIII (March 1958), 151-60.

in the towns that evidence for their existence must be found.

Although social relationships in the towns have not been studied methodically, it can be inferred from some visible processes that traditional ties remain extremely important. Most towns are divided into ethnically distinct neighborhoods. Agboville, which began as a center for the construction of the Ivory Coast railroad, attracted Baoulé construction gangs as well as Dioula or Senegalese traders who came to cater to their needs. A nearby Abbey village was eventually incorporated into the city. Twenty years later these component groups had retained their identity and lived in separate quarters of the city known under the name of the tribe that dwells within (Mossikro, Dioulakro) or under the name of a tribal ancestor or founding father (Brou Nguessankro, Kouakoukro). There are no Abbey or Attié, the natives of the region, in Mossikro and Godekro, and no northerners or westerners in Obodjikro and Sambregnankro, the quarters inhabited by the natives.[84]

A similar pattern was noted in Daloa by Raulin. When the city was created as the administrative center for a new *cercle*, the African sector was divided into streets on a grid pattern; the streets were further subdivided into lots for sale to African settlers. "It appears well established that the Administration did not purposefully assign to buyers given sectors of the city according to their ethnic origins. . . . Neighborhoods became differentiated in a spontaneous manner. This is quite normal and understandable if we consider the focus of attraction that each one of these neighborhoods provides for the members of the group that lives there. . . . Africans—regardless of origin—who arrive in Daloa settle near the lots inhabited by their compatriots. By compatriots, one should understand not only the ethnic group in the wider sense of the word, for example, the Malinké or the Bambara group, but the geographical origin. For example, the Malinké

[84] R. Grivot, "Agboville, esquisse d'une cité d'Afrique Noire," *Etudes Eburnéennes*, IV (1955), 84-107.

of Odiénné do not mix with the Malinké of Touba, and the Dioula of Sikasso do not cohabit with those of Bougouni. Each of the ethnic and geographic subdivisions has its own neighborhood, its traditional headman, and its specialized activities."[85]

Selective immigration to the city continues to occur on the basis of the needs of the social and economic leaders of the ethnic subcommunities. A Malinké from Odiénné who acquires a piece of land in the surrounding countryside or who expands his trading activities imports young tribesmen to work for him.[86] This pattern prevails among Africans who work for European and Lebanese employers as well. Each of these small enterprises has a foreman, a sort of labor boss for the outfit. He acts as the intermediary between the non-African management and the African workers; he has a great deal of autonomy in the hiring of personnel and it is, of course, quite normal for him to give preference to his own relatives and tribesmen.[87]

These observations suggest that opportunities for the development of new social relationships of a universalistic type in the urban centers appear to be more limited than might be assumed on the basis of their heterogeneous character. The major exception to the ecological pattern noted above is Treichville, where the French administration carefully attempted to prevent the development of ethnic neighborhoods.[88] But precisely because of this, voluntary associations have appeared to recreate ethnic solidarity.

The development of regional communities that include an urban center and surrounding rural areas has not led to a lessening of ethnicity because of the reactions of the natives to the growth of towns dominated by foreigners. In Gagnoa,

[85] Raulin, p. 121. [86] *Ibid.*

[87] This is based on personal observation.

[88] The unpublished results of a survey carried out during 1959 by research groups sponsored by the Ministry of Public Works indicate that the borough is not subdivided into ethnic wards.

where relationships between the native Bété and the immigrants have long been less than cordial, "in recent times this suspicion has become more manifest. Ever since a degree of self-government has been granted to Africans, the inhabitants of the rural areas are not unaware that the new center of authority will be in the towns, as it has been in the past, and that it is at that center that decisions concerning their own fate will be taken. Since the Bété knows that the population of Gagnoa is made up mostly of non-Bété foreigners, he fears, rightly or wrongly, the rule of the non-Bété and he rebels against the Dioula."[89] Similarly in the Agboville region, where Grivot had noted in 1942 that the Abbey natives might eventually be eliminated from their own region's development by the foreign townsmen,[90] the situation has become so tense that clashes between these groups occur almost every year. In 1959 the Abbey even organized vigilante groups to prevent the townsmen from leaving the city.

Within rural areas, similar relationships prevail between natives and foreigners or between geographically contiguous groups. During the 1920's and 1930's, the native Dida in Divo were contemptuous of the Baoulé and Dioula immigrant farmers who engaged in work reserved for women in their own society. Except for exacting compensatory payment for the use of their lands, the Dida had little to do with the foreigners.[91] Twenty years later, the foreign settlers refused to continue these payments or even to negotiate with the Dida. The Baoulé and Dioula found renewed unity in their own midst when they applied pressure on their members to prevent some of them from having dealings with "the enemy."[92] In 1959, when a truck driver (a member of one of the immigrant groups) ran down and accidentally killed a Dida child, he was lynched by the villagers. His own countrymen

[89] Raulin, p. 88.
[90] Grivot, *Etudes Eburnéennes*, IV (1955), 98.
[91] R. Grivot, *Le Cercle de Lahou* (Paris: Larose, 1948), p. 70.
[92] Raulin, pp. 4-5.

retaliated by burning several Dida villages.[93] In the Gouro region, tensions have grown recently because the natives are becoming conscious of the immigrants' economic power. Claims over proper compensation for the use of land cannot be settled on the basis of customary law, which is different for the two tribes involved; but neither can they be adjudicated on the basis of French civil law, because property transactions were not carried out on the basis of legal contracts. The settlement of disputes is left to the play of interpersonal relationships. Here also, Raulin noted, there is a tendency of unification on both sides to present a common front to the other.[94]

That immigrants and natives emerge from the confrontation with a renewed sense of distinctiveness can be explained in general as Deutsch has suggested: "An isolated minority in a strange new country might increase its efforts to recall its past and to standardize its behavior so as to erase again and again the eroding effects of the new environment on its traditional culture. If such a group can at the same time find some special niche in the common society, so that even its social and economic experiences will be less similar to those of other groups than they otherwise would be, then this group may retain its separate cohesiveness for long periods of time."[95]

Throughout this chapter it has been stressed that differentiations between traditional societies have been intensified by the cumulative effect of uneven Western impact and, in recent years, by differential rates of cultural and economic change. New ecological patterns and communications between groups have not reduced but rather increased the

[93] Based on informants' report, 1959.

[94] Raulin, pp. 45-58.

[95] Deutsch, p. 95. This process is not limited only to immigrants and natives, where it appears very dramatically, but also between neighbors of the same general group, such as the Ehotilé and the Abouré, both Akan. For an example of this, see Rougerie, *Les Pays Agni . . .*, pp. 54-59.

awareness of differences based on traditional culture. Today the Agni or the Abouré are different from the Bété or the Gouro not only because they eat different foods, speak differently, or settle their disputes according to different norms, but because they are wealthier, more educated, and more Christian. The Malinké and the Sénoufo in the past were of two different northern civilizations, but now the Malinké are also more likely to be Moslems, traders, and urbanites, while the Sénoufo are subsistence farmers and continue to practice their traditional religion. It is in this sense that Ivory Coast society can be characterized as one in which cleavages tend to be consistent rather than crisscrossing.

This pattern may change in the long run. To some extent, it began to happen during the interwar period, when Ponty graduates and others began to think in terms of the territory, as well as in terms of their own region. They acquired a vision of the Ivory Coast as a unit alongside seven others in French West Africa. Yet at the same time they became the champions of their tribe. These individuals were the leaders not only of a territorial, and even a superterritorial movement, but also of tribal associations. Although they coalesced into a vast movement, they were also pulled back by their traditional loyalties. These divergent views and loyalties are mainly responsible for the unity and the disunity of political organizations in the Ivory Coast.

CHAPTER II

THE ORIGINS OF POLITICAL ORGANIZATIONS

✧ THE *Parti Démocratique de Côte d'Ivoire* and other organizations originated through the transformation of voluntary associations into political instruments. This occurred in the Ivory Coast after World War II, when the colonial system was modified to allow for African participation in the government. Although the sources of nationalism were generally the same as elsewhere in West Africa, specific features of the colonial system gave rise to particular grievances that conditioned the character of postwar politics.

SOURCES OF DISCONTENT

The Prewar Colonial Regime

Before 1945, as Professor Kenneth Robinson has stated, the political history of French West Africa was essentially "administrative history—the history of the impact of metropolitan ideas and interests on the practical day-to-day problems of administration in a poor, thinly populated, and undeveloped country."[1] The system was based on a fundamental distinction between citizens and subjects. At first only Africans born in one of the four communes of Senegal that had obtained special privileges under the French Revolution and Frenchmen were considered citizens. African subjects could, in theory, become citizens through a procedure akin to individual naturalization. But since educational facilities necessary to acquire the proper qualifications were rare, this form of legal assimilation was extremely restricted.

[1] Kenneth Robinson, "Political Development in French West Africa," *Africa in the Modern World* (ed.) Calvin W. Stillman (Chicago: The University of Chicago Press, 1955), p. 147.

In 1921 the Ivory Coast had only 308 African citizens, including many Senegalese among them.[2] By 1936, there were only 2,000 naturalized citizens in the entire federation of French West Africa.[3]

Neither citizens nor subjects had much opportunity to participate in government. The only local body in which they were represented was the Administrative Council created in 1895, a body with advisory powers only.[4] From 1920 on, it had 5 official members and 4 unofficial appointed ones. The latter included 2 subjects, usually traditional chiefs who had demonstrated their loyalty to the Administration.[5] After 1925, the subjects had 3 representatives on the Council; they were chosen by a very limited electorate which was concentrated mostly in the then capital city, Grand Bassam. Citizens alone elected a representative to the *Conseil Supérieur des Colonies*, another consultative body, created in Paris in 1883.[6] The most important check on the colonial administration was probably the Chamber of Commerce, which had a few Senegalese among its members. This body acquired a reputation of great influence and was said to be able to make and unmake governors. Its president reminisced in 1959: "I was more influential twenty-five years ago than I am now. . . . The Chamber of Commerce was then the only body that could control government. We worked through our friends in the metropole whenever necessary. . . . As you can see, . . . in the old days the center of gravity of politics was within my own bailiwick."[7]

The limitations on African participation in the government at higher levels were by no means compensated at the

[2] French West Africa, *Annuaire 1922*, p. 65.

[3] Robinson, "Political Development in French West Africa," p. 141.

[4] Its membership and authority varied somewhat from time to time. For details, see Amon d'Aby, *La Côte d'Ivoire . . .*, pp. 50-51.

[5] *Ibid.*

[6] *Ibid.*, pp. 52-54.

[7] Interview with M. François Massieye, president of the Chamber of Commerce, Ivory Coast, 1959.

local level. Grand Bassam and Abidjan had official mayors and appointed municipal councils, which included a few Africans from 1915 onward; four other towns were granted consultative commissions in 1919.[8] Elsewhere, each district had a *conseil des notables*, of which Buell wrote: "Inasmuch as these councils have for president a Frenchman who controls the agenda, and inasmuch as the members are picked mostly from chiefs, they do not have the freedom of discussion which exists, for example, in the Transkei. . . . In addition, the French councils have no money to dispose of in the form of a budget to promote native welfare. They are thus deprived of the experience which the necessarily precise discussion of financial affairs involves."[9]

Government was then essentially in the hands of French officials, accountable to their superiors in the hierarchy rather than to local conciliar organs. This hierarchy included, in descending order, the following levels: the Ministry of Colonies; the General-Government of French West Africa, headed by a governor-general;[10] the government of the Ivory Coast colony, headed by a lieutenant-governor, later governor; the *cercle*, with a *commandant de cercle*; and the *subdivision*, headed by a *chef de subdivision*. This hierarchy impinged more directly upon the population than its British equivalent. For example, in 1926 at a time when 25

[8] Amon d'Aby, *La Côte d'Ivoire* . . ., pp. 46-47.

[9] Buell, I, 1000.

[10] The Ivory Coast was administered from 1895 to 1957 as one of eight colonies, later territories, in a unit known as French West Africa. This larger unit was created in 1895 to coordinate French action in the entire area. In 1905 the *Gouvernement-General*, with headquarters at Dakar, Senegal, was endowed with a budget of its own that received all the indirect taxes collected in the colonies. Dakar provided them in exchange with some common services. The executive of French West Africa was the hierarchical superior of the individual executives of the colonies; nevertheless, the latter retained their individual character as well. Sometimes, French West Africa was called a "group" of colonies; more generally, it was called a "federation," a designation used in this study. For a fuller discussion, see Oswald Durand, "Organisation Administrative," *Afrique Occidentale Française*, I, 244-46.

subdivisions were closed for lack of personnel, the Ivory Coast had 1 colonial official for about 18,000 people. Southern Nigeria had, at the same time, only 1 official for about 70,000 people.[11] This is one sense in which it is appropriate to speak of French direct rule.

More generally, this designation stems from the French approach to the question of traditional authorities. A former governor of the Ivory Coast has described that aspect of the colonial system as follows: "Unlike the British, the French are not superstitious about monarchy. Nowhere did they strengthen chiefdoms by granting them tribunals and an autonomous treasury. The chief is not regarded as a potentate, but as a useful administrative auxiliary. The French administrator does not find personal contact with Africans repugnant and instinctively practices direct administration."[12] The practice of recruiting as "chiefs" individuals from other tribes and even other territories, instituted at the time of military pacification, was modified later on because it proved to be impracticable.[13] The new system included two main levels; the village or the *quartier* (city ward), and above it, the *canton* (county). The village or ward headman maintained law and order, prevented forest fires, protected the crops, arbitrated minor disputes of a civil or commercial nature, and most important of all, collected the *impôt de capitation*, the personal head-tax. His remuneration consisted of a rebate on collections. He was appointed by the *chef de subdivision* from a group of candidates chosen by the population of the village, and in practice, he was usually the individual who would rule

[11] Buell, I, 648, 983.

[12] Hubert Deschamps, *L'éveil politique africain* (Paris: Presses Universitaires de France, 1952), p. 81.

[13] Hardy, p. 179. New directives were issued for French West Africa in 1917, but implemented in the Ivory Coast only in 1934. Unless otherwise indicated, the section on chiefs is based on the scheme elaborated by Governor Reste in Ivory Coast, *Programme d'action . . .*, pp. 177-94.

according to tradition, if there was such an office in the village.

Unlike the village chief, the *chef de canton* was frankly an agent of the native authority, appointed by the governor upon recommendation of the *commandant*.[14] He supervised village chiefs in the execution of their duties, established census rolls from which the tax burden of each village was assessed, and—at least until 1945—recruited manpower for the various administrative levies discussed below. He was a salaried official, paid according to his rank in the hierarchy. The secular aspects of this role, however, were sharply qualified by the following directives concerning recruitment of individuals to fill it. Governor Reste asserted in 1934: "In fact, if there exists in the region a family that furnished traditional rulers in the past, kinglets of some importance, an individual from within this family will have more prestige than any other. He should be chosen if his character is not objectionable. And he should be chosen as much as possible according to ancient customs governing the transmission of authority."[15] In practice, wherever the French found a clearly differentiated, functioning traditional political system, the county was made to coincide with the territorial boundaries of the chiefdom. This was the case, for example, in Kiembara County of Korhogo *cercle*, among the Sénoufo, and throughout the Agni-dominant *cercles* of Aboisso and Abengourou. The latter was divided into three counties which corresponded to Ndénié, Béttié, and Diabé States respectively. There, the traditional rulers became the official chiefs as well.

Generalizing about the Ivory Coast experience of this system, Amon d'Aby concludes: "The traditional chiefdoms no longer exist, but the new auxiliaries have continued to be recruited among the successors to these chiefs. In other words, the thrones have been upset, but their occupants

[14] *Ibid.*, p. 178. [15] *Ibid.*, p. 187.

have been maintained; the traditional chief has been dethroned, but the same man has been designated as the administrative chief."[16] Because the chiefs were so closely associated with the colonial administration and were dependent for their continued tenure of office on official support rather than on traditional legitimacy or on some form of popular consent, they drew to themselves many of the grievances directed against the colonial regime as a whole. Paradoxically, because the chiefs' official role was narrowly defined, the French did not bother to regulate other aspects of their activities. They were given no official functions in the administration of justice but continued to mete out punishment and to levy fines, sometimes of great importance, among their own subjects.[17] This was an additional source of grievance among the more *évolué* strata in the country, who had no recourse against arbitrariness.

The distinction between citizens and subjects appeared in a particularly sharp fashion in the sphere of law enforcement.[18] For subjects, there was nothing but administrative justice. Since 1912, the entire system of native justice had been in the hands of French administrators and practically no distinction was made between criminal and civil law. Most affairs were handled at the level of the *subdivision*, where a French official of the lowest category in the hierarchy could impose fines up to 5,000 prewar francs (then about $1,000) in criminal cases. The *commandant de cercle* could even impose the death penalty. Although there was a possibility of appeal, its use was discouraged by imposing a fine upon the appellant if he lost the case. The only check on the administration was review *pro forma* only by a *tribunal d'homologation*, which did not hear new

[16] Amon d'Aby, *Le problème des chefferies* . . ., p. 33.
[17] Buell, I, 1008. This was confirmed by many informants.
[18] This section is based on information contained in the indispensable Buell, I, 1006-1020, and Amon d'Aby, *La Côte d'Ivoire* . . ., pp. 67-72.

evidence. Since little was known about local law, and since the administrators usually did not speak the local language, they relied on the opinions of native assessors, usually local chiefs whom they had appointed, and who often had a stake in the controversy under consideration. Civil servants were not eligible as assessors. Hence, educated Africans were excluded from participation in the administration of justice, although as subjects they remained under its jurisdiction.

In order to be in a position to act rapidly when the judicial procedures were too slow, the administrators were given the authority to punish various offenses through the exercise of simple police powers, without any trial whatsoever. Under the system known as the *indigénat*, sanctions amounted to as much as twenty-five-dollar fines and two-week jail sentences; apparently, several such sanctions could be heaped upon the same defendant. One of the offenses punishable in this way was "lack of respect for authority." This was invoked to suppress any associations that had or that might potentially have a critical tendency. This sword of Damocles also thwarted most attempts to establish an African press.

Forced Labor

In 1959 the memory of forced labor, a practice abolished in 1946, still evoked more indignation and resentment among Ivoiriens than any other aspect of the prewar colonial system. Several practices were included under this general heading. First, the French instituted in Africa a system of *prestations*, similar to the one still in force at home before the war, whereby local governments could levy a tax in the form of a contribution of manpower to cover the cost of highway repair.[19] Under this rule, every adult male was required to contribute twelve days' work a year to the *commandant*. Although individuals were allowed to meet this obligation

[19] Brian Chapman, *Introduction to French Local Government* (London: George Allen and Unwin, 1953), pp. 182-83.

through a cash payment, few were able to do so. Furthermore, there were many abuses; since the administration kept no rolls, recruitment was arbitrary.[20] The system was used to construct roads, as well as to maintain them. Second, the French decreed in 1926 that some of the Africans liable to military service—the *deuxième contingent*—could be conscripted locally for a period of three years and forced to work for the public works department of the government.

The most notorious practice, which aroused world-wide criticism of French colonialism, began in the 1920's. The administration at this time impressed manpower for work on European and African coffee and cocoa farms. This system of recruitment was instituted because by the time commercial agriculture was launched, migratory currents toward Ghana had already drained the northern part of the country and much of Upper Volta of available manpower. As conditions were much more attractive in the British colony, French Africans resisted all attempts to stem this current.[21] Although those who were recruited in this fashion were paid by their employers, wages were extremely low, and the government strictly supervised the performance of the contract they were forced to accept. In the face of widespread criticism abroad, the French acknowledged the existence of forced labor in their colonies, but justified it as follows: "The use of coercion in the matter of native labor has aroused criticism and protest everywhere. Some call it 'return to slavery.' The pity expressed by these defenders of oppressed races, who reaffirm the thesis of the good savage and the bad civilizers, no longer knows any limits. . . . Yet, they do not suggest any substitute. The regime of forced labor is an established fact. In our opinion, the only way to abolish

[20] Buell, I, 1037-39.

[21] Labouret, pp. 226-32. In 1930 about 200,000 workers from French territories migrated annually to the Gold Coast. For the general aspects of this question, see Jean Rouch, "Migrations au Ghana," *Journal de la Société des Africanistes*, XXVI (January 1956), 82.

it is to maintain it temporarily, to organize it properly in order to reduce its drawbacks as much as possible, and to give it an educational role."[22] This institution was particularly resented because it worked mainly to the benefit of Europeans established in the Ivory Coast on a semi-permanent basis.

European Settlers and the Land Problem

The French government actively encouraged European settlement in the Ivory Coast because, as an official publication expressed it, the country had unlimited possibilities of development, but "the native population . . . is much too weak to exploit this wealth, given the rudimentary means at their disposal."[23] In order to attract colonists, the French government appropriated large amounts of land in its own name and redistributed it in the form of freehold grants. Settlers who planted cocoa and coffee for a period of five years could obtain twice the amount of land they had developed on a freehold basis at the end of that period.[24] Although in theory the ownership rights of the African population were protected, the burden of proof of traditional ownership was on them, and they were effectively reduced to the status of tenants at will.[25] Although this system prevailed throughout French Africa, more than half of the concessions granted in the federation of French West Africa were located in the Ivory Coast.[26]

Many Europeans to whom concessions were granted in this manner accumulated land for speculative purposes and never engaged in agriculture. After the war, it was discovered that important tracts around Abidjan and elsewhere, which

[22] René Mercier, *Le travail obligatoire dans les colonies africaines* (Paris: Larose, 1933), pp. 15-16.

[23] French West Africa, Gouvernement-Général, *La Côte d'Ivoire en 1920* (Paris: Larose, 1920), p. 9.

[24] Edgard Maguet, *Concessions domaniales dans les colonies françaises* (Paris: Larose, 1930), pp. 44-45, 177-78.

[25] Buell, I, 1023-24.

[26] Thompson and Adloff, p. 348.

were needed for urban expansion, were owned by Europeans who had never even resided in the Ivory Coast, but who had purchased this land for very small amounts of money from luckless erstwhile *colons*. An even greater source of African discontent were those Europeans who stayed on. It is estimated that before World War II there were about two hundred European farmers who owned about one-third of all cocoa trees and an even larger share of coffee trees.[27] They competed directly with African producers but had many advantages over them. First, although African farmers also received a quota of impressed manpower, Europeans always had preference in this respect. Secondly, French farmers had greater access to the technical know-how developed by the Department of Agriculture of the colonial government than did Africans.[28] The result was that they had a much greater acreage yield and higher quality products. Whether for this or for less economic reasons, they also obtained preferential prices from purchasers. When premiums to encourage production were distributed, they alone could usually meet the bureaucratic requirements involved.

The type of immigration that took place was another reason for the resentment of the French. The French made no attempt to discourage individuals who had but vague notions concerning possible employment, little or no capital, and sometimes not even their return fare. Many became shopkeepers or were employed in low-level jobs by the administration or by business firms, where they competed with educated Africans. In 1959 there were still European truck drivers, service-station attendants, barbers, and grocers in

[27] Hubert Fréchou, "Les plantations européennes en Côte d'Ivoire," *Cahiers d'Outre-Mer*, XXIX (January-March 1955), 271.

[28] The annual report of the Department of Agriculture for 1938, for example, reports the progress of many experiments carried out by the government on European farms and deplores the fact that African farms are incapable of improvement. Ivory Coast, Service de l'Agriculture, "Rapport annuel" (1938), p. 132. (Typescript on file at I.F.A.N., Abidjan.)

the Ivory Coast, known by most Frenchmen and Africans as *petits-blancs.*[29] Finally, although the French take great pride in their racial equalitarianism, racial segregation was blatantly practiced. The Plateau in Abidjan was restricted to European residence only; the bridge separating the mainland from Treichville was barred to Africans at nightfall.[30]

The Popular Front and Vichy

A period of great liberal spirit, rapidly followed by an extreme reaction, helped bring African discontent to the point of explosion. During the entire history of French colonial rule, policies in the dependencies followed the fluctuations of political fortunes in the metropole. Colonial appointments were distributed among French parties according to the balance of power within a governmental coalition.[31] One important consequence of this spoils system was the staffing of many posts by left wingers during the period of the Popular Front. Individual officials mitigated colonial rule with a great deal of sympathy toward individual Africans. In 1937, for the first time, Africans—at least those who were literate—were allowed to organize trade-unions. A branch of the French Socialist Party (S.F.I.O.) was established at Grand Bassam. Existing rules for the attribution of land grants were reinterpreted to afford greater protection to African traditional owners; freehold grants were replaced by long-term leaseholds.[32] Most important of all, at this time communications were being established between the

[29] Based on personal observation. The same fact also struck Buell's attention more than twenty years earlier. Buell, I, 985.

[30] Dresch, p. 222.

[31] "Even the office of governor was used in this fashion. As late as 1911, an energetic minister found the cadres of this rank full of 'elderly gentlemen who had been planted there in the early days of the creation of our empire in return for electoral services that they had rendered at Béziers or Chateauroux.'" Dennis W. Brogan, *The Development of Modern France* (London: Hamish Hamilton, 1940), p. 252.

[32] Before it was widely applied, however, this decision was fought by the colonial interests and rescinded.

emergent African elite and their French superiors in the civil service. The Ivory Coast poet and novelist, Bernard Dadié, who had then recently graduated from William Ponty and was serving in Dakar, has vividly summarized the impact of the Front on such as himself:

"Relationships between Europeans and Africans seemed to become more cordial, more human. . . . Was this cordiality attributable to the newly inaugurated Popular Front policies? Europeans and Africans stood side by side in all public gatherings: on May First, at the Governor's Ball, etc. . . . Climbié [the novel's hero] read newspapers of all shades of political opinion, talked politics with certain leaders, with young administrators sent by the Popular Front to implement the new policies. These young Frenchmen talked to him about Karl Marx, Engels, Dialectics, Scientific Materialism. He listened to them. To tell the truth, he found all these difficult to understand. He was forced to consult the dictionary. At Ponty, none of these problems had ever been studied. These names were not known there. Philosophy, sociology, civic education? Not in the curriculum!"[33]

The Popular Front administration was thoroughly purged when France swung to the right. The reaction that culminated in the Vichy regime was projected in enlarged form on Africa. The paternalistic attitudes fostered by the Maréchal in the metropole were translated into an attempt to restore the authority of the chiefs at the expense of the educated strata. The Vichy government's racial attitudes, which led to the institution of segregation at home, gave official sanction to existing practices in Abidjan and elsewhere. When S.T.O., the forced labor system, was established in France, the old system in Africa was reinforced and made even more arbitrary. Africans were compelled to produce quotas of commodities needed by the metropole without adequate compensation. Such practices intensified discontent. "Long

[33] Bernard Dadié, *Climbié* (Paris: Editions Seghers, 1956), p. 105.

after the fall of the Vichy government and even after the Liberation, the memory of this difficult period continued to be successfully exploited for electoral purposes" in the Ivory Coast.[34]

The reinforcement of old restrictions and the imposition of new ones were perceived more keenly by those who had tasted the liberal attitudes of the Front than by any other group. The most significant consequence of Vichy was that it forced the African elite to identify with the masses. Earlier, graduates of William Ponty and some rich planters had been able to move up in the new system of social stratification. But now, even those who had become naturalized citizens were treated as common African subjects. African planters, who had shared in the benefits of the forced labor system, were not only forced to abandon their plantations because of a lack of manpower but were themselves liable to be recruited for work on European plantations. Wartime shortages of imported goods affected the elite more seriously than anyone else, including Europeans. Among the most vivid memories of this period related by members of the elite was the fact that because of shortages, they were forced to return to a more African way of life. Food was particularly important. During the war, local students staged a strike because the *pensionnat* of the Ecole Primaire Supérieure stopped preparing French-style meals; the few educated African women resented having to breast-feed their babies because no canned milk was available to them. In Africa, as in other societies, the upwardly mobile are particularly sensitive to status symbols.

To regain lost privileges—and because they had been made aware of the unfortunate lot of their countrymen—the elite enlisted the support of fellow Africans with whom few had identified before the war. In addition, French-speaking Africans were faced with one overwhelming fact: Frenchmen

[34] Amon d'Aby, *La Côte d'Ivoire . . .*, p. 44.

themselves had become the subjects of a foreign invader. They were not invincible.

The Growth of Voluntary Associations

A major phenomenon in the new towns during the interwar period was the rise of ethnic associations. These groups, whatever name they are called, have in common an organization based on traditional social groupings—the lineage, the clan, the village-group, or the tribe.[35] Although their original objectives were sports and leisure activities, they rapidly took on the additional goal of modifying traditional societies according to the aspirations of their leaders—the educated young men of almost every tribe, *commis* in the service of the government or of private firms. Membership included not only tribesmen who had migrated to the towns, but also others at home who were dissatisfied for one reason or another with chiefly rule. From their point of view, the chiefs were no longer adequate as mediators between the population and the colonial rulers. These "new men" attempted to take over the leadership of ethnic groups by substituting an association for the traditional political community. The chiefs, in fear of being eliminated altogether, often gave in to pressures, and thus the associations began to participate in tribal affairs.[36]

These groups were antitraditional, insofar as they challenged the traditional authority structure, and at the same time, neotraditional, in that they allowed tribal ties to be carried over into a new environment. In Treichville, where there

[35] For a general discussion of the characteristics and of the functions of such associations in Africa generally, see Hodgkin, pp. 84-92. These and other voluntary associations in the Ivory Coast have been studied by Immanuel Wallerstein in "The Emergence of Two West African Nations: Ghana and the Ivory Coast" (Unpublished Ph.D. dissertation, Department of Sociology, Columbia University, 1959).

[36] Unless otherwise indicated, this account is based on Amon d'Aby, *La Côte d'Ivoire . . .*, pp. 36-37, and *Le Problème des chefferies . . .*, pp. 36-37, as well as on interviews with participants in 1959.

were no ethnic neighborhoods, they protected their members against the isolation and the dangers of a heterogeneous environment. Their leaders acquired the experience of modern forms of administration. Although the groups were bureaucratic in form, with a president, a general secretary, a treasurer, and other officials specialized according to function, they also incorporated traditional concepts of leadership based on ascription. In some cases, for example, offices were inherited according to prevailing norms in a particular society. In addition to their functions for city dwellers, these groups also provided then, as they do today, communication links between the towns and the hinterland. Political communications could thus rapidly reach every corner of the country through this network.

Such associations underwent a double process of fragmentation and regrouping. The name they usually bear is somewhat misleading because it often refers to the *cercle* or the *subdivision* from which the members originate rather than to a particular tribe. Yet, when one looks closely at the *Association des Originaires de Daloa*, for example, it is clear that only Bété, the natives of the district, belong to it. Over the years, these associations became differentiated not only according to the larger ethnic group with which the members identify, as for example the Baoulé, but also according to the eight Baoulé tribes, and sometimes even subgroups of villages within a larger traditional political entity. In 1959 over two hundred distinct societies of this type were enumerated in Treichville alone.[37] But at the same time, a process of regrouping was at work. For societies in which there is little organization above the village level, such associations have created a tribal consciousness that is not founded on the existence of a traditional unit. This often occurred as the result of status competition between

[37] This estimate is based on a tally of names and scheduled meetings reported in *Abidjan-Matin*, the daily newspaper, during a period of nearly one year in 1959.

Africans, sometimes on the basis of French-imposed criteria. One political leader, who began his public career as founder of such an organization, summarized the process as follows: "We were dissatisfied with the outlook of the people in Abidjan who considered us as their inferiors. This was because our part of the country [the west] had contact with the French much later than most others. They used to say that we were cannibals, and that we did not even make up a tribe. Therefore, the few other intellectuals and myself organized a sort of federation in Abidjan to include all the people from our villages and from surrounding areas who spoke about the same language."[38]

Some ethnic groups coalesced further into larger associations, roughly coextensive with the culture circles discussed in Chapter II. These larger groups were the building blocks of early electoral coalitions after the war. The first of these was the *Association pour la Défense des Intérêts des Autochtones de la Côte d'Ivoire* (A.D.I.A.C.I.), founded in 1934 by the leaders of the Agni and other Akan groups of the southeast.[39] Although they hoped to gain support from other Akan tribes, they made little headway outside their own immediate region because they found the path to their goal blocked by the Baoulé, who soon organized the *Union Fraternelle des Originaires de Côte d'Ivoire.* In 1944 the westerners in Abidjan founded the *Union des Originaires des Six Cercles de l'Ouest,* which included most Kru ethnic groups on the other side of the Bandama River. The *Odienné Idéal,* which began as its name indicates with members from a single *cercle,* later incorporated other Malinké Moslems from Séguéla and elsewhere. Foreign Africans had their own associations, such as the *Union Fraternelle des Sénégalais,* or

[38] Interview with Mr. Séry Koré, 1959.

[39] Amon d'Aby, *La Côte d'Ivoire* . . ., p. 37. It is interesting to note that this name was an exact French translation of Aborigines Rights' Protection Society, an early association of a similar nature in Ghana, unable, like this one, to provide effective leadership for a nationalist movement.

the *Union Voltaique.* There were recurrent, but largely unsuccessful, attempts to regroup all foreigners into one single body.

When literate Africans were allowed to organize trade-unions in 1938, these bodies rapidly included every white-collar occupational group. The *Syndicat des Instituteurs* and the association of auxiliary doctors, pharmacists, nurses, midwives, and veterinarians, which bore the unlikely name, *Synmedvetpharsa*—incorporating all the occupations included—as well as various government clerks' unions were particularly outstanding because they counted as their members most of the graduates of William Ponty and the Ecole Primaire Supérieure. From the same strata also emerged cultural associations, devoted to the theatre and to the study of "folklore," as African customs were termed before the war.[40] Their leaders and members, who often also belonged to the ethnic associations already discussed, were united by the bonds formed during the years together at school, by common residence in administrative quarters, and often by marriage ties, since few *évolués* would consent to marry into a *non-évolué* family. They transcended not only ethnic and regional affiliations but territorial ones as well, because graduates of William Ponty were liable to serve anywhere in the federation. These individuals constituted a ready-made freemasonry when the time came to launch political movements in the Ivory Coast and in the whole of French West Africa.

Other economic associations involved self-employed Africans. Although entrepreneurial opportunities were limited, there were some in transport and in farming. The *Syndicat*

[40] Amon d'Aby, himself a playwright, devotes a special chapter to the theatre in *La Côte d'Ivoire* . . . The three authors he mentions, beside himself, all became leading lights in the P.D.C.I. The theatre tradition that began in school around 1934 has remained a lively one; the country's troupe has been repeatedly acclaimed in Paris. One of the authors became Minister of Interior in 1960. There is an interesting parallel between this and the *Ballet de Keita Fodéba* in Guinea.

des Transporteurs, a guild-like organization, has existed since the 1930's in one form or another, notwithstanding recurrent split-offs and reorganizations. The ability to transport individuals to the polls and to rallies gave its members, who own trucks and *rapides*[41] used for public transportation, a great deal of weight in parties and movements. Attempts to organize coffee and cocoa growers began during the 1930's under the leadership of southeasterners, who were also involved in the establishment of the A.D.I.A.C.I. The purpose of the early efforts was to create a cooperative that could secure loans from the government-controlled agricultural credit fund.[42] However, little progress was made; chiefs were suspicious of this possible challenge to their influential position and the ethnic antagonism between the Agni and other farmers elsewhere hindered effective action. After its failure, Ivory Coast farmers joined the European-dominated *Syndicat Agricole de la Côte d'Ivoire*, for membership in *some* such organization was necessary in view of the corporatism embedded in the French colonial structure.[43] This was not a happy marriage because during the war, European members methodically discriminated against Africans.

African hopes to again launch an organization better suited to the defense of their particular interests were boosted when Governor Latrille, appointed by the French Committee of National Liberation to replace his Vichy-designated predecessor, attempted to break the hold of the pro-Vichy Europeans on the economy by sponsoring the creation of a countervailing organization, the *Syndicat Agricole Africain* (S.A.A.).[44] The

[41] These are converted trucks with benches and windows.

[42] Amon d'Aby, *La Côte d'Ivoire* . . ., p. 110.

[43] On many economic questions, the government consulted quasi-official bodies, such as the Chamber of Commerce and the Chamber of Agriculture, themselves made up of representatives of the various trade and agricultural associations. Sometimes these consular chambers directly managed a government program, such as the allocation of scarce imports.

[44] Amon d'Aby, *La Côte d'Ivoire* . . ., pp. 110-12.

S.A.A. grew from the top down. Its eight cofounders appointed agents at the level of every *subdivision*. These representatives, who were required to be literate in French, were usually leading planters who were also county chiefs, as was one of the founders, Félix Houphouet-Boigny. Membership was officially restricted to farmers who had at least two hectares (about five acres) of land, but in practice it was open to smaller farmers willing to pay the annual 300 fr. dues. By the end of 1944, membership had grown to 8,548 with nearly half of the members concentrated in the two Baoulé-dominant *cercles* of Bouaké and Dimbokro. Most of the other members were scattered throughout the forest zone, with the exception of the southeast. This area, which produced 53 per cent of the coffee and cocoa grown in the Ivory Coast, accounted for only 10 per cent of the membership. It was obvious that the Agni remained outside the mainstream of African organizational life.[45]

Of the 8 founders, 4 were from the southeast, 3 were Dioulas, and only 1 was a Baoulé. The Baoulé, Houphouet-Boigny, derived support from the largest group of members and was easily elected president when the organization held its first congress in Abidjan in September 1944. At the first congress, which was held in order to define the aims of the organization, the most important resolutions adopted were: to secure premiums for African producers; to organize cooperative sales in order to eliminate middlemen; to obtain a quota of imported cloth and agricultural implements; to secure a more equitable allocation of manpower for its members. The Africans in the S.A.A. also considered an alternative solution to the manpower problem—obtaining the elimination of administrative recruitment altogether. This

[45] All information on the S.A.A. was obtained from interviews with members of its permanent secretariat. Data concerning membership was computed from the registers in the organization's archives. Production figures are drawn from Table 3 above.

they felt would place them in a more competitive position because they would be able to negotiate directly with traditional chiefs in the north for the services of their young men. Furthermore, payment could be arranged by sharing the crop among the workers, thus freeing farmers from the hold of money-lenders. In the first months of its existence the S.A.A. thus engaged in a multitude of activities and grew in importance beyond the confines of its membership. Although it had no members in the savanna regions, contacts were established there when negotiations for manpower were undertaken. After the war, its membership lists were used to draw up electoral registers, and during the first political campaign, it served as an admirable machine to promote the candidacy of its president.

Political Beginnings

The leaders of Free France, indebted to the Empire, where the fight for liberation had been carried on after the metropole fell in 1940, pledged a new deal for the colonies.[46] The debt was symbolically repaid by holding a policy conference on this subject at Brazzaville in 1944.[47] Although the ultimate goals of French policy remained ambiguous, the prewar *Conseil Supérieur des Colonies* and other consultative bodies were abolished, and subjects were invited to participate alongside citizens in the forthcoming French Constituent Assembly. The election in October 1945 of a man to represent Ivory Coast subjects in Paris was the first opportunity most Africans had of manifesting their political concerns and their preferences at the territorial level.

The October election had been preceded in August by elections for the Abidjan Municipal Council, postponed since

[46] Charles de Gaulle, *The War Memoirs of General de Gaulle*, Vol. I, *The Call to Honour* (New York: The Viking Press, 1955), pp. 44, 107.

[47] The Brazzaville Conference is summarized in Adloff and Thompson, pp. 30-33. For an Ivory Coast reaction, see Amon d'Aby, *La Côte d'Ivoire . . .*, pp. 44-46.

1939 because of the war.[48] European and African citizens, as well as some subjects, voted on a common roll for a slate to be composed of 9 subjects and 9 citizens. The subjects, who were a majority of the electorate, could win if they united in support of a single ticket. In contrast to the leaders who advocated a slate that included some Europeans and to others who proposed various lists of candidates dominated by a single ethnic group, Houphouet-Boigny put forward the radical notion of excluding whites altogether and formed instead a coalition of Ivory Coast tribes and foreign Africans. His slate comprised 8 Ivoiriens, including only 1 Baoulé beside himself, 6 Senegalese, 2 Dahomeyans, and 2 Guineans. Most other African tickets withdrew and Europeans abstained in protest. Houphouet-Boigny's *Bloc Africain* secured 1,495 out of 1,523 votes cast.[49]

In October citizens and subjects voted for separate representatives. To win on the first ballot, a candidate needed at least one-fourth of the total registered votes and an absolute majority of the votes cast; if he failed to obtain this a run-off election would be held. Of the 31,384 voters in the *deuxième collège*, made up entirely of subjects, 15,101 were in the Ivory Coast proper and 16,282 in Upper Volta districts.[50] Since the Mossi Empire formed a fairly homogeneous unit that controlled a large bloc of votes, a candidate from Upper Volta might easily be elected unless Ivoiriens agreed on a single man. A nominating committee composed of leaders

[48] Abidjan had become in 1939 a *Commune Mixte du Deuxième Degré*, entitled to elect its own municipal council on the basis of universal suffrage for citizens and restricted categories of subjects. Amon d'Aby, *La Côte d'Ivoire* . . ., p. 47.

[49] This section is based on the account contained in Amon d'Aby, *La Côte d'Ivoire* . . ., pp. 47-50, supplemented by interviews with participants.

[50] Upper Volta, 1 of the 8 colonies of French West Africa, was carved into several parts in 1932. The major section was attached to the Ivory Coast, probably in order to facilitate control over the flow of manpower to the southern forest zone. The territory was reconstituted as a separate entity in 1947.

of voluntary associations in Abidjan failed to reach a consensus, however,[51] and 5 Ivoiriens competed on the first ballot. Beside Houphouet-Boigny, they included A. Boni and K. Binzème, 2 southeasterners who had studied law in France; A. Digna-Bailly, a Bété who had spent many years abroad and had even been active in French Socialist politics at the municipal level in Paris; and Tidiane Dem, a northern businessman, the son of one of Samory's lieutenants. There were also 6 Upper Volta candidates, headed by Tenga Ouedraogo, Chief Page in the Mossi Empire. Three Europeans and 1 Senegalese brought the total to 14.[52]

Electoral results, organized in Table 6 by Ivory Coast and Upper Volta districts, clearly show that support centered from the very first around Houphouet-Boigny in the Ivory Coast proper and around Tenga Ouedraogo in the north. Houphouet-Boigny's plurality was insufficient, and a run-off election was held the following month. The trend already noted was accentuated at that time. It is important to analyze the sources of Houphouet-Boigny's earliest success in order to understand the basis of his political strength in the country.

In the Houphouet-Boigny camp preparations for the 1945 elections had begun much earlier through the formation of an efficient electoral committee, made up of about 30 leaders of major voluntary associations. Among them were officials of the S.A.A. and of Baoulé ethnic associations. Support from these sources, however, accounted for only about half of the votes Houphouet-Boigny obtained.[53] Other important blocs in the coalition accounted for the remainder. Ouezzin Coulibaly,

[51] Amon d'Aby, *La Côte d'Ivoire . . .*, pp. 55-56.

[52] Unless otherwise indicated, all information on this election is based on documents and results on file at the Ministry of the Interior, Ivory Coast, and used with the permission of the Ivory Coast government.

[53] Dimbokro and Bouaké *cercles* account for 23 per cent and 18 per cent of the votes cast for Houphouet-Boigny on the first and second ballots respectively. If other regions of S.A.A. concentration are added to these Baoulé areas, only about 45 per cent of the votes Houphouet-Boigny received can be accounted for.

TABLE 6

Elections of a Representative of the Second College to the First French National Constituent Assembly, 1945

Candidates	*Ivory Coast Districts*		*Upper Volta Districts*		*Total*	
	Votes	*Per Cent*	*Votes*	*Per Cent*	*Votes*	*Per Cent*
	First Ballot, October					
Houphouet-B.	8,456	79.0	4,224	38.8	12,680	49.8
T. Ouedraogo	566	5.2	9,150	62.2	9,716	38.2
Others (12)	1,708	15.8	1,325	9.0	3,033	12.0
Total valid votes	10,730	100.0	16,283	100.0	25,429	100.0
	Second Ballot, November					
Houphouet-B.	9,067	83.5	3,913	24.2	12,980	50.7
T. Ouedraogo	862	7.9	10,759	73.0	11,621	45.4
Others (8)[a]	940	8.6	55	.5	995	3.9
Total valid votes	10,869	100.0	14,727	100.0	25,596	100.0

[a] Five candidates withdrew and one new one entered on the second ballot.

leader of the Teachers' Union, brought in much of the non-Mossi Upper Volta vote; the U.O.C.O.C.I., represented on the electoral committee by E. Djaument and S. Koré, channeled support from the west; Senegalese, to whom Houphouet-Boigny was related by marriage, helped bring in the votes of foreign Africans who had been under obligation to the *Bloc Africain* since the August 1945 elections. Cohesion in this heterogeneous alliance was heightened by the desire to stop Upper Volta.[54] Its organizational tasks were facilitated by the benevolent neutrality, if not the outright support, of the Ivory Coast Governor and his second-in-command, a French communist. These two men naturally took an interest in insuring the success of the S.A.A., an organization they had helped create.[55]

[54] Amon d'Aby, *La Côte d'Ivoire* . . ., p. 56.
[55] The following example, based on documents in Ivory Coast archives,

Houphouet-Boigny also showed great political acumen in the choice of campaign issues. His manifesto reflected widespread grievances and advocated mostly social and economic measures, including expansion of educational facilities, school-building programs, scholarships for study abroad, elimination of all "adapted" aspects of the curriculum to insure equality with French education, and establishment of institutions of secondary education in the Ivory Coast proper. The platform also demanded the creation of a good network of roads, bridges, railroads, harbors, and air transport, "built with machines rather than with heavy physical labor";[56] better working conditions and salaries, paid vacations and retirement pay; promotional opportunities for civil servants; low-cost housing developments; easier procedures for African land registry; and finally, the abolition of forced labor. Concerning the constitution, it advocated implementation of the resolutions of the Brazzaville Conference including: citizenship for all *évolués*, elimination of the *indigénat*, creation of new communes, and formation of a local elected assembly (made up of Europeans and Africans) which would determine priorities in development and control the local budget. None of the other candidates opposed any of these suggestions, but none was as outspoken in advocating them.[57] Kouame Binzème, for example, emphasized almost exclusively constitutional

---

illustrates the political role of the Governor. While establishing the electoral register in his district, a *commandant* asked the Governor whether members of the S.A.A. who did not meet the property qualifications to vote should be registered. He added that "for 300 fr., Africans now think they can buy citizenship." The Governor's curt answer was: Register all members of the S.A.A. Although it is reported also that communist organizers helped the Houphouet-Boigny organization, no evidence was found. A *Groupe d'Etudes communistes* was created only in April 1946, according to the declaration filed.

[56] Houphouet-Boigny's campaign manifesto is on file in the archives of the Bureau of Political Affairs, Ministry of Interior, Ivory Coast.

[57] Several members of the Houphouet-Boigny electoral committee admitted this in interviews, 1959. It was confirmed by one of Binzème's supporters.

problems, which were less interesting than the tangible measures for economic and social betterment to many of the new voters.[58]

Another element in Houphouet-Boigny's success was his personal position in Ivory Coast society. The Ivory Coast leader, a Baoulé of the Akoué tribe and a member of a chiefly lineage, was born in 1905 in Yamoussoukro, a small village of Dimbokro *cercle*.[59] He graduated from William Ponty and became a *médecin africain* in 1925, one of the first Baoulé to reach the apex of the educational system. As a Ponty *major*, first in his class, he had status among the educated strata; but unlike Binzème, Boni, Bailly, and a handful of others who had studied in France and lived abroad for several years, he had not removed himself from the mainstream of Ivory Coast life. He served in the colonial medical service in various parts of the Ivory Coast until 1940. While stationed at Abengourou, where he took interest in efforts being made to organize cocoa and coffee growers,[60] he married his first wife, who was of royal Agni lineage through her mother's line and a Senegalese through her father. Through this marriage, he acquired kinship ties with other Akan and among foreign residents as well. When his maternal uncle died in 1940, he inherited large amounts of land in Yamoussoukro and was appointed *chef de canton* of the Akoué. By taking the lead in organizing the *Association des Chefs Coutumiers*, he extended his influence among traditional leaders outside his own ethnic group. At the time of his emergence as leader of the S.A.A., he was one of the richest African farmers in the entire country. He not only symbolized the achievements

[58] Amon d'Aby, *La Côte d'Ivoire* . . ., p. 56.

[59] Houphouet-Boigny's traditional status is somewhat controversial. Some of his critics have suggested that his maternal family came to occupy a Baoulé stool only because of French administrative interference. I have included in this biographical account only information that seems generally accepted. It was obtained in an interview with President Houphouet-Boigny in 1959 and checked with a variety of informants.

[60] In 1933. Amon d'Aby, *La Côte d'Ivoire* . . ., p. 110.

of the emerging Ivory Coast *bourgeoisie* but had the personal means to finance a political campaign.

The most important factor, however, was his ability to take advantage of personal position, political opportunities, and widespread grievances, to create a sort of federation of ethnic groups. His mastery of ethnic calculus might well make him a successful politician in any American metropolis. The knowledge that the Baoulé could not stand alone was the source of a dream of territorial unity. As Houphouet-Boigny himself said, "If unity had not been in our heart, we should have discovered it in our head."[61]

These elements were overshadowed by his achievements during the First National Constituent Assembly. On March 1, 1946, a bill was tabled "by M. Houphouet and some of his colleagues"[62] proposing the abolition of all forms of forced labor in Overseas France. Viewed from France, then searching for a new regime, this was but a minor item; it called for neither floor debate nor even for a roll-call vote at any stage of its passage. But viewed from Africa, and especially from the Ivory Coast, its promulgation on April 3, 1946, marked African emancipation from a state akin to that of slavery. Not only did this remove at one stroke the most hated symbol of colonial rule, but it had been achieved by one of the Ivory Coast's own sons. Overnight, Félix Houphouet-Boigny became a mythical hero who had imposed his will upon the French. For many years, people throughout the country—encouraged by the Houphouet-Boigny organization—firmly believed that unless he were returned to office, forced labor would be reinstated. The gratitude he earned from his countrymen has remained a foremost element in his political power and it has prevailed over the hesitations of many

[61] Quoted from interview notes.

[62] For the history of the bill, see: France, *Annales de l'assemblée nationale constituante élue le 21 octobre 1945, Débats*, II (January-March 1946), 548; III (March 12-30, 1946), 1320; IV (April 1-17, 1946), 1514 (Paris: Imprimerie des journaux officiels, 1946).

followers who questioned his later policies. Fifteen years later, a member of the Legislative Assembly, when asked how and why he became involved in politics, explained: "It was very simple. The peasants of my region suffered a great deal from forced labor. In my own family, there were twenty-four men and boys, but most of the time there were few around to work for the family. The others were out slaving for the commandant. When politics began, President Houphouet said he would do everything to eliminate this barbarous practice. I decided that this was for me, and I followed him. We didn't know whether he could do it, but he kept his word. Since then, I have followed him blindly and I shall continue to do so as long as he remains faithful to this principle."[63]

With this added advantage, Houphouet-Boigny towered over all his opponents in the June 1946 elections (made necessary by the defeat of the first draft constitution in the May 1946 referendum) for a representative to the Second Constituent Assembly.[64] His manifesto, much the same as it had been in 1945, now embraced constitutional proposals put forward by the left in the Assembly, a French Union based on the free consent of its members, in which all would have equal rights. Houphouet-Boigny now ran under the banner of the *Parti Démocratique de Côte d'Ivoire*, founded officially in April, and allied in the Constituent Assembly with the French Communist Party. His major opponents, who had earlier created an agricultural association designed to supplant the S.A.A. in the southeast and in the north, now formed a coalition under the name of *Parti Progressiste de Côte d'Ivoire*,[65] hoping to secure substantial support in

[63] Interview with El Hadj Moussa Kone, 1959.

[64] For details of the work of the Committee on Overseas France and the fate of its proposals, see Chap. VII, "100,000,000 Frenchmen," in Gordon Wright, *The Reshaping of French Democracy* (New York: Reynal and Hitchcock, 1948), pp. 142-50.

[65] Its two main leaders were K. Binzème and T. Dem. The agricultural association was the *Syndicat des Planteurs et des éleveurs Africains.*

these areas. But the P.D.C.I. candidate was invincible. In June 1946 he obtained 98 per cent of the votes cast in Ivory Coast districts, compared with 83 per cent in November 1945; abstentions dropped from 27 per cent in November to 18 per cent in June.[66] There was no opposition in Upper Volta, where the leading candidate had withdrawn from the race in exchange for Houphouet-Boigny's pledge of support for northern demands for separate status. In less than a year Houphouet-Boigny had achieved personal domination of the Ivory Coast political stage.

Conclusions

The founders of the P.D.C.I. forged unity out of an amalgam of heterogeneous components by constructing an indirect party in which individuals were not members of the party but of social groups that belonged to the party.[67] About one-third of the estimated 80,000 members and supporters in 1946 belonged to the S.A.A.;[68] the remainder were affiliated through some of the other groups mentioned in this chapter. Cohesion stemmed from the multiple links among the leaders. The issues they defined did not lead to disagreement, mostly because they were very general and encompassed the grievances of almost every group in the society. The members were remarkably disparate, including normally antagonistic elements, such as chiefs and young men; westerners, renowned for their dislike of strangers and foreigners; individuals who had been influenced by the Socialist party; and new recruits in the *Groupe d'Etudes Communistes*. Because the coalition was not involved in an intensive struggle with an out-group,

[66] The second college electorate (Ivory Coast districts only) grew from 14,971 in November to 18,958 in June. Percentages were computed from data on file in the Ministry of Interior.

[67] Duverger, pp. 6-17.

[68] In December 1946, 71,916 voted for the R.D.A. candidates. This figure is of the same order of size as the 65,000 members claimed by the R.D.A. in the Ivory Coast at the Bamako Conference of October, 1946. The figure we use is a maximum estimate.

local antagonisms that threatened to disrupt it could be tolerated. No attempts were made to integrate chiefs and young men, or Bété and Dioula, at the local level. As Simmel has suggested, "the group in a state of peace can permit antagonistic members within it to live with one another in an undecided situation because each of them can go his own way and avoid collisions."[69]

In the latter part of 1946 changing political conditions in France and the reactions of European *colons* in the Ivory Coast to the emergence of African political organizations led to active efforts on the part of the colonial government to destroy the P.D.C.I. In a sense, the organization was at war. Simmel has suggested that "a state of conflict . . . pulls the members so tightly together and subjects them to such uniform impulse that they either must go completely along with, or completely repel, one another. This is the reason why war with the outside is sometimes the last chance for a state ridden with inner antagonisms to overcome these antagonisms, or else to break up definitely."[70] The consequences of this state of war for the P.D.C.I. and more generally for the Ivory Coast will be considered next. But first, it is necessary to examine the institutional framework of the French Union, which conditioned Ivory Coast politics from 1946 on.

[69] Simmel, *Conflict*, p. 92.
[70] *Ibid.*

PART II

THE RISE OF THE PARTI DÉMOCRATIQUE DE CÔTE D'IVOIRE

CHAPTER III

THE INSTITUTIONAL FRAMEWORK OF POSTWAR POLITICS

✧ ALTHOUGH France pledged in the preamble to her new constitution "to guide the peoples for whom she has assumed responsibility toward freedom to govern themselves and democratically to manage their own affairs," the nature of the French Union that emerged from the labors of the constituent assemblies of 1945 and 1946 was highly ambiguous. The prewar colonial system was considerably modified, but self-government was ruled out, as it had been at Brazzaville in 1944. Full integration of African tropical dependencies into the French Republic was never seriously considered. However, the local councils instituted in the dependencies were modeled after the ones in French departments, and all the territories were represented in the parliament of the Fourth Republic, one and indivisible. A federal solution was rejected, but the Assembly of the French Union could be seen as the nucleus of a federal or confederal community. This chapter is not concerned with the sources of these ambiguities nor with the operations of the French Union as a whole, but only with the consequences of these institutional arrangements for the territory that is the object of this study.[1]

PARTICIPATION AND REPRESENTATION

The Electorate

All French subjects were made citizens in 1946, but a distinction continued to exist between citizens of French status (*citoyens de droit français*)—a category that included metro-

[1] The best general studies of the institutions of the French Union are contained in the works of Prof. Kenneth Robinson, P. F. Gonidec, and L. Gray Cowan, cited in the bibliography.

politan Frenchmen and former African citizens—and citizens of local status, the former subjects. Citizens of French status had universal suffrage and constituted the first college of electors. Only some of the others could participate in elections; they constituted the second college. From November 1946 on, these colleges voted for the same *députés* to the French National Assembly but for different representatives at the local level.

The second college grew slowly in the Ivory Coast through the designation of additional categories of individuals as electors. In October 1946 the categories included the following: members and former members in good standing of local assemblies (such as municipal councils and *conseils des notables*); members of voluntary associations properly registered with the government; government employees; other white-collar workers employed for over ten years; veterans and recipients of honors; licensed traders and businessmen; holders of hunting or driving permits. In 1947 all those who were certified to be literate in French were added.[2] In 1951 new categories included: heads of family who had fulfilled their tax obligation; mothers of two children "living or dead for France"; recipients of pensions. The following year, all heads of household were included. Figure 1 summarizes this growth and indicates the gap between the actual electorate at any given time and what it might have been under universal suffrage. The African electorate grew approximately from 1 out of 80 adults in October 1945 to 1 out of 10 in November 1946. It reached 1 out of 7 in 1952, and finally included approximately 1 out of 2 in 1956.[3] The grant of universal suffrage in June 1956 coincided with other major reforms in the French Union system.

Until the right to participate in elections was obtained by all Africans, almost every political organization focused upon

[2] For a detailed discussion of these categories and the French justifications for their use, see Cowan, pp. 98-99.

[3] This last increment was due to a broader interpretation of existing rules rather than to additional categories of voters.

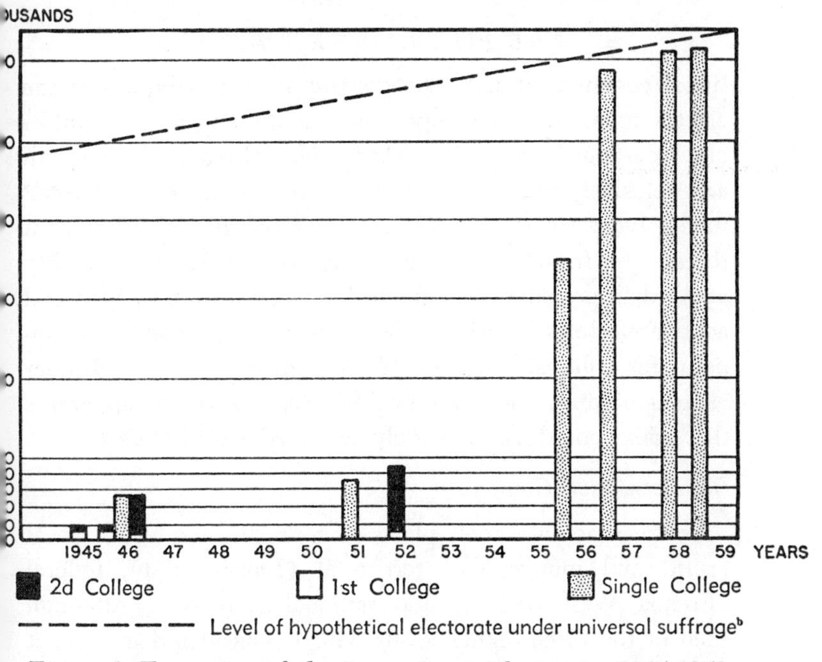

Figure 1. Expansion of the Ivory Coast Electorate, 1945-1959, Territorial Assembly and National Assembly[a]

universal suffrage as a major demand. Although the electorate was small, electoral performance was regarded as an important index of the strength of political groups by the French authorities as well as by the African participants themselves. Every movement, in order to survive, must also operate as an electoral machine. The nature of the electorate facilitated their organizational tasks, since those who were eligible to vote tended to be more educated, more involved in business activities, and more active in voluntary associations than the bulk of the population. They constituted that sector of the population which was "mobilized" into the network of na-

[a] All data on the electorate were obtained from records on file in the Bureau of Political Affairs, Ministry of the Interior, Ivory Coast.

[b] Hypothetical electorate was obtained by computing the estimated proportion of adults of both sexes for each year from the population figures contained in: Godin, "Problèmes démographiques," *Marchés Tropicaux*, April 18, 1959, pp. 1021-24.

tional communication.[4] The geographical distribution of the electorate was also an important conditioning factor. Unlike other parts of West Africa, where political parties began with an exclusively urban clientele because they alone could vote,[5] in the Ivory Coast the electorate was distributed throughout the country from the very beginning. In 1945 the municipality of Abidjan provided only about 2 per cent of the total second college electorate for Ivory Coast districts. Although the impetus for political action could come from Abidjan and other centers, organizations were impelled to construct an apparatus that could coordinate a widely scattered electorate.[6]

Representative Councils

Political activity took place at four distinct levels: local (rural and municipal),[7] territorial (Ivory Coast), federal (French West Africa), and national (France). Although each of the three higher levels will be considered in turn, it is important to remember that a political organization had to act on all fronts at once.

[4] Deutsch, pp. 100-101.

[5] Compare, for example, with Senegal, where the older urban parties were overwhelmed when participation was suddenly extended to the hinterland. Paul Mercier, "Political Life in the Urban Centers of Senegal: A Study of a Period of Transition," *Political Research: Organization and Design*, III (June 1960), 3-20.

[6] The more developed parts of the country, in particular the southeast, were slightly overrepresented in terms of their proportion of the total population. Generally, there were no great divergences between the distribution of the electorate and that of the population as a whole.

[7] Until 1955, municipal government remained largely in the sphere of the executive. There were three categories of communes in French West Africa: *commune mixte du premier degré*, with an appointed municipal council and an official mayor; *commune mixte du second degré*, with an elected council on a restricted suffrage basis; and *commune de moyen exercice*, with a council elected on the basis of universal suffrage; the last two also had official executives, but with some elected assistant mayors. There were none in the highest of these categories in the Ivory Coast before 1953, when Abidjan, Bouaké, and Grand Bassam were promoted to that rank. There is no adequate explanation for this lack of development of local government, except to note that the French are less concerned with "grass-roots democracy," perhaps, than are Anglo-Saxon countries.

TERRITORIAL. The main focus here was the Territorial Assembly,[8] whose political importance was much greater than its constitutional authority. Originally, these organs were modeled after the equivalent institutions of French departments and were viewed as auxiliaries of the executive branch of government. Their primary concern was with regional economic questions rather than with political matters. "They were, according to Napoleonic principles, purely deliberative —that is to say that the initiative of administrative measures was completely beyond their reach. Furthermore, the Assemblies did not truly have decisional authority. In the most important matters, their deliberations became authoritative only after the intervention of the executive."[9] The Assembly could deliberate on the following items: control over the disposal of property belonging to the territory; classification of roads and waterways; attribution of scholarships; provisions for public relief; determination of sources of territorial revenue. In this last matter, its decisions were subject to final review by the French *Conseil d'Etat*.[10] On a variety of other subjects, the Assembly had to be consulted by the executive: land grants above a certain size; organization of administration; education; economic representation; and regulation of hunting and fishing. What would happen if the executive neglected to take into consideration the Assembly's recommendations remained unwritten in the basic decrees.

[8] It was known as *conseil général* until 1952, and *Assemblée Territoriale* from 1952 to 1958, after which it became in turn *constituante*, *législative*, and *nationale*. In order to avoid confusion, I shall refer to it as Territorial Assembly until 1958, and its members will be called assemblymen.

[9] P. F. Gonidec, "L'évolution des territoires d'Outre-Mer depuis 1946," *Revue Juridique et Politique de l'Union Française*, VIII (June-September 1957), 433.

[10] Decree 46-2375 of October 25, 1946, which sets forth the authority of the assembly, and on which the discussion is based, is reprinted along with other pertinent documents in Ivory Coast, Assemblée Territoriale, "Création, formation, règlement intérieur" (Abidjan, n.d.), pp. 10-32. (Mimeographed.) This decree was subsequently modified by Law 52-130 of February 6, 1952, also reprinted therein, pp. 34-43.

Although the Assembly shared the initiative with the executive in allocating public revenue, its authority in this domain was severely restricted. "Mandatory" expenditures, earmarked for government services considered vital by the colonial administration, and which amounted to nearly one-half of the entire territorial budget, could not be modified at all.[11] Whenever the Assembly tried to reduce the effectiveness of the coercive apparatus, for example, by reducing budgetary allocations in this category, the executive could simply reinstate the cuts by transferring funds from other chapters in the budget. Furthermore, the Assembly could not initiate new expenditures or reduce revenue without compensating for its decision by cutting other expenditures or finding new sources of income.

The Assembly could also express its opinion on every other matter pertaining to the administrative and economic life of the country, as long as it remained nonpolitical, a term that remained itself undefined. Its motions, called *voeux*, were binding upon no one at all. Through its president, the Assembly could also request information from the executive on matters within its jurisdiction, and could communicate its views on the state of things in the Ivory Coast directly to the Governor-General of French West Africa or to the Minister of Overseas France. Finally, it could delegate its members to inquire into specific questions within its jurisdiction; for example, a committee could be sent to interview the population in order to ascertain in what manner transactions concerning the sale of land were carried out. As an electoral college, it chose 5 Ivory Coast representatives to the *Grand Conseil* in Dakar and 4 representatives to the Assembly of the French Union, as well as 3 representatives to the Council

[11] Mandatory expenditures in the first budget, submitted in the fall of 1946 for fiscal year 1947 amounted to 42 per cent. This was computed from Ivory Coast, *Budget pour l'Année 1947* (Abidjan: Imprimerie du Gouvernement, 1946).

of the Republic. The last two sets of individuals were not necessarily drawn from its own ranks.

Notwithstanding their limited authority, "as the representatives of the people in the territories members of the assemblies increasingly came to regard themselves not as local councilors, but as legislators in their own right . . . ."[12] This was true for both European and African members. Although there were many clashes between them, they all agreed that their powers were too narrow, and efforts to widen the authority of the Assembly as well as to make the executive more accountable to it were never abandoned.

Until 1957, the Assembly was made up of two sections elected by the first and second college respectively, with a varying number of members as indicated in Table 7.[13] Although the Africans were always in the majority, European representation was much greater in relation to the electorate or to the population ratio. This was, needless to say, one of the most important sources of continued African discontent.

TABLE 7

Membership of the Territorial Assembly, 1946-1957

Period	*First Section*		*Second Section*		*Total*
	Seats	*Constituencies*	*Seats*	*Constituencies*	*Seats*
1946-1948[a]	20	3	30	10	50
1948-1952[b]	18	2	27	7	45
1952-1957	18	8	32	17	50

[a] Until 1948, part of Upper Volta was included in the Ivory Coast. These districts had 2 members of the first section and 15 members of the second section.

[b] After the departure of Upper Volta Assemblymen, the others remained in the Assembly until 1952. The second college elected 12 additional members for Ivory Coast districts in May 1948.

[12] Cowan, p. 108.

[13] In 1947 and 1948 they were elected by a simple majority system with second ballot. From 1952 on, by a simple majority and a single ballot. Under both systems, there were multi-member constituencies. Proportional representation was never used.

In the Assembly, the two sections voted together on all matters, with the exception of the selection of representatives to the Council of the Republic. The Assembly was ruled by a *bureau* elected annually and headed by a president whose functions made him the most important elected official in the territory, aside from the *député*.[14] As presiding officer, he recognized members who wished to speak, controlled the mechanics of voting, corresponded with the executive, and acted as spokesman for the members. But his political importance transcended the formal aspects of his role. The annual contest for the position of president served as a test of strength of political groups and alliances in the Assembly were made and unmade for this purpose.

Although the two sections consistently took opposite stands on all issues, the second section would always have a majority. If cleavages did not differentiate consistently between African and European members, competition would become more delicately balanced; if but a few members of the second section sided with the first, majorities could be reversed. Therefore, the struggle between the Houphouet-Boigny organization, which attempted to develop and maintain solidarity among the African members, and its opponents, who tried to find chinks in this armor, supplied one of the major political themes in the Ivory Coast during the early postwar years. Although few of the Assembly's decisions were binding on the colonial administration, the symbolic value of political control over this body was very great. This was acknowledged indirectly by the administration which used

[14] The *bureau* also included 2 vice-presidents, 3 secretaries, and a *questeur*. The Assembly was organized into committees along functional lines. Normally, there were two ordinary sessions held in the fall and in the spring. The Governor, sometimes at the request of the president, could call for extraordinary sessions as well. The order of business was determined by a conference of the presidents of the various committees. Between sessions, much of the Assembly's work was carried out by a standing committee made up of 3 members of the second section and 2 of the first.

all available means to obtain a docile majority. Because of the importance of action in the Assembly, political organizations needed not only effective electoral machinery but vigorous and skillful parliamentary manipulators as well.

FEDERAL. From 1947 on, the territorial assemblies of each of the 8 territories elected 5 representatives to the *Grand Conseil de l'Afrique Occidentale Française* located in Dakar, Senegal. Although this enhanced the truly federal character of French West Africa, it was offset by the continued hierarchical relationship that prevailed in the executive sphere between the territorial and the federal levels. The powers of the council were substantially the same for the federation as a whole as were those of the territorial assemblies for its components.[15] In addition, however, the council controlled the allocation of federal subsidies and tax reimbursements to each of the territories.

Neither geography, nor social structure, nor economic factors provided unity in French West Africa.[16] But the continued existence of a federal level of government encouraged communications between African leaders and contributed to the formation of superterritorial parties. Coalitions were created in order to control the *bureau* of the *Grand Conseil*. Yet, the structure of the French Union also reinforced territorial identity. The territories, rather than the federation, were represented in Paris. Ivory Coast representatives in Dakar fought representatives of Upper Volta or of Sudan over the allocation of scarce financial resources.

It was generally agreed in the Ivory Coast that the federal level was not only superfluous but harmful as well. Before World War II, European businessmen were the most ardent spokesmen of "financial autonomy" for the colony.[17] In 1945,

[15] Cowan, p. 111.

[16] Elliot J. Berg, "The Economic Basis of Political Choice in French West Africa," *The American Political Science Review*, LIV, No. 2 (June 1960), 400.

[17] This referred to the desire to retain all indirect taxes, currently

TABLE 8

Ivory Coast Representation Abroad, 1945-1960[a]

Name of Organ	*Dates of Tenure*	*Number of Seats*	*Mechanics of Election and Electorate*
Grand Council of French West Africa (Dakar)	1947-1952 1952-1957 1957-1958	5 5 5	Elected by territorial assembly from its midst; sections voting together; list voting, proportional representation.
National Constituent Assembly (Paris)	1945-1946 1946	2 2	Elected directly by population, separately by two electoral colleges, one member each; simple majority, second ballot system.
National Assembly (Paris)	1946-1951 1951-1956 1956-1959	3[b] 2 2	Elected directly by population, both colleges voting together; proportional representation, voting by party lists.
Council of the Republic (Paris)	1947-1948	5[b]	Elected by territorial assembly, not necessarily from its midst; 3 for second section, 2 for first; proportional representation, list voting.
	1948-1955 1955-1959	3 3	Same electoral mechanics as before; 2 for second section, 1 for first.
Assembly of the French Union (Versailles)	1947-1953 1953-1958	4 4	Indirect election by territorial assembly, sections voting together, not necessarily from its midst; list voting, proportional representation.
Senate of the Community (Paris)	1959-1960	11	Elected by territorial assembly from its midst; list voting, majority rule.

[a] Only representation up to 1957 is discussed in this chapter; the table includes later representation as well because terms of office did not terminate at the same time.

[b] Reduction of representation in the National Assembly and the Council of the Republic afterwards was due to the reconstitution of Upper Volta.

collected by the federal government and reallocated to the territories on the basis of need, within the territory. The issues involved and the character of the tax structure after the war will be discussed in Chapter VI.

for example, the Vice-President of the Chamber of Commerce argued bluntly that Ivory Coast money must remain in the Ivory Coast.[18] The *Parti Progressiste* sent a memo to the members of the first Constituent Assembly arguing in favor of the elimination of the General-Government because of the unfair taxation structure that deprived the Ivory Coast of most of its revenue. In the first year of its existence, the Territorial Assembly unanimously endorsed a motion presented by a European member demanding the abolition of the federal government.[19] Even the territorial executive shared this attitude. Shortly before the Assembly proceeded to elect representatives to the Grand Council, the Governor stated that in Dakar, the Ivory Coast would give much but receive very little. He continued: "Our hopes will be with our representatives who will have to defend jealously, and if necessary, without respite, we ask of them, the wealth that has been acquired by our peoples and which many others will want to divide among themselves. Ours is not the faith of Saint Martin, who offered his cloak to the poor. . . . The cloak we entrust you with, gentlemen, we ask you to return it to us without too much damage."[20]

President Denise, general secretary of the P.D.C.I., said that he feared lest the members of the financial committee of the Assembly required a prolonged stay in a sanatorium as a result of their immense effort in fighting budgetary anemia during 1947. The causes of the disease? Again, it was the General-Government: "Like a giant squid that strikes a swimmer in the high seas, the General-Government sucks up most of our resources and dumps upon us, little by little,

[18] Amon d'Aby, *La Côte d'Ivoire* . . ., pp. 127-31.

[19] Ivory Coast, Conseil général, "Procès-Verbaux des débats," January 9, 1947 (in the archives of the Ivory Coast National Assembly). Cited hereafter as "Debates."

[20] *Ibid.*, October 9, 1947. During the same session, a government spokesman stated that the Ivory Coast had contributed 700 million francs to Dakar in 1947 but had only received 250 million in return.

all the departments that bring in no revenue, while retaining all those that pay for themselves. . . . After we deduct from our meagre budget the cost of administrative manpower . . .; after we deduct the costs of materiel, what remains to be expanded on the country's development? Practically nothing. . . . Unless Dakar stops taking all our blood and is willing to transfuse some of it back into us, it might have to pay for the flower and wreaths of our first-class funeral."[21] This issue gained in intensity during the next ten years, until the very existence of the federation was at stake. Paradoxically, the Ivory Coast provided the incentive both for the creation of the most important federation-wide political movement, the *Rassemblement Démocratique Africain* (R.D.A.) and for the eventual destruction of the federation itself. At this level, as well as within the territory, themes of unity and of disunity ran concurrently.

FRANCE. The most unique feature of the French Union system, which distinguished it sharply from either the British or the Belgian colonial systems, was the grant of representation to the overseas peoples in the metropolitan parliament. The consequences of involvement in French domestic politics for African leaders have been particularly evident in the case of Houphouet-Boigny.

Although the Ivory Coast was grossly underrepresented, with approximately one deputy per 1,250,000 population compared with one per 80,000 in France, representation in the National Assembly was of great political importance. First, it gave the territory at least a limited opportunity to participate in decision making at the most important level in the Fourth Republic. Secondly, African deputies benefited from parliamentary immunity, an invaluable protection during periods of bitter political warfare.[22] Thirdly, participation

[21] *Ibid.* M. Auguste Denise, as may be gathered from his language, attended William Ponty medical school and acquired a reputation as a brilliant surgeon before he entered full-time politics.

[22] Williams, pp. 193-94. He refers to the case of an African deputy,

in the game of internal French politics could be used to political advantage by shrewd tacticians, especially since the narrowness of governmental majorities sometimes enabled overseas representatives to cast decisive votes.[23] This could even lead, as it did in the case of Houphouet-Boigny, to membership in a French government with all the perquisites attached to ministerial office. The experience of the politics of negotiation and of the effective use of log-rolling tactics, acquired during Houphouet-Boigny's fourteen years in the National Assembly, influenced his political style even in spheres far removed from the French parliament.

Contact with political groups in the National Assembly provided links between African leaders and metropolitan French parties. In order to secure positions on committees of the National Assembly (apportioned to political groups on the basis of proportional representation), African representatives found it necessary either to constitute a group of their own or to affiliate themselves, through direct membership or *apparentement*, with French metropolitan groups. Which group to join in Paris became an important question, a question decided not only on the basis of ideological preferences but on the grounds of political expediency as well.[24] The political fortunes of African members fluctuated not only with those of the organization that elected them but also with those of the parliamentary group to which they belonged. *Apparentement* with the communists became very costly for Houphouet-Boigny

---

probably Ouezzin Coulibaly, who was made editor of his party's newspaper in order to overcome the dangers of repeated suits for libel that jeopardized the paper's existence. A *parlementaire* could be arrested only if caught in the act of committing a crime, or with the expressed leave of the house to which he belonged. Houphouet-Boigny escaped arrest in this manner in January 1950.

[23] Gonidec, p. 435.

[24] Concerning the activities of African representatives in Paris, see P. Guillemin, "Les élus d'Afrique Noire à l'Assemblée nationale sous la IVème République," *Revue Française de Science Politique*, VIII, No. 4 (December 1958), 861-77.

and others when that party returned to a position of permanent opposition in mid-1947.

Representation in the National Assembly also contributed to the territorialization of politics. In elections to the Territorial Assembly there were many small constituencies where individuals could make a bid for ethnic support, but in order to elect its deputies the country acted as a single constituency. Political organizations were thus forced to find ways to transcend the boundaries of tribes and regions, as Houphouet-Boigny's electoral committee had done in 1945. The system also reinforced sociological or psychological factors that contributed to the personalization of politics. In the Ivory Coast, as in other territories, the *député* was constantly in the limelight. He might begin as *primus inter pares* in a territorial party, but he was in a position to transform the party into a personal machine.

The Council of the Republic and the Assembly of the French Union were less important politically. The legislative powers of the Council of the Republic were severely restricted.[25] The Assembly of the French Union was an advisory body that had to be consulted on laws and decrees concerning Overseas France. It drew little public attention in France, and there is no evidence that its suggestions were ever taken into consideration in policy making.[26] But it served as a friendly forum where overseas representatives could make themselves heard above the din of domestic French politics

[25] Williams remarked: "The Council never has the first word, for it has no right to initiate, and never has the last, for its advice can always be overridden by the Assembly." In practice, it was a *chambre de réflexion* that had some influence on government policy rather than on legislation. Williams, p. 276.

[26] This was because its decisions could not affect the existence or the policies of government. Its debates were hardly reported in the press. *Ibid.*, p. 295. Nevertheless, the Assembly's debates are of great value to students of Overseas France because they contain a wealth of documentation not available elsewhere. The detailed history of the organ might reveal that its influence was greater than is suggested here; but this history remains to be undertaken.

that drowned out overseas problems in parliament. Nevertheless, these two organs provided additional opportunities to elevate party leaders to the rank of *parlementaire*, with the perquisites of status, economic advantages, and political security the position carried. The Ivory Coast had a total of nine such offices until 1948, at which time the number was lowered to seven. (See Table 8.) Indirect elections by the Assembly, with list voting and proportional representation, gave party leaders control over recruitment to these posts. This facilitated their use in political bargaining.

It is important to note, in conclusion, that although Ivoiriens participated in politics at these several levels, the focus for political organization remained territorial. All direct elections were waged on a territorial base; indirect elections required control of the Territorial Assembly. The system had much in common, structurally, with the system in the United States which gave the state legislatures control over the elections of Senators. Like the national parties in the United States, which have remained in some ways confederations of state machines, the *Rassemblement Démocratique Africain*, of which the P.D.C.I. was a component, was essentially an alliance of territorial parties.

The Executive

The Command Hierarchy

Representative organs in Africa had little control over the colonial bureaucracy. In France legislative oversight was restricted, and the cabinet retained the right to rule by decree in many matters concerning Overseas France.[27] The executive thus retained a great deal of discretion in decision making. At the lower levels, officials had relatively little authority within the colonial administration; in relation to the public, however, they remained almost absolute rulers.[28]

[27] Under Article 72 of the constitution. See Schachter, p. 395.
[28] This was noted in the case of British colonial structure as well.

The role of the *commandant* has been surrounded by a veritable mystique. To the Africans in the *cercle*, he was an authoritarian demiurge. Writers on French colonial policy have characterized his role as "humanitarian," "authoritarian," and "revolutionary," explaining that these attributes were inseparably linked.[29] With less flourish, he may be compared to the prefect of metropolitan France, of whom Chapman has written: "He is the representative of the State in the department and as such he is the direct representative of every Minister, not only the Minister of the Interior; all ministerial directions and requests should go through his hands even though they are to be carried out by members of another administrative service. He is therefore titular head of all state services within the Department, whether technical or administrative. The departmental chiefs of these services . . . may propose, but the Prefect decides. Even the most senior service heads can never for long deny their subordination to the Prefect."[30]

As the colonial system shifted from the prewar authoritarian to the postwar "welfare state" type, the role of the *commandant* underwent a similar change. At the time of French penetration, he had been the jack-of-all-trades; during the period of intensive colonization between the wars, he was the expert producer; after the war, he became the civic educator and

D. Apter and R. Lystad, "Bureaucracy, Party, and Constitutional Democracy: An Examination of Political Role Systems in Ghana," *Transition in Africa: Studies in Political Adaptation* (eds.) Gwendolen M. Carter and William O. Brown (Boston: Boston University Press, 1958), p. 21.

[29] Robert Delavignette, "Le Commandant de Cercle," *Service africain* (Paris: Gallimard, 1946), pp. 15-34. In 1931 Delavignette also wrote a narrative of his own experience as *commandant* among the Sénoufo of the Ivory Coast and Upper Volta, *Les paysans noirs* (Paris: Editions Stock, 1947).

[30] Brian Chapman, *Introduction to French Local Government* (London: George Allen and Unwin, Ltd., 1953), pp. 102-3. Apter has remarked that the continental model is also relevant in British Africa. (Apter, *The Gold Coast in Transition*, p. 132.)

community developer.[31] This was reflected in the curriculum of the Ecole Coloniale, later called the Ecole Nationale de la France d'Outre-Mer (E.N.F.O.M.), where most administrators obtained diplomas. The emphasis gradually shifted from administrative law to civil engineering, and more recently, to training in the social sciences and in the coordination of voluntary activities.[32]

Although after the war most French officials were career personnel, there was room within the limits of the civil service rules for political considerations in recruitment, assignment, and promotions. Overseas France was included in the parcelling out of the French bureaucracy into spheres of influence of the major political parties; after the war, as at the turn of the twentieth century, colonial appointments at the gubernatorial and higher levels were shared on a principle of proportional representation.[33] This explains why the Ivory Coast administration was weighted toward the Communists during the period of *tripartisme*, while at the same time Senegal remained a Socialist stronghold, and Upper Volta was predominantly M.R.P. In 1951 a modified statute for the governors eliminated practically every guarantee of stability of appointment and tenure of office.[34]

The politicization of the bureaucracy endowed the otherwise rigid French Union system with a great deal of flexibility. Every major shift in the relationship between France and the P.D.C.I. was reflected in the appointment of an appropriate governor. No less than 13 chief executives were appointed in the Ivory Coast between 1943 and 1960, with an average

[31] Henri Labouret, *Colonisation, Colonialisme, Décolonisation* (Paris: Larose, 1952), p. 176.

[32] Interviews with M. Bouteille, Director of E.N.F.O.M., and with other officials of the school, Paris. October 1958.

[33] Once again, there is a parallel with the prefect: "Other public officials in France must possess many proper qualifications; a Prefect requires only the trust and confidence of the Government. There can therefore be no security of tenure nor any right to permanence in this post." Chapman, pp. 100-101.

[34] Williams, p. 386.

tenure of about 18 months. Governor Latrille was recalled at the beginning of 1947; his successor, Oswald Durand, actively fought the P.D.C.I. Between 1948 and 1951, the chief executive was Laurent Péchoux, a Socialist appointee, specialist of tough anticommunist tactics. He was sent home on leave and never returned, when negotiations between the R.D.A. and the French government began in 1951. After a series of interim appointments, Pierre Messmer, later Minister of Defense in the De Gaulle government, was sent to the Ivory Coast to transform the territory into the showcase of the French Union.

At lower levels, this policy was reflected in the numerous transfers of administrators from one territory to another. Although this resulted in discontinuities in policy and hampered the implementation of many programs that required careful nurture, such as cooperative agricultural enterprises, it compensated for the lack of any constitutional reform between 1946 and 1957. The same colonial system was vastly different under Latrille, under Péchoux, or under Messmer. Finally, although the Territorial Assembly had no control over the executive, Ivory Coast deputies in Paris could influence administrative appointments after they became reconciled with the regime. In this manner, the bureaucracy became somewhat accountable to African representatives before this accountability was implemented through formal changes in the institutional framework.

The Specialized Services

The structure of the specialized services further reduced the accountability of the executive to representative bodies in Africa and contributed to the growing antagonism between the Ivory Coast and Dakar. This arose from the existence of several categories of personnel and from a distinction between the levels of government to which the departments were accountable.

Any government department contained three levels of officials: university-trained *cadres généraux*, who could serve anywhere in the French Union; *cadres communs supérieurs*, with a secondary school education,[35] who served throughout the federation; and *cadres locaux*, with a primary or upper primary schooling, who were restricted to service in the Ivory Coast. Rules concerning recruitment and promotion were established by Paris, Dakar, or Abidjan for each of these respective levels. Appearances notwithstanding, however, "with some exceptions, the administrative services of the Overseas Territories were State services, i.e., regulated by centralized authorities and placed under their authority. Administrative terminology, which distinguished between general cadre, superior cadre, and local cadre, might have induced an error by leading someone to believe that there were, before 1957, purely local services, accountable to local authorities. In reality, even agents of local cadre were at the service of the State. The head of the territory, who was competent to determine their *statut* and to recruit them, acted as representative of the state. Most of the expenditures for personnel were obligatory expenditures for local budgets. In the final analysis, the outcome was almost perfect centralization."[36]

The confusion Gonidec mentions was compounded because some services were paid out of the French budget, and others from that of French West Africa or of the Ivory Coast. Distinctions between the categories of services were not clearly defined and shifted from time to time. Within a specific functional sphere such as education, some schools in the Ivory Coast were supported by Dakar and others by

[35] William Ponty, although not a full secondary school, was nevertheless assimilated to the secondary level for this purpose.

[36] P. F. Gonidec, "L'évolution des Territoires d'Outre-Mer depuis 1946," *Revue Juridique et Politique de l'Union Française*, XII, No. 1 (January-March 1958), 43. These distinctions have been emphasized because they led to many confused discussions at the time of the *Loi-Cadre* reforms of 1956 and 1957.

Abidjan; in agriculture, field services were territorial, but experimental farms were federal. Department heads, who appeared before the Assembly at the request of its president to account for the operations of their services, sometimes refused to answer questions concerning aspects that were "federal" rather than "territorial"; sometimes they refused to appear at all because they claimed to be accountable only to Dakar. Although Ivory Coast representatives on the Grand Council could obtain the information desired at that level, the Territorial Assembly often felt frustrated in its attempts to bring officials to account. In this, too, they sometimes had the support of the territorial governor; although he was nominally the head of all services in the Ivory Coast, he sometimes found that the heads of "federal" services refused to obey his directives.[37] This situation supplemented and reinforced other sources of antifederal attitudes already discussed.

Africanization

Recruitment to the command and the specialized bureaucracies was based on educational achievement rather than on racial ascription. In practice, however, Africans were restricted to the middle and lower levels since they had only limited opportunities to obtain a university education. Berg has summarized the situation as it existed a few years after the war: "There were about 42,500 civil servants in French West Africa in 1951, including some 5,300 Europeans. Only about 2,000 of these Europeans were doing genuinely higher level administrative or technical work, of the sort that normally requires higher education. About 30,000 of the 37,000 African civil servants were in the lowest classifications—the junior clerk grades; 5,500 were in the middle levels, in jobs for which teacher training school or some secondary school attendance is an entry requirement. The higher ranks of the civil service

[37] This discussion is based on an analysis of the operations of the Territorial Assembly, as seen through its debates.

included 2,000 Africans, but most of these were not connected with administration; they were African auxiliary doctors, midwives, pharmacists, veterinarians."[38]

Not a single Ivory Coast African occupied a decision-making position in the executive of his territory until after the *Loi-Cadre* reform of 1956. Until 1950, those in the middle ranks of the administration received lower pay than their European colleagues for the same work. This fact, together with the continued presence of Europeans who did not perform genuinely high functions in the government bureaucracy, was a source of grievances among the elite. Furthermore, the system did not enable Africans to acquire administrative skills. This later reduced the courses of action open to African leaders because the advantages of independence had to be balanced against the cost of the possible sudden departure of French civil servants and the ensuing difficulties that might be encountered in the performance of governmental services.

Although promotional opportunities in the civil service were limited, nevertheless, almost all educated Africans gravitated toward the colonial bureaucracy. There were no positions for them in private firms, manned by Europeans at even lower levels than those in the government; furthermore, some were under obligation to serve because they had received scholarships. As previously suggested, these individuals were crucial from the point of view of political action for the P.D.C.I. leadership came almost entirely from their ranks. But this made the party extremely vulnerable to administrative pressures.

The Chiefs

Although legislation to revise the status of the chiefs was under consideration in Paris from 1947 on, no decision was ever taken, and the system remained essentially what it had

[38] Berg, pp. 397-98. Before the *Loi Lamine-Gueye* of 1950, auxiliary doctors etc. belonged to the middle ranks of the services.

been before the war.[39] However, the relative importance of the chiefs declined. Elected representation meant that assemblymen supplanted the chiefs as principal go-betweens for the population and the authorities. Even the chiefs' administrative functions were reduced: forced labor was abolished; census taking and road building were now carried out by specialized departments of the government. Only the head-tax continued to be collected by village chiefs.

Since no provisions were made for special representation of traditional authorities in the central organs of government, chiefs who wanted to remain the spokesmen of their people had to become involved in the electoral process and in politics generally. Many of the chiefs who were also farmers were active in the S.A.A. or in similar organizations that opposed it. Some became party officials. Later, because they were administrative creatures, the chiefs were also subject to governmental pressures to leave the P.D.C.I. or to support other parties. In this manner the entire *chefferie* was politicized. This tendency was compounded by the introduction of an element of popular consultation in their appointment as the result of the implementation of Governor Reste's directives.[40] Although these factors undermined traditional institutions in the Ivory Coast, they facilitated the institutionalization of secular structures of anthority.

CONCLUSIONS

The ambiguity of the ultimate goals of the French Union made agreement upon the next step of constitutional change

[39] Cowan, p. 187. Thompson, p. 212. Until 1956, rules concerning the status of chiefs were in the domain of the law and could be made only by the National Assembly.

[40] In 1955 the administration stated in an article in the local press that although consultations often took place among village chiefs and community leaders to select a county chief by means of secret ballot, this should not be confused with elections. The article pointed out that if today the population elected its chiefs, tomorrow it would try to elect tax collectors or sheriffs. (*Abidjan-Matin*, August 9, 1955.)

difficult to reach once the basic institutions had been established in 1946. During the next decade, the framework discussed in this chapter remained relatively unchanged. Modifications involved only the liberalization of existing rules: a few Africans were recruited into the upper ranks of the executive; suffrage was gradually extended; additional money was spent on social welfare services; efforts were made to promote better personal relationships between officials and members of the African elite.

The lack of change was due also to the centralization of the French system. Relationships between an individual territory and the metropole were defined in the constitution of the Fourth Republic; fundamental modifications required constitutional change, rather than a simple law of parliament. Unlike the British, the French could not—or perhaps would not—advance one territory at a time along its own schedule of reform.[41] Although many attempts were made to revise the constitution, French politicians had other fish to fry. Settlement of the status of *L'Afrique Noire* did not require in their eyes a very high priority, because its future never created a crisis in French domestic politics as did that of Algeria, Tunisia, or Indochina. *Immobilisme* in France during most of this period retarded reform even when agreement on the next step *was* reached. For example, the municipal law of 1955, giving the Ivory Coast its first self-governing municipalities, took three years to wend its way through the French legislative labyrinth.[42]

In a book published in 1953 a prominent French analyst of colonial affairs dismissed postwar agitation in all of French

[41] The exceptions to this generalization were Togo and Cameroun. As mandated territories, these were not considered to be parts of the Republic, one and indivisible, and therefore special constitutional arrangements could be made there. However, reforms in these two territories in 1955 furnished the impetus for reform in other African territories as well.

[42] Kenneth Robinson, "Local Government Reform in French Africa," *Journal of African Administration*, VIII, No. 4 (October 1956), 179-85.

West Africa by writing that there was no nationalism there, "only a few scattered instances of social unrest due to the propaganda of the R.D.A., a Communist-inspired party.[43] In a way, this was a fairly accurate summation, if nationalism is equated with demands for outright independence. The opportunity to participate in politics at the metropolitan level afforded by the French Union system retarded demands for independence because African leaders stood to lose their status as representatives or members of the government of a major world power in the process. Nevertheless, the impetus of change in Africa was so great that it carried all of French-speaking Africa toward independence.

Emerson has suggested that colonialism was a school for democracy. With the customary lag, he indicates, the practices and doctrines prevalent in the metropole were applied in the territories. In the British colonies, notwithstanding some drawbacks, "the legislative council was a halfway house which gave some taste of democratic procedures and stimulated demands for more."[44] Apter has demonstrated that in the Gold Coast the British parliamentary pattern was a source of political institutional transfer "carefully constructed under the guidance and control of the colonial service and the nationalists."[45]

Did the institutions of the French Union have similar effects? The ambiguous nature of the system emerges once again in this respect. Representative councils, such as the territorial assemblies and the Grand Council, stemmed not from France's parliamentary and democratic tradition but from her Napoleonic past. Nevertheless, African politicians learned to use parliamentary tactics in these assemblies; those who went to France became socialized to parliamentary life

[43] G. Hardy, *Histoire Sociale . . .*, p. 244.

[44] Rupert Emerson, *From Empire to Nation* (Cambridge: Harvard University Press, 1960), p. 231.

[45] Apter, *The Gold Coast in Transition*, p. 19.

there as well. In one respect, the French went beyond the British in a democratic direction: when territorial representation was established, the councils were completely elected and had an African majority from the very start.

But some important characteristics made the system less of a school for democracy than its British counterpart. In many ways, the Minister of Overseas France ran his territories much as a Minister of the Interior might have managed the politics of a *département* in nineteenth-century France. The administration did not hesitate to participate actively in elections. The French were always more concerned with finding an *interlocuteur valable* than with the development of responsible parties and of an opposition. The Ivory Coast administration first encouraged the growth of an opposition to the P.D.C.I., but later when it acknowledged Houphouet-Boigny as spokesman for the entire country, it showed little concern with the fate of its own political creatures. By remaining neutral in the face of the P.D.C.I.'s electoral tactics in 1956 and by giving the party official support at that time, the French helped create a firm one-party system in the Ivory Coast earlier than anywhere else in West Africa.

More fundamentally, France did not furnish an exemplary democratic parliamentary system that could deal effectively with the crucial problems faced by new nations. The Fourth Republic stood as a negative model, indicating to African leaders what they must avoid in order to shoulder successfully the burdens of self-government. When the Ivory Coast came of age, the direction of change in France was away from a parliamentary democracy and toward a type of monarchical republic, with a dominant executive and a powerless parliament, and with restricted political competition. This evolution reinforced the predispositions of Ivory Coast leaders and endowed their own constitutional preferences with greater legitimacy.

CHAPTER IV

THE PARTY MILITANT

DURING the five-year period extending from the summer of 1946 to the summer of 1951, the P.D.C.I. transformed itself from an indirect party with limited membership into a highly articulated mass organization engaged in a multitude of activities inside and outside the confines of the institutional framework of the French Union. This was conditioned by specific political and economic events, which will be discussed briefly in the first section of this chapter.[1] However, the process and the results of this transformation are of primary importance because the P.D.C.I. retained the structural characteristics it developed during this period for many years. Furthermore, when the P.D.C.I. and other political groups mobilized support among the masses, the cleavages discussed earlier were politicized. Particular attention will be devoted to the consequences their appearance had for the P.D.C.I. as an organization and for the later development of Ivory Coast politics.

THE SOURCES OF TENSION

The factors that precipitated the formation of an atmosphere of political warfare between the P.D.C.I. and the colonial administration included the reaction of European residents to the rise of African organizations, changing conditions in postwar France, and increasing economic difficulties.

European residents reacted to the economic and political challenge of the Houphouet-Boigny electoral committee and of the S.A.A. by seeking allies throughout the French Union.

[1] The historical context as well as the specific events that took place in French West Africa and in the Ivory Coast during this period have been the object of an excellent study by Ruth Schachter. I have attempted as much as possible not to duplicate her pioneer work in this chapter. At times, however, duplication is necessary to make the remainder of this study comprehensible.

In 1946 the first college representative[2] lectured on the dangers arising from the stiff African stand against separate electoral colleges and helped organize a colonial interest group, the *Comité de l'Empire Français.* After forced labor was abolished and African subjects were made citizens, this group called a meeting of the "Estates-General of French Colonization" to arrest further reforms. The situation in the Ivory Coast was viewed with special alarm. It was reported that Africans had abandoned their European employers without notice in the midst of the harvest and that economic activities were at a standstill. The group's organ, *Marchés Coloniaux*, blamed the local administration which, it said, showed little concern with the situation. The organization therefore directed its pressures at the level of the Ministry of Overseas France.[3]

The reforms proposed by the First Constituent Assembly, which represented a high-water mark of progressive thought on colonial problems, were defeated in the May referendum. By contrast, the French Union that emerged from the second draft approved in October was a signal retreat. Houphouet-Boigny held the *Marchés Coloniaux* crowd responsible for this; they were a group which "viewed everything from a merchant's

[2] The deputy in the first constituent assembly was Governor Reste, the architect of the policy toward chiefs. Reste, a Radical-Socialist, was a relatively mild defender of European economic interests. He was replaced in the Second Constituent Assembly by A. Schock, who belonged to the lunatic fringe of the extreme right. First college politics, which are not discussed in the confines of this study, were highly competitive. There were 9 candidates for a single seat in June 1946, representing, as might be expected, every shade of the French political rainbow, including a royalist and a communist. Reste's activities are reported in *Marchés Coloniaux*, February 23 and March 9, 1946. The characteristics of first college politics are drawn from issues of *La Côte d'Ivoire*, a *colon*-oriented newspaper published in the Ivory Coast at that time, and from electoral manifestoes and results in the archives of the Ministry of the Interior.

[3] Ernest Milcent, *L'A.O.F. Entre en Scène* ("Bibliothèque de l'Homme d'Action" [Paris: Editions Témoignage Chrétien, 1958], p. 35). The organization prepared a pamphlet outlining the most effective tactics in dealing with the Ministry of Overseas France. *Marchés Coloniaux*, June 1, 1946.

point of view and for whom colonization was not a civilizing enterprise but simply a way of selling trash to Africans in exchange for timber, coffee, and cocoa."[4] It was as a reaction to the activities of the colonial lobby that he and other African representatives in Paris sought to coordinate their efforts by convening a congress at Bamako, French Sudan (now Republic of Mali) in October 1946, a few days after the constitution of the French Union was approved by referendum.

More than 500 participants converged upon the Sudanese capital—the crossroads of West Africa. Under pressure from metropolitan parties, which feared the creation of a nationalist movement similar to Ferhat Abbas' Algerian Manifesto, most Africans who were affiliated with the M.R.P. and the S.F.I.O. stayed away. Communist influence thus grew by default. Because of this, the *Rassemblement Démocratique Africain* issued from the congress was directly affected by political trends in France and abroad during the next two years. The fact that Houphouet-Boigny was elected president of the coordination committee appointed to launch the movement, and another Ivory Coast leader, Fily Sissoko, was named secretary-general, clearly indicated that at this point, the R.D.A. was an extension of the P.D.C.I. to the superterritorial level.[5]

The congress demanded revision of the constitution in the direction of the proposals of the left in the First Constituent Assembly. Then, as later, the R.D.A. advocated greater control over the territorial executive, the extension of suffrage, the elimination of separate electoral colleges. In the realm

[4] In a speech in Paris, reported in *Marchés Coloniaux*, October 12, 1946. The magazine followed this report by an attack on "the vicious M. Houphouet," and wondered how a big African planter could call himself a proletarian simply because he belonged to Mr. Thorez' political party. I suggest that his own personal wealth made his ideological commitment the more impressive among the masses.

[5] Milcent, pp 36-40. See also Thompson and Adloff, pp. 84-85. This Fily Sissoko must not be confused with Fily Dabo Sissoko, a Sudanese leader.

of economics it asked rapid social and economic development of the territories with the help of France, the elimination of colonial privileges and coercive methods of administration, and a reform of the taxation system to eliminate the head-tax. Its ultimate goal was the creation of a Franco-African political community based on equal rights and duties for all members. These resolutions, which provided also the nucleus of the P.D.C.I.'s objectives, were widely publicized. When running for election to the National Assembly in November 1946, Houphouet-Boigny repeated them and pledged in his campaign manifesto "to remain faithful to the spirit of Bamako."[6]

The R.D.A. was born during a period of national and international crisis. Within a few months, France had to cope with open warfare in Indochina (December 1946), unrest in North Africa, and a rebellion in Madagascar (March 1947). Tensions between East and West were mounting as well. In the metropole, the uneasy tripartite alliance was tottering. After the communist ministers were dismissed from the French government in May 1947, "the most important date in the post-war history of France,"[7] the party launched a counter-attack in the form of strikes designed to cripple economic recovery. By the end of 1948, the French domestic crisis was so acute that the Socialist Minister of the Interior conducted government operations against striking coal miners in the north on a military basis.[8] The occurrence of a simultaneous strike among the railroad workers of French West Africa from October 1947 to January 1948 and the presence of many communist organizers in R.D.A. circles suggested that the communist organizational weapon was being extended to West Africa. The French government viewed the Ivory Coast, the

[6] Houphouet-Boigny, "Proclamation de Foi," November 1946 (on file in the archives of the Ministry of the Interior, Ivory Coast).

[7] Williams, p. 20.

[8] For an account of France during this period, see Franz Borkenau, *European Communism* (New York: Harper and Brothers, 1953), pp. 525-29, and Herbert Luethy, *France Against Herself* (New York: Frederick A. Prager, Inc., 1955), p. 152.

bastion of the R.D.A., as another skirmish in its own Battle of Prague. Governor Latrille had already been recalled in February 1947. The following April, in one of his first official acts, his successor ordered his staff to beware of agitators who were going about interpreting the new laws, to take all necessary measures to eliminate them, and to make it clear to the population that Africans who love their country should denounce these individuals to the administration.[9] Civil servants, employees of private firms, and chiefs were enjoined to leave the party.

It is probable that the French government's evaluation of the R.D.A.'s orientation was correct at the time. As long as the communists were in the government, it was hoped that the Franco-African community to which the movement aspired would be of the popular democracy type. Afterwards, when restated by the general-secretary of the R.D.A. in 1948, the organization's goals sounded much more ambiguous. It sought ". . . the emancipation of the various African countries from the colonial yoke through the affirmation of their economic, political, social, and cultural personality, and by means of a free membership in a union of peoples and of nations based on the equality of rights and of duties."[10] Whether or not this implied a demand for independence does not matter, for this and other pronouncements placed the movement well beyond the pale of what the French government considered legitimate political aspirations.[11] At the close of the second R.D.A. Congress in Abidjan in 1949, the secretary-general declared that under present conditions African reforms take a lower priority among the goals of the organization

[9] The order is reprinted in Ivory Coast, *Journal Officiel*, April 17, 1947.

[10] Quoted in Milcent, p. 43.

[11] Interpretations of the meaning of this and other statements are conflicting. For a suggestion that it did imply independence, see M. A. Déjaument, "Notes sur l'évolution politique du R.D.A.," paper presented at the round table of the Association Française de Science Politique on African political parties in March 1959. I am grateful to Mr. Thomas Hodgkin for bringing it to my attention.

than the achievement of international peace, as defined in Stockholm.[12]

The economic context contributed to the growth of mutual suspicion between Africans and Europeans.[13] The continuance of wartime controls of imports and the shortage as well as the high price of consumer goods were widely attributed by Africans to the machinations of European importers. Inflation was coupled with low prices for coffee and cocoa. In the fall of 1948 the French government purchasing agency for cocoa accumulated a surplus and stopped buying. Commercial firms bought from producers at half the price announced at the beginning of the season. The following year, government restrictions on trade were lifted; the Ivory Coast was at the mercy of world market fluctuations; prices continued to drop. The 1948-1949 coffee season was good; because of the great demand in France, buyers bought any kind of coffee at any price. The following year, however, the French government purchasing agency withheld its decision concerning the price it would pay for the new crop and the quantity it would buy. Farmers were in desperate need of cash, yet nobody bought coffee between November 1949 and February 1950, usually months of intense economic activity. Europeans viewed

[12] Gabriel d'Arboussier, "Rapport au Comité de Coordination," May 1, 1949 (mimeographed). He explains that the R.D.A. must prevent French efforts to transform Africa into a base for the Atlantic Pact nations.

[13] A major source of information on the events of this period in the Ivory Coast is the report of a committee of the French National Assembly appointed to investigate the disturbances that occurred in 1949 and 1950. This report was never discussed in the Assembly, however, because shortly after it was filed, negotiations between the French government and the R.D.A. were completed. France, *Assemblée nationale, Documents parlementaires, Annexe No. 11348, Rapport fait au nom de la commission chargée d'enquêter sur les incidents survenus en Côte d'Ivoire, par M. Damas, député* (Session of 1950, Sitting of November 21, 1950). It will be cited as *Annexe, No. 11348.* The parallel with the economic situation in Ghana is striking. Concerning the latter, see Great Britain, Colonial Office, *Report on the Commission of Enquiry into Disturbances in the Gold Coast, 1948* (London: Her Majesty's Stationery Office, 1948), p. 8.

African reluctance to sell at low prices as part of a producers' boycott; Africans, encouraged by their political leaders, believed that Europeans were trying to punish them for engaging in politics.[14] Everyone blamed the territorial administration; the Governor turned to the Minister of Overseas France; and the highest official in the colonial hierarchy wrote to his colleague, the Minister of Economic Affairs, who could not make up his mind concerning the proper price of coffee: "The consequence of this situation is grave discontent throughout the country, scientifically exploited to develop anti-French arguments. You are not ignorant of the events in the Ivory Coast. They originate in the low prices paid by the traders to the producers because the traders cannot sell coffee to the businessmen, who themselves cannot find markets in France. I cannot allow this situation to continue because I should be encurring a very grave political responsibility."[15]

The Transformation of the P.D.C.I.

At the end of 1946, no African could be elected in the Ivory Coast without the endorsement of the P.D.C.I. When new offices were created, the party widened its base of support by coopting representatives of all political factions in the country. In the November 1946 elections to the National Assembly, Houphouet-Boigny had taken on as his running mates 2 Upper Volta leaders who represented the Mossi and the non-Mossi population respectively.[16] Other potential contenders were promised seats in the Council of the Republic,

[14] These views were expressed at meetings of the Chamber of Agriculture and the Chamber of Commerce reported in *La Côte d'Ivoire*, May 28 and June 19, 1949.

[15] The letter is quoted in *Annexe, No. 11348*, p. 606.

[16] Both were Ponty graduates. Ouezzin Coulibaly, cofounder of the Teachers' Union, had taught there as well. He was defeated in 1951, but later became Ivory Coast senator and once again deputy in 1956. He retained that post until his death in 1958, even while serving as Prime Minister of his native Upper Volta from 1957 on. The other was Kabore Zinda, a pharmacist, who died a few months after the election.

the Grand Council, and the Assembly of the French Union.[17] The P.D.C.I. was unopposed.[18] The following month, all 15 candidates for Ivory Coast seats in the second section of the Territorial Assembly who ran under the banner of the *Rassemblement Africain* were elected, but not a single one of their 24 opponents obtained a seat.[19] The P.D.C.I. rapidly secured a political monopoly by means of bargaining with potential contenders, rather than through open competition. Nevertheless, the party appeared to have widespread support throughout the country. During 1947, an attempt was made to transform this coalition-like organization into a solid monolith, suited to militant action and capable of withstanding the onslaught of its political enemies. One year after Bamako, on October 11, 1947, the P.D.C.I. held its first territorial congress. The executive committee which issued from that meeting then proceeded to organize the party throughout the country. These activities continued throughout the following year and were stepped up in the fall of 1948 in preparation for the second congress of the R.D.A., held in Treichville from January 2 to 6, 1949. A cadre school, conducted with the help of the *Groupe d'Etudes Communistes,* trained party or-

[17] Most of them were duly elected to these posts afterwards. The coalition elected Sékou Sanogo, a Malinké Moslem, and Louis Druart, a European sympathizer, along with Houphouet-Boigny, to the Grand Council. The 3 senators were Etienne Djaument, leader of the Western U.O.C.O.C.I.; Guissou, from Upper Volta; and Franceschi, a French communist. The three members of the Assembly of the French Union it was able to elect, on the basis of proportional representation, were Mamadou Coulibaly, another Moslem northerner; Léon Robert, another European sympathizer; and Gabriel d'Arboussier, a West Indian-Sudanese mulatto, later secretary-general of the R.D.A. Allegedly, one of the senate seats had been promised to K. Binzème, leader of the *Parti Progressiste*; this was the reason given for their split from the coalition at the beginning of 1947. Amon d'Aby, *La Côte d'Ivoire . . .*, p. 59.

[18] The electoral results, computed from the files of the Ministry of the Interior, were: registered, 187,905; valid votes, 125,752; P.D.C.I., 125,752. This is for all districts, including Upper Volta.

[19] The results for the 15 Ivory Coast constituencies of the second section only were: registered, 128,525; valid, 76,911; *Rassemblement Africain,* 67,876 (94 per cent); others, 9,035 (6 per cent).

ganizers.[20] Final decisions concerning party structure were taken at the congress.

Party Organization[21]

The organizational scheme followed the model of the French Communist Party, modified in the light of African conditions. Although the structure described here has persisted, organizational practice has always diverged from theory in several important respects which will be noted in the course of the discussion. The P.D.C.I. was to be a direct party, highly articulated vertically, based on cell-like units, and operating on the principle of democratic centralism.[22] A major difference from the model, however, was that the P.D.C.I. was not intended to be a vanguard organization with restricted membership, but rather an all-encompassing mass organization.

The basic units of the party are the village and the ward committees. Membership is open; dues-paying members elect a bureau headed by a secretary. At the level of the *subdivision*, the committees form a *sous-section*, and in 1949 there were between 60 and 70 of these.[23] The bureaus of all the committees elect the bureau of the *sous-section*, headed by a secretary-general. In addition to the basic committees, the party organization at the local level also includes ancillary associations: women's groups, particularly active during market demonstrations or at rallies; youth groups, such as *La Goumbé*,

[20] There were 130 day and 75 night students in December 1948. Rassemblement Démocratique Africain, "Rapport à l'Organisation." Abidjan, January 1949. (Mimeographed.)

[21] Unless otherwise indicated, all information in this section was obtained from interviews with P.D.C.I. officials who had been in the party since its inception.

[22] The nomenclature is that used by Duverger, pp. 4-60.

[23] Ward is used here to translate *quartier*; the word does not necessarily indicate an electoral unit. In 1949 the Ivory Coast had 16 *cercles* further divided into 43 *subdivisions*. Some of the larger districts had more than one *sous-section*. In Abidjan, Treichville and Adjamé were each separate *sous-sections*.

a dancing society whose members are young Moslems in Abidjan and in the hinterland. Some *sous-sections* created their own police force, the *Service d'Ordre,* to maintain order at meetings, to deal with hecklers from opposition groups, and also to retaliate against them.

There are no horizontal links between the committees or between *sous-sections.* The latter communicate only upward, to the territorial organs of party government.[24] A number of delegates, proportional to the membership in each *sous-section* (as defined by the number of dues-paying members), makes up the annual territorial congress which elects the *Comité Directeur*, the territorial executive committee. During electoral periods, a territorial conference constituted by an equal number of delegates from each *sous-section* is called by the *Comité Directeur* to nominate candidates.[25] The inner core of the *Comité Directeur* is the *Bureau Politique*, the highest executive organ of the P.D.C.I., whose members must reside in Abidjan, where they direct party affairs between congresses and meetings of the *Comité Directeur.* It is headed by a secretary-general. Other secretaries have specific responsibilities for various aspects of party government: finances, legal affairs, propaganda, organization, or the press. At one time, the secretary-general and a few other members constituted the *Bureau Permanent*, which manned the party headquarters near the Treichville market place.

The P.D.C.I. is itself a *section* of the *Rassemblement Démocratique Africain.* The formal links with the superterritorial movement were through P.D.C.I. representatives to the interterritorial congress, scheduled to meet every two years, and through membership in the *Comité de Coordination*, the R.D.A. executive committee between congresses. The *sections* are

[24] There was at one time an intermediate level in each region, but these were eliminated for fear that defections at that level might jeopardize all *sous-sections.* One official added that the regional committees were becoming too independent vis-à-vis the *Comité Directeur.*

[25] Schachter, p. 388.

autonomous, but their *Comité Directeur* must apply the general program of the R.D.A. decided upon at the congress.[26]

Party officials, working under the fire of the colonial authorities, sacrificed organizational theory to effectiveness. The result was a different kind of organization altogether. At the basic level, ward committees were never created in Abidjan. Instead, the *sous-sections* of Treichville and Adjamé, the largest in the entire party, were made up of ethnic subcommittees. One of the founders of the Treichville branch has explained this process: "During the elections [of 1945 and of 1946] we had found that the ethnic associations that existed in the city functioned efficiently for electoral purposes as well. In preparation for the battle we would be waging, we thought that it was necessary to create highly solidary units, equivalent to the communist cells in France. Ethnic organization was the most natural and the most practical for this purpose. Regardless of where they lived and worked in the city, people of the same tribe came together for social purposes. So, we transformed the ethnic associations into party subcommittees. Where they did not exist, we helped the tribes to organize original ones. Only in this way could we communicate with the members, collect dues, and pass down party directives in the various local languages."[27]

The Treichville *sous-section*, with about 20,000 members at the end of 1948, was made up of over 100 ethnic subcommittees. Some of them, such as the 17 different Baoulé units, were regrouped into a single central committee. However, in other towns, where neighborhoods are ethnically homogeneous, ward committees are in effect ethnic committees as well. As one party leader put it, the P.D.C.I. was constructed as a sort of "federation of tribes."

Organizers felt that only after urban units had been firmly

[26] R.D.A., IIème Congrès Interterritorial. "Résolution d'Organisation." Abidjan, January 1949. (Mimeographed.)

[27] Interview with M. Mathieu Ekra, 1959.

established could they penetrate into the villages. This method of attack was strongly criticized by an official of the French Communist Party who warned, in the summer of 1948, that the failure to organize the peasant masses in the struggle against imperialism constituted a dangerous deviation.[28] Party officials then launched an organizational drive into the villages. They now claim that about one-half of the 8,000 or so villages in the country had organized committees by the end of 1949. Another discrepancy between theory and practice concerned the *sous-section.* Instead of being the apex of a hierarchical organization of committees, the *sous-section* became a sort of caucus of the indirect type,[29] with a membership made up of representatives of the various ethnic groups that make up the town and its environs.

Party membership was to be defined on the bases of the purchase of a party card and the payment of annual dues. In Treichville alone, about 20,000 party cards had been sold by the end of 1948; three years later the total stood at nearly 32,000. Party leaders report that territorial membership grew from about 80,000 at the end of 1946 to 350,000 or 500,000 at the end of 1948, and reached 850,000 or 1,000,000 at the beginning of 1951.[30] But the concept of membership on which these figures are based corresponds more accurately to the notion of supporters. When pressed, officials admit that these are not all *militants,* but that nearly all adults were considered to be *sympathisants.*

Party finances were derived from the proceeds of the sale

[28] R. Barbé, in a circular addressed to the members of the Groupes d'Etudes Communistes active in the P.D.C.I. and the R.D.A., dated July 20, 1948. Reprinted in *Annexe, No. 11348,* pp. 938ff.

[29] The caucus "functions in a rather large geographical area, usually corresponding to the chief electoral division," Duverger, pp. 18-19.

[30] Territorial figures are cited in *Annexe, No. 11348.* They were submitted to and confirmed by officials in 1959. According to the last one cited, two-thirds of the adult population of both sexes "belonged" to the P.D.C.I., a manifest exaggeration. It was impossible to gain access to registers of dues payments, with the exception of the Treichville branch.

of cards and dues collections; money was distributed among the several party levels, with but little formal accounting. The cards cost 100 C.F.A. francs, an amount equal to the minimum annual head-tax most individuals had to turn in to the government. In addition, however, the P.D.C.I. also benefited from the personal wealth of some of its leaders, including especially Houphouet-Boigny and A. Denise, who drew substantial income from their agricultural holdings. Help in kind was also forthcoming from African traders, who often put their vehicles at the party's disposal, and from Syrian and Lebanese merchants, who had always paid some form of informal tribute to local notabilities in exchange for the privilege of buying and selling goods in the area.[31]

The principle of "democratic centralism" was never operational. Recruitment took place mainly from the top downward. The leadership that emerged at the territorial level in 1947 was substantially the same as that of the Houphouet-Boigny alliance of the previous year. One important modification, however, was the elimination of individuals closely identified with the S.A.A. and other "bourgeois" enterprises. The S.A.A. nevertheless remained closely affiliated with the party. Originally, many of the leaders of the *sous-sections* were civil servants stationed in the towns of the hinterland,

[31] The Levantine population of the Ivory Coast grew from about 100 in 1921 to 1,500 in 1956. Syrians and Lebanese are truly intermediary between the African and the European population, not only by their economic activities, but also in terms of their way of life and status in the society. Their success as traders is due to the fact that they do not operate on a strictly contractual basis, as European firms do, but establish personal relationships with Africans; they also use their extended and extensive family to establish a network of correspondents. In the past, they paid tribute to the chiefs. But more recently, they transferred their allegiance to the party secretary-generals, the new men of power. Although they usually took out insurance by contributing to all parties, they have generally maintained excellent relations with the P.D.C.I. (Georges Gayet, "Les libanais et les syriens dans l'Ouest Africain," *Ethnic and Cultural Pluralism in Intertropical Communities* [Bruxelles: International Institute of Differing Civilizations, 1957], p. 170).

self-designated or appointed by the *Comité Directeur* to found party branches. They in turn appointed leaders in villages or in wards. In most cases, once some members were recruited, some form of election was held to confirm the make-up of the bureau. But because the party was engaged in an intensive struggle at the very time that leadership selection took place at all levels, membership control through a system of regular elections was never applied. Although the tenure of all the bureaus, from the lowest committee to the *Comité Directeur*, was limited to a single year by party regulations, the original leaders held office permanently. When gaps appeared in the structure as the result of jailing, defection to the opposition, retirement, or incapacity of some of the cadre, they were filled on an *ad hoc* basis, and sometimes not at all. No territorial congress was held again until 1959. Meanwhile, the *Comité Directeur* convened at irregular intervals a sort of general committee made up of the secretary-generals of the *sous-sections*. Under these circumstances, the P.D.C.I. clearly never developed a tradition of internal democracy.

Formal relations with the R.D.A. have always been overshadowed by the presence at the helm of the movement of Houphouet-Boigny himself.[32] The interterritorial movement did not really have any authority over the *sections*. Although there were no formal horizontal links between them, the P.D.C.I. often gave financial or organizational assistance to other territorial parties in Guinea or Sudan. It is useful to view the P.D.C.I. and other *sections* of the R.D.A. as autonomous territorial parties, linked, through their leaders, into a limited political alliance.

The party's organizational drive stimulated a climate of agitation from the end of 1947 on. Two aspects of its activities

[32] He has never held any office in the P.D.C.I. except that of honorary president, a position similar to that of life chairman of the C.P.P. The highest executive office is that of general-secretary, occupied by A. Denise from 1947 to 1959.

were viewed by the chiefs and by French officials as an attempt to supplant the entire established administrative structure. Party tribunals were created in various parts of the country to deal with community affairs.[33] These bodies competed with the *tribunaux coutumiers* manned by the chiefs under French supervision. Publicly, the *Comité Directeur* discouraged them, because they made party officials liable to prosecution on the grounds of interference with government and because they antagonized the chiefs and tradition-minded individuals everywhere. But the national leadership had little control over the activities of the local cadre. Party secretaries often took advantage of the situation to extend their authority over many spheres of life unrelated to the party's concern. Relationships with chiefs remained ambiguous. Houphouet-Boigny often repeated that since he was himself a chief, traditional rulers had nothing to fear from the R.D.A. But the activities of the P.D.C.I. cadre and rank-and-file drove many chiefs, who had earlier participated in the alliance, into the arms of the French administration to obtain protection. In 1951 the *Association des Chefs Coutumiers*, which claimed a membership of 100 out of 104 of the chiefs in the higher categories, openly declared itself against the R.D.A. and pledged loyalty to France.[34] Many individual chiefs became active in parties sponsored by the administration to offset the P.D.C.I. In many communities, disputes over the legitimacy of the incumbent chief, inheritance claims, or land rights, involved "traditionalist" and "modernist" factions. When this occurred, the P.D.C.I. organizer was often the spokesman for the "new men," who viewed the party as an opportunity to gain the status they could not achieve in traditional society or as a

[33] For example, in Bouaké, Béoumi, and Tabou. *Annexe, No. 11348*, pp. 354, 364, 434.

[34] *La Côte d'Ivoire*, February 24, 1951. The *Association* stated that it had never properly functioned since its birth in 1945 "because of the anti-French ambitions of the political party that has worked against us for the past five years."

lever suitable to remove the obstacles that tradition erected in their path.

A similar process developed as the result of the sale of party membership cards. Often, when chiefs attempted to collect the head-tax, they found many who reported that they had already fulfilled their obligation "by paying to Houphouet-Boigny." Local party cadre, who retained part of the cost of the card for use by their bureau, sometimes told prospective members that its purchase could indeed be a substitute for payment of the *minimum fiscal*, the annual personal tax. In a literal sense, the P.D.C.I. competed with the chiefs and the administration for the allegiance of the population.[35]

Moreover, as the P.D.C.I. extended its activities throughout the country and in all strata, its organizers clashed with other political entrepreneurs who were also in search of mass support. Many of them were members of the Houphouet-Boigny coalition who had split off when the P.D.C.I. underwent its metamorphosis into an ideologically committed organization.

Politics in the Assembly

Between 1947 and 1949, the party in the Assembly abandoned its reformist orientation, characterized by a willingness to compromise and a concern with practical issues. Its adoption of a more revolutionary orientation was signaled by a constant testing of the limits of the organization's powers and attempts to develop ideological unity among the members. Demands were transformed into issues; at the beginning, the party worked within the rules, later it attempted to cut the Gordian knot.

During the first year of the Assembly's life, competition for control of the *bureau* and for the election of senators was

[35] Instances of this procedure are found throughout the various testimonies in *Annexe, No. 11348*. Once again, this was often done against the directives of the territorial leaders.

keen, but the two sections otherwise agreed on many items. Europeans and Africans were united against the territorial executive in their concern to control the purse. All advocated a reduction of purely administrative expenditures in favor of more tangible items such as school buildings, roads, and better health facilities. When a European planter complained that the premium distributed to coffee growers was too low, the Assembly unanimously approved a motion of protest directed to the Ministry of Overseas France. The Assembly's united stand against Dakar has already been mentioned.[36] The atmosphere was indeed so cooperative that President Denise declared in April 1947 that although he had feared many differences of opinion between Africans and Europeans, he was pleased to find that "we are all Africans together, concerned with the best interests of the Ivory Coast."[37]

The euphoria was shortlived. Militancy penetrated the Assembly in mid-1948, when 12 new assemblymen were elected to replace Upper Volta representatives. Once again, all P.D.C.I.-sponsored candidates won. Seven of them were members of the *Bureau Politique* elected by the October 1947 congress, including G. Coffi Gadeaü, organizational secretary, and J. B. Mockey, political secretary. Four of these party officials were strangers from Guinea, Soudan, Senegal, and Dahomey respectively, symbolizing the P.D.C.I.'s superterritorial concerns. These new members took the lead in formulating new issues, as reflected in the three cases that follow.

LAND ISSUE. Although the land grant system instituted before the war remained unchanged, the Territorial Assembly had to be consulted before final decisions concerning appli-

[36] See above, pp. 89-92.

[37] Ivory Coast, Conseil général, "Debates," April 1, 1947. Although regulations prescribed publication of the Assembly's minutes in the *Journal Officiel*, this was seldom done. Most sessions' proceedings are available only in typescript form in the archives; some were never translated from stenographers' notes. The above account is based on an examination of whatever transcripts were still legible after over ten years' storage in a damp tropical basement.

cations could be taken by the executive. At first, it was only concerned with the proper enforcement of existing rules. In November 1947, for example, it turned down a petition to transform a leasehold obtained by the Gonfreville weaving plant in Bouaké in 1943 into a permanent freehold because the company had not invested sufficient amounts and because the local population claimed that there was a shortage of agricultural land in the area.[38] Eight months later, when, under pressure from his superiors, the Governor asked the Assembly to reconsider its decision, the P.D.C.I. leadership not only refused but demanded that the entire system of grants be reevaluated.[39] At first, the Assembly refused to accept administrative reports concerning the willingness of traditional owners to give up their rights and organized, instead, independent investigations by its own members. President Denise demanded that such investigations be made mandatory.[40]

In the fall session, J.-B. Mockey presented a brief that challenged the very principles on which the system rested. In his introductory remarks, he emphasized the P.D.C.I.'s pan-African and revolutionary spirit: "Before we broach this problem, we want it to be known that we are not so much concerned with the present as with the future. What I am going to say for the Ivory Coast is valid for all the other territories of the Federation and for all of Tropical Africa."[41] He declared that the decree which defined unused land as "vacant and masterless" was based on an erroneous assump-

[38] Ivory Coast, Conseil général, "Debates," November 6, 1947.

[39] *Ibid.*, July 15, 1948. It was apparent from the discussion in the Assembly that pressure was being applied by the Chairman of the Board of Gonfreville, M. Durand-Réville, senator from Gabon, and one of the founders of the Comité de l'Empire Français in 1945.

[40] *Ibid.*, July 26, 1948. As we have seen, the Assembly was empowered to designate investigatory committees but it could not establish this procedure on a permanent basis. Members complained that they had been ignored or even insulted by administrators when they attempted to perform their assigned tasks.

[41] *Ibid.*, November 27, 1948.

tion since every single square meter of land in the country in fact belonged to a family; even if temporarily fallow, it was not without master. Article 713 of the French civil code, which stipulated that the State became the owner of such land and could dispose of it at will, he continued, was utterly dishonest because it violated the protectorate treaties negotiated with Ivory Coast tribes a century ago. Finally, the practice of attributing freehold grants to outsiders was an outright crime because it would eventually lead to land shortages and to famine. Therefore, he concluded, the P.D.C.I. demanded the abrogation of the decree of 1935 that had instituted the system; replacement of freehold grants by long-term leases; and registration of all land in the name of the Ivory Coast rather than in the name of France.[42]

The last motion was viewed by France as a challenge to her sovereign rights.[43] Before the final vote, a European member stated: "Mr. President, . . . I take the liberty of bringing to your attention the fact that the Assembly is about to indicate its independence from the French State. This would be highly improper. So far, there is nothing in the structure of the French Union that challenges French sovereignty in the territories. I want to call the Assembly's attention to the grave political consequences of the decision it is about to take."[44] This warning notwithstanding, the African members were adamant. Most of them voted to approve all three motions.[45]

THE QUESTION OF SEPARATE COLLEGES. Although Africans could have controlled all Assembly offices from the begin-

[42] *Ibid.* Mockey stated that this practice was almost as vile as that which the American settlers adopted toward Indians and asked whether the French too would exterminate the rightful owners of the soil in order to impose their rights. These debates were reprinted as a pamphlet and were widely circulated in French West Africa. Mockey's arguments were allegedly prepared with the help of Louis Druart, a European sympathizer in the Assembly.

[43] Thompson and Adloff, pp. 345-51.

[44] Ivory Coast, Conseil général, "Debates," November 28, 1948.

[45] *Ibid.* The results of the vote are included in Table 9.

ning, since they had a majority of the members, they agreed in 1947 to share them with the first section. They retained the presidency but granted the office of first vice-president to a European; in addition, they elected European chairmen in all committees in order to benefit from their experience. From July 1948 onward, this policy was sharply modified. When the *bureau* was renewed after the by-elections, the second section elected to the first vice-presidency one of the two pro-African European members. They then abandoned the office of second vice-president to the remainder of the first section. Furthermore, the Assembly's committees elected a majority of African chairmen.

In March 1949, during the regular annual renewal of Assembly officers, the Europeans retaliated by boycotting the entire proceedings and refusing even to accept committee assignments. Since the standing committee needed two members of the first section in its midst in order to operate, it could not legally meet. The P.D.C.I. then elected Europeans to these offices in absentia. When these men also resigned, African members flaunted the basic decree governing the Assembly's operations by meeting regularly to conduct business alone, in open defiance of the principle of mandatory European representation.

THE BUDGET ISSUE. In 1947 the Assembly had agreed to raise personal taxes because it acknowledged the need to develop the country. The following year, however, when the administration requested an additional increase, all African members objected. As an alternative, the P.D.C.I. proposed an increase in business taxes. Although this suggestion was endorsed by the Assembly, its decision was nullified by the *Conseil d'Etat*.[46] The party rightly viewed control of the purse as the most crucial function of any representative body. If its authority to do this in the Ivory Coast was curtailed, then the grant of local representation to the African population was

[46] *Ibid.*, November 22 and 23, 1948.

meaningless.[47] In 1949 the P.D.C.I. therefore waged a last-ditch stand on the issue of the budget. However, as it was now in the minority in the Assembly, success required skillful maneuvering and dilatory tactics.[48]

When it submitted the estimates for 1950, the government once again requested an increase in the personal tax, amounting this time to an increase of 80 per cent over the previous year. In the face of many objections to this proposal, President Denise suggested that the Assembly begin by considering expenditures. Throughout the discussion, the 13 P.D.C.I. votes were cast first in favor, then against, various items in order to confuse the opposition as to their ultimate intentions. Expenditures were finally approved, with the exception of the Governor's secret fund and other items earmarked for the government's coercive activities.[49] When revenue came up for consideration, the P.D.C.I. surprised its opponents by agreeing to a 60 per cent increase in personal taxes. The 6 African members who had withdrawn from the coalition, seeing an opportunity to espouse a popular cause, announced that they would abstain from voting on the budget if the increase were approved. They carried out their promise when the entire budget came up for decision. But in a sudden reversal of its previous position, the P.D.C.I. cast its votes against it. Since only 11 Europeans voted in favor, the budget was defeated.[50]

[47] Interview with M. G. Coffi Gadeau, 1959.

[48] The party was in the minority because of defections which had taken place throughout the preceding months. This case is based on Assembly debates on November 5 to 12, and December 27, 1949, supplemented by the interview with M. Coffi Gadeau, one of the principal actors, and other participants.

[49] The secret fund was notoriously used for political purposes. Other items voted down were funds for the maintenance of the prisons where many P.D.C.I. leaders were by then detained. Since these were obligatory expenditures, they were reinstated by executive action.

[50] The element of surprise was crucial. The P.D.C.I. members sat in the back rows of the Veterans' Hall where the Assembly met. President Denise called for ayes by show of hand; the six non-P.D.C.I. Africans abstained. When they realized that the P.D.C.I. had not voted in favor (as they had expected) and asked for a new vote, Denise turned down their request.

The P.D.C.I.'s triumph was short lived. The following month, the budget was approved during an extraordinary session of the Assembly. Houphouet-Boigny warned the government at that time that they would run into difficulties when they tried to collect any taxes at all during the forthcoming year.[51] The party thus clearly indicated that it intended to extend its opposition activity beyond the narrow confines of the Assembly. It challenged the legitimacy of the entire system of government.

In the long run, by articulating scattered demands, transforming them into issues, and focusing them upon political institutions common to the entire country, the activities of the P.D.C.I. in the Assembly facilitated the transition from a traditional to a secular political system, in much the same way as in the Gold Coast.[52] But in the short run, and from the point of view of the party itself, the consequences were much less desirable. Between July 1948 and December 1949, while these issues were being developed, the party's majority in the Assembly deteriorated, as Table 9 indicates.

As there were no intervening elections, the change must be attributed solely to switches in the allegiances of representatives originally elected as members of the P.D.C.I.-sponsored coalition. These defections were due mainly to pressures exerted by the administration upon the members, including the threat of sanctions against those who remained faithful to the party and promises of rewards for those who changed sides.[53] Why did these pressures not result in greater

[51] Ivory Coast, Conseil général, "Debates," December 27, 1949.

[52] Apter, *The Gold Coast in Transition*, especially Chapter 11, "The Legislative Assembly in Action," pp. 234-56.

[53] Sanctions included reduction in grade, non-promotion, assignment to undesirable areas, or dismissal from the service for civil servants. It was usually not difficult to find some violation of regulations for which African government employees could be prosecuted. Thus, many of those who were indicted were not accused of political crimes, but rather of *délits de droit commun*, and were treated as common criminals. For non-civil servants, sanctions included withdrawal of licenses to do business, repeated inspections etc. Rewards included the opposite:

TABLE 9
The Decline of the P.D.C.I. Majority

Position of Members[d]	*July 1948*[a]	*Nov. 1948*[b]	*Mar. 1949*[a]	*Nov. 1949*[c]	*Dec. 1949*[c]	*Mar. 1950*[a]	*Mar. 1951*[a]
Pro-P.D.C.I.	31	19	22	13	9	9	9
Neutral	—	2	—	6	1	2	2
Anti-P.D.C.I.	6	8	16	11	27	28	26
Total present	37	29	38	30	37	39	37

[a] Assembly votes for the office of President. A. Denise was the P.D.C.I. candidate in all cases. He was opposed by Kacou Aoulou in 1948 and by Capri Djédjé afterwards.

[b] Vote on the three motions concerning the land issue.

[c] Vote on the budget estimates for 1950.

[d] "Pro-P.D.C.I." position is defined as support for its presidential candidate or support for the position it advocated on a specific issue. "Neutral" includes abstentions or blank votes. "Anti-P.D.C.I." involves support for another presidential candidate or opposite stand on an issue it advocated.

solidarity among African members? A reasonable explanation can be found in the characteristics of the P.D.C.I.-elected representatives who reflected the nature of the party as a whole. Although all of them had run for office under the *Rassemblement Africain* banner, there was only minimal group consensus prior to the outbreak of conflict with the government. As Coser has suggested, "in such cases disintegration of the group, rather than increase in cohesion, will be the result of outside conflict."[54] Many candidates had been brought into the alliance through common electoral objectives, rather than because they shared a common ideological outlook. All agreed in principle with the objectives stated at Bamako—what African around 1948 or 1949 would

extra promotions, preferential allocation of trucks and other scarce items, and even outright money gifts. Two P.D.C.I. members said in 1959 that they had been offered money from Governor Péchoux's office in 1949, had accepted the gift, but then fooled the authorities by voting with the P.D.C.I.

[54] Coser, p. 93.

not—but were not necessarily committed to run the personal risks that an all-out struggle for the achievement of these objectives entailed. Many of them attributed the threats directed against the P.D.C.I. from 1947 on to its identification with the French Communist Party and its involvement in issues that were not directly relevant to their own concerns. Therefore, they ceased to regard preservation of the organization as worthwhile.[55] The validity of this interpretation is confirmed by differences in behavior between two groups. Only 5 out of the 15 members elected in December 1946—before the transformation of the P.D.C.I.—remained faithful, as against 8 out of the 12 elected in May 1948, *after* the party had assumed its new ideological orientation.

Political Competition

The Competitors

With an eye on future elections, leaders who left the party sought to create new political organizations. They had no choice but to voice their appeal in ethnic terms. The P.D.C.I., by moving into the organizational vacuum which had existed after the war, had pre-empted the position of a nationalist movement and had created a sort of confederation of ethnic associations. Any new parties would have to be created by chipping away at this edifice and in particular, by retrieving some of its component ethnic blocs. In this, the P.D.C.I.'s challengers obtained the help of the French, who had long before seen the usefulness of exploiting ethnic divisions to conquer Africa.[56]

The *Progressiste* leaders in the Assembly, J.-B. Amaokon

[55] At a meeting of the P.D.C.I. representatives in March 1949, 9 members decided to leave the party unless it severed its communist ties at once. *Annexe, No. 11348*, p. 473.

[56] The use of this tactic was advocated in a military manual designed for troops engaged in the pacification of the Western Sudan. (Colonel Mangeot, "Manuel à l'usage des troupes opérant au Soudan français," *Bulletin du Comité d'Etudes Historiques et Scientifiques d'A.O.F.* [1922], p. 590.)

Boa and Kacou Aoulou revived their party, which was based mostly on the Agni of the southeastern *cercles* of Abengourou and Aboisso. Etienne Djaument, who had brought the support of the U.O.C.O.C.I. to Houphouet-Boigny's candidacy in 1946 and had become a senator the following year, withdrew from the P.D.C.I. in 1948. He then created the *Bloc Démocratique Eburnéen* with the support of his Nehyo tribesmen in Sassandra and other Kru groups in nearby regions. Capri Djédjé, elected President of the Territorial Assembly against A. Denise in 1949, together with Digna Bailly, candidate to the French Constituent Assembly in 1945, founded a section of the French Socialist Party (S.F.I.O.) among their Bété tribesmen in Gagnoa and Daloa *cercle.* Moslem northerners, including Sékou Sanogo, Ivory Coast representative to the Grand Council, Yoro Sangaré, Tidiane Dem, and others, expanded the ethnic association *Idéal d'Odiénné* into the *Entente des Indépendants de Côte d'Ivoire.* Even among the Baoulé, political hopefuls—including one of Houphouet-Boigny's brothers-in-law—organized an ethnic party, the *Union des Indépendents de Côte d'Ivoire.*[57]

Most of these organizations claimed that they, rather than the P.D.C.I., remained faithful to the spirit of Bamako.[58] Within the context of Ivory Coast politics in 1949, however, they were reformist in tone in that they were willing to work within the existing framework. Hence, they were viewed as traitors by many other Africans. Many leaders and followers were sheer opportunists who took advantage of the administration's desire to build up countervailing organiza-

[57] With the exception of the *Parti Progressiste,* all of them were created between April and December 1949. Names of leaders and parties are drawn from registration forms on file in the archives of the Ministry of the Interior, Ivory Coast. Additional information was obtained from examination of electoral results and from interviews with leaders of these parties.

[58] See for example the statements by E. Djaument in *Annexe, No. 11348.*

tions. However, some were genuinely concerned about the apparent takeover of the P.D.C.I. and the R.D.A. by external agents. Little is known about the organization of these parties. Most of them had only one or two branches, in Abidjan and in the *cercle* dominated by the ethnic group they represented. Few reached the stage of organizing village committees, although in almost every community in the country, some individuals became *Indépendants, Socialistes,* or *Progressistes.* In some cases, P.D.C.I. secretaries defected to the opposition and took the entire membership with them. Civil servants, who were particularly vulnerable to administrative pressures, readily became organizers for the new parties. Many years later, P. Yacé (since 1960 the general secretary of the P.D.C.I.) reminded an audience of government employees that "it must be acknowledged that the action of the R.D.A. . . . did not receive, during our time of difficulties, the support it might have expected from the civil servants. They were much more numerous in 1951 among the ranks of the Progressive Party, the Independents, or the Socialists, than in the R.D.A. camp."[59]

Political Conflict

The agitation conducted by the P.D.C.I., the aggressive tactics of the new political groups, and the repressive actions of the French administration took place within the context of the economic crisis discussed earlier. A series of clashes in the Ivory Coast between February 1949 and February 1950 resulted in an estimated 52 deaths, several hundred injuries, and perhaps 3,000 arrests and detentions. The highlights were street fights in Treichville in February 1949, leading to the arrest of 8 leading members of the P.D.C.I. executive in Abidjan, and three-cornered encounters between P.D.C.I. supporters, their African opponents, and French-led police or armed forces in Dimbokro and Séguéla at the

[59] *Fraternité,* February 12, 1960.

end of January 1950. This last incident followed an abortive attempt to arrest Houphouet-Boigny.[60]

An analysis of these events indicates that they followed a common pattern, observed in many other communities. They usually were triggered by a specific event which was often unrelated to explicit political issues. Typical cases include a showdown between two factions that had been engaged in a dynastic controversy in Abengourou since 1943, a fight in the market place over the price of goods in Séguéla, and a clash over the purchase of agricultural produce by a middleman in Bouaflé. However, other incidents were directly related to the political situation. Fighting broke out when the administration tried to arrest a local P.D.C.I. leader, when hecklers from one side interfered with meetings of the other side, when P.D.C.I. faithful ostracized "traitors" in a given community, as they did with Sékou Sanogo's wives in Séguéla. Most of the events were localized in urban areas and pitted natives against immigrants. They were not always on the same political side. In Abengourou most immigrants backed one faction of the Agni community involved in a stool fight and were pro-R.D.A.; the secretary-general of the *sous-section* was a Dioula. In Bouaflé, however, the P.D.C.I. secretary-general was a native Gouro, who led the Gouro

[60] These events are narrated in detail by Ruth Schachter in *A History* . . ., based on information contained in *Annexe, No. 11348*, in the French press, and in unpublished materials including records of the trials of P.D.C.I. leaders. Even while doing research in the Ivory Coast ten years later, it was impossible to avoid repeated lengthy reports of the glorious days of the "time of politics," as many call the period under consideration. Although it is possible for an African nationalist leader to refer to the events surrounding the outbreak of the French Revolution as a "routine street demonstration," the same individual will not regard his own agitational past in the same way. In a discussion in the Ivory Coast Legislative Assembly in which the French Revolution was characterized in this way, one of the members warned that if the word *banale* were kept in the record, others might use the same word to characterize the events in the Ivory Coast in 1949 and in 1950. (Ivory Coast, *Journal Officiel de la République de Côte d'Ivoire, Débats de l'assemblée législative*, No. 13 [1959], pp. 178-82.) Cited hereafter as *Débats de l'assemblée législative*.

in an attack against the principal Dioula trader, who was champion of the *Indépendant*-minded immigrants. The regularity in this pattern lies in the fact that specific events, related or unrelated to politics, revived latent controversies. Factions within a community would then rapidly align themselves as they had in the past. In the first stage of controversy, as Coleman has generalized, "it seems that movement from specific to general issues occurs whenever there are deep cleavages of values or interests in the community which require a spark to set them off—usually a specific incident representing only a small part of the underlying differences."[61]

P.D.C.I. organizers and opposition leaders in search of support often gave these controversies a political character. Pro-government witnesses told the investigatory committee of the National Assembly that incidents often followed visits by a leading member of the R.D.A.; R.D.A. witnesses contended that disturbances occurred in the wake of appearances by French officials or opposition leaders. Whatever the case may have been, the visitors related the local issues to the broader ideological questions of the future of Africa and relationships to France. They attempted to mobilize support for the territorial organizations aligned on this basis. This also follows a typical pattern of conflict. During a second stage, new and different issues appear, unrelated to the original bone of contention. Involuntary issues appear, formerly repressed because of the working relationship between individuals. But once the stability of the relationship is upset, the suppressed topics come to the surface. Coleman also notes that sometimes the diversification of issues is purposive and serves to solidify opinion and to bring in new participants by providing new bases of response.[62]

During a third stage, disagreement shifts to antagonism:

[61] Coleman, *Community Conflict*, p. 10.
[62] *Ibid.*

"A dispute which began dispassionately, in a disagreement over issues, is characterized suddenly by personal slander, by rumor, by the focusing of direct hostility. . . . Once set in motion, hostility can sustain conflict unaided by disagreement about particular issues."[63] This process of generalization, he suggests, is due to the need for consistency. It is particularly acute in communities that do not create among their members the potential for cross-pressures.[64] In the Ivory Coast, when community conflicts reached this stage, individuals fell back on primordial attachments to kinship or ethnic units. As indicated in Chapter II, lines of ethnic cleavage tend to coincide with other differentiations as well. The potential for cross-pressures that might inhibit conflict is low. In the process of becoming involved, some groups strengthened their attachment to the P.D.C.I., while others identified strongly with new organizations. This reinforced pre-existing lines of cleavage in the country, giving them an additional political dimension. Now, many of the Agni, who distinguished themselves from the Baoulé by their relatively higher economic and educational status, were also *Progressistes,* while the Baoulé for the most part coalesced around their R.D.A. champion, Houphouet-Boigny. Because these political identifications were related to consistent cleavages, they retained their intensity long after the issues that had sparked political controversy had disappeared. Indeed, the major reason for French repression of the R.D.A. disappeared in the fall of 1950, when the movement renounced its *apparentement* to the Communist Party.

The Aftermath

At the end of 1949 the P.D.C.I. had lost its majority in the Territorial Assembly; members of the *Bureau Politique,* with the exception of those who benefited from parliamentary immunity, were in jail or in hiding to escape prosecution; at

[63] *Ibid.*
[64] *Ibid.*, p. 22.

all other levels the cadre were out of action or vacillating. Was the party to retreat or to launch a final offensive? The latter view prevailed. P.D.C.I. leaders in the Grand Bassam jail staged a hunger strike in December 1949 to speed up their trial and to obtain improved conditions for the prisoners. Over 500 women marched from Abidjan to Bassam, a distance of about 30 miles, to demonstrate in front of the jail. Simultaneously, the P.D.C.I. launched a boycott of the purchase of imported goods, followed by a strike by domestic help and by the vegetable and fruit vendors in Abidjan. Individual secretary-generals directed riots against opposition groups. Violence flared everywhere.[65]

The serious character of these incidents led to reconsideration by all sides involved. The French government banned all political meetings in the Ivory Coast but seemed unwilling to engage in a showdown with the R.D.A. The situation was investigated. From February 1950 to June of the same year, the High-Commissioner of French West Africa, the Minister of Overseas France, and finally a committee of the French National Assembly visited the territory to ascertain the causes of the trouble. At the same time, negotiations began with R.D.A. leaders through persons interposed.[66] Houphouet-Boigny was also reconsidering. Although he had attended the Twelfth Congress of the French Communist Party in the spring, he was already thinking of severing the ties that bound him to the Thorez machine. The outbreak

[65] In the events surrounding the abortive attempt to arrest Houphouet-Boigny at the end of January, an Ivory Coast R.D.A. senator, Biaka Boda, disappeared. When after an intensive search he could not be found, he was presumed dead. It is interesting to note that this period coincided exactly with the launching of "positive action" in Ghana on January 8, 1950. Padmore, p. 80. There is no evidence of collusion between the C.P.P. and the P.D.C.I., although many stories were circulated about it in Paris at the time.

[66] One of the go-betweens was A. Boni, a candidate in 1945, then serving in the Ministry of Overseas France in Paris. He later became Minister of Justice of the Ivory Coast Republic.

of the Korean War contributed to his decision.[67] Furthermore, the conflagration sent coffee and cocoa prices rocketing, thus reducing economic discontent overnight.[68] Houphouet-Boigny's decision was announced publicly in October.[69] In March 1951 the R.D.A. *parlementaires* indicated their return to the fold by endorsing a candidate to the office of prime minister for the first time since January 1947.[70]

Incidents had ceased by mid-1950, but tensions remained great in anticipation of the 1951 election of two deputies to represent the Ivory Coast in the National Assembly. After the *désapparentement*, the French government retained an ambivalent attitude toward the P.D.C.I. The Prime Minister, René Pléven, leader of the U.D.S.R., welcomed the R.D.A. action and attempted to promote a reconciliation.[71] A reconciliation was quite possible because for the first time since 1947 the M.R.P. did not control the Ministry of Overseas France. François Mitterand, a hardy perennial in the Fourth Republic's garden, also a member of the U.D.S.R., acted as chief mediator.[72] As Minister of Overseas France, he invited

[67] Houphouet-Boigny has often expressed his fear of the "yellow peril," because, he has explained, Africa might be seen by the overcrowded masses of Asia as a natural locus for expansion. It is possible that the active involvement of China in world affairs, signaled by the outbreak of the Korean War, frightened him.

[68] For the causes of this phenomenon, see Edwin P. Reubens, "Commodity Trade, Export Taxes, and Economic Development," *Political Science Quarterly*, LXXI, No. 1 (March 1956), 42-70.

[69] The process involved will be discussed in the following chapter. The announcement was made in the Ivory Coast in *La Côte d'Ivoire*, November 18, 1950.

[70] Guillemin, p. 870. They voted for Guy Mollet (who did not make it) on March 6, and for M. Queuille (who did) on March 9.

[71] *Le Monde*, December 30, 1950.

[72] Pléven, then Prime Minister, had been Commissioner for the Colonies at the Brazzaville Conference in 1944 and had more understanding than most French politicians of African questions. His and Mitterand's party, the U.D.S.R., was "the most important of the minor parties . . . situated very close to the center of gravity of French politics." (Williams, pp. 143-46.) Its support was necessary in almost every coalition under the Fourth Republic. Concerning the

R.D.A. deputies to attend the inaugural of the Abidjan harbor in January 1951, notwithstanding criticism by the Europeans, the local administration, and African opponents. Governor Péchoux, who, in the eyes of most Africans, was the most important symbol of the repression, was sent home on indefinite leave. At the same time, the French remained watchful, as Mitterand later revealed: "In order not to give rise to false hopes, it was necessary to avoid a confusion between progressive reform and a reaction stemming from weakness. This is why I thought it wise to explain to Mr. Houphouet-Boigny that in any case, the coercive means at the disposal of the governors would be increased in order to be prepared to deal with deviations that might be caused by the adversaries of this policy."[73]

The French also worked to undermine the P.D.C.I.'s electoral monopoly. The Ivory Coast electorate grew from 107,963 in November 1946 to only 189,154 in June 1951, the lowest rate of increase in all of French West Africa.[74] Furthermore, this was the result of a complex operation which involved eliminating from the electoral registers many who were thought to favor the P.D.C.I. and facilitating the processing of those who would probably support other parties. Nearly half of the voters were struck from the rolls in the Baoulé *cercles*; in the Agni-dominant *cercle* of Aben-

---

negotiations with the R.D.A., Mitterand has written his own account of the process that led eventually to the *apparentement* of the R.D.A. to the U.D.S.R. in 1952. He stated that having visited Accra, he was aware of the effects that the enlightened British policies toward nationalists might have on Houphouet-Boigny, since he and Nkrumah were of the same tribe. Between Accra and Abidjan, he wrote, osmosis was at work. It was therefore necessary to act rapidly, in order to avoid also the opening up of a second front while France was tied down in Indochina. François Mitterand, *Présence française et abandon* (Paris: Plon, 1957), pp. 165-200.

[73] Mitterand, p. 185.

[74] The 1946 figure cited here is for Ivory Coast districts only. During the same period, the electorates of Senegal and Guinea tripled; those of Sudan and Dahomey grew sixfold; Mauritania's quadrupled. Thompson and Adloff, p. 59.

gourou and in the Malinké area of Odiénné the electorate was multiplied nearly tenfold.[75] The administration overtly promoted anti-P.D.C.I. candidates and later in a report to its hierarchical superior took credit for the relatively poor showing of the Houphouet-Boigny organization.[76]

Although the R.D.A.'s *désapparentement* removed with one stroke the major source of disagreement among Ivory Coast leaders, most of the new political entrepreneurs turned down Houphouet-Boigny's offer of a reconciliation before the elections.[77] They attempted to create out of the scattered organizations that had arisen in 1949 a new alliance of ethnic and regional associations that would replace the P.D.C.I. Unification proved to be impossible in the face of competition among the various groups. Since there were only 2 offices at stake and election was on a list basis, ethnic leaders paired off to diversify their appeal. The leading ticket, combining the north and the southeast, was made up of the *Indépendant* Sékou Sanogo and the *Progressiste* Kacou Aoulou; they ran

[75] For example, registration figures for 1946 and 1951 respectively were: Abengourou, 1,040 and 10,416; Odiénné, 1,339 and 9,000; but Dimbokro, 3,522 and 2,618; Bocanda, 4,022 and 2,618. Figures obtained from records on file in the Ministry of the Interior, Ivory Coast.

[76] In a report to the High Commissioner for French West Africa after the elections, the Ivory Coast government stated that the relative defeat of the P.D.C.I. was due to the patient work of the administration of the territory during the preceding four years. But the ambiguity of the French position by 1951 also emerges from the report. A draft submitted to the Governor suggested that the R.D.A.'s current policy was nothing but a stratagem devised to gain some respite, and that the administration should continue to destroy it while it could. The draft bears the penciled comments: "Do this over in softer language. . . . One can think this, but the Governor believes that it is not opportune to say so at this time." (Letter on file in the archives of the Ministry of the Interior, Ivory Coast.) During the campaign, the administration used all the pressures already mentioned in connection with the assembly, as well as strategic placement of polling places, making it more convenient for opponents of the R.D.A. to vote. This is, of course, in the French tradition, as Stendhal has recounted in *Lucien Leeuwen.*

[77] Europeans, too, refused to believe the R.D.A.'s good intentions. *La Côte d'Ivoire*, Novembre 29, 1950; *Le Monde*, December 30, 1950.

under the name of the *Parti de l'Union Française*. Two other teams combined a westerner and a northerner.[78] Notwithstanding the efforts of its opponents, the P.D.C.I. secured 61 per cent of the votes cast.[79] It had a majority in 36 out of 48 *subdivisions* throughout the country, with highest support in Baoulé-dominant areas. The 12 *subdivisions* it failed to carry included 6 predominantly Agni, 2 Bété, 3 Sénoufo and Malinké districts in the north, and 1 in the extreme west. On the basis of proportional representation, the party retained only 1 of the 2 seats. Houphouet-Boigny was elected once again, but his running mate, Ouezzin Coulibaly, lost. The second seat went to Sékou Sanogo, whose party had obtained 32 per cent of the votes.[80] The entire R.D.A. won only 2 other seats in French West Africa.[81] (See Map 2.)

Conclusions

Houphouet-Boigny's victory in spite of repression clearly demonstrated that the colonial administration could not easily break the hold of his organization over the Ivory Coast. His personal stature was enhanced by his ability to avoid arrest, attributed by many to special powers rather than to the legal device of parliamentary immunity. The French now had two alternatives: to go far beyond the coercive

[78] Digna Bailly, a Bété and Vamé Doumouya, a Dioula from Bouaflé formed the *Union Républicaine*; Djaument and Kassoum Coulibaly, a northern Sénoufo, competed as the *Entente Ethnique Eburnéenne*. There were three additional tickets that were in effect P.D.C.I. fronts. The idea was to have as many slates as possible in order to gain access to the polling places and to obtain permission to hold meetings. The candidates on these lists instructed their followers to vote for Houphouet-Boigny and Ouezzin Coulibaly.

[79] The results were as follows: registered, 189,154; votes cast, 111,287; valid votes, 109,759; P.D.C.I., 67,200; *Union Française*, 35,336; *Union Républicaine*, 5,881; *Entente Ethnique Eburnéenne*, 1,341; *Union Démocratique*, 1.

[80] After the elections the P.D.C.I. attempted to obtain the invalidation of his election. This was defeated by a vote of 285 to 48 in the French National Assembly on August 24, 1951.

[81] Milcent, p. 63.

NATIONAL ASSEMBLY ELECTIONS, 195

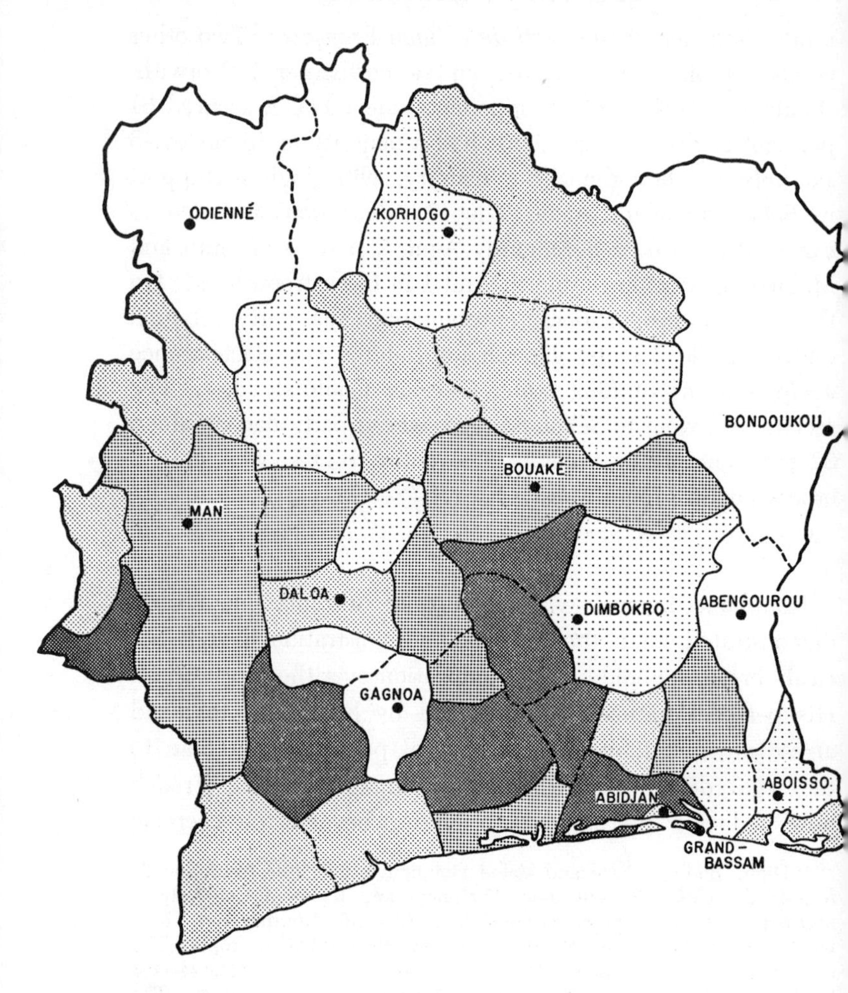

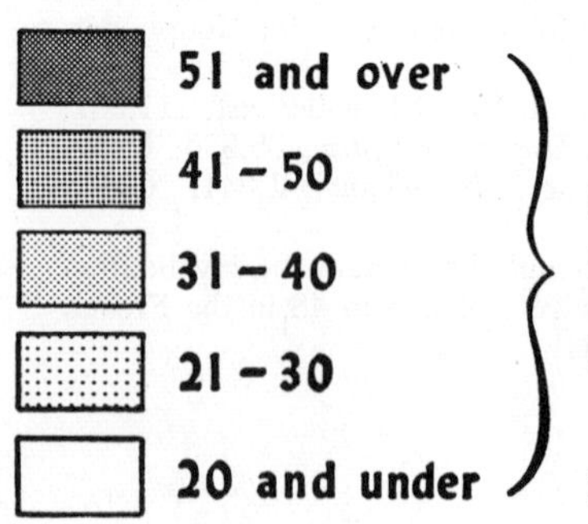

Per cent of registered electors who supported PDCI candidates (by subdivision)

Map 2

measures already used to destroy the P.D.C.I. or to agree to negotiate with its leader as an *interlocuteur valable.* They chose the second line of action, thus acknowledging the legitimacy of his claim to represent the people of the Ivory Coast. But this was a Pyrrhic victory. The party had lost its political monopoly and was faced with stronger challengers than ever before. Its organization was nearly destroyed. Houphouet-Boigny admitted that "there is no doubt that nearly the entire mass of peasants and workers magnificently demonstrated their will to resist. But the cadre gave in everywhere: first the chiefs, then the civil servants, the white-collar workers, the petty businessmen, all those whose daily bread was assured by the administration or by the colonists."[82]

The situation of the other *sections* of the R.D.A. was even more precarious. In the face of the threat of complete destruction, Houphouet-Boigny sounded the retreat. When the secretary-general of the R.D.A. questioned the wisdom of his decision, Houphouet-Boigny answered charges of treason as follows: "The R.D.A. is a movement and not a political party. It must take into account in its organizational structure as well as in its tactics, African realities and among other things, the lack of differentiation of the population into antagonistic classes and the specific reactions of our masses. . . . Communism is not the goal of the R.D.A. . . . Hence, since communism was not our goal . . . and since the overwhelming majority of the French people, outside a minority of selfish and narrow-minded reactionaries, are not at all irreducibly opposed to African emancipation, did we have the right to facilitate the task of the reactionaries who labeled the R.D.A. communist in order to secure the support of a large portion of the French people against us?"[83] In justifying his decision,

[82] In an address to the Coordination Committee of the R.D.A. at Conakry, 1955. Quoted in Milcent, p. 52.

[83] Félix Houphouet-Boigny, "Réponse à d'Arboussier," *L'Afrique Noire,* No. 27, July 24, 1952. Houphouet-Boigny was accused of treason

Houphouet-Boigny appealed to the same arguments that had been invoked by such party leaders as E. Djaument when they left the P.D.C.I., namely that the communist tie jeopardized rather than helped achieve the goals defined at Bamako in 1946. Shortly after the elections, he sought a political truce and asked all groups to cooperate for the social and economic development of the country. This marked the beginning of an entirely new phase of political development which will be discussed in the next section.

The development of Ivory Coast politics as of mid-1951 can also be assessed from the point of view of national integration. Nationalist movements such as the Convention Peoples Party of Ghana ". . . formed a major element in the socialization of what was a predominantly localized and fragmented set of tribal and regional areas. . . ."[84] More generally, it is held that the nationalist party is "the most important mechanism to reduce the conflict between ethnicity and national integration."[85] But the case of the P.D.C.I. indicates that a nationalist movement can contribute to national integration at one level of social life while creating obstacles to it at another level.

Bonds forged among the top leaders of the party replaced traditional ties. Many individuals had first come to the movement as leaders of ethnic associations. Later, their activities as members of the *Comité Directeur* took them beyond their own regions and their proper tribe. Some were jailed and became "martyrs," heroes known and respected throughout the country. When elected to higher office abroad, in Dakar or in Paris, they defended the interests of the Ivory Coast rather than those of a particular tribe. At the uppermost levels, party structures thus facilitated the transformation of ethnic leaders

in the Soviet press; his was a "national bourgeois" deviation. ("Soviet Views on Africa," *Soviet Survey*, April-June 1959, p. 40.)

[84] Apter, *The Gold Coast in Transition*, p. 212.

[85] Immanuel Wallerstein, "Ethnicity and National Integration," *Cahiers d'Etudes Africaines*, No. 3 (1960), p. 138.

into truly national leaders, dedicated to the formation of a new political community coextensive with the entire territory. They channeled the support they retained among their own tribesmen to the organization as a whole and thus the links that were established within the P.D.C.I. among the various groups contributed to national integration.

At lower levels, however, the structures created in 1947 helped maintain ethnic ties even when economic and social change might have diminished their importance. In Treichville, where members of the P.D.C.I. might have developed non-ethnic associational ties from their occupational activities or neighborhood contacts, the party helped them avoid this altogether. The movement did not generate a new kind of social life. Elsewhere, basic party units coincided with ethnic wards, and party life also reinforced ethnicity. This is confirmed by Raulin, who observed of a town in the Ivory Coast hinterland that "public meetings, and more generally the entire set of political activities, take place separately, each committee leader taking care of his own ward. There is no communication at the base between the different wards and in this sense, the party, which might have constituted a factor of integration for the immigrants, plays absolutely no such role; the specificity of each of the ethnic groupings is a fact acknowledged and recognized by the Africans themselves."[86] Community conflicts led to a search for consistency which was found eventually in a reinforcement of primordial ties. The growth of territorial nationalism was accompanied by the renascence of ethnic subnationalism. Alongside the territorial movement, new political organizations appeared which were dependent for their continued existence on tribal identification.

It is true, as Wallerstein has indicated, that ethnicity is not necessarily incompatible with national integration. He has shown that ethnic groups tend to diminish the importance of kinship role; that they serve as mechanisms of resocializa-

[86] Raulin, p. 126.

tion; that they help to keep the class structure fluid and so prevent the emergence of castes; and finally, that they can function as outlets for political tensions by permitting individuals to challenge persons rather than the authority of the office these persons occupy. "In rejecting the men," Wallerstein concludes, "they implicitly accept the system."[87] To the above list, the contribution of ethnicity to secularization can be added. Although much political activity took place within tribes rather than across tribal lines, the introduction of a dimension of secular political loyalty undermined traditional structures and facilitated the institutionalization of new forms of government. Amon d'Aby has written that "by agreeing to participate in a given political group, the chief saw his authority being weakened and a large part of his subjects put themselves under the authority of the political leaders."[88]

Ethnicity can also have dysfunctional consequences. Wallerstein notes especially that ethnic groups are particularistic in their orientation and diffuse in their obligation and that this can result in problems of nepotism and corruption. Furthermore, the persistence of ethnic affiliations can create dangers of separatism.[89] It is impossible to draw a balance sheet of consequences of political activity during this period. From the point of view of participants in the system, the contributions of conflict and ethnicity to national integration are less visible than the obstacles they created. The experience of militancy revealed the dangers of separatism in the Ivory Coast by reviving the centrifugal tendencies stemming from the sharp cultural differentiations that exist in the country. Separatism, in this sense, affected the P.D.C.I. rather than the territory. But for political leaders, the movement and the nation were identical. What was harmful to the P.D.C.I. could not possibly be beneficial to the Ivory Coast. The

[87] Wallerstein, pp. 134-37.
[88] Amon d'Aby, *Le problème des chefferies . . .*, p. 37.
[89] Wallerstein, pp. 134-37.

memory of conflicts during this period instilled among many Ivoiriens a fear of the consequences of political competition and mass mobilization for action.

Finally, the consequences of this political phase upon the development of democracy can be examined. The behavior of the French administration was calculated to instill a respect for the forms of democracy but not for its spirit. Elections were something to win, not a contest to be waged according to rules of fair play; there were few limits to the pressures that could be applied upon assemblymen to secure a majority in the council. On the other hand, the end of the P.D.C.I.'s political monopoly did signify the introduction of political competition in the Ivory Coast. The results of the 1951 election, albeit engineered, indicated that the new organizations had some popular strength. Although they had been supported by the colonial administration, they were not merely its creatures. Because these political groups were based on genuine differentiations in Ivory Coast society, their chances of survival were fairly good. Their continued existence might insure, in turn, the persistence of political competition. Yet, the willingness of the leaders of these parties to collaborate with the colonial government during the militant years left in its wake a memory of disloyalty that deprived them of legitimacy. The leaders and their followers were cast beyond the pale of the new society. In order to return, they had to recant and make amends. They were therefore highly vulnerable to pressures for reintegration into the unified movement the P.D.C.I. began to construct in 1952.

Within the P.D.C.I., militancy resulted in the growth of autocratic control in the hands of Houphouet-Boigny. The party's governmental mechanisms were never made operational because of the state of political warfare that presided over their creation. Later, they were suspended because of the need to underplay party activity. By 1951, nearly all the leaders of the P.D.C.I. were in jail, with the exception of those who benefited from parliamentary immunity. Ouezzin Coulibaly lost his immunity in 1951 after his defeat and was subject to prosecution; senator Biaka Boda was dead; two of the three P.D.C.I. representatives in the Assembly of the French Union were not Ivoiriens; the third was willing to defer to his chief. Houphouet-Boigny thus stood alone at the helm of his party.

PART III

THE EMERGENCE OF A ONE-PARTY SYSTEM

CHAPTER V

UNION FOR DEVELOPMENT

BY 1957, the year Africans obtained a measure of self-government, the P.D.C.I. had regained the ground lost between 1948 and 1951. In the process of reconstructing its political monopoly, the organization underwent once again a major transformation. This time, although it retained the appearance of a militant movement, the P.D.C.I. became a machine concerned primarily with electing men to office and distributing tangible incentives to its members. This process of transition from militancy to the new phase coincided approximately with the duration of the second legislature, from 1951 to 1956. During these four and a half years, as the P.D.C.I. began to change it derived less support from shared grievances than from the tangible satisfactions for which it was able to take credit. The economic environment in which it operated became crucial. Hence, important economic considerations conditioned the stand of Ivory Coast leaders who participated in decisions that modified the institutional framework of the French Union from 1956 on.

THE APPEAL TO UNION

Professor Kenneth Robinson has suggested that during the period of the second legislature, "the *immobilisme* of metropolitan politics was paralleled by something of a 'pause' in political activity in French West Africa."[1] In the case of the Ivory Coast, this was a deliberate choice. Houphouet-Boigny stated at the time that "during a period of crisis, *immobilisme* is a positive policy, to be preferred over action that might lead to an irreparable misstep."[2]

[1] Kenneth Robinson, "Senegal: The Elections to the Territorial Assembly, March 1957," *Five Elections in Africa* (eds.) W. J. M. Mackenzie and Kenneth E. Robinson (Oxford: At the Clarendon Press, 1960), p. 319.

[2] In a speech at the Conakry meeting of the R.D.A. Coordination Committee, quoted in Milcent, p. 65.

The process of *désengagement* was as complex as the *engagement* had been earlier. Its major public turning point was a mass rally held in the Abidjan football stadium on October 6, 1951. Reviewing the history of the R.D.A., Houphouet-Boigny acknowledged that the *apparentement* of his party to the communists had been a source of disunity. Now that this stumbling bloc had been removed, "union for a constructive policy [was] a vital necessity."[3] The road to cooperation, he continued, albeit a difficult one to follow, was the road to salvation. United, Europeans and Africans could do a great deal to promote the best interests of the Ivory Coast. If order was restored, then the French administration could once again devote its energies to the performance of its proper functions of guidance and of development, rather than those of gendarme and promoter of political parties. In the weeks that followed, he enlarged upon these themes before European and African audiences. He pledged to support France on the international scene under any circumstances[4] and promised that the R.D.A. would help promote the social and economic development of the country by voting for higher taxes if necessary. Capitalists would always be welcome, he added, as long as they devoted themselves to the common enterprise of development.[5]

This reorientation took place within the context of a spectacular economic boom that enabled many Ivoiriens to enter the ranks of coffee and cocoa growers and to engage in profitable trade. In 1954 Houphouet-Boigny gave economic achievement an even greater priority over political reform among the goals of his organization. In a speech welcoming the new Governor, he listed the country's hopes: rapid com-

[3] The text of Houphouet-Boigny's speech was reprinted in *La Côte d'Ivoire*, special issue of October 10, 1951. This in itself was unusual because *La Côte d'Ivoire* was the organ of the local Europeans and had been violently anti-R.D.A. throughout.

[4] Earlier the R.D.A. had followed the communist line and had announced it would help France only in case of a "defensive" war. *Ibid.*, October 27, 1951.

[5] *Ibid.*, November 17, 1951.

pletion of the Abidjan harbor, betterment of local roads, construction of the Treichville bridge, modernization of agriculture, and rapid expansion of educational facilities. He concluded: "In the final analysis, political wisdom commands us to undertake these different tasks. The populations of the Overseas Territories realize that the constitution of 1946 has brought to overseas men rights and duties which are to the citizen what the skeleton is to the man. We must instill life into this skeleton, give it a healthy body by elevating the African economically and socially to the height of his juridical promotion."[6] This reversal in the order of priorities expected of a nationalist movement in Africa became one of the distinguishing characteristics of the Ivory Coast regime. To Kwame Nkrumah's dictum, "Seek ye first the political kingdom and all things else shall be added unto you,"[7] Houphouet-Boigny might have opposed the advice he gave his own Baoulé countrymen in one of his first tours of the country after launching the policy of union: "If you don't want to vegetate in bamboo huts, concentrate your efforts on growing good cocoa and good coffee. They will fetch a good price, and you will become rich."[8] Nevertheless, the achievement of the goals defined by this new Guizot required political action at several levels.

In France, the R.D.A. went far beyond a simple reconciliation with the regime and became a governmental party. Shortly after the beginning of the second legislature, its representatives in the National Assembly announced their *apparentement* to the U.D.S.R. whose leader, René Pléven, was once again prime minister.[9] One tangible and immediate result

[6] Ivory Coast, Assemblée territoriale, "Debates," March 1, 1954.

[7] Quoted in Emerson, p. 83.

[8] At the opening of the Dimbokro Fair, in a speech quoted in *France-Afrique Abidjan*, March 17, 1953.

[9] The alliance was of mutual benefit since the U.D.S.R. had fallen below the crucial number of 14 members necessary to obtain representation in the Committee of the National Assembly. Williams, pp. 146, 236. In the Assembly of the French Union and in the Council of the Republic, the R.D.A. affiliated with the *Rassemblement des Gauches Républicaines*.

was the release of most of the high-level P.D.C.I. leaders detained at the Grand Bassam jail. From then on, the deputies remained on the side of the angels by approving 12 of 14 candidates for the office of prime minister.[10]

In the Ivory Coast, the first opportunity to implement the new policy was the renewal of the Territorial Assembly in March 1952.[11] At the beginning of the campaign, the P.D.C.I. announced that rather than stand alone, it would seek a broad union with other African groups and also with Europeans willing to cooperate, under the name of Union for the Economic Development of the Ivory Coast (U.D.E.C.I.). Houphouet-Boigny promised his African opponents that this appeal did not signify an attempt to create a single political party. The future, he stated, lay in open competition between political parties, with a neutral administration acting as the umpire. "Each and everyone of you can remain within his own party. After all, we see shopkeepers who smile at one another all day long but who nevertheless compete to get the largest number of customers. It is something like that we want to bring about here."[12] Much later, however, the P.D.C.I. admitted that this appeal to union had been a tactical move to disorganize its adversaries.[13]

Some opponents responded to the call without delay. Digna Bailly announced that now there were no obstacles to cooperation since he had fought Houphouet-Boigny not because he

[10] Guillemin, pp. 870-71.

[11] The *conseil général* was renamed *Assemblée Territoriale* shortly before the renewal. The proportion of African members was slightly greater. In the Ivory Coast, there were 5 additional second college seats. Law 52-130, reprinted in Ivory Coast, *Journal Officiel*, February 11, 1952.

[12] *La Côte d'Ivoire*, January 2, 1952.

[13] "At the time of the territorial elections of March 1952 the president of the R.D.A. disorganized the opposition by taking on his own tickets active elements among his foes. The latter were quite willing to submit themselves to this procedure since there were many disputes among themselves over the choice of candidates . . . and since they were very conscious of the great chances of success of any candidate coopted by the P.D.C.I." (Mamadou Coulibaly, "Notre Combat," *Fraternité*, August 5, 1960.)

was a Baoulé, but because he had played into the hands of the communists. "In politics, one must know how to forget, and to forget quickly," he announced.[14] The Bété leader, who had been defeated in June 1951; a Senegalese, who had been an unsuccessful candidate in the first college elections of 1947; 2 *Indépendants*; and 4 Europeans of U.D.S.R. or of Socialist background endorsed the manifesto of the U.D.E.C.I., which stated: "The political parties R.D.A., S.F.I.O., and independent candidates who make up the list of Union for the Economic Development of the Ivory Coast declare their solidarity for the purpose of conducting the current electoral campaign on the basis of a minimal program of economic growth and of social peace. This *apparentement* is tied to the solemn promise . . . to leave each party its freedom of action and each person his proper individuality in the future Territorial Assembly."[15]

Not all anti-P.D.C.I. leaders were willing to be coopted, however. Sékou Sanogo commented after the announcement of the R.D.A.'s *apparentement* to the prime minister's own party: "I am disgusted. What do I look like, now that Houphouet-Boigny, whom I have been fighting for years in the name of France, has become a part of the government majority?"[16] He and his running mate of 1951, Kacou Aoulou, sought re-election to the Territorial Assembly in opposition to U.D.E.C.I. candidates. Others, such as E. Djaument, agreed that the policy of union was desirable but felt that "we should continue our political emulation in order to insure a democratic future for this country."[17] Altogether, 42 candidates challenged the union's 32 nominees.

To the members of his own party, Houphouet-Boigny had directed the following appeal in October 1951: "I demand of all our militants that they respect the laws and that they

[14] *La Côte d'Ivoire*, October 13, 1951.
[15] *Ibid.*, March 15, 1952.
[16] *Ibid.*, January 16, 1952.
[17] *Ibid.*, February 2, 1952.

obey the legitimate authorities. Let us prove our sincerity through our actions. Only in this way will we be able to lift the veil of suspicion that still hovers over us. Do not give to anyone the opportunity to criticize your behavior. Be conscious of your rights, but be even more conscious of your duties."[18] This was repeated in addresses throughout the country. None of the P.D.C.I. leaders openly disagreed with the new party line.[19] Ten of the thirteen assemblymen who had remained faithful were included in the U.D.E.C.I. slate. But there were important omissions: the three men who had steered most of the issues discussed in the previous chapter through the Assembly, Mockey, Gadeau, and Paraiso, were left out; other party "martyrs," such as M. Ekra, B. Dadié, J. Williams, were not nominated. The new recruits were mostly S.A.A. officials, more business-minded than most members of the P.D.C.I. executive, and party leaders who had not been in the forefront of the battle. This was part of the price the party had to pay to accommodate its new European and African partners.[20] Nevertheless, regardless of their personal feelings and their ideological preferences, the "martyrs" joined other members of the *Comité Directeur* and a general assembly of all secretary-generals in expressing publicly their

[18] *Ibid.*, October 10, 1951. A few days later, he asked them to fight "against their bad instincts" as he himself had been doing since his youth by giving up mangoes, tobacco, and alcohol. He also promised to restrain his temper. "I don't ask you to follow me on this path, but I want you to behave in such a way that the R.D.A. policy becomes one of non-violence. . . . Let us stop our fratricidal struggles. . . . Let us struggle not against our brothers, but against illiteracy, alcoholism, slums." (*Ibid.*, October 13, 1951.)

[19] One member of the party executive explained later, in an interview, that although some disagreed with Houphouet-Boigny's reorientation, they were at his mercy because they had been freed as the result of administrative action, rather than through due process of law, as part of a bargain Houphouet-Boigny had made with the French.

[20] This was really a temporary party purge since although all those who were not nominated remained on the party executive, the latter was inactive. Several were included on municipal tickets in 1954, after the end of the cooling off period.

approval of the U.D.E.C.I. candidates and pledging to support wholeheartedly the new policy of union.[21]

The Union fared well in the elections, obtaining a total of 72 per cent of the valid votes cast, compared with 61 per cent for the Houphouet-Boigny—Ouezzin Coulibaly ticket the previous year.[22] This was due to a large extent to the administration's relative neutrality.[23] The P.D.C.I.-sponsored coalition captured all but 4 of the 32 seats in the second section of the new Assembly. Most of the outstanding opposition leaders, including Sékou Sanogo, E. Djaument, Kacou Aoulou, and Capri Djédjé were defeated in their home constituency. At its first meeting, the Assembly elected Houphouet-Boigny president; he received 27 votes against 22 for his Senegalese opponent, A. Diop.[24] The party's strategy had clearly proved successful, even though support for the coalition was still short of what it had been in 1946.[25]

The policy of union was implemented at the municipal level as well in 1954. The case of Abidjan was particularly significant, because it had been on a similar electoral occasion nine years earlier that Houphouet-Boigny had launched the *Bloc Africain* by opposing the inclusion of Europeans on the municipal ticket. Now, a slate called the "Union for the Defense of the Interests of the Abidjan Commune" was created inviting

[21] The statement was issued at the end of a meeting held in Abidjan, February 19 to 24, 1952. (*La Côte d'Ivoire*, March 8, 1952.)

[22] The results were: registered vote, 203,174; valid votes cast, 92,947; U.D.E.C.I. candidates, 67,876; others, 25,071.

[23] For example, in Abengourou, Odiénné, and Bondoukou, where it is generally held that opposition groups had benefited from administrative assistance in 1951, the total vote recorded for the P.D.C.I.'s opponents dropped from 15,272 in 1951 to 6,794 in 1952. However, these constituencies still returned anti-P.D.C.I. candidates.

[24] One U.D.E.C.I. member, Ouezzin Coulibaly, was absent. (Ivory Coast, Assemblée Territoriale, "Debates," April 28, 1952.)

[25] The 67,876 votes it obtained represented a smaller absolute number than the 71,916 cast for the R.D.A. candidates in Ivory Coast districts in December 1946. Furthermore, the Union's proportion of the electorate (rather than of votes cast) dropped from 56 per cent in 1946 to 36 per cent in 1951, and to 33 per cent in 1952.

the participation of Europeans who proclaimed as their purpose "to work outside of politics in order to abolish racism, and to work for the greater glory of the French Union starting at the grass-roots level."[26] Fourteen of the 45 Union candidates to the 45-member municipal council were Europeans. Frenchmen and Africans were listed together on the tickets in the city's three wards: in Treichville, the ticket had 22 Africans and 5 Europeans; in the Plateau, 6 Europeans and 3 Africans; and in Adjamé, the other African section of the city, 6 Africans and 3 Europeans. The Union candidates included several prominent P.D.C.I. leaders (among them 3 of the "martyrs" of Bassam) whose presence was no longer objectionable to the European partners. As was always the case, the Africans represented a variety of ethnic groups and territorial origins; in this instance, 9 of the 31 were foreigners. The Union won without any difficulty.[27]

Houphouet-Boigny emphasized at the time that even municipal politics were related to the over-all policies of his organization. He stated that unity had to be sought at the local level as well as in Paris. The ties that bound Africa to Europe were strong ones; occasional antagonisms were nothing but family quarrels, which could not withstand considerations of enlightened self-interest. Asked to comment on the situation in the Gold Coast, then rapidly moving toward independence, he explained that this was but one possible solution, which the Ivory Coast regarded with great interest, but which he did not think was the best one for Africa. He reminded his questioner that "it is a mistake to put Black Africa in the same category as Indochina and North Africa. These old countries have the nostalgia of the past; they cannot escape the pressures

[26] *France-Afrique-Abidjan*, May 28, 1954.

[27] European opponents charged that its success was due to the fact that many African soldiers had been brought in to vote on the Plateau at the last minute in order to insure a victory in that ward for the Union list. In Treichville and in Adjamé, there was no serious competition. *France-Afrique-Abidjan*, issues from May 25 to June 8, 1954.

of nationalism that shake up the postwar world. But no nation can be completely independent. This century is, indeed, the century of the interdependence of all peoples."[28]

The greatest difficulties in the implementation of the policy of union were encountered at the remaining institutional level of government, that of French West Africa. Although the superterritorial R.D.A. continued to exist during the period under consideration, activities at the federal level came to a standstill. After the 1952 elections demonstrated beyond the shadow of a doubt that Houphouet-Boigny's reorientation had not been merely a tactical move, the former general secretary, Gabriel d'Arboussier, attempted to provoke a showdown between Houphouet-Boigny and those who objected to the *désapparentement* of 1950 and to the new alliance with the U.D.S.R.[29] But the president of the R.D.A. maneuvered to avoid a confrontation of the various territorial sections until he was sure of his ground. The R.D.A.'s position was not discussed until Houphouet-Boigny finally agreed to a meeting of the Coordination Committee at Conakry in July 1955. There, he demanded and obtained the expulsion of all territorial sections that had refused to follow his lead.[30] He exhorted members of the R.D.A. everywhere to exercise a great deal of patience, as he and his followers had been doing for the past three years in the Ivory Coast.

The R.D.A. was less concerned with the past than with the future. At Conakry its leaders advocated reform of the French

[28] *Ibid.*, June 12, 1954.

[29] Gabriel d'Arboussier had been asked to resign at the time of the *désapparentement* and conformed to this request. He later took back his resignation. After the Dakar headquarters of the R.D.A. denied his right to speak for the party, on May 15, 1952, D'Arboussier publicly attacked Houphouet-Boigny. The latter published an answer in *L'Afrique Noire*, July 24, 1952. For an account of this dispute, see Milcent, pp. 78-87.

[30] They included the *Union Démocratique Sénégalaise*, the *Union des Populations du Cameroun* (Um Nyobe), and the *Parti Progressiste Nigérien* (Djibo Bakary). The R.D.A. thus remained essentially a confederation of three major organizations: the Ivory Coast, Guinea, and Sudan territorial *sections.*

Union in a federal direction; this was to be implemented through deconcentration and decentralization. The Coordination Committee also adopted resolutions demanding the abolition of separate colleges and the grant of universal suffrage. In the economic sphere, which was defined as being of primary importance, the R.D.A. asked from France increased public and private investments.[31] These resolutions formed the standard against which African leaders evaluated the proposals for reform, known as the *Loi-Cadre*, tabled by the French Government and issued from the National Assembly elections of January 1956.

Economic Issues

Postwar Economic Growth

After World War II, the economy of French West Africa expanded at a rate unmatched in its earlier history.[32] Within this larger unit, the Ivory Coast's growth was even more dramatic. Toward the end of the 1950's, the territory resembled Ghana, the richest and the most highly developed country in West Africa, more than the federation, as the indicators summarized in Table 10 show.[33] Although the Ivory Coast had only 13 per cent of the federation's population, its share of the gross product of French West Africa was 26 per cent. Per capita income was approximately twice as high.[34] Another important indicator of the degree to which the Ivory Coast outdistanced other territories is its share of the total external trade of French West Africa. It had 10 per cent of the imports

[31] This account of the Conakry meeting is based on Milcent, pp. 87-92, and on reports in *Abidjan-Matin*, July 13 and 15, 1955.

[32] For a thorough discussion of the phenomenon, see Berg, pp. 391-405. Although concern here is more with the results than with the causes, it may be noted that it was due to a large extent to a vast outpouring of French public and private investments.

[33] The exception is education. The Ivory Coast would resemble Ghana even more if it were not also included in the federation, thus inflating figures for the latter.

[34] Marcel Capet, *Traité d'économie tropicale. Les économies d'A.O.F.?* (Paris: Librairie Générale de Droit et de Jurisprudence, 1958), p. 271.

TABLE 10

Some Indicators of Economic Development in French West Africa, the Ivory Coast, and Ghana[a]

	F.W.A.	Ivory Coast	Ghana
Exports per capita ($ U.S.)	18.2	47	51.6
Imports per capita ($ U.S.)	20.3	33	52.9
Percentage of total population engaged in non-agricultural wage earning	1.4	2.8	4.6
Electricity consumption per capita (KWh.)	7.7	9.4	49
Road density (miles of road per thousand square miles of area)	27.1	51	49
Number of inhabitants per motor vehicle	270	120	120
Railway density (miles of railway track per thousand square miles of area)	1.4	3.0	7.0
Per capita passenger miles traveled on railways	15	11[b]	35
Number of inhabitants per doctor	33,000	20,000	25,000
Percentage of school-age children attending schools	13	28	86

[a] Data for French West Africa and for Ghana are based on the year 1956 and obtained from Berg, p. 393. Data for the Ivory Coast were obtained from Côte d'Ivoire, Ministère du Plan, *Inventaire . . .*; Ministère du Plan, *Plan quadriennal, 1958-1962*; Ministère de l'Intérieur, Service de l'Information, *La santé en Côte d'Ivoire* (1956). They are for 1957, or 1958.

[b] This figure includes Upper Volta.

in 1920, 17.5 per cent in 1936, and 30 per cent in 1956. Its exports grew from 19.6 per cent of the total in 1936 to 25.8 per cent in 1947, and finally reached 45.5 per cent in 1956.[35]

The Fiscal Structure and the Federal Issue

Because of the taxation system that prevailed in French West Africa, the Ivory Coast's relatively greater economic expansion did not benefit the country as much as its leaders had anticipated.

As was mentioned earlier, since 1905 a large share of the indirect taxes collected in the territory had been turned over

[35] French West Africa, Gouvernement-Général, Service du Plan, *A.O.F. 1957*, p. 127.

to the federal government, which performed in exchange a variety of services for the Ivory Coast and other territories. From 1938 on, there had been a tendency toward further centralization of services in Dakar. To meet these new expenses, the Government-General appropriated all the remaining indirect taxes levied by the territories, leaving them only direct taxes.[36] The former were much more substantial than the latter. In any given year, approximately three-fourths of the total revenue raised in the Ivory Coast was drawn from indirect taxes, such as customs and excise taxes on imports, duties on exports, taxes on business transactions, postal revenue, and other items.[37] After the war, many of the services were returned to the territories, but Dakar did not give up the sources of revenue it had earlier appropriated. Since the territories could not meet expenditures from direct taxes alone, they were dependent upon rebates or subsidies from the federal government. According to the decree instituting it, the Grand Council of French West Africa was to use what money it needed to meet expenditures for the federation and then reallocate the remainder to the territories in proportion to their contribution.[38] In fact this was not done. Every year, the redistribution was the occasion of a great debate in the Grand Council, pitting the richer against the poorer territories.

During the 1920's, complaints stemmed from Senegal and Guinea. In the 1930's, as the Ivory Coast moved to the fore economically, it in turn became critical of Dakar. The major argument was always couched in terms of balance-sheet arithmetic. Kouamé Binzème, the *Progressiste* leader, demonstrated in 1946 that during the preceding decade, the Ivory Coast had collected 1,541 million in indirect taxes; of this,

[36] Jean Déboudaud, "Budget et impôts," *Afrique Occidentale Française*, I, 253-260.

[37] For a complete breakdown of the various taxes in force in the Ivory Coast and the level of government for which they were collected, see Roland Lecuyer, *La législation fiscale en Côte d'Ivoire* (Abidjan: Editions de la Côte d'Ivoire, 1955).

[38] Déboudaud, p. 256.

the federation returned in the form of expenditures in the territory or as subsidies only 704 million; the balance in favor of the federal budget was thus 837 million, a sum which represented about 40 per cent of the total of all Ivory Coast budgets during this period.[39] The postwar record is summarized in Table 11. The proportion of the Ivory Coast's contribution that was returned to the country varied from year to year, with a high of 32 per cent in 1949 and a low of 7 per cent in 1950 (column C). In later years, this figure

TABLE 11

Postwar Revenue in the Ivory Coast
(in million C.F.A. fr.)[a]

Year	*Taxes Collected to the Benefit of F.W.A.* (A)	*Amount Returned to I.C.* (B)	*Per Cent (B) of (A)* (C)	*Taxes Collected by I.C. for Own Benefit* (D)	*I.C. Budget Total* (E)	*F.W.A. Expenditures in I.C.* (F)
1949	3,030	954	32	919	1,873	557
1950	4,458	293	7	2,003	2,296	790
1951	7,070	684	10	2,160	2,844	1,246
1952	7,306	913	12	3,123	4,036	2,040
1953	8,120	2,054	25	2,901	4,955	2,842
1954	11,060	2,268	20	3,576	5,844	2,191
1955	10,972	2,729	25	4,073	6,802	2,185

[a] Ivory Coast, Ministère du Plan, *Troisième plan quadriennal 1958-1962*, pp. 87-88.

leveled off to around 20 to 25 per cent. Looking at it in a different way, the Ivory Coast contributed a larger share of the total F.W.A. revenue than she received every year. In 1949 the country was the source of 23.4 per cent of the total, but the recipient of only 17.8 per cent of the amount that was returned to the territories. In 1954 these figures were 36.5 per cent and 18.0 per cent respectively.[40] In addition to

[39] In a study cited in Amon d'Aby, *La Côte d'Ivoire . . .*, pp.128-31.

[40] Berg, p. 403. His figures and mine are slightly different because different sources were used. The argument is much the same.

the money returned, however, the federal government also performed services in the Ivory Coast (column F).

Nevertheless, the disadvantage to the Ivory Coast of the tax structure is evident. In 1955, for example, it could be argued that the total amount of revenue from direct and indirect taxes raised in the territory was 15,045 million C.F.A. frs. (columns A+D). The total spent was 8,987 million (columns E+F). The Ivory Coast thus considered that it had a net "loss" of 7,058 million, an amount nearly as large as what was spent *in toto*, and larger than its own annual budget for that year. By 1958, considering the record of the preceding decade, the Ivory Coast maintained that between 1949 and 1956, the federation had collected 65,229 million from Ivory Coast sources. It had spent 13,827 million in the territory in the form of various services and had returned in cash another 15,191 million. The final balance was a "deficit" of 36,028 million from the territorial point of view. This was more than twice the total amount contributed by the French to the Ivory Coast's development in the form of F.I.D.E.S. funds. If the Ivory Coast had kept this revenue during the period under consideration, it would have been able to double its annual budgetary income without increasing taxes.[41] But the territorial leaders became more vociferous during the 1950's, when economic development became the primary goal of the Houphouet-Boigny coalition. These considerations were an important determinant, although by no means the sole one, of their attitudes toward the future of the federation when it was discussed with other issues as part of the *Loi-Cadre* reforms.

[41] These arguments were spelled out by the Minister of Planning *after* the *Loi-Cadre* had already brought about changes in the structure under consideration. This does not detract from their value in explaining the Ivory Coast stand on the issue of federation earlier as well. (Ivory Coast, Ministère du Plan, *Troisième plan quadriennal 1958-1962* [Abidjan: Imprimerie du Gouvernement, 1958], pp. 87-88.)

Agricultural Economics and Relations with France

The Ivory Coast's relative wealth stems almost entirely from agriculture and within this sphere, from two commodities—cocoa and coffee. It was estimated that about 70 per cent of the gross national product in 1957 was in the agricultural sector.[42] As Table 12 shows, the proportion contributed by coffee and cocoa grew after the war. In 1956 they constituted about 90 per cent of the total, with coffee alone by far the most valuable product. The table also offers additional evidence of

TABLE 12

The Place of Coffee and of Cocoa in the Total Ivory Coast Export Economy[a]

Commodity	*Per Cent of Total*		
	1947	*1956*	*1958*
Coffee	55.8	57.5	59.0
Cocoa	19.0	32.0	20.0
Timber	4.9	4.8	11.0
Bananas	4.6	1.3	4.0
Others[b]	15.7	4.4	6.0
Total	100.0	100.0	100.0
Total value (in million C.F.A. frs.)	1,933.5	26,287.3	32,017.7

[a] Sources: Data for 1947 and for 1956, Ivory Coast, Ministère du Plan, *Inventaire économique de la Côte d'Ivoire, 1947-1956* (Abidjan: Imprimerie du Gouvernement, 1958), p. 91; data for 1958, Ivory Coast, Ministère du Plan, Service de la Statistique, *Bulletin statistique, supplément trimestriel* (Deuxième Trimestre, 1959), tables following p. 23.

[b] Includes small amounts of gold, diamonds, and other mineral products, as well as additional agricultural commodities such as palm oil and pineapples.

the very large postwar economic growth of the territory, although part of the increase in the total value of exports must be attributed to successive devaluations and inflation, rather than to an increase in real value.

[42] S.E.R.E.S.A., "Rapport d'une mission dans le secteur agricole," 1959, p. 24 (on file at I.F.A.N.).

Notwithstanding this vast expansion, the Ivory Coast economy has remained truly colonial. Most Africans are engaged in the primary production of export commodities, and a very small share of the country's production is absorbed locally. In every sector of the economy, with the exception of primary production itself, the managers have remained European. Imports and exports are ultimately handled by foreign business concerns with their center of operations outside the country. Most important, the Ivory Coast has continued to do business mostly with the metropole. In 1947 the franc zone accounted for 83 per cent of its exports and 69 per cent of imports;[43] a decade later, they were still 74 per cent and 73.5 per cent respectively.[44] As Berg has indicated, this is a phenomenon commonly found in French West Africa as a whole. It has made the federation into a high price area, because the area has had to pay higher than world prices for the goods it imports. But as a counterbalance, the area's exporters sell at higher than world prices in French markets protected by tariffs, quotas, and exchange controls.[45] From the point of view of this study, it is important to note that this was partly the result of the Ivory Coast's own efforts in solving problems stemming from a crisis in the market for her major commodity, coffee.[46]

With coffee alone amounting to nearly 60 per cent of the value of exports during the entire postwar period, private and public prosperity have been closely linked to the fate of this commodity.[47] The world market for coffee, like that

[43] Ivory Coast, Ministère du Plan, *Inventaire . . .*, p. 86.

[44] Ivory Coast, *Bulletin statistique, supplément trimestriel* (Deuxième Trimestre, 1959), p. 27.

[45] Berg, pp. 398-99.

[46] Coffee is by no means the sole problem the country faced; I am using it here because it is, in fact, the most important commodity, but mostly because it illustrates a process of decision making and strategy relevant to an understanding of Ivory Coast politics during this period.

[47] It is produced by a large number of relatively small farmers. An important share of the non-agricultural sector is related to activities concerned with its processing and marketing. In the public sector, taxes

for most primary agricultural commodities, is subject to widely fluctuating cycles.[48] After having reached an all-time low in 1940, coffee prices rose steadily.[49] In the Ivory Coast as well as elsewhere, a sort of "coffee rush" set in. This was accelerated during the Korean War boom when prices rose from 89.2 cents a kilogram in 1950 to about 120 cents in 1954.[50] Between 1950 and 1956, while the area devoted to cocoa growing in the Ivory Coast increased by 50 per cent, the amount of land used to produce coffee more than doubled.[51] Coffee production rose from 45,300 metric tons in 1948 to 93,800 in 1956 and was expected to reach nearly 150,000 tons in 1960.[52] Nevertheless, the Ivory Coast's prosperity has remained very fragile. Production eventually became greater than the total amount France could absorb and it was necessary to find other outlets. But although it is the world's third largest source of coffee, the Ivory Coast produces only about 3 per cent of the total output. Even by means of stock controls, it cannot alone control price trends on the world market.[53] Furthermore, because the Ivory Coast coffee is low in quality and of a type that is not usually prized by consumers, it cannot compete with equivalent commodities from other countries except by selling for much less. This can be

---

on coffee exports amount to between 15 and 21 per cent in various years (Lecuyer, pp. 23, 28) and supply an important share of the total public revenue. Furthermore, the situation of the coffee market and the prices fetched by the sale of this commodity determine the balance of trade and especially the value of imports, from which another important share of government revenue is derived.

[48] Reubens, pp. 53-54.

[49] For background on the coffee market, production, cycles, see the article under that heading in *Encyclopaedia Britannica*, 1956, Vol. v.

[50] Communauté Economique Européenne, Direction Générale des Pays et Territoires d'Outre-Mer, *Etude sur le marché du café* (Document de Travail VIII/D/112/o-F, January 1960), p. 12.

[51] Ivory Coast, *Inventaire . . .*, pp. 35-36.

[52] *Ibid.*

[53] This is in contrast to Ghana, which produces nearly 40 per cent of the world's cocoa and can somewhat compensate for prices by manipulating the flow of products into the market.

advantageous during periods of high prices such as the Korean boom; but the advantage is lost in bad times, when prices for *all* coffee drop and purchasers can obtain high quality products of the type they prefer for relatively little money.[54] The boom was effectively followed by a bust that heralded a steady deterioration of prices. Within a few months in 1954, the price paid for Ivory Coast coffee on the world market fell from 121 to 77 cents per kilogram. In 1960 it reached an all-time low of 33 cents.[55]

In the past, economic crises had exacerbated tensions between Africans and Europeans. However, in 1954 the situation was considerably changed. Europeans no longer competed against African producers, but engaged in complementary activities; political communications had been established at the leadership level between the two communities. The crisis now fostered unity. Together, African producers and European businessmen faced a hostile outside world. Under the leadership of the president of the Chamber of Agriculture, R. Desclercs, French residents reacted to the catastrophe by seeking protection for Ivory Coast products in an "economy of the French Union." A motion tabled in the Assembly demanded that the French government reinstate the 20 per cent tariff protection against foreign coffee that had existed before World War II and establish restrictive quotas on imports. Houphouet-Boigny wielded his majority in the Assembly to obtain unanimous approval of the motion. The only dissent came from a European member who warned that if successful, this policy would make the Ivory Coast more dependent than

[54] I take this as a given in this study, without attempting to account for the fact itself. Data on quality are contained in *ibid.*, p. 36. The Ivory Coast produces *Robusta* coffee, generally suitable only for mixing with milder types and for the production of soluble coffee.

[55] C.E.E., *Etude . . .*, p. 14. For 1960, see "L'évolution du marché des produits tropicaux en 1960: Café," *Marchés Tropicaux*, March 4, 11, 1961. Current prices are quoted on the commodity page of the *New York Times*, "R" Contract.

ever on France.[56] In spite of this, a grand alliance was formed to win the Battle of Coffee, as the operation was called locally. In the spring of 1955 the Chamber of Agriculture and the S.A.A. repeated the Assembly's demands and formulated new ones: a 20 per cent tariff on foreign coffee; a 12 per cent premium on exports to compensate for the difference between French and world prices; a quota system whereby French importers must purchase 4 tons of African coffee for each ton of foreign coffee; and finally prohibitions on the import of all Brazilian coffees that competed with Ivory Coast *Robustas*.[57] The operation was manned in Paris by Georges Monnet, a former Minister of Agriculture, and an Ivory Coast representative in the Assembly of the French Union since 1947.[58]

The union at home facilitated action in France, where the Ivory Coast could be viewed as a pressure group within the French structure of decision making. The first skirmish in the Battle of Coffee was won when the Ivory Coast obtained a lowering of the price base for calculation of export taxes, thus reducing the outgoing price by 9 francs; a 10 per cent tariff wall; a three-month suspension of licenses to import coffee liable to compete with its own; and a premium on exports set first at 6 per cent and then raised to 12 per cent. Hailing these measures, the Governor stated that success was due to "the union without cleavages of all elected representatives of the Territory, of the Administration, and of the Consular Assem-

[56] Ivory Coast, Assemblée territoriale, "Debates," December 22, 1954. The lone dissenter was Reinach, a Socialist who had been elected as one of four European members of the second section in 1952.

[57] *Abidjan-Matin*, March 14, 1955 and minutes of the S.A.A. meeting of March 31, 1955 (on file in the archives of that organization).

[58] Monnet, the creator of the "Office du Blé" in France during the Popular Front, has substantial business interests in the Ivory Coast, including a coffee plantation and pineapple canneries. He had been elected by the first section of the Assembly in 1947 and reelected in 1953. (*France-Afrique-Abidjan*, October 31, 1953.) He was Minister of Agriculture of the Ivory Coast from 1959 to 1960; eventually he was replaced by an African minister but remained Houphouet-Boigny's advisor for agricultural questions.

blies. . . ."[59] This was a far cry from the situation in the country only five years earlier.

The African and European members of the Assembly, who had unanimously resisted all past attempts to withhold a portion of the income derived from coffee to build up a stabilization fund that would compensate for extremely low prices, agreed to reverse their position in exchange for a French promise that such a fund would obtain support from the metropolitan treasury. The existing *Caisse du Café* and *Caisse du Cacao*, hitherto concerned exclusively with research and the construction of feeder roads, were quickly transformed with almost no debate into *Caisses de Stabilisation.*[60] They obtained a subsidy, as France had promised, a few months later.[61] In return for this and other measures, however, the Ivory Coast had to sell 1 ton of coffee on the world market for every 10 tons sold to France, a process known as *jumelage à l'exportation.* The next objective in the Battle of Coffee was the elimination of this obligation.[62] Monnet argued further that protectionism was necessary but not sufficient. What the Ivory Coast really needed, he asserted, was a guaranteed price for its products, as in the case of Senegalese peanuts or the olive oil of southern France.[63]

Before further action could be taken, the National Assembly was dissolved and a new election was called. It was a triumph for the P.D.C.I. and for the entire R.D.A., which emerged as the most important party in French-speaking Africa. Its president entered the Guy Mollet government and was the first

[59] Ivory Coast, Assemblée territoriale, "Debates," March 28, 1955.

[60] For background on the *Caisses*, see Thompson and Adloff, p. 474. They bear little resemblance to the marketing boards of British Africa. Ivory Coast, Assemblée territoriale, "Debates," April 7, 1955. The vote was 26 in favor, none against, 9 abstentions.

[61] *Abidjan-Matin*, October 2, 1955.

[62] Motions to this effect were debated and adopted by the Territorial Assembly. Ivory Coast, Assemblée territoriale, "Debates," April 20, 21, 22, 1955.

[63] *Abidjan-Matin*, April 4, 1955.

African to hold full ministerial rank.[64] Before leaving the territory for Paris, Houphouet-Boigny stated the major theme of his policy for the next few years: "We are very happy that the policy of Union has been successful so far. But the climate of good relations between the Ivory Coast and France will deteriorate very rapidly if the country does not obtain for its peasants the same kind of protection that wheat-growers and wine-producers get in France, or peanut-producers in Senegal."[65] When the announcement of Houphouet-Boigny's promotion came, *La Concorde*, the voice of the Ivory Coast coalition, commented that now that he was a minister he ought to be able to win this final stage in the Battle of Coffee.[66]

Success of this strategy required the maintenance of a close

[64] Others, such as Senghor, had already held the office of *Secrétaire d'Etat*, i.e., junior minister.

[65] *Abidjan-Matin*, January 17, 1956.

[66] *La Concorde*, February 9, 1956. Although this study is not concerned with French politics, it is interesting to consider why France was willing to grant these benefits to the Ivory Coast. First, the metropole was in need of good friends in the colonies, after having already suffered loss of prestige as the result of Indochina, Tunisia, Morocco, and Algeria. Market protection was a relatively cheap price to pay for this, since its cost could be passed on to the French consumer. Secondly, some French businessmen stood to profit from coffee sales; others would benefit from the retention of an Ivory Coast market for their own exports. It is important to note, however, that resistance was growing in France to such arrangements. French importers of Brazilian and other foreign coffee of course objected most vehemently. (*Abidjan-Matin*, April 13, 1955.) *Le Monde* argued that the coming of the Common Market signified that France could no longer afford to hang on to the concept of imperial protection; if it is necessary to subsidize commodities such as peanuts or coffee, this should be done through treasury grants for everyone to see and discuss. (Reprinted in *La Concorde*, June 28, 1956.) In a series of articles in the mass-circulation magazine *Paris-Match*, Raymond Cartier developed a doctrine of decolonization based on economic arguments that eventually came to be known under his name. *Cartierisme*, sometimes also called "anti-colonialism of the right" argued that in an artificial economy such as that of the French Union, poor territories cost France a great deal because they produce nothing, but rich ones like the Ivory Coast are even more costly because they produce something. (*Paris-Match*, issues during 1956; reprinted in *La Concorde*, August 16, 1956.) France must therefore give her colonies their freedom in order to avoid becoming the colony of her colonies.

relationship between the Ivory Coast and France, because a claim based on equity could reasonably be formulated only by a territory that considered itself as much an integral part of France as the department of Hérault or Tarn et Garonne. These considerations, together with the antifederation arguments discussed earlier, determined the Ivory Coast's stand on proposed reforms that transformed the French Union into the *Communauté* in less than three years.

THE LOI-CADRE REFORMS

Welfare Colonialism

It was widely acknowledged during the life of the second legislature that some reforms in the institutional framework of tropical Africa were necessary if France were to avoid facing there the fate she had met in North Africa and in Indochina. Yet, although several projects were under study, little was done until 1955.[67] In that year Togoland, where the French operated under the scrutiny of the United Nations and under international pressure, was given a measure of self-government.[68] Municipal reforms, achieved after much delay, promoted three Ivory Coast cities to the status of *commune de plein exercice,* with a municipal council elected on the basis of universal suffrage, and with an elected mayor.[69] Further reforms, including the grant of universal suffrage to the territories and additional representation for tropical Africa in

[67] In 1954 the Minister of Overseas France suggested that the territorial assemblies be given greater powers and that their members be granted some executive responsibility. (Kenneth Robinson, "Constitutional Reform in French Tropical Africa," *Political Studies,* VI, No. 1 [February 1958], 47.) Revision of the constitution in a federal direction was also under consideration. (André Blanchet, *L'Itinéraire des partis africains depuis Bamako* [Paris: Plon, 1958], p. 132.)

[68] Robinson, "Constitutional Reform in French Tropical Africa," p. 47.

[69] The cities were Abidjan, Bouaké, and Grand Bassam. Six new *communes de moyen exercice* were created as well. Concerning these reforms, see particularly L. Gray Cowan, *Local Government in West Africa,* pp. 152-57, 173-90, 218-20, 242-44, and 271-78.

the National Assembly, were pending at the time of the dissolution of the Assembly at the end of the year.[70]

Meanwhile, there were important modifications of the system in the realm of social and economic welfare. A Labor Code for Overseas France, passed in 1952, satisfied many of the demands formulated by the growing body of wage earners and salaried employees.[71] But the most significant changes came not as the result of a law at all, but through the evolution of the attitudes of colonial officials and the activities of the government. This was heralded in the Ivory Coast in 1954, when Governor Pierre Messmer, shortly after his arrival, gave precedence to Houphouet-Boigny, then president of the Territorial Assembly, at the opening of the spring session. After Houphouet-Boigny emphasized in his welcoming speech the economic goals of the country's representatives, Messmer replied: "Beside the magnificent economic development and the promise of social progress I see here . . . the political problems of the Ivory Coast appear to me to be secondary considerations, as long as public peace is not troubled. In this sphere, the gravest difficulties, I believe, are behind us. They were unavoidable. That is the price of adaptation to a new political regime. It is useless to seek to pin down responsibility for these events. We know from experience that new institutions can never be established without creating somewhat of a stir. Today, heads have cooled off. I ask of everyone in the Ivory Coast to make a renewed effort to reduce political passions to their proper place, a modest one, and to cultivate that which unites rather than that which divides."[72]

By 1956, the administration's role came close to the one advocated by Houphouet-Boigny in his appeal of October 1951: it was much less a gendarme than an agency for education and for development. This was reflected in the distribution

[70] *Abidjan-Matin*, December 7, 1955.

[71] P. Hugnet, *Code du travail d'Outre-Mer: Texte et commentaires* (Paris: Recueil Sirey, 1953), *passim*.

[72] Ivory Coast, Assemblée territoriale, "Debates," March 1, 1954.

of personnel among the various governmental services, summarized for 1949, the height of the repression, and 1956, the year preceding the institutional reforms effected by the *Loi-Cadre*, in Table 13. There was an absolute decrease in the

TABLE 13

The Transformation of the Colonial System[a]

Sector of Activity	1949		1956	
	Number	*Per Cent*	*Number*	*Per Cent*
Command and General Administration	885	19	1,688	23
Law Enforcement	1,479	32	1,232	16
Health, Education, and Welfare	1,457	32	2,675	36
Economic Development	790	17	1,913	25
Total	4,611	100	7,488	100

[a] The data in this table were computed from the tables of organization that accompany the annual budgetary estimates prepared by the government for submission to the Assembly. The categories were obtained by summarizing the various services of government. "Law enforcement," for example, includes police forces, personnel engaged in the adminis tration of prisons, and *gardes de cercle,* the local equivalent of the *gendarmerie.* Ivory Coast, *Budget pour l'Année 1949* (Abidjan: Imprimerie du Gouvernement, 1948) and Ivory Coast, *Budget pour l'Année 1956* (Abidjan: Imprimerie du Gouvernement, 1955).

number of personnel engaged in activities relating to law enforcement, even though the total number of government employees increased by 62 per cent. The change in activities appears even more clearly when the growth factor is considered.[73] This factor was 1.62 for the entire administration, but 1.89 for the category of command and general administration; .83 for law enforcement; 1.85 for health, education, and welfare; and finally, 2.53 for activities related to economic development.

[73] This "growth factor" is an index obtained by computing number of personnel in 1956/number of personnel in 1949. A figure below 1.00 indicated an absolute decrease.

The Loi-Cadre

The elections of 1956 signaled the beginning of the end for the Fourth Republic, which went down after having failed to solve the Algerian question.[74] Before its death, however, the regime opened the way for basic reforms in tropical Africa. A few days after Algerian mobs pelted the Prime Minister with tomatoes and threats, the Minister of Overseas France, Gaston Defferre, told the National Assembly that there was an emergency south of the Sahara as well. "The natives are restless. . . . The question is not whether we should plagiarize the British, but there is no doubt that the fact that they transformed the political and administrative regime of their territories has contributed to the growth of the impatience of the peoples of French West and of French Equatorial Africa."[75]

Because it was necessary to act more rapidly than could be done through normal legislative procedures, the government asked parliament to pass an enabling act, or *Loi-Cadre*, which would state broad directives to be implemented by decree.[76] Although the French did not consult conciliar organs in the

[74] "The dissolution had been decided by the parties of the center right to save or even to broaden their majority; they lost it. There was no majority on the left or on the center left either. There were nothing but minorities." (Jacques Fauvet, *La IVe République* [Paris: Librairie Arthème Fayard, 1959], p. 307.)

[75] France, Assemblée nationale, *Débats parlementaires*, March 21, 1956, p. 1108.

[76] The government project was sent to the Assembly in February 1956 and debated there in March. After consideration in the Council of the Republic the following June, it was adopted in second reading by the National Assembly and promulgated as Law 56-619 on June 23, 1956. (For the text, see Ambassade de France, New York, *African Affairs 14a* [August 1956].) The decrees to implement it were published in December 1956 and debated in the National Assembly in January, in the Council of the Republic the following month, and adopted by the National Assembly in March. After further consideration by the Council of the Republic, they were promulgated on April 4, 1957. For a full analysis of the reforms, see P. F. Gonidec, "L'évolution des Territoires d'Outre-Mer depuis 1946. 3. Les nouvelles institutions des Territoires et des Groupes de Territoires," *Revue Juridique et Politique de l'Union Française*, No. 1 (1958), pp. 43-92, and K. Robinson, *Constitutional Reform. . .*

territories, African leaders participated in decision making in Paris. The Ivory Coast, in particular, was able to promote its own views through the participation of Houphouet-Boigny in every government of the Fourth Republic's last two years.[77]

The first set of issues concerned the nature of participation. Universal suffrage was granted by the *Loi-Cadre* itself without much discussion. But the issue of separate representation for Europeans and Africans was more controversial. The original government project, prepared with the approval of Houphouet-Boigny, whose party had specifically advocated elimination of separate colleges throughout its existence, would have postponed the institution of the single college until after territorial executives were chosen, in order to insure European representation at that level. Although the Overseas Affairs Committee of the National Assembly amended this to provide for immediate abolition of separate representation, the National Assembly reinstated the government's version over the protests of all African members.[78] Notwithstanding a spirited defense of the concept of special European representation by Senator Armand Josse, spokesman for the more conservative Ivory Coast Frenchmen,[79] the Council of the Republic

[77] Gaston Defferre, speaking in defense of the government proposal, announced that it had been prepared with the help of the minister-delegate to the presidency, Houphouet-Boigny. France, Assemblée nationale, *Débats parlementaires*, March 21, 1956, p. 1112.

[78] Debates on this and other issues lasted three days. The final vote, cast at 4 a.m. on March 23, 1956, was 466 in favor of the government proposal, 99 against, and 13 voluntary abstentions. All R.D.A. representatives voted in favor; the Indépendants d'Outre-Mer, led by Mamadou Dia and Senghor, abstained. The high vote must not be taken to reflect attendance, since the *boitier* system enabled one man to cast the votes of his entire political group. At one point, the debates indicated that only 48 members were physically present. (*Ibid.*, March 20, 1956, pp. 1066-88; March 23, 1956, p. 1222.)

[79] A. Josse, a barrister and businessman, had been one of the most outstanding opponents of the R.D.A. during the militant years. He helped prosecute R.D.A. leaders. Nevertheless, he earned the respect of Houphouet-Boigny because of his frankness. Later, he served as an adviser to the African government when it engaged in constitution making.

amended the bill once again in the more liberal direction.[80] The single college was finally adopted by the National Assembly in second reading.[81]

The second set of issues concerned decentralization. This was more difficult to achieve because it required the prior resolution of a constitutional difficulty: how could authority devolve to decision-making organs in Africa without violating the constitutional prescription specifying that parliament alone was empowered to make laws? This was resolved by applying a doctrine developed earlier for Cameroun, a French trust territory. A distinction was made between different spheres of governmental activity: some services would be performed by the state, and others by the federations or the territories. Each category of services would be accountable to a distinct level of government.[82] Once this principle was established, important new issues arose: the composition and the accountability of the new African executives, as well as the domain of each of the three levels of government, the state, the federation, and the territory.

There was general agreement on the desirability of territorial executives. The Defferre project embodied the formula

[80] The amendment instituting the single college was passed by 167 votes against 143. The final vote in the Council of the Republic was 211 in favor, 77 against. (France, Conseil de la République, *Débats parlementaires* [June 7, 8, and 12, 1956].)

[81] On June 19, 1956. The final vote was 470 to 105.

[82] It is necessary to clarify one important point. Before the *Loi-Cadre*, all services were in effect state services. There were, however, different cadre often called "local," "federal," as well as "state." All of them were accountable to the state. (Gonidec, pp. 43-44.) The *Loi-Cadre*, by changing this pattern of accountability, truly brought about decentralization. But some of the services formerly managed by the federation became state services outright. This led to repeated complaints that the law created further centralization into the hands of the rue Oudinot, the Ministry of Overseas France. In a non-constitutional sense this was somewhat correct. If these services had remained in the hands of the federation, they might be controlled by Africans if they obtained self-government at the federal level. By passing them on to the state, France avoided this possibility.

worked out for Togoland the previous year, which provided for a Council of Government headed by the governor.[83] It would have 6 nominated official members and 6 members chosen by the Territorial Assembly from its own midst, but responsible to the governor rather than to the Assembly. But in mid-1956, faced with the forthcoming independence of British Togoland, the French granted to their own trust territory fully responsible self-government.[84] In order to head off any further African demands this might engender, the decrees published in December 1956 amended earlier proposals to include a majority of elected members. The Overseas Committee of the National Assembly, as might be expected, would not accept less than what Togoland had received. As Gabriel Lisette said, it was inconceivable that France's legitimate children should receive less than what she had given to her foster children.[85] In the face of governmental opposition to this request—on the grounds that what was constitutionally feasible in Togoland was not feasible in the territories—the Assembly worked out a final compromise, whereby the Council of Government would be headed by the governor, but all other members would be elected by the Assembly. The leader of the elected group would have the title of vice-president. There were no provisions for responsible government, but the Council would be allowed to resign if it felt that it no longer enjoyed the confidence of the Territorial Assembly.[86]

The governmental project emphasized decentralization to the benefit of the territories and to the detriment of the federation, a proposal in line with the Ivory Coast's preferences.

[83] Kenneth Robinson, "Constitutional Reform . . .," p. 48.

[84] Decrees of August 24, 1956.

[85] France, Assemblée nationale, *Débats parlementaires*, January 29, 1957, p. 370.

[86] Once again, the R.D.A. voted in favor and the I.O.M. abstained. The final vote, on February 2, 1957, was 296 in favor, 263 against, and 7 voluntary abstentions. (*Ibid.*, February 2, 1957, p. 557.)

There would be no federal services *sui generis*, but rather common services performed at the request of the individual territories, without an elected executive at the federal level. Why did the French, who after all had created the federation, propose measures that would facilitate its ultimate disappearance? Gonidec, writing shortly after the *Loi-Cadre* was implemented, suggested that "the Parliament and the Government reckoned that it would have been politically dangerous to decentralize to the level of the federations. It is certain that French West Africa, with its twenty million people, its important economic potential, and the movement for unification that is taking place at the political and the trade union level, . . . would have constituted a unit capable of imposing its views upon the Metropole if it had benefited from the measure of decentralization granted to the territories. One can therefore understand why the Government doggedly defended . . . the principle of decentralization to the territorial level."[87]

This maneuver was clearly perceived by Leopold Senghor, deputy from Senegal, who immediately accused the French government of attempting to "balkanize" Africa.[88] He continued to demand the institution of federal executives while the law continued its way through the legislative process.[89] After it was promulgated, the standing committee of the Grand Council of French West Africa directed a motion requesting the creation of federal services and of an executive to the Minister of Overseas France.[90] When the decrees implementing the law indicated that the government was adamant, the Grand Council refused to vote the budget for 1957 and

[87] Gonidec, pp. 82-83.

[88] In an interview published in *Afrique Nouvelle*, March 20, 1956.

[89] *Ibid.*, March 27, 1956. In order to make the idea of a federal executive acceptable to Abidjan, Senghor even proposed the creation of two federations centered on Dakar and Abidjan respectively. (*Ibid.*, January 3, 1956.)

[90] On July 2, 1956. It was signed by Jean Delafosse, an Ivoirien, among others. (*Ibid.*, July 10, 1956.)

asked the territorial assemblies to follow suit.[91] The Ivory Coast, of course, refused. Faced with the prospects of partial self-government, the territory's leadership was more acutely conscious than ever of the financial disadvantage of federation. The governor encouraged antifederal thinking by stating in a press conference: "Our budget of seven billion francs is ridiculously low. We are on the eve of the institution of the new *Loi-Cadre* system, which will bring about inevitably new financial burdens. If we want the Ivory Coast to pursue her economic and social expansion, it appears not only fair, but also good business, to return to this country all the income she collects from customs."[92] *La Concorde* added that the Ivory Coast's poor relatives were developing a parasitic outlook and were probably not doing enough to lift themselves up by their bootstraps.[93]

Although the advocates of a federal executive were unsuccessful, they succeeded in obtaining the creation of a limited number of interterritorial services and a provision that would enable the territories to create additional ones if they so desired. In the main, however, the new arrangements undermined the federation, in keeping with French and Ivory Coast desires.[94] Under the *Loi-Cadre* decrees, the territories would retain the gross amount of duties on exports, as well as most indirect taxes, with the exception of tariff and excise taxes on imports.[95]

The principle of decentralization to the territories was firmly established. But the scope of the reform was a function of the allocation of services between the territories and

[91] *Ibid.*, December 18, 1956.
[92] *La Concorde*, July 13, 1956.
[93] *Ibid.*
[94] Some of Houphouet-Boigny's critics accused him at the time, as well as later, of being a "stooge" of the French government on this issue. I believe that it is sufficient to note that their interests coincided.
[95] Details of the new financial structure are contained in Jean Roche, "Aspects financiers de la Loi-Cadre," *Annales Africaines* (Paris: Imprimerie Guillemot et de Lamothe, 1958), pp. 80-84.

the state. It was clear throughout, as one might expect in any federal system, that the state would continue to control the most important services: external affairs and defense, monetary and financial systems, customs, guarantees of civil liberties, representation of the central power. But in addition, France also sought to retain categories dealing with the maintenance of the solidarity of the constituent parts of the Republic and with its economic, social, and cultural expansion. The latter included, among others, higher education, broadcasting, and geological and mining services. Senghor expressed the general feelings of the African representatives when he states that if African territorial governments were given only toys and lollipops, while the most important services remained in the hands of the French, such governments would have only the appearance of power.[96] His protests and the concerted African efforts to transfer at least customs and higher education to the territories were to no avail in the face of French determination.[97]

In their final version, the decrees implementing the *Loi-Cadre* gave the territorial assemblies greater control over the budget by reducing obligatory expenditures. They also wielded new authority over the regulation of local (territorial) public services and their employees, over registry services, and over customary law and traditional authorities. In the midst of the large number of specified attributes, it is important to note in the light of past history that ownership of "vacant and masterless" land was transferred to the territory. The Assembly's decisions in these various fields were sanctioned

[96] France, Assemblée nationale, *Débats parlementaires*, February 1, 1957, p. 484.

[97] The votes on these issues show how little Africans could do in the face of French resistance to specific reforms. The Overseas Affairs Committee had reported out a project in which customs had been transferred from the category of state services to the territories, but the Assembly voted by 405 to 156 to put it back in the original category. An amendment to transfer higher education was also defeated by 400 to 161. (*Ibid.*, January 30, p. 371; February 1, 1957, p. 484.)

by penalties as severe as 3 months' imprisonment and fines of 300,000 frs. The reforms also facilitated the entrance of Africans into the higher ranks of the civil service. An additional series of decrees concerned the economic and the social spheres. Mandatory provident societies, the *Sociétés de Prévoyance*, were to be gradually replaced by government-managed, semi-voluntary organizations, the *Sociétés Mutuelles de Développement Rural.* The territories were also empowered to offer special conditions to potential investors, to establish family allocations and workmen's compensation. Finally, the Institute of Higher Studies in Dakar was promoted to the status of university, the first one in French-speaking Africa.[98]

CONCLUSIONS

Far from solving the question of the future relationships between France and her overseas possessions and the problem of the relationships between the territories themselves, the *Loi-Cadre* opened the way for further evolution of these major issues.

Concerning the future of federation in French West Africa, the consequences of the *Loi-Cadre* may be viewed from the point of view of the Ivory Coast, the main preoccupation in this study. The transfer of income from indirect taxes to the territorial budget enabled the country to increase its revenue rapidly and at little cost. The annual estimates grew as follows, beginning in 1955, the last year under the old system (in thousands of C.F.A. fr.):

1955	6,356,445,000
1956	7,620,657,928
1957	8,402,429,000
1958	11,786,223,000[99]

[98] Gonidec, pp. 80-92.

[99] An unspecified share of the increase was due to normal economic expansion. Figures are taken from annual budgetary estimates for years indicated. (Ivory Coast, *Budget pour 1955* [Abidjan: Imprimerie du Gouvernement, 1954]; *ibid.*, 1956, 1957, and 1958.)

This only whetted the country's financial appetite. Shortly after the *Loi-Cadre* institutions began to operate, the Ivory Coast demanded to retain import duties as well. In the debates over the budget for 1958 one member of the Assembly even suggested that the territory purposely unbalance its budget in order to benefit from federal subsidies, since this was the rationale behind the pro-federation stand of other members of the federation.[100] Politically, this was translated into further efforts to destroy the federation. In the process, the Ivory Coast became increasingly isolated from the mainstream of political thought in French West Africa.

The *Loi-Cadre* left the future of Franco-African relationships as ambiguous as it had always been. Maurice Duverger asserted that the reforms had clearly paved the way for the creation of a federation, although no one would openly admit it.[101] Professor Robinson noted that the reforms were equivocal, but that in contrast with the changes initiated in 1946, "they were made to seem less far-reaching than they will probably prove to be."[102] He concluded that the law evidently ruled out "colonial subordination and full integration," and that orthodox federalism was unlikely. Some form of "association" would lead to independence or to a durable alternative.[103] Gonidec discerned the future more clearly: "In rather curious fashion, France is coming close to the policy of autonomy followed by Great Britain. This tendency is very clear in the case of Togo and Cameroun. Undoubtedly, for the Overseas Territories, the juridical fiction of the unity of the French State is still maintained. But one can already state that France has stepped unto a path that leads to the creation of autonomous units, distinct from the French State."[104]

[100] Ivory Coast, Assemblée territoriale, "Debates," January 28, 1958.
[101] In an article in *Le Monde*, reprinted in *Afrique Nouvelle*, February 12, 1957.
[102] Robinson, *Constitutional Reforms* . . ., p. 65.
[103] *Ibid.*
[104] Gonidec, p. 92.

The only question that remained in doubt, he concluded, was whether France had the ability to preserve bonds "as light as air and as strong as steel," such as the ones Britain had developed with her former colonies.[105] This was indeed the issue that would dominate the political scene during the next three years.

The institutions of the *Loi-Cadre* were rapidly superseded. Less than a year after the election of the African territorial executives, the Fourth Republic came to an end, opening the way for basic constitutional reform. In the long run, the *Loi-Cadre* was more significant in the light of the transformations it brought about in the structure of African political organizations. This law, together with the municipal reforms noted earlier, enhanced the importance of territorial political activity. In the Ivory Coast universal suffrage doubled the electorate. Elections to the Territorial Assembly, whose membership had been increased to 60, were of utmost importance since the members would determine control of the territorial executive and indirectly of the Grand Council of French West Africa, where the fate of the federation would be sealed.[106] Regardless of the constitutional limitations imposed upon the territorial executive, the presence of Africans at the helm of the country's government meant, from the point of view of the rank-and-file, that responsibility for government had been effectively transferred to the hands of their own leaders. The new political format, the enlarged electorate, and the assumption of responsibility for government, accelerated trends of change in the P.D.C.I. that had begun when the party abandoned its militant orientation.

[105] *Ibid.*

[106] The number of seats was determined by a law promulgated on November 15, 1955. (*Ibid.*, p. 82.)

CHAPTER VI

THE PARTY TRIUMPHANT

MOST African leaders shared the goal of political unification of French West Africa. Although the R.D.A. and the *Indépendants d'Outre-Mer* agreed in 1956 that the formation of a single African parliamentary group would give its members accrued bargaining power in the precariously balanced French political system, competition for leadership of such an organization and controversy over the future of the federation during passage of the *Loi-Cadre* arose as major obstacles to unity.[1] Creation of a single all-encompassing movement was advocated once again by Leopold Senghor at the founding congress of *Convention Africaine* in January 1957.[2] Speaking as the official R.D.A. observer, Ouezzin Coulibaly, who had been reelected a few days earlier to the second Ivory Coast seat in the National Assembly, stated: "No underdeveloped country which reached its political maturity was able to do so without giving primacy to either a single political party, or to one with such an overwhelming majority that

[1] The negotiations during 1956 are summarized in Milcent, pp. 96-97.

[2] Under the leadership of L.-S. Senghor and his *Bloc Populaire Sénégalais*, the *Indépendants d'Outre-Mer* representatives met at Dakar in January 1957 to launch *Convention Africaine*, a new superterritorial movement. In reaction to this and in an effort to become independent of the metropolitan party, the Senegalese Socialists, under Lamine-Gueye, organized a *Mouvement Socialiste Africain*. This third political formation (in addition to C.A. and to the R.D.A.) held its first congress at Conakry at the same time. The C.A. sought a merger with the R.D.A., but the latter sought unity on its own terms, i.e., by absorbing the lesser organizations. The M.S.A., which would almost surely be absorbed by one of the other two in any unification scheme, disagreed with the goal of a single movement. During the same period, African trade-unions were also seeking to become autonomous of their metropolitan *centrales* and met to launch the *Union Générale des Travailleurs d'Afrique Noire* (U.G.T.A.N.) at Cotonou, in January 1957. For the political history of this period, which forms the background to that of the Ivory Coast, see particularly Milcent, pp. 93-145; K. Robinson, "Senegal: The Elections . . .," pp. 327-31.

it controlled every sector of social life."[3] Although this goal was never realized at the level of French West Africa, it was already within the reach of the P.D.C.I. The new institutions further facilitated its attainment, and by the time the Ivory Coast became a self-governing republic in 1958, the one-party system was firmly established.

The P.D.C.I. as a Machine

Between 1952 and 1957, the P.D.C.I. recovered its strength throughout the Ivory Coast. In the Territorial Assembly, emphasis on economic issues of concern to the entire country helped develop unity among the members. This was reflected eventually in unanimous support for Houphouet-Boigny's candidacy as president. As Table 14 shows, there was a

TABLE 14

The Growth of a Unified Coalition: Presidential Votes in the Territorial Assembly, 1952-1956[a]

Candidates	*1952*	*1953*	*1954*	*1955*	*1956*
Houphouet-Boigny	27	34	38	38	39
Abstentions	—	—	11	9	—
Others[b]	22	12	—	—	—
Total votes cast	49	46	49	47	39

[a] Data obtained from record of vote in the Territorial Assembly, Ivory Coast, Assemblée territoriale, "Debates," April 24, 1952, April 12, 1953, April 4, 1954, March 28, 1955, and March 29, 1956.

[b] The other candidates were Amadou Diop (1952) and J.-B. Amoakon Boa (1953).

yearly progression from support for opponents, to voluntary abstentions, and finally, to outright support for Houphouet-Boigny. Furthermore, the U.D.E.C.I. group, which had begun with 28 members in 1952, had grown to 36 in 1956. The additions included 3 of the 4 Africans elected by the opposition and 5 first section Europeans.[4]

[3] Quoted in Blanchet, p. 58.

[4] Based on an examination of the annual declarations of membership

In January 1956 Houphouet-Boigny and his running mate, Ouezzin Coulibaly, secured 87 per cent of the valid votes cast and a majority in all but 2 of the 49 *subdivisions*. The remainder was scattered among 13 opposition tickets.[5] An observer viewed this overwhelming victory as "a plebiscite in favor of one man, M. Félix Houphouet-Boigny, and . . . a tactical demonstration, proving the existence of a real organization, which one is almost tempted to call a native para-government."[6] The P.D.C.I. was clearly no longer a protest movement based on shared grievances; it had now acquired the characteristics of a political machine concerned with electing men to office and with distributing tangible incentives to its members.[7] Like a typical machine, it was largely issue-free. Houphouet-Boigny announced during the 1956 campaign that the party would not present a precise program, but that its candidates pledged themselves to seize every opportunity to serve the Ivory Coast well in Paris.[8]

Structure

The gap between the organizational theory invoked by the founders of the P.D.C.I. and political reality, which had existed ever since the party was created, was widened during this period. The P.D.C.I. emerged as an organization for the masses rather than as a mass organization. The party press and the territorial organs of government, curtailed in

---

by the groups in the Assembly, on file in the archives of the National Assembly, Ivory Coast.

[5] Opposition will be discussed below. The results were: registered, 875,594; valid votes, 583,410; P.D.C.I., 506,494; all others, 76,916. The 2 deviant *subdivisions* were the Bété-dominant areas of Gagnoa and Issia.

[6] M. Vignaud, "Les élections du 2 janvier 1956 en Côte d'Ivoire," *Revue Française de Science Politique*, VI, No. 3 (July-September 1956), 570-82.

[7] For a discussion of the characteristics of machines, see James Q. Wilson, *Negro Politics: The Search for Leadership* (New York: Free Press of Glencoe, 1960).

[8] *Abidjan-Matin*, December 31, 1955. See also Vignaud, p. 577.

1951 to facilitate strategic manipulation by Houphouet-Boigny, were never reactivated. The basic units seldom met except during electoral campaigns. There was much less emphasis on the payment of dues as the criterion of membership. In Treichville, where 32,000 members had purchased party cards between 1949 and 1952, only about 8,000 paid their dues between 1952 and 1955. Many sympathizers refused to pay dues because they felt that since the R.D.A. was now with the government, their membership obligation was fulfilled by paying taxes.[9]

Party life was restricted almost exclusively to the activities of the *bureau* of the *sous-section.* At that level, increasingly caucus-like, authority was concentrated in the hands of the general secretary. After many of the civil servants who had founded party branches withdrew under administrative pressure, local leaders were issued from a different stratum altogether. In many communities, the new general secretary was a Dioula, a Moslem trader from the northwestern part of the country or from Sudan. These individuals, who are the intermediaries between farmers and Levantine or European merchants, wield great influence within the bazaar economy of the Ivory Coast—an economy based on manipulative skills, control over the flow of cash and credit, and on ownership of the most common means of transportation.[10] Many Dioulas have, in addition, purchased land and now engage in commercial agriculture. These men are linked to one another through a network of commercial channels through which other communications can flow as well. Thus, economic skills

[9] This as well as the remainder of this section is based mainly on interviews with general secretaries of selected *sous-sections*, including Abidjan, and a sampling of areas in the southeast, the north, and the west. There are few party records in existence and even fewer available to outsiders.

[10] D. Apter, "Political Organization and Ideology," *Labor Commitment and Social Change in Developing Areas* (eds.) Wilbert E. Moore and B. Feldman (New York: Social Science Research Council, 1960), p. 173.

and the influence they provide can easily be adapted to political use. A Dioula general secretary can make a farmer's vote a condition for obtaining cash advances before the beginning of the cocoa or coffee trading season. He can transport voters to the polls. He knows a great deal about local disputes and can exploit them to the party's advantage. In 1956 Vignaud reported that the general secretaries prepared the way for campaign caravans by working with a flying squad of high-level party leaders from Abidjan to iron out local difficulties and to reconcile factions. Houphouet-Boigny's arrival was only the climax of these preparations. On election day, staff members of the local party manned the polling offices, supervised operations and brought the sick to the polls.[11]

When the R.D.A. became part of a government coalition in France, businesslike relations were established between the general secretary and the *commandant* or the *chef de subdivision* in the field. In many ways, the general secretary replaced the African chief as the intermediary between the colonial hierarchy and the population-at-large. French administrators consulted him in the allocation of government projects and services in their district. His advice was sought at the time of the annual revision of electoral registers.[12] Because of this cooperative arrangement, the party leadership could exert, with impunity, social pressures upon its opponents. Many *Indépendants* and *Progressistes*, the "traitors" of 1948-1951, were ostracized and allowed to participate in community activities only after they publicly recanted, and promised to support P.D.C.I. candidates; in addition, they were required to pay a heavy fine to the general secretary.[13]

[11] Vignaud, pp. 578-81.

[12] *Ibid.*

[13] In Séguéla, *Indépendants* were not allowed to be buried in the cemetery; almost everywhere, P.D.C.I. followers prevented their opponents from buying and selling in the market place; in Man, there were even punitive expeditions against known deviants. P.D.C.I. leaders

Cooptation

Control over this electoral machine gave the P.D.C.I. a practical monopoly over access to public office, which it used to absorb most of its opponents. Cooptation was facilitated by the multiplication of offices as the result of municipal reform, the elimination of separate sections in the Assembly, and African participation in the executive. Having been promised offices for themselves and for their followers, the leading opposition candidates of January 1956, Kacou Aoulou, Sekou Sanogo, and Etienne Djaument, responded to Houphouet-Boigny's renewed call to territorial unity the following May by declaring that from now on their own parties were one and the same as the R.D.A.[14] Amalgamation was clearly visible at the municipal level, where, although nomination was tantamount to election, the P.D.C.I. leaders took great care to make their ticket representative of all groups in the community. Presenting the final slate to the electors of Bouaké, Houphouet-Boigny stated:

"The R.D.A. Executive Committee met with us. Respectful of our fundamental rules, of our most sacred principles, and taking into account the promises which I made in your name, namely fraternal cooperation with our brothers, all our brothers, who have come from all the territories of the French Union, Metropolitan as well as African, we have decided that the thirty-one seats would be allocated as follows:

"Seven will be granted to our metropolitan brothers, who will be able to make a free choice, thus taking their share of responsibility in the management of the future municipal government of Bouaké.

---

at the territorial level publicly deplored these actions but explained privately that this was a legitimate way to make up for economic sanctions and other deprivations incurred by the party faithful during the time of troubles. See also Schachter, note 1, p. 388.

[14] *Afrique Nouvelle*, May 15, 1956.

"The *originaires* of the Ivory Coast will have fifteen seats, the *non-originaires* nine.

"This is the decision we have taken. It is now your duty to give us the best of your children in order to accomplish the task the masses expect of us: the demonstration of our ability to manage honestly the interests thay have entrusted to us."[15]

Each of the two major categories of Africans, Ivoiriens and foreigners, included leading members of the P.D.C.I. *bureau* of the *sous-section* as well as selected spokesmen for the *Indépendants, Progressistes,* or Socialists. The same procedure was followed in Abidjan and in Grand Bassam, as well as in the six smaller towns where elections were held the following month.

Everywhere, the coalition was adapted to local circumstances. In Abengourou, after a general reconciliation was effected in September 1956,[16] the municipal slate included the two pretenders to the paramount chief's stool of the Agni State of Indénié (they had been feuding since 1944) as well as the *Progressiste* assemblyman elected in 1952 and his defeated P.D.C.I. opponent. Each of the major ethnic communities in the city, including the Europeans, were asked to caucus to select their own candidates for inclusion on the final ticket. Because of this, the general secretary explained, it did not matter that voters had no choice: "This is a truly democratic procedure. After all, we took a great deal of care to give some representation to every group in the community. What more can anybody ask for? By representing every group, we gave to every voter someone of his own kind to vote for and to be represented by."[17] This technique to

[15] Ivory Coast, Service de l'Information, *Discours et Allocutions de M. le Ministre Houphouet-Boigny* (Abidjan, n.d.). Speech at Bouaké November 3, 1956.

[16] *La Concorde*, September 27, 1956.

[17] Interview with M. Cheick Diop, general-secretary of the Abengourou *sous-section* of the P.D.C.I., 1959.

obtain support, which some local leaders say they learned from communist organizers in 1945, is nevertheless strikingly similar to that which is in wide use in American metropolitan communities, where ethnic diversity comes close to that of the Ivory Coast. Edward J. Flynn of the Bronx explained his own approach in much the same terms as Cheick Diop in Abengourou: "The Bronx is a cosmopolitan place. . . . Therefore, when the organization is forming a ticket to present to the people, it is important that the candidates represent and come from these . . . groups. . . . Our whole system of government is based on proportional representation."[18]

The selection of 60 candidates to represent all the components of the Ivory Coast coalition in the Territorial Assembly in 1957 was complicated by the inflationary consequences of the *Loi-Cadre.* It was estimated at the time that there were as many as 700 hopefuls.[19] Although little is known about the process of selection itself, the characteristics of the candidates finally designated by the *Comité Directeur* and approved by a general assembly of the general secretaries of the party offer additional clues concerning the nature of the coalition itself.[20] Although Europeans were no longer entitled to separate representation, 12 seats were set aside for them on the various tickets. Little concern was given to the candidates' past pro-African political record; one of the Frenchmen elected by the second college in 1952 was dropped, while Senator Josse, who had fought the *Loi-Cadre* to the finish, was nominated. The fact that three-fourths of the

[18] Quoted in *Politics in the United States* (ed.) Henry A. Turner (New York: McGraw-Hill Book Company, Inc., 1955), pp. 267-68.

[19] *La Concorde*, February 21, 1957. The 60 seats were apportioned among 19 electoral districts, corresponding to the *cercles*, with from 1 to 6 members each according to population. Concerning electoral procedures in general, see Kenneth Robinson, "Senegal: The Elections . . .," pp. 346-56.

[20] For the characteristics of the candidates, see Tables 20-23 below. All information concerning candidates discussed here was obtained from their biographical records on file in the Legislative Assembly, and was supplemented by interviews is most cases.

individuals chosen were members of one of the consular chambers, compared with only about one-third in the previous Assembly, indicated that the main criterion here was economic representativeness.[21] Following the pattern repeatedly noted in this study, African candidates were ethnically diversified. Of the 48 candidates 4 were foreigners; all major native tribes were included, although the southeast was somewhat overrepresented in terms of its share of the total population and the northeast fell short of its proportional share.[22] Seven of the 24 Africans who had held office previously had earlier been identified with opposition parties.[23] The 24 African newcomers to the Assembly included 8 high-level P.D.C.I. leaders; 9 individuals active mostly in ethnic associations at the local level—including 4 identified with opposition groups; 3 trade-union officials; and finally, 5 younger men, representing a new political generation. The make-up of the slates was carefully balanced within each constituency as well. In Abidjan the P.D.C.I. pointed out to the voters that the 5-man ticket included 2 outstanding party militants and 1 trade-unionist, along with 1 representative of the older European generation and 1 newcomer, *génération jeune patron.*[24] The voters may have noted also that the 3 Africans included 1 member of the Ebrié tribe, the original inhabitants of the city; 1 from an inland tribe, representing the immigrants; and a third, who championed one of the major groups in the *cercle des Lagunes* outside the city proper.[25]

[21] This was further emphasized when one man who had retired was replaced by his business partner.

[22] There were 12 southeasterners, 8 Baoulé, 12 westerners, 7 Malinké from the northwest, and 4 northeasterners, mostly Sénoufo.

[23] Among them there was one from each of the major regional opposition groups: Kacou Aoulou (southeast), Tidiane Dem (north), and Etienne Djaument (southwest).

[24] *La Concorde*, March 21, 1957.

[25] The leading candidate was Philippe Yacé, who had rapidly risen in the party hierarchy after having been appointed general secretary

The same concern with obtaining support by extending representation to a variety of ethnic and interest groups was reflected in the composition of the first Ivory Coast government (see Tables 21, 22, and 23). Auguste Denise, general secretary of the P.D.C.I., who became vice-president of the Council, explained that its members had been chosen to appeal to everyone, "whether or not they are R.D.A."[26] Beside Denise, two other members of the *Bureau Politique* were in the government, one as Minister of Interior, the other as Minister of Economic Affairs. Agriculture and finances were entrusted to the president of the S.A.A. and to one of the few Africans who had achieved prominence in the business community. Other ministers were identified with major voluntary associations including labor, youth, cultural, and professional organizations. These 10 Africans were also ethnically diversified: 6 were from the southwest, 2 were Baoulé, and 2 were westerners.[27] The government also included 2 European experts, probably in order to inspire confidence among potential investors.[28]

Cooptation to the Assembly or to the government had much more than symbolic value. In addition to social status, these positions carried great economic rewards. After the elections, the Assembly established for itself and for the government the highest salary scale in all of French West Africa, with an

---

of the Treichville branch when the incumbent was arrested in 1949. A Ponty graduate, he had been active in the Teachers' Union and was the leader of the most important African Veterans' Association. There are some indications that he is currently Houphouet-Boigny's heir designate.

[26] *Abidjan-Matin*, May 18, 1957.

[27] The north was conspicuously absent, a fact brought to Mamadou Coulibaly's attention when he visited his home region, Odiénné. He answered his countrymen that they must be patient since Houphouet-Boigny had been guided by political imperatives in his choice of ministers. (*Ibid.*, August 1, 1957.)

[28] They were: J. Millier, Minister of Public Works, formerly Director of Public Works for the Ivory Coast; and Raphael Saller, Minister of Planning, formerly first college senator from Guinea and a F.I.D.E.S. administrator.

average annual expenditure of $10,000 for each assemblyman and $12,000 for each minister.[29] Because many of the members were civil servants who had lost the government housing to which they were entitled when they resigned after the elections, the Assembly asked for and received interest-free loans, guaranteed by the public treasury, to build homes for the assemblymen. Additional advantages included land grants, substantial credit on the part of European firms, the use of private automobiles, civil honors, and trips to Paris at public expense.[30]

The party as an organization also benefited from this distributive system. Officeholders were under obligation to contribute part of their salary to the party.[31] Furthermore, most of the P.D.C.I.'s activities were indirectly supported by public funds; public buildings were commonly used for party meetings. By appointing 15 of its members, who happened to be also high-level party leaders, to tour the country in order to ascertain the demands of the population, the Assembly could legitimately pay their expenses and supply them with government transportation. If there was any doubt about the political nature of this trip, it was dispelled by P. Yacé, who reminded

[29] This included basic salary, per diem while the Assembly was in session, travel expenses, and other perquisites. The salary scale, decided at a closed meeting of the Assembly on August 1, 1957, was not publicized. The above figures are drawn from the budgetary estimates for 1958. A comparison with other French West African countries is supplied by Roche, p. 75.

[30] The loans were approved by the Assembly in June 1958. (Ivory Coast, Assemblée territoriale, "Debates," June 19, 1958.) Businessmen invited newly elected members in 1957 and again in 1959 to buy freely. This, according to some informants, was written off as normal business expenditures. As a minister, Houphouet-Boigny was entitled to his quota of *Chevaliers de la Légion d'Honneur*, a common form of patronage in metropolitan France. In 1957 the Ivory Coast sent 62 people at public expense to attend the Bastille Day celebrations in Paris. (*Abidjan-Matin*, July 10, 1957.)

[31] There are conflicting reports on the exact amount, but it is generally held to be 10 per cent. There may have been an increase to 15 per cent in 1959. Some of the European members returned their entire salary to the leadership.

the members that notwithstanding the monolithic party situation and the elimination of competition, they must remain vigilant because many problems persisted and required study.[32]

The Economic Weapon

Economic development, the recovery of revenue formerly earmarked for the federation, the maintenance of prosperity through protected markets and favorable prices for coffee, all contributed to the distributive capability of the regime. Increased control over the allocation of government projects and services enabled the party to wield economic pressures as sanctions against deviators and to encourage loyalty through economic rewards. In 1955 a projected electric plant in Abengourou was built in Dimbokro instead—after the Abengourou representative refused to join the U.D.E.C.I. in the Assembly. The Agni of Indénié were told that unless they voted this representative out at the first available opportunity, they would continue to be penalized.[33] After Digna Bailly left the U.D.E.C.I. in 1955, a campaign was launched in his district to force him to resign on the grounds that his continued presence in the Assembly jeopardized the economic future of the Bété region.[34] Political considerations influenced the annual allocation of tangible projects such as schools, roads, dispensaries, and public buildings to the various *cercles*. In

[32] Ivory Coast, Assemblée territoriale, "Debates," December 20, 1957. The following year, the entire Assembly was sent on an official mission to prepare the referendum.

[33] Interviews with party officials and former opposition sympathizers in Abengourou, 1959.

[34] He had been elected on the U.D.E.C.I. ticket in 1952 but left it after an unsuccessful bid in 1955 to fill the senate seat traditionally allocated to the west. (*Abidjan-Matin*, July 5, 1955.) Soon afterwards, the region began to stir. (*Ibid.*, October 13, 1955.) The campaign asking him to resign was carried in both *Abidjan-Matin* (issues of July 20 and July 23, 1956) and *La Concorde* (issue of July 26, 1956). These techniques were similar to those used by the French administration against the P.D.C.I.

September 1957 the vice-president of the Assembly requested a special allocation to provide a new road in his own constituency. When this was turned down as economically unsound by the public works committee, Yacé repeated his request and explained to the Assembly that he was surprised that anyone even mentioned economic considerations since all knew very well that there were important political reasons for granting his request.[35] A newcomer to the Assembly in 1957, who represented an area where there had been a closely contested election, spoke for many of his colleagues when he declared:

"I stand up to protest against the allocation of new schools that the financial committee has just made to the detriment of Gagnoa, where, as everyone knows, there is a political problem.

"During the last political campaign, many promises were made to the voters, many improvements were pledged to Gagnoa if the R.D.A. ticket came through. We were elected, but for the past year, nothing has been done.

"This is very unfortunate for Gagnoa.

"I ask insistently of our Ministers that they think over the particular situation of Gagnoa and that they give favorable consideration to all our demands because of this problem."[36]

In the very first year of its existence, the Ivory Coast government also altered the tax structure with an eye to political considerations. By eliminating the *impôt des planteurs,* to which most farmers were liable, and exonerating transporters, including many local party officials, from the payment of the *patente,* or business tax, the party secured renewed support from important groups. These decisions were hailed by Jean-Baptiste Mockey, Minister of the Interior and political secretary of the P.D.C.I. as the greatest achievement of the entire year.[37]

[35] Ivory Coast, Assemblée territoriale, "Debates," September 11, 1957.
[36] *Ibid.*, January 29, 1958.
[37] *Ibid.*

Internal Controls

Control over this machine-like organization is maintained through an elaborate system of mutual checks and internal competition among the various elements. At the local level, the general secretaries, often immigrants from other parts of the country, do not derive their authority from local support but rather from their office in the party hierarchy. They are dependent for their appointment and for their continued existence upon the territorial executive and particularly upon Houphouet-Boigny personally. Although these persons are often unpopular and resented because of their economic role, Abidjan has always insisted that all communications be channeled through them.[38] Although many general secretaries aspired to hold elective office at the territorial level, few were nominated as party candidates in 1957. Instead, most regions were represented by educated favorite sons, who by virtue of their occupations had long lived away from home and seldom had any control over local party organization. Many of them later attempted to supplant the general secretary or to replace him with one of their own lieutenants. This competitive situation provided dual channels of upward communications and increased the flow of information to the uppermost echelons of the party. Furthermore, political cadre and representatives were interdependent. The *député*, as the assemblyman came

[38] Here also there is a striking parallel with an organization such as Tammany Hall, "a political bureaucracy in which rights appertained not to individuals but to the positions they occupied. 'Have you seen your block captain?' It did not matter that your captain was an idiot or a drunk, or a devout churchgoer who would be alarmed by the request at hand; the block captain had to be seen first. Then the election district captain. Then the district leader. The hierarchy had to be recognized. For the group as a whole, this served to take the risks out of politics. Each would get his deserts—in time." (Daniel P. Moynihan, "When the Irish Ran New York," *The Reporter*, June 8, 1961, p. 33.) In the same way as upward mobility in the U.S. has undermined the strength of some machines, many younger and better educated individuals in the Ivory Coast resent having to deal with the party through such people.

to be called, could not be elected without support from the local organization, which was controlled by the general secretary; but the latter had to work through the representative in Abidjan to gain access to the *ministre*, from whom all tangible benefits flowed. Finally, occasional conflicts between general secretaries and representatives increased their dependence on the highest level of the party hierarchy for arbitration.[39]

A similar process operated at this highest level. Most of the members of the *Comité Directeur* had spent their adult life away from their native region—in some cases outside the Ivory Coast—and did not have an independent base of political support; hence, they derived their authority from their office in the party. Of those who had joined the party during its formative years, many were civil servants who had been jailed in 1949 and afterwards prohibited from administrative employment for several years. For their own and their family's subsistence, they were heavily dependent upon the party and on Houphouet-Boigny himself. Some served as members of his personal staff in Paris;[40] others were sent to be trained at institutions of higher education in order to qualify for administrative positions open to Africans from 1956 on;[41] and almost all owed their amnesty and reinstatement in government service to Houphouet-Boigny's intercession.

Houphouet-Boigny cumulated an increasing number of elective positions. In 1957 he was at the same time member and president of the Territorial Assembly; member of the municipal council and mayor of Abidjan; member and president of the Grand Council of French West Africa; member of the National Assembly and a minister of the French Republic.[42]

[39] Information on which this section is based was obtained from case studies in Treichville, Abengourou, Korhogo, and Daloa, as well as on additional reports from informants and on interviews with most members of the 1957-1959 Assembly.

[40] E.g., Jean-Baptiste Mockey and Albert Paraiso.

[41] E.g., Pierre Huberson, Mathieu Ekra, and Amadou Bocoum.

[42] Lest this be taken as the indication of a personality cult, it must

Although he spent much time in Paris and operated in Africa through deputies, no single person could speak for him in the Ivory Coast. In the government Auguste Denise and Jean-Baptiste Mockey often disagreed with each other and both clashed with Philippe Yacé, who presided over the Assembly during the leader's absence. None of the three had the authority to settle controversies. In order to solve particular problems, it was always necessary to travel to Paris to consult Houphouet-Boigny or to obtain his opinion during one of his brief visits to the Ivory Coast.

Shortly after the first government was formed, government and assembly leaders went to Paris "to coordinate their activities in the spirit of the union policy."[43] Although solidarity in the upper ranks of the party had developed through shared experiences in jail, in school, at work, or through personal ties,[44] there were also built-in competitive elements arising from a constant jockeying for position within the hierarchy and from differences in outlook or in interest. Competition for the position of heir designate, in particular, served to provide Houphouet-Boigny with adequate information from at least three major channels; this competition also enhanced his role as the indispensable final arbiter of disputes and helped maintain flexibility in the entire apparatus.[45]

---

be noted that cumulation of office in this way is a common pattern in French politics, exemplified by Gaston Defferre, of *Loi-Cadre* fame, who was at the same time Socialist mayor of Marseilles, a *député*, and a minister.

[43] *Abidjan-Matin*, July 30, 1957.

[44] Many were brothers-in-law, including at one time J.-B. Mockey and M. Ekra, both married to P. Yacé's sisters. It was not possible to extricate the family and in-law ties within the leadership, but it appears from occasional observations that this constitutes a very extensive network. It is understandable when one remembers that the "elite" in the Ivory Coast tends to intermarry for social reasons and that it is relatively small to begin with.

[45] In an interview in 1959 Houphouet-Boigny was asked to discuss his own functions in the system. He emphasized that of the referee more than other aspects. To put this in its proper perspective, one might think of two teams of prisoners playing baseball, with the warden as umpire.

Obstacles to Unanimity

The opposition that the P.D.C.I. encountered stemmed mainly from the cleavages that had been translated into political organizations between 1949 and 1951. There were new groups, however, based on occupational and ideological differentiations.

Persistence of Ethnic Competitors

In January 1956 the leading opposition tickets agreed with the R.D.A.'s pronouncements at Conakry the preceding July. All the candidates also pledged to secure better prices for coffee, higher wages, greater social security benefits and additional housing facilities.[46] Although their main concern was not openly expressed, it was to promote the interests of the less developed regions of the country, the north and the southwest, which corresponded to three non-Akan culture circles. Most of the candidates stood as champions of the Bété, the Sénoufo, or the Malinké.[47] Their organizations had been sustained between elections through voluntary associations. The *Idéal d'Odienné*, which had been at the root of the *Parti des Indépendants* in 1951, now provided support for the two Moslem candidates of the *Liste d'Entente du Nord*. Similarly, the *Liste d'Union du Mahou* was the electoral extension of the *Association des Originaires de Séguéla*, whose President was the leading candidate. Notwithstanding the reconciliation effected between the P.D.C.I. and some opponents in May 1956, many of these groups reappeared in 1957 in different form and sometimes with different leaders. In Aboisso, for example, after Kacou Aoulou was nominated as a P.D.C.I. candidate in the Territorial Assembly elections,

[46] Electoral manifestoes are contained in *Abidjan-Matin*, December 14 and 16, 1955.

[47] Out of 26 opposition candidates, there were 4 foreign Africans; 1 from the southeast; 9 northerners (Sénoufo and Malinké); 8 westerners (mostly Bété). Information concerning origins was not available for the 4 others.

some of the Agni of Sanwi State supported the *Liste pour la Défense des Intérêts du Pays Sanwi* promoted by one of his erstwhile *Progressiste* associates, C. Brou Quoiho.

Altogether, the P.D.C.I.-sponsored coalition was unchallenged in 9 out of the 19 *cercles* in 1957; seven constituencies had 1 opposition slate and the remaining 3 had 2 each. Of these 13 opposition groups 10 were clearly identifiable as local ethnic parties. The *cercles* in which they appeared had been traditionally anti-R.D.A. As Table 15 shows, 7 of the 9 *cercles* that ranked highest in terms of support for anti-P.D.C.I.

TABLE 15

The Persistence of Opposition, 1951-1957[a]

	Cercles *Ranked by Opposition Strength in 1951 Elections*	*Opposition in 1957*	
		Yes	*No*
High	1. Odiénné	—	x
	2. Abengourou	x	—
	3. Grand Bassam	x	—
	4. Daloa	x	—
	5. Bondoukou	x	—
	6. Gagnoa	x	—
	7. Aboisso	x	—
	8. Agboville	x	—
	9. Korhogo	—	x
Low	10. Man	—	x
	11. Bouaflé	—	x
	12. Dimbokro	—	x
	13. Lagunes (Abidjan)	x	—
	14. Séguéla	—	x
	15. Grand Lahou	x	—
	16. Bouaké	x	—
	17. Sassandra	—	x
	18. Katiola	—	x
	19. Tabou	—	x

[a] All the data in this table are based on electoral results on file in the Bureau of Political Affairs, Ministry of the Interior, Ivory Coast. Because some of the *cercles* that existed in 1957 had not yet been created in 1951, results for several subdivisions were combined for the earlier date. The ranking is based on opposition percentage of the total valid vote.

groups in 1951 had opposition in 1957 as well. Of the 9 *cercles* where the P.D.C.I. was unchallenged in 1957, all but 2 had been among its strongholds in 1951. Development helped sustain opposition. There was a fairly clear relationship between degree of development and the presence of opposition in 1957, as indicated in Table 16.[48] When the two attributes, high opposition in 1951 and high development are combined, the relationship is very strong. Abengourou, Grand Bassam,

TABLE 16

Development Sustained Competitiveness[a]

	Cercles *Ranked by Degree of Relative Development*	*Opposition in 1957*	
		Yes	*No*
	1. Abengourou	x	—
	2. Grand Bassam	x	—
	3. Lagunes (Abidjan)	x	—
	4. Aboisso	x	—
High	5. Agboville	x	—
	6. Sassandra	—	x
	7. Gagnoa	x	—
	8. Dimbokro	—	x
	9. Daloa	x	—
	10. Grand Lahou	x	—
	11. Tabou	—	x
	12. Bondoukou	x	—
	13. Bouaké	x	—
Low	14. Katiola	—	x
	15. Man	—	x
	16. Bouaflé	—	x
	17. Séguéla	—	x
	18. Odiénné	—	x
	19. Korhogo	—	x

[a] See note a for Table 15.

[48] The index used for this ranking is the percentage of children of school age who are actually attending school. It was obtained from E. Boka, p. 1026. I use it as an index of relative development, because the ranking obtained corresponds almost exactly to ranking by estimated per capita revenue in the *cercles*. If the latter were used, Daloa ranks 11th, and Bondoukou moves up to 4th place. Since they both had opposition in 1957, it neither strengthens nor weakens the relationship.

Daloa, Aboisso, and Agboville—the only *cercles* that had both high opposition in 1951 and high degree of development—all were competitive in the 1957 elections.[49]

These relationships were empirically observable as well. In the areas of greater development there had been a growth of ethnic tensions from 1955 on, involving most often clashes between natives of the region and immigrants. Shortly before the municipal elections of November 1956, there were skirmishes in Bouaké, the Ivory Coast's second city, between Ivory Coast and Sudanese Dioulas as well as between Baoulé and all immigrants. Many Baoulé objected to the selection of Djibo Sounkalo from Upper Volta—the long-time political boss of the city—as candidate for mayor. Out of this discontent grew the *Mutualité des Autochtones de Côte d'Ivoire* devoted to the defense of the interests of natives; this group presented candidates in 1957 under the name of R.D.A. *Mutaciste*.[50] Some of the P.D.C.I.'s opponents in January 1956 obtained support because of Houphouet-Boigny's choice of Ouezzin Coulibaly, also from Upper Volta, as a running mate.[51] Spokesmen for various youth organizations complained that everyone spoke of the need to eliminate *racisme*, but that meanwhile, foreigners secured the best jobs in the local civil service and in private companies.[52] There was prolonged

[49] The idea for this hypothesis was obtained from the article by Seymour M. Lipset in which he examines the relationship between democracy, defined in terms of competitiveness, and development in Europe and in Latin America. ("Some Social Requisites of Democracy: Economic Development and Political Legitimacy," *The American Political Science Review*, LIII, No. 1 [March 1959], 69-105.) Coleman has applied a similar approach to comparisons between underdeveloped countries (*The Politics of the Developing Areas*, pp. 538-44). My own use of it to make internal comparisons is very provisional and requires further refinement, although in its present state it is useful to summarize some aspects of Ivory Coast politics.

[50] *La Concorde*, October 25, 1956. *Abidjan-Matin*, September 4 and October 4, 1956. *Mutaciste* was taken from the initials of the organization. It is interesting to note that they insisted on calling themselves R.D.A.

[51] Vignaud, p. 579.

[52] *La Concorde*, August 23, 1956.

fighting between Mossi from Upper Volta and Abbeys around N'Douci in October 1956.[53] Elsewhere, these conflicts involved several Ivory Coast tribes. The Sénoufo, Djimini, and Tagouana of the northeast complained that the Malinké of the northwest were continuing the process of conquest begun by Samory and were trying to subject the entire north to their commercial and cultural imperialism.[54] In Gagnoa and Daloa, Raulin observed around this time the growth of tension between the Bété natives and Baoulé or Dioula immigrants.[55] A fight broke out in Gagnoa in October 1955; there was violence during the campaign of December of the same year; it flared again in the fall of 1956, during the period of municipal electioneering; and finally again in March 1957, when Digna Bailly and Capri Djédjé campaigned against the P.D.C.I. nominees. Bété spokesmen told the Baoulé immigrants that they ought to know how the natives felt since they had themselves already begun to fight back a foreign invasion in Bouaké.[56] Difficulties began to appear in the Grand Lahou region as well, where Dida natives and Dioula or Baoulé immigrants had peacefully coexisted for about twenty years.[57]

Ivory Coast xenophobia has often been seen as the root of its antifederation stand. Wallerstein viewed this isolationism as a form of ethnic separatism.[58] Other R.D.A. sections accused the P.D.C.I. of *racisme* and attributed its antifederation efforts not to the desires of the leaders but to the pressures of the rank-and-file.[59] The reverse is also possible. When econom-

[53] This began when a Mossi driver accidentally killed an Abbey child. He was lynched, and later warfare broke out between native and immigrant villages. (*Abidjan-Matin*, October 11, 12, 15, 1956.)

[54] *La Concorde*, October 19, 1956.

[55] Raulin, pp. 87-92, 119-21, 124-30.

[56] Related by informants, 1959. Many of the Baoulé of the savanna colonized other parts of the country suitable for coffee growing.

[57] Raulin, pp. 24-26.

[58] Wallerstein, p. 138.

[59] The Ivory Coast stand on the federal issue was explained in those terms in *L'Essor*, the organ of the *Union Soudanaise*, territorial section of the R.D.A. The article implied that the xenophobia of Ivoiriens was

ic arguments formulated by Ivory Coast leaders to justify their demands were translated into simpler terms at the mass level, they reinforced latent resentment of foreign Africans and legitimized the expression of such sentiments. In any case, the two probably reinforced one another. Although it is impossible to determine whether ethnic antagonisms had actually grown in comparison with an earlier period, there is no doubt that they had grown in the eyes of the country's leadership. P. Yacé told the Assembly at the end of 1957:

"We would be violating the trust our people has given us if we did not emphasize another problem which threatens this country's economy. We must deal with it right away, before it becomes too difficult. . . . It is no secret that the Ivory Coast has sixty small races and dialects . . . not including foreigners. . . .

"The danger is localism directed against immigrants. Some are not allowed to acquire property. Others . . . are not welcome because they are Moslems. . . . In the Center, there is a reaction against all those who are not pedigreed Ivoiriens. . . . This problem was formerly found only in the cities, where it was translated into politics. . . . Now, there is a danger that it will reach villages and rural areas."[60]

The leaders were concerned with this problem because ethnic loyalties provided support for opposition groups and interfered with the attainment of the goal of a single party. Secondly, the eruption of antiforeign antagonism into open conflict lent some support to the accusations formulated by the federalists toward the Ivory Coast; in order to offset them, it was necessary to continue to grant representation to foreign residents at the municipal and at the territorial level, thus

well known to anyone who had lived there. (Quoted in *La Semaine en A.O.F.*, September 27, 1958.)

[60] Ivory Coast, Assemblée territoriale, "Debates," December 20, 1957.

contributing fuel to the flames of native resentment.[61] Thirdly, *racisme* was genuinely thought to be incompatible with the values of modernity and progress promoted by the party. Ouezzin Coulibaly, on the day of the municipal elections, voiced his appeal to the voters in these terms: "There has been propaganda to abstain based on *racisme* because there are Sudanese, Voltaics, Senegalese, or Metropolitan candidates on our lists. . . . Africans, do not follow the partisans of Hitler. Follow Houphouet-Boigny against *racisme*. Vote overwhelmingly against *racisme*, for unity, and for evolution."[62] Fourthly, ethnic conflict threatened to destroy the image that the leadership was trying to create of an Ivory Coast that was peaceful, politically stable, and safe for the purpose of investments. Yacé's statement clearly alludes to this problem. At the very time that the party became responsible for government, its leaders were increasingly faced with the shortcomings of unity in the country. Awareness of the obstacles that lay in the path of national integration was a crucial element in shaping their decisions concerning the future of the Ivory Coast in 1958.

New Opposition Groups: Youth and Labor

Not all groups that challenged the P.D.C.I. were ethnic. As the party's economic alliance with French business interests grew, its relations with labor unions deteriorated.[63] The

[61] A. Denise answered Ivory Coast critics by stating that it was the only one that had foreigners in its Territorial Assembly. (*Afrique Nouvelle*, October 29, 1957.)

[62] *La Concorde*, November 15, 1956.

[63] Labor unions are mostly white-collar ones. When first organized, they were grouped into *centrales* affiliated with a political party, like their metropolitan counterparts. The employees of the private sector were mostly C.G.T.-oriented and worked with the R.D.A. during the militant years. Most of the civil servants' unions were *autonome*, because pressure was brought to bear against those who belonged to the communist-oriented C.G.T. from 1948 on. There were, in addition, smaller *centrales*, one affiliated with the C.F.T.C. (Catholic-oriented) and C.G.T.-F.O. (Socialist). For strikes and during collective bargaining periods, there was a regrouping across *centrales* by sector, as in the case of the

first political clash occurred in November 1956 when the *Comité Intersyndical du Secteur Privé*, which grouped all unions in the private sector of the economy, complained that the presence of several notoriously reactionary European employers on the municipal ticket in Abidjan indicated that the workers' interests were being sacrificed unfairly to the goal of national unity. The Committee instructed the workers to demonstrate their discontent by striking the name of the employers from the ballots, thus making them invalid,[64] and called for a three-day strike. Civil servants joined in. On the third day violence erupted in Treichville, involving Africans and Europeans for the first time. The party leadership intervened to re-establish order.[65] After much negotiation, they promised to take labor's wishes into consideration. They kept their bargain; two of the members of the provisional committee of the newly organized trade-union movement, U.G.T.A.N., were included among the P.D.C.I.-sponsored candidates to the Territorial Assembly in 1957.[66] A third was named Minister of Labor and of Social Affairs the following May. Although the executive committee of U.G.T.A.N. told union members to vote for the R.D.A. in March 1957, the civil servants went

---

Comité Intersyndical cited above. (Wallerstein, p. 163, and E. Berg, "Labor Problems in an African Dependency," paper on file at the library of the African Studies Program, Boston University, October 1956.)

[64] *La Concorde*, November 15, 1956.

[65] On the third day of the strike one African was hurt by a bullet fired by a European civilian. It was reported that there were nineteen wounded, a score of private cars destroyed, and many store windows broken in Treichville during the strike. (Reports are found in *Abidjan-Matin*, November 18 and 22, 1956; *La Concorde*, November 22; *Marchés Coloniaux*, December 1; *Afrique Nouvelle*, November 27, 1956.)

[66] In the Ivory Coast the U.G.T.A.N. regrouped most C.G.T. and C.G.T.-*autonome* unions. It was launched in 1957. The three members of the provisional executive coopted to the Assembly and the government were Camille Gris (general secretary of the C.G.T. and leader of the Commercial Employees); Amon Tanoh (general secretary of the Teachers' Union); and Gaston Fiankan (general secretary of the Railroad Workers' Union). For U.G.T.A.N., see Ruth Schachter, "Trade Unions Seek Autonomy," *West Africa*, January 19 and 26, 1957.

on strike because they were dissatisfied with the particular choice of labor representatives.[67] Behind this, however, there was more basic disagreement with the general policies pursued by the P.D.C.I., including especially relations with France, recruitment of Africans to higher ranks of the civil service, and continued employment of Africans from other territories in the local services.

There was some overlap between the leadership and membership of the civil servants' unions and youth organizations. Ever since the R.D.A.'s *désapparentement* of 1950, the gap between the older educated generation in Africa and the younger one studying in Paris, continuously subjected to the influences of the French Marxist milieu, continued to grow. Students abroad were increasingly vocal in their attacks against Houphouet-Boigny's policies. Most of those who returned to the Ivory Coast after completion of their studies attempted to enter politics but found that militants of an earlier hour had already staked out claims over all the available political ground. Around 1951, the first wave of returning professionals who had studied in Paris just before, during, and immediately after World War II attempted to establish a special party unit devoted to the study of political and economic problems. They encountered opposition among the lesser educated, older elite, who regarded the newcomers as a threat.

Therefore, their energies were channeled into cultural and professional organizations. In 1954 they founded the *Cercle Culturel et Folklorique de la Côte d'Ivoire* (C.C.F.C.I.), with membership restricted to Ivoiriens; through this association they also met a few intellectually-oriented P.D.C.I. leaders, such as J.-B. Mockey, as well as members of the opposition, such as Kacou Aoulou.[68] A similar association, the *Cercle*

[67] *Abidjan-Matin,* March 25, 1957.

[68] The first executive committee of the C.C.F.C.I. included the first two Ivory Coast medical doctors, J. Vilasco and Djessou-Loubo, and the

Africain d'Etudes et de Recherches Economiques et Sociales was open also to foreign Africans and to Europeans. The *Association des Ingénieurs et Techniciens Africains* was a sort of trade-union for technical personnel but was also concerned with the training of skilled workers. All these associations served as political stepping stones for their leaders. When the *Bureau Politique* of the P.D.C.I. finally authorized the creation of a *Comité d'Etudes R.D.A.* in 1957, the president of the C.C.F.C.I., Dr. Djessou-Loubo, and the president of the Engineers' Association, Alcide Kacou, became its leading lights. They both appeared later that year in the first Ivory Coast government as Minister of Health and Minister of Technical Education respectively.

Other university-trained people joined the leaders of the younger generation that had not studied abroad but were active in labor unions and other voluntary associations to found the *Union de la Jeunesse de Côte d'Ivoire* (U.J.C.I.) in 1955. Its explicit purpose was to promote the political aspirations of "youth." The leadership of this organization was predominantly from the center (Baoulé) and the west (Bété) and did not include northerners or foreigners. When internal dissensions arose over the stand to be taken on the *Loi-Cadre* in mid-1956, the faction that was most opposed to the Houphouet-Boigny formulae gained control. From then on, the U.J.C.I. was considered an opposition group. It was closely related to the two major students' associations, the *Association Générale des Etudiants et Elèves de Côte d'Ivoire* and the *Association Générale des Etudiants de Côte d'Ivoire en France,*

---

first two engineers, A. Kacou and C. Donwahi. Vilasco, Djessou-Loubo, and Donwahi were past presidents of the Ivory Coast Students' Association in France. The association sponsored lectures, theatrical performances, discussions, and published irregularly a magazine, *Ebur.* The first issue explained that although the group has been accused of "regionalism," it was open to all. Nevertheless, no foreigners ever appeared on the roster of leaders. Most of the information in this section was obtained in interviews with leaders of the associations mentioned, 1959.

which met in Abidjan in July 1956, to unify their movement under the name of *Union Générale des Etudiants de Côte d'Ivoire.* The congress indicated that the youth organizations were much less concerned with educational problems than with more general issues. The students accused the R.D.A. of not paying enough attention to educational problems and of selling out to the colonialists. They condemned the *Loi-Cadre*, objected to the Territorial Assembly's decision to grant a leasehold to an Indochinese rubber firm, and announced their preference for public investments over private ones.[69]

Shortly after this congress, one of the leaders of the *Association des Parents d'Elèves* that had cosponsored it founded a monthly newspaper, *Attoungblan*, which announced in its fourth issue the creation of a new political party. Its French name, *Front de Libération Noire*, had the same initials as the Algerian rebel organization; its African name, *Kotoko*, meant "independence." *Attoungblan*'s vituperative prose was calculated to arouse nationalist sentiments—discouraged by the P.D.C.I.—as well as ethnic subnationalism among specific groups. The newspaper took a pro-Nasser stand during the Suez crisis, hailed the coming of independence for the Gold Coast as the only suitable solution for Africa, advocated the wearing of native dress, spoke of African unity, but approved at the same time of the separatist claims of the traditionally oriented Agni of Sanwi State. It instructed its readers to abstain from voting in the municipal elections "in order to avoid being the accomplices of slave traders, stateless Jews, and all sorts

[69] The exchange between student and P.D.C.I. leaders was printed in *Abidjan-Matin*, August 14, 1956, and *La Concorde*, August 2 and 13, 1956. Concerning the land grant in question, the company and Europeans in the Assembly had supported a freehold grant. The Governor proposed to grant them a 99-year lease. Although the Committee of the Assembly preferred 25 years, the final compromise was 60 years. This was by no means a reversal of P.D.C.I. policies of 1948, since the land grant system had been modified in the direction the party had advocated at that time. (Ivory Coast, Assemblée territoriale, "Debates," February 16 and 17, April 19, 1957.)

of anti-nigger capitalists."[70] The F.L.N.'s manifesto was published in December 1956. It asserted that no incumbent or past political leader would be allowed to hold office in the party, that Europeans must abandon the R.D.A. before it was too late and negotiate with F.L.N. leaders, and that since the French would never willingly liberate Africa, it would be necessary to take direct action. Finally, the F.L.N. asserted that it opposed all violent action, that it agreed with the Bandoeng Pact, and that Nkrumah, who did not betray his people, was a great leader. It concluded by demanding immediate independence for the Ivory Coast.[71]

In March 1957, the editor of *Attoungblan* and the former president of A.E.C.I.F., an attorney, led an opposition ticket in Abidjan. Another former student leader, now a member of the U.J.C.I. executive, challenged the P.D.C.I. in Agboville. Although both groups were explicitly concerned with nationalist issues and demanded immediate independence, they also encouraged ethnic subnationalism in order to secure electoral support, particularly among the Attié of Adzopé *subdivision* in Agboville.[72] The third "youth" opposition was active in Grand Lahou *cercle*, where yet another former student leader, A. Usher Assouan, ran against the P.D.C.I. general secretary, who had been designated as a candidate. He announced, however, that he did not disagree with the overall policies of the party leadership. This was the only successful challenge to the P.D.C.I.'s supremacy.[73]

[70] *Attoungblan*, November 1956.

[71] *Ibid.*, December 1956.

[72] Agboville *cercle* consists of two *subdivisions*, Agboville and Adzopé, inhabited by the Abbey and the Attié respectively. The ticket led by C. Assi Adam, an Attié, obtained 42 per cent of the votes in the *cercle*; he received 62 per cent in his own Attié region against only 21 per cent in the Abbey-dominant *subdivision*.

[73] A. Usher Assouan later became a vice-president of the Assembly and has been Ivory Coast Ambassador to the United Nations since 1961. He had a 56 per cent majority in the *cercle*, with particularly strong support in Lakota *subdivision*.

CONCLUSIONS

Gauged by its electoral performance in 1956 and 1957, the P.D.C.I. machine was highly effective. In the municipal contests of November and December 1956 the lists it sponsored were unchallenged in all but two towns, as Table 17 indicates. Only in Gagnoa did the party's opponents win

TABLE 17

Municipal Elections, 1956

City	*Registered*	*Votes Cast*	*Valid*	*P.D.C.I.*	*Others*
	Communes de Plein Exercice, November				
Abidjan	69,116	33,047	32,990	32,990	—
Bouaké	20,038	9,788	9,183	9,183	—
Grand Bassam	8,123	4,094	4,050	4,050	—
	Communes de Moyen Exercice, December				
Daloa	9,025	6,930	6,905	6,905	—
Gagnoa	8,414	6,008	5,953	2,803	3,150[b]
Dimbokro	8,381	4,329	4,297	4,297	—
Man	7,127	4,562	4,456	4,456	—
Abengourou	3,613	2,686	2,683	2,683	—
Agboville	7,206	4,332	2,222	2,222	(a)

[a] The 2,051 ballots cast for the opposition in Agboville were declared invalid because the list did not include a sufficient number of candidates. The entire election was later invalidated, but no new ones had yet been held as of mid-1963.

[b] This gave Digna Bailly's party control over 2 of the 3 wards of the city, with 14 out of the 27 seats in the municipal council.

enough seats on the municipal council to gain control over the office of assistant to the mayor. In March 1957, the U.D.I.E.C.I. obtained 89 per cent of the votes cast and captured all but two of the 60 seats in the Territorial Assembly.[74] Its triumph was complete immediately afterwards,

[74] The U.D.I.E.C.I. had majorities in 18 out of the 19 *cercles* and in 50 out of 55 smaller units for which electoral results have been broken down, the exceptions in the latter case being the *subdivisions* of Adzopé, Bondoukou, Lakota, Issia, and Gagnoa. The results of the election were: registered, 1,483,044; valid votes, 807,410; U.D.I.E.C.I., 720,278; all others, 86,542. (Ivory Coast, Service de l'Information, *Bulletin Spécial. Résultat des Elections à l'Assemblée territoriale*, Abidjan, April 4, 1957.)

however, when the two successful opposition candidates announced that they were R.D.A. and joined the other members to elect Houphouet-Boigny president.[75] (See Map 3.)

The P.D.C.I. leadership nevertheless were worried by the election results. Participation, which had reached 67 per cent in January 1956 fell to 54 per cent in 1957. It was particularly low in the cities, where one might perhaps expect a higher turnout than in rural areas. The three *communes de plein exercice,* which had an average turnout of 49 per cent in November 1956, had a level of participation less than half that of the territorial average in 1957. In Abidjan alone, as Table 18 shows, the turnout dropped from 57 per cent in

TABLE 18

Decline of Participation in Abidjan

Election	*Registered*	*Voting*	*Void*	*R.D.A.*	*Opposition*
January 1956 (National Assembly)	51,895	29,645	631	23,910	5,098
November 1956 (Municipal)	69,116	33,047	757	32,290	—
March 1957 (Territorial)	73,796	15,399	352	13,571	1,476

January 1956, to 48 per cent in November of the same year, and finally to only 21 per cent in March 1957. Only half as many persons voted in 1957 as in January 1956.

What did the decline of participation indicate? First, it must be noted that at the territorial level there had been nearly a doubling of the electorate between January 1956, and March 1957; this was brought about by the implementation of universal suffrage. Since earlier categories of electors had been chosen in accordance with criteria that distinguished those who were more educated, more economically active,

[75] Houphouet-Boigny received 59 votes; he himself abstained. *Abidjan-Matin,* April 3, 1957. Ivory Coast, Assemblée territoriale, "Debates," May 15, 1957.

ERRITORIAL ASSEMBLY ELECTIONS, 1957

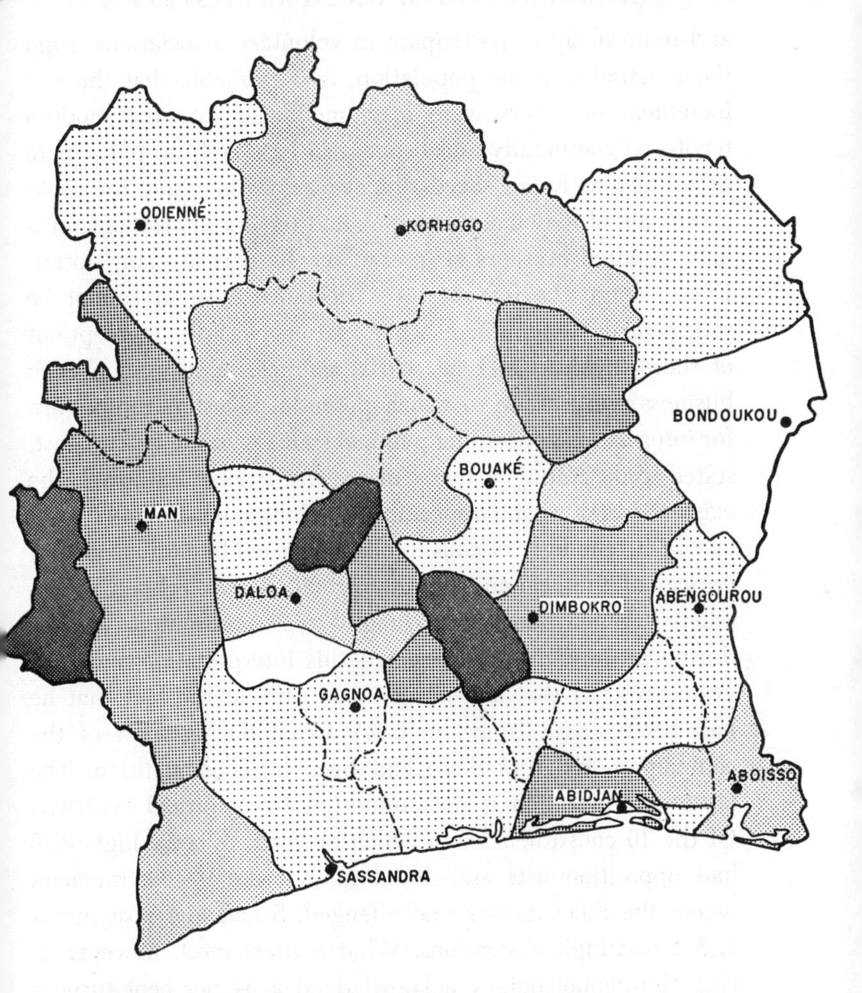

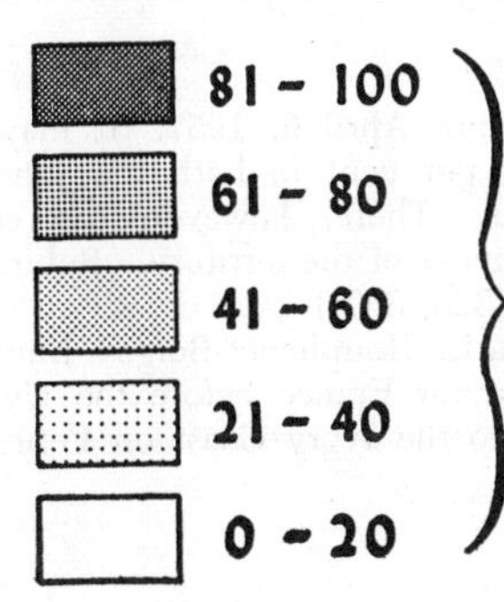

Per cent of registered electors who supported PDCI candidates (by subdivision)

Map 3

and more likely to participate in voluntary associations, from the remainder of the population, it is probable that the last increment of voters were least mobilized into the modern territorial community and hence also less likely to participate in political activities. Secondly, at least in the cities, the rapid succession of national, municipal, and territorial elections, may have resulted in a loss of interest on the part of many voters. Even though the reasons for a declining turnout cannot be satisfactorily determined, what matters was the perceptions of those involved in Ivory Coast politics. A leading French business publication, to which potential investors might turn for information concerning political stability in the Ivory Coast, stated unhesitatingly that "mass abstentions indicated the existence of a silent opposition to Houphouet-Boigny's policies."[76] In the light of calls to abstain issued by various groups critical of the regime, this interpretation was echoed everywhere. When Houphouet-Boigny was confronted with it during an interview, he rejected this interpretation and suggested instead that abstentions were due to the fact that he had been absent from the Ivory Coast during most of the campaign[77] and that there had been little competition. The latter interpretation is not supported by empirical evidence. Of the 10 constituencies in which abstentions were highest, 6 had opposition lists and 4 did not; of the 9 constituencies where the P.D.C.I. was unchallenged, 5 had low abstentions and 4 had high abstentions. What matters most, however, is that Houphouet-Boigny acknowledged a 54 per cent turnout as insufficient.

[76] *Marchés Tropicaux et Méditerranéens,* April 6, 1957. It may be noted that turnout in Senegal was 54 per cent in both the January 1956, and the March 1957, elections. There, however, the cities participated more actively than the remainder of the territory. (Robinson, "Senegal: The Elections . . .," pp. 316, 326, 387.)

[77] After spending most of 1956 in Paris, Houphouet-Boigny traveled to New York to appear as a spokesman for France before the United Nations in January 1957. He returned to the Ivory Coast on February

This revealed the major political problem the P.D.C.I. faced at the time it became responsible for the government of the Ivory Coast. Between 1952 and 1957 the party had become a successful electoral machine through the skillful use of various techniques, including cooptation, patronage, and economic pressures. This might have been sufficient if the party had operated within a well-established constitutional framework whose legitimacy was firmly institutionalized. Under such conditions, relatively low participation might even be considered politically advantageous. But the P.D.C.I. was not merely a machine. It claimed to be also an all-encompassing movement that based its legitimacy on overwhelming support from all strata of the population. From this point of view, the 1957 elections indicated that the U.D.I.E.C.I. fell far short of what it must achieve, since it had obtained support from slightly less than half of the adult population.[78]

Furthermore, in order to conduct external relations successfully and to inspire confidence among potential investors, it was necessary to demonstrate that the regime was stable and that there was complete internal unity around Houphouet-Boigny. From this point of view, the fact that more than that there was complete internal unity around Houphouet-liability. It grew in importance where the Ivory Coast leaders were forced to choose between alternative definitions of relationships with France in 1958 and decided to forego the opportunity of becoming fully independent. This decision and the grant of self-government to the territories of French West Africa in 1958 brought about a further transformation of the P.D.C.I.

---

15 but left soon afterwards to tour other parts of French Africa on behalf of the *Loi-Cadre* policies. He returned only a few days before the elections and did not campaign in the hinterland. (*La Concorde*, February 15, 1957; *Abidjan-Matin*, March 30, 1957.)

[78] Votes cast for the P.D.C.I. represented 49 per cent of the registered electorate, which included almost the entire adult population of both sexes.

PART IV

THE IVORY COAST REPUBLIC: ONE-PARTY GOVERNMENT AT WORK

CHAPTER VII

THE RELUCTANT NATION

THE political development of French dependencies was irresistibly influenced by the most important event in modern African history, the grant of independence to the Gold Coast in March 1957. In retrospect it is clear that any status short of international sovereignty rapidly became unacceptable to other African countries. Although the Ivory Coast followed suit shortly afterwards and became fully independent in August 1960, it did so after much hesitation. The Ivory Coast was a reluctant nation. Its leaders, faced with the overwhelming responsibility of transforming an underdeveloped country still imperfectly integrated into a modern nation-state, attempted to gain some respite by sharing this responsibility with the former colonial power for as long as they could without jeopardizing their political control at home.

DEMANDS FOR CHANGE

Although African politicians agreed to work within the framework of the *Loi-Cadre*, they pressed for further reforms even before the law was implemented. Senghor characterized France's attitude as "a kind of hesitation waltz in which you move two steps forward to go one step back, and in which the left hand takes back half of what the right hand gave."[1] Labor unions, assembled at Cotonou, saw the law as "a mystification, a façade which fools no one. Its sole object is to divide us, to mask and to perpetuate the colonial regime."[2] Even Houphouet-Boigny, whose duties as Minister of State included supervising the proper execution of the decrees, acknowledged that they did not constitute an end in them-

[1] *L'Unité*, March 5, 1957.
[2] Quoted in *Présence Africaine*, No. 18-19 (February-May 1958), p. 120.

selves but only one step in a momentous turn of African history.[3]

The next step required a revision of Title VIII of the constitution of the Fourth Republic, which defined the framework of the French Union. *Convention Africaine* advocated a gradual loosening of the ties between France and her African dependencies. Senghor and his associates asked that the territories be granted internal autonomy as members of a French federal republic. This new political community would eventually give way to a confederation of associated states, a sort of "Commonwealth à la française." But the first objective was to reconstitute African unity, threatened by the *Loi-Cadre*, at the level of the primary federations in Africa. The *Mouvement Socialiste Africain* abandoned the traditional assimilationist orientation of the Senegalese Socialists in favor of an undefined form of free association between metropolitan France and self-governing overseas territories.[4]

In the absence of any congress since 1949, the R.D.A.'s stand was defined only through the Conakry resolutions of 1955 and through the pronouncements of its president. Houphouet-Boigny's often repeated vision of the future was a Franco-African federal community of free and equal members.[5] More explicitly than other leaders, he rejected independence as the ultimate goal. When Kwame Nkrumah of Ghana visited the Ivory Coast a few days after his own country had become

[3] In a speech at Porto-Novo, Dahomey, on February 25, 1957, quoted in *Présence Africaine*, p. 120. During an earlier tour of Africa, Houphouet-Boigny had indicated his wholehearted approval of a law which granted universal suffrage to Africans, something which he asserted had not been accomplished even in great democracies. (Ivory Coast, Service de l'Information, *Discours et Allocutions* . . ., 1956.)

[4] These positions were defined at their founding congress held in Dakar and Conakry respectively in January 1957. (Robinson, "Senegal: The Elections . . .," pp. 329-30.

[5] *La Concorde*, February 26, 1957. This theme was repeated when Houphouet-Boigny spoke before the United Nations as a member of the French delegation and in an article based on this speech appearing under his name in *Foreign Affairs*, July 1957, pp. 593-99.

an independent member of the Commonwealth, Houphouet-Boigny asserted that during this century of "interdependence of peoples," undeveloped and weak African countries stood to gain very little from "nominal independence." He challenged his visitor to a rendezvous ten years hence to determine which political path would have had more beneficial effects for the African masses.[6]

It was not clear whether Houphouet-Boigny spoke for France, for the Ivory Coast or for the entire R.D.A., which had reached the summit of its power in 1957 and had emerged as the largest political organization in Africa.[7] Pressures were mounting within the party to clarify its stand. The third interterritorial congress was scheduled to meet in Bamako in October 1956, the tenth anniversary of the birth of the movement. It was postponed several times, allegedly because of the forthcoming municipal and territorial elections.[8] In reality, party leaders were trying to settle privately controversies concerning the future of the federation, relations with France, the Algerian question, and Houphouet-Boigny's accountability to the movement before facing congressional

[6] During this visit they also discussed border problems stemming from an undefined boundary in the Ehy and Tendo Lagoon, where Gulf Petroleum was searching for oil. (*Afrique Nouvelle*, April 9 and 30, 1957.)

[7] The entire R.D.A. fared very well in the territorial elections. Its sections obtained absolute majorities in the Ivory Coast, Sudan, Guinea, and Upper Volta, as well as substantial minorities in Niger and Dahomey. Altogether, it obtained 54 per cent of the popular vote in French West Africa. (French Embassy, New York, *African Affairs*, No. 18, May 1957.) For the first time since 1947, it gained control of the Grand Council of French West Africa, hitherto dominated by Senegalese parties and their I.O.M. allies. The R.D.A. was able to elect a full slate of officers, headed by Houphouet-Boigny, who thus became president of an organ whose existence he challenged. (Milcent, p. 128.) It is no wonder then that while the C.A. and M.S.A. spoke of a merger to create a unified party, the R.D.A. sought to attain unity by absorbing all others. Sékou Touré bluntly invited the C.A. and M.S.A. simply to join the R.D.A. after the elections. (*Afrique Nouvelle*, April 16, 1957.)

[8] *Afrique Nouvelle*, September 25, 1956.

delegates and publicizing party disunity.[9] These efforts came to nought when, in the face of Ivory Coast opposition, Sékou Touré and Gabriel d'Arboussier joined non-R.D.A. members of the Grand Council in support of a motion to expand federal services and to create a federal executive.[10]

From the bitter struggle that developed at Bamako, where the R.D.A. finally met from September 25 to 30, 1957, it was obvious that Houphouet-Boigny's views represented only those of the Ivory Coast section of the movement.[11] His report to the congress, in which he advocated the progressive transformation of the French Union into a Franco-African federation and the immediate elimination of all intervening levels of government between the territories and the metropole, was received with hostility by most delegates.[12] In the debates that followed, the majority leaned in the direction of the proposals transmitted by Sékou Touré, general secretary of the Guinea section. They proposed recognition of the right to independence for all territories and asserted that in order to increase Africa's bargaining power, an African community must be created before seeking to bring to life a Franco-African federation. The *aile marchante* of the movement also objected to Houphouet-Boigny's continued participation

[9] At a controversial meeting held in April 1957, the coordination committee of the R.D.A. decided to hold the congress in July. It was reported that disagreement among the leaders was so intense that Houphouet-Boigny threatened to resign and that only lack of unanimity on a successor prevented the others from accepting his decision. (Blanchet, p. 48.) It was later announced that the congress was postponed once again until September 1957. (*Afrique Nouvelle*, April 23, 1957.)

[10] This occurred during Houphouet-Boigny's absence, when the Grand Council was meeting under the chairmanship of Gabriel d'Arboussier, who had returned to the R.D.A. fold in 1956 and who had been elected first vice-president of the Council following the R.D.A. triumph in 1957. (*Afrique Nouvelle*, September 3, 1957.)

[11] The account of the congress is based on the thorough analysis contained in A. Blanchet and on the excellent short summary by Thomas Hodgkin, "After Bamako," *Africa Special Report*, II, No. 11 (December 1957), 2-7.

[12] Troisième Congrès Interterritorial du R.D.A., "Rapport Moral," delivered September 26, 1957. (Mimeographed.)

in the French government because this might be interpreted as R.D.A. support for the colonial war waged in Algeria.

To stave off a split in the movement, the congress reached—albeit with great difficulty[13]—compromise solutions on all these issues. The final political resolution stated:

"The congress considers that the independence of peoples is an inalienable right which allows them to dispose of the attributes of their sovereignty according to the interests of the popular masses.

"But it considers that interdependence is the golden rule of the life of peoples and manifests itself in the twentieth century by the constitution of large political and economic wholes."[14]

R.D.A. representatives were instructed to seek the creation of a federal state with France and to propose a law "tending toward the democratization of the existing federal executives" in Africa. Settlement of the Algerian problem by means of negotiations "with the genuine representatives of the Algerian people" was held to be a prerequisite for any redefinition of Franco-African relations and a step that would have to precede the creation of any federation.[15] Houphouet-Boigny was reelected President, but the composition of the new

[13] They required postponement of the final session for three days, during which Houphouet-Boigny withdrew from the congress and the Ivory Coast delegation was ostracized by the other sections. A. Denise later stated that the Ivory Coast would have asked Houphouet-Boigny to resign and would have seceded from the movement if the congress had insisted on endorsing Sékou Touré's proposed motion supporting the creation of a federal executive. (*Afrique Nouvelle*, October 29, 1957.) It has been suggested that Houphouet-Boigny was less anti-federal than the Ivory Coast party (Blanchet, pp. 91-93), although there is little evidence for this interpretation. Houphouet-Boigny was faced with a double dilemma, the first arising from a conflict between his position as an African leader and as a member of the French government, the second stemming from his role as president of a superterritorial movement and that of boss of isolationist Ivory Coast. These dilemmas were never really resolved.

[14] Troisième Congrès Interterritorial du R.D.A., "Résolution de Politique Générale," September 1957. (Mimeographed.)

[15] *Ibid.*

bureau of the coordination committee indicated that he was now only *primus inter pares.*[16] He was also enjoined to represent the party's views rather than his personal opinions in Paris.

Bamako and other developments indicated that as African protest movements became government parties, older alignments based on loyalties formed during the early years of political activity were giving way to newer positions based on territorial interests. The preferences of territorial organizations on contemporary issues were determined by the ideological orientation of individual leaders rather than by decisions taken in common by the superterritorial movements. Within the R.D.A., the Bamako compromise on the federal issue was short lived.[17] When the Grand Council once again advocated the creation of a federal executive in April 1958, the Ivory Coast withdrew altogether and the Territorial Assembly vowed that its representatives would not return to Dakar.[18] After

[16] He was surrounded by four vice-presidents, Modibo Keita (Sudan), Sékou Touré (Guinea), Doudou Gueye (Senegal), and Gabriel Lisette (Tchad). There were, in addition, 4 secretaries, but no general secretary; 2 treasurers; and 2 other members. The Ivory Coast was less important at this level than it had been at the beginning of the movement's existence. With the growth of the *Parti Démocratique de Guinée* and the *Union Soudanaise* within their respective territories, with leadership of outstanding stature, the P.D.C.I. was just another section.

[17] Less than two months later, the Ivory Coast Territorial Assembly challenged the legality of the Grand Council's action the previous August. (Ivory Coast, Assemblée territoriale, "Debates," November 14, 1957.) In January 1958 the Guinea Territorial Assembly, dominated by the P.D.G. reasserted its support of the Grand Council's action. (*Cahiers A.O.F.*, February 1, 1958.)

[18] Houphouet-Boigny avoided a showdown within the R.D.A. and possible defeat for his own faction by not attending the opening of the Grand Council. He denied having been a candidate for reelection and was replaced by Gabriel d'Arboussier. (*Abidjan-Matin*, March 28, 1958.) It is significant that the Ivory Coast's reaction occurred while the Territorial Assembly was in the midst of approving the government's plan for 1958-1962, in which the necessity of retrieving territorial revenue with which the federation had absconded (from the Ivory Coast point of view) was fully spelled out. Houphouet-Boigny was absent during the discussion in the Territorial Assembly on April 9, 1958, but later endorsed the Assembly's action. (*Ibid.*, April 19, 1958.)

the R.D.A. coordination committee proposed a new compromise whereby the proposed federal executive would be replaced by an "executive delegation" in addition to the High Commissioner and each territory would be free to join the federation or be directly attached to the Franco-African unit, the Ivory Coast agreed to return to the Grand Council.[19] Nevertheless, it was clear that the Guinean and Sudanese sections were much closer on this issue to the newly created *Parti du Regroupement Africain* (P.R.A.), a merger of the C.A., M.S.A., and other smaller parties, than to the Ivory Coast section of their own party.[20] Similarly, the Ivory Coast did not feel bound to endorse the demand for recognition of the right of independence formulated by spokesmen for the R.D.A., C.A., and M.S.A. at a February 1958 meeting in Paris.[21] In the final months of the Fourth Republic, while African demands for constitutional revision became more insistent, few leaders believed that France would willingly relinquish part of her sovereignty to a political community in which her former dependencies would have equal status, as Houphouet-Boigny's federal formula would require. However, while they began to seek other solutions, the Ivory Coast became increasingly separated from the mainstream of African political thought.

The Community

When De Gaulle returned to power in May 1958 not only Title VIII but the entire constitution was revised. As the "man of Brazzaville," the General enjoyed almost unlimited trust among African political leaders and was a mythical

[19] Blanchet, pp. 101-102.

[20] The P.R.A. was launched at a meeting held March 26 and 27, 1958, in Dakar, following an earlier all-parties conference in Paris in February. The R.D.A. attended but still refused to merge with the others.

[21] The resolution is reprinted in Blanchet, p. 198. He reports (p. 96) that Houphouet-Boigny publicly disassociated himself from this resolution in a speech in France.

figure of power among the masses.[22] But his intentions concerning the future of tropical Africa were not clear. His chief constitutional architect, Senator Michel Debré, preferred a federal solution but disapproved of complex federal schemes. He advocated a simple system in which each territory would choose between the *status quo*, integration as a department, or autonomy. In the last case, the extent of its autonomy would be determined by a constitutional provision listing the mandatory areas of common decision.[23] These views were very similar to those of Houphouet-Boigny, who had survived the sinking of his ship to become a member of the De Gaulle cabinet. He was the only African member of the government advisory group that prepared the first constitutional draft published at the end of July.[24]

The institutions which France "offered to the peoples of the

[22] De Gaulle had been hailed as the liberator throughout Africa in 1944 and 1945. Many teenagers, boys and girls, in the Ivory Coast of 1959 bore his name. In French Equatorial Africa, his name was associated with the origins of a religious cult, N'Gol. He had visited the Ivory Coast in 1953 and Houphouet-Boigny was known to admire him greatly. For the circumstances of his return to power, see in particular J.-R. Tournoux, *Secrets d'etat* (Paris: Librairie Plon, 1960).

[23] Nicholas Wahl, "The French Constitution of 1958: II. The Initial Draft and Its Origins," *The American Political Science Review*, LIII, No. 2 (June 1959), 366. Other proposals circulating in France at that time included Mitterand's, set forth in his book, leaning toward federation, and the ones published by a high French official under the pseudonym "Africanus" in June 1958, advocating the transfer of legislative powers to the Overseas Territories as had been done for Togo at the beginning of the year, according to a formula that would bear the name of "confederation." (Africanus, *L'Afrique noire devant l'indépendance* [Paris: Plon, 1958].)

[24] The draft was published in *Le Monde*, July 31, 1958. This study does not attempt to present a detailed history of the making of the constitution. The major steps were: (1) preparation of the government draft, published at the end of July; (2) study of this draft by a consultative constitutional committee, on which sat several African representatives, and recommendations for change in the government's proposals, completed on August 14; (3) reconsideration by the government, interrupted by De Gaulle's trip to Africa, further consultation, and publication of the final draft on September 4; (4) referendum held in France and in Africa on September 28, 1958. The account is based on daily issues of *Le Monde*, unless otherwise indicated.

Overseas Territories who manifested the will to belong to them," as the preamble stated, repeated Debré's three choices.[25] The new unit would be headed by the president of the French Republic. Its organs would include an executive, which remained undefined; the upper house of the French parliament, where the territories would be represented; and a court of arbitration to settle conflicts between the members. Common matters decided at the federal level would include foreign affairs; defense; currency; common financial and economic policy; exploitation of strategic raw materials; control over justice and higher education. No provision was made for future changes in the status of the members, and no mention was made anywhere of the right to self-determination or independence.[26]

These proposals obviously fell short of the compromise formulated at Bamako as well as the proposals put forth by the interparty group in Paris in February 1958. Meanwhile, African opinion had shifted toward a demand for more radical change. In June the congress of the Federation of African students in France (F.E.A.N.F.) branded Houphouet-Boigny a traitor and rejected in advance any solution short of outright independence.[27] U.G.T.A.N. leaders, who constituted the radical wing of both the R.D.A. and the P.R.A., indicated that beyond their explicit demand for recognition of the right to independence, they had in mind rapid evolution toward a sort of loose association of fully independent nations.[28] By the time the constitutional draft was published, the P.R.A. had held its first congress at Cotonou and took

[25] See particularly the preamble, Article 22, and Articles 65-73. (*Ibid.*, July 31, 1958.)

[26] The federation could negotiate agreements with other independent states to create a community, but there was no possibility for the territories to become associated states.

[27] Reported in *Le Monde*, June 29-30, 1958.

[28] This position was expounded by Sékou Touré and Djibo Bakary, leaders of U.G.T.A.N. The latter was elected general secretary of the P.R.A. provisional committee with Zinsou of Dahomey. (Blanchet, p. 149.)

an unequivocal stand in favor of recognition of the right to independence, *fédération primaire* in Africa, followed by *confédération* of these consolidated units with France.[29] In this light, most Africans saw the constitutional draft as truly reactionary, because it was even more backward than the constitution of 1946, which at least stated that France pledged to lead her dependencies toward freedom. Senghor remarked that it appeared as if Africans were being pushed to the point where only a total break of relations with France was possible.[30] Only the Ivory Coast seemed satisfied with the government proposals. Prime Minister Denise, returning to Abidjan after having consulted with his leader in Paris, announced that France's offer was sufficient for anyone who did not actually intend to seek outright independence. Further bickering would be harmful, he added, because Africa must inspire confidence among those who were willing to help her economically.[31]

The more prevalent African views were embodied in the recommendations made by the Overseas Affairs subcommittee of the constitutional consultative committee, which added confederation to the three choices already included. This addition was not acceptable to De Gaulle. In a personal appearance before the subcommittee, flanked by Michel Debré and Houphouet-Boigny, the General stated that those who rejected the government's three choices demonstrated for outright secession. Indirectly, this was the first acknowledgment of the existence of the ultimate solution—independence.

[29] At this congress, Senghor and others who advocated a two-step process including first federation, then a loosening of ties into a confederation, were faced with pressures for outright independence stemming mostly from Djibo Bakary and his partisans. Because of this and also because it was concerned with outbidding the R.D.A., the P.R.A. became more demanding. (*Le Monde*, July 27, 1958.)

[30] Senghor's reactions and others were reported in *ibid.*, July 31, 1958, and following days.

[31] In a speech before the Territorial Assembly on August 7, 1958. He was now Prime Minister because all vice-presidents of the councils of government had been promoted to president in July 1958.

But, said De Gaulle, the territories that seceded would do so at their own risk; France would have to act in consequence.[32] Although the implications of such a move were not spelled out, it was thought that they would involve immediate recall of all French administrators serving abroad, the end of all economic and financial aid, and perhaps even more drastic measures. Many Africans and qualified French observers felt this was not a recognition of the right of independence, as requested, but a form of blackmail, a manifestation of "anti-colonialism of the right."[33] In the face of this warning, the constitutional consultative committee bypassed the controversy between "federation" and "confederation" by proposing the creation of a Community. The revised draft provided for mechanisms to enable members to redefine their status every five years and the preamble asserted that the Community was to be based on the right of its members to self-determination.[34]

Although the government was not scheduled to publish a final draft until the early days of September, its principal provisions, announced in anticipation of De Gaulle's forthcoming tour of Africa, indicated that it embodied most of the committee's recommendations. The paramount issue was

[32] *Le Monde*, August 10-11, 1958.

[33] "Let them be independent and be damned" summarized a widespread attitude in France during the summer and early fall of 1958. This was gathered from a regular examination of the popular press and from many conversations with individuals who were not particularly concerned with African problems. I have already noted the growth of *Cartierisme* since 1956. De Gaulle's views were strongly criticized by A. Blanchet in *Le Monde* (August 19, 1958) as belonging to this same sector of opinion and *indigne* of the General.

[34] This Community would have an assembly made up of the delegates of the legislative assemblies of member states, represented on the basis of population and in proportion to the extent of their burden in managing common affairs, a provision which would insure French paramountcy. This proposal was eventually embodied in the senate of the Community, as will be shown below. The committee's proposals were submitted to the government on August 14. The text of the recommendations and the cover letter by Paul Reynaud justifying the changes were published in *Le Monde*, August 17-18, 1958.

now whether the proposed constitution would grant the right to independence. African leaders questioned De Gaulle on it at every stop he made. In Madagascar the General asserted that all choices were available, including "secession." The following day, at the historical city of Brazzaville, where the French Union had been launched fourteen years earlier, he announced for the first time unequivocally that a "no" vote in the forthcoming referendum on the constitution would be interpreted by France as a demand for independence. His Minister of Overseas France hastened to add that France would not veto such a move.[35] At De Gaulle's next stop, Abidjan, Gabriel d'Arboussier asserted that since he had kept his promise to the peoples of the Overseas Territories, there was no longer any doubt of Africa's affirmative vote.

But on the following day, a dramatic confrontation between the General and Sékou Touré in Conakry contributed to a drastic change in the course of French West African political history.[36] The Guinean leader firmly reasserted his demands; in addition to the right of independence, he wanted equal status with France in a truly federal community, the regrouping of African territories, and complete internal autonomy. Whether he found the constitutional proposals acceptable was not yet clear to many observers, but the harsh tone of his speech overshadowed important conciliatory elements in its content. To De Gaulle, however, the answer was obvious. He grew visibly impatient during Sékou Touré's address and perceived him as a challenger who must be met in battle. As his response indicated, he continued to view independence as "secession" and anticipated that the ideological rift between himself and Sékou Touré was beyond healing. A few minutes

[35] Reports of De Gaulle's trip, the announcements he made, and African reactions were adequately reported in *Le Monde* and in *The New York Times*, issues of August 21 through 28, 1958.

[36] This account of the events in Conakry is drawn from Jean Lacouture, *Cinq Hommes et la France* (Paris: Editions du Seuil, 1961), pp. 349ff. Lacouture was correspondent for *Le Monde* at the time and is held in very high regard as an analyst of colonial questions.

later, he told his entourage that France and Sékou Touré could never get along and hence that they must prepare for France's permanent departure from Guinea on the morning of September 29. After the General had spoken, things had become equally clear to the leader of Guinea: "We want freedom, they promise us punishment . . ."[37] All attempts at mediation failed. On the following day, the Guinean leader announced that his country would vote "categorically and unanimously 'no' " in the referendum.[38]

After the General's return to Paris, the government amended the constitutional draft once again to take into account his Brazzaville declarations. The principle of self-determination was included in the preamble, which also stated that "the Republic hereby offers to the Overseas Territories that express the desire to adhere to them, new institutions based on the common ideal of liberty, equality, and fraternity, and conceived with a view to their democratic evolution."[39] This acceptance was to be expressed by voting "yes" in the referendum. Those who voted "no" were cast beyond the pale of the Community. Afterwards, the territorial assemblies of the members must decide within four months whether to retain the *status quo*, to become departments, or to be promoted to the status of autonomous republics. The territories could join the Community either as single units or as a group, such as a primary federation.[40] Article 86 provided for change of status of the members later on at the request of the French Republic or by means of a resolution of their legislative assembly, confirmed by referendum. For those who voted "yes" now but changed their mind afterwards, the constitution stated unequivocally that "under the same

[37] *Ibid.*, p. 353.
[38] *Ibid.*, pp. 353-57.
[39] Preamble and Article 1. The text of the constitution is reprinted in Herman Finer, *The Major Governments of Modern Europe* (Evanston: Row, Peterson, and Company, 1960), pp. A8-A17.
[40] Articles 76 and 91.

conditions [as the ones given above] a member state of the Community may become independent. It shall thereby cease to belong to the Community."[41]

Although the constitution was clear concerning freedom of choice, it was highly ambiguous concerning the structure of the Community. Matters to be decided in common, similar to those listed in the government's first draft, were specified in Article 78. But no legislative organs were provided to deal with them. The member states would no longer be represented in the French parliament. They would participate instead in the senate of the Community.[42] This new organ was only an advisory body. It could deliberate on common matters at the request of the president of the Community but the constitution did not make it mandatory for the president to formulate this request. Only if the French parliament and the assemblies of the other member states agreed to abandon some aspect of their sovereignty in the legislative sphere to the benefit of the senate would this organ make executory decisions. In reality, the senate turned out to be nothing but an abortive successor to the ill-fated Assembly of the French Union.[43]

The lack of a Community legislature enhanced the importance of the executive. It consisted of an executive council, whose

[41] Article 86.

[42] Article 83. The membership and procedures of the senate of the Community were left to be specified in an organic law. France had a majority of the seats, with 186 out of a total of 284. (*Le Monde*, May 2, 1959.)

[43] The senate never acquired the power to make executory decisions. It did not even have a home of its own but met at the Palais du Luxembourg, the traditional home of the upper house of parliament. As such, it was even less noticeable than the Assembly of the French Union had been. Three weeks after the referendum, a very high official in the Ministry of Overseas France could not explain to an interviewer what the senate would do, if anything. It never did do much. The French government approved of a project to give the senate decision-making authority in matters of racial discrimination (*Abidjan-Matin*, November 5, 1959), but this was never implemented. At any rate, the senate was dissolved in 1960 after the birth of the "renovated Community."

organization and procedures were left to be defined by an organic law. This body was headed by the president of the French Republic, in whose election the members of the Community would participate. It would include the prime minister of the French Republic, the heads of government of all the other member states, and the ministers responsible for common affairs.[44] Those who were actually appointed to these posts were the ministers of the French Republic.[45]

The third Community organ was a court of arbitration empowered "to rule in litigations occurring among members,"[46] but otherwise undefined by the constitution. After a whole year of observing and analyzing the new institutions at work, a French constitutional specialist could only conclude that the Community was undefinable.[47] Considering these ambiguities, it is not surprising that at the time of choice in September 1958, all major African leaders interpreted the new constitution in accordance with their predispositions. To the newer wave of African nationalists, such as Djibo Bakary and Sékou Touré, it was nothing but a repetition of the French Union and hence was unacceptable. For Senghor, Tsiranana, and other advocates of a French-style commonwealth of nations, the Community was a tolerable transitional framework.[48] Houphouet-Boigny endorsed it without reservations as a move toward closer federal ties between France and Africa.

The Ivory Coast's Choice

"Communauté, Oui; Indépendance, Non"

When he returned to the Ivory Coast to lead the campaign

[44] Articles 6, 81, and 82.

[45] P. F. Gonidec, "La Communauté," *Public Law* (Summer, 1960), p. 186.

[46] Article 84.

[47] Gonidec, "La Communauté," p. 188.

[48] For details of these reactions, see issues of *Le Monde*, September 4 through 27, 1958. Comments in the African press are summarized in *La Semaine en A.O.F.*, weekly publication of the Information Office of the Government-General in Dakar, issues of September 1958.

for a "yes" vote in the referendum, Houphouet-Boigny urged his countrymen once again to reject nationalism: "It is as a free man, conscious of the worth of this country, conscious of reality, who refuses to walk backwards into History, it is as a free man who believes that at the very time when the great powers refuse to be isolated, at a moment when, for example . . . Frenchmen and Germans . . . want to build a bridge over a great gap filled with blood, sweat, and tears . . . that I declare that it would be going backwards . . . if in Africa we were to limit our evolution to the narrow confines of a nation."[49] Houphouet-Boigny's genuine devotion to the ideal of Franco-African community and his own exalted position in the French political structure undoubtedly contributed to his choice. But among the various justifications formulated during the campaign and afterwards, two major themes emerged: economic necessity and the problem of national unity.[50]

Because the P.D.C.I. was a political machine, heavily dependent on its distributive capacity for continued support, and because relatively great prosperity brought about an even more rapid growth of newly perceived needs among many strata of the population, economic considerations were even more pressing in 1958, after Africans had acquired some experience of governmental responsibility, than they had been earlier. The Community was thought to be a solution to the problem of economic development involving relatively

[49] Ivory Coast, Ministère de l'Intérieur, Service de l'Information, *Discours Prononcé par M. le Ministre d'Etat Houphouet-Boigny au Stade Géo-André à Abidjan le 7 septembre 1958* (Abidjan: Imprimerie du Gouvernement, n.d.), pp. 4-5. Hereafter cited as Speech of September 7, 1958.

[50] Although concern here is with an analysis of the Ivory Coast's choice, it must be noted that she shared a decision made by 11 of the other 12 territories of French-speaking Africa. The Ivory Coast's refusal of independence in 1958 was thus by no means an isolated or a deviant phenomenon. For one general interpretation of the motivations guiding the affirmative vote of most French-speaking Africa, see Berg, pp. 391-405.

little political cost. As indicated in Chapter VI, the Ivory Coast was dependent on France for the continued prosperity of its essentially agricultural economy. Although of all French West African territories, it was probably the most likely to survive if left to its own devices, this would involve major dislocations and readjustments and require a policy of austerity that might endanger the regime. Furthermore, the metropole was the most important source of capital investments. During the preceding decade, the French treasury had provided 48 per cent of the total of public investments made in the territory.[51] Houphouet-Boigny did not doubt that once the Community was established, the French contribution would increase.[52] During the campaign, he asserted that it was because the Ivory Coast could not possibly insure by its own means a decent standard of living for the entire population that he had agreed to enter into a larger political and economic community. He explained that he did not find *Communauté* control over common matters objectionable since it meant

[51] Seresa, *Rapport* . . ., p. 14. The total from all sources was 36.8 billion C.F.A. francs for the years 1947-1956. At first sight, the Ivory Coast appeared to be less dependent on France than French West Africa as a whole, where the French treasury provided 72 per cent of the total of public investments during the same period. (Berg, p. 396.) But since the non-French contribution to the Ivory Coast total was obtained mainly from import and export taxes, themselves a function of the country's ability to market her commodities abroad, indirectly France subsidized the Ivory Coast's ability to help herself. Most of the funds contributed by France were channeled through the *Fonds d'Investissement et de Développement Economique et Social* (F.I.D.E.S.). This prompted some observers to attribute to the African governments of 1957-1958 the motto, "Semper F.I.D.E.S. . . ." (Blanchet, p. 182.)

[52] During the inaugural ceremonies of the bridge bearing his name, which links Abidjan and Treichville and was built entirely with F.I.D.E.S. funds, Houphouet-Boigny told the Minister of Overseas France that Africa expected France to make greater sacrifices than ever after the Community was established. (Ivory Coast, Assemblée territoriale, "Debates," March 15, 1957.) He told his own countrymen that France was willing to help because he had explained to her leaders the meaning of the Agni proverb, "A father must feed his child until he grows teeth, so that the child will feed him when he loses his own." (Speech of September 7, 1958, p. 13.)

in effect that the metropole would bear the burden of the cost of defense and foreign affairs and would undertake to build a university in Abidjan. If this were slavery, he concluded, then he was willing to remain in bondage all his life.[53] Through the voice of his spokesman, Auguste Denise, he further argued that private capital would flow more freely once capitalists realized that they did not have to fear the consequences of nationalism in the Ivory Coast.[54]

As suggested earlier, P.D.C.I. leaders, after taking over the reins of the government, became more aware of the unfinished task of national integration. Beyond Houphouet-Boigny's economic arguments loomed a growing concern over the problem of internal unity. During the campaign for the referendum, he spoke repeatedly of the recrudescence of tribalism and of internal struggles that threatened the existence of newly independent countries. If this occurred in Ghana between closely related tribes, was it not likely to take particularly violent forms in the Ivory Coast, an artificial creation with sixty-odd tribes that could communicate with one another only through the medium of the French language?[55] He made explicit his fear that the sudden transfer of control over law, order, and the administration of justice to the hands of Africans not yet experienced in the ways of democracy, might have disastrous consequences. Membership in the Community would, on the contrary, foster unity within the Ivory Coast and more generally in Africa: "Is it not true that the unity of each of our tribes, the unity of the Baoulé among others, is better realized in the midst of the Ivory Coast, a

[53] This was an allusion to Sékou Touré's statement that he preferred freedom and a plate of manioc to buttered bread to be eaten in bondage. (*Ibid.*, p. 14.)

[54] Ivory Coast, Assemblée territoriale, "Debates," August 7, 1958.

[55] This example was cited by President Houphouet-Boigny in an interview in March 1959. He emphasized that the case of Ashanti and northern opposition to the C.P.P. in Ghana around 1955 and 1956, which had led to the postponement of independence for a whole year, had been foremost in his mind, along with the memory of Hindu-Moslem conflicts in India.

French creation, in the same way as the unity of Brittany is better assured in the context of France? In the same way we think . . . that unity in Africa will be better fostered within a larger political and economic unit. Today, the Community offers us an ideal framework for this purpose."[56]

Many P.D.C.I. officials were less wholeheartedly committed to the ideal of Franco-African federation than their leader. Because their activities were centered in Africa rather than in France, they were more attuned to the state of popular opinion and to the irresistibly attractive notion of independence. Less involved in the French parliamentary system than Houphouet-Boigny, they had retained a more suspicious attitude toward the colonial power. Nevertheless, they accepted his choice as a necessary one at the time. Those who were particularly responsible for party organization knew that its machinery was adequate only for electoral purposes. It could not possibly take over the tasks of day-to-day administration and of economic development, as it would probably be required to do if France retaliated against a "no" vote.[57] They viewed the Community as an opportunity, albeit a temporary one: after all, they explained, the Ivory Coast would retain her new bridges and roads, her schools and hospitals, regardless of the future state of her relationships with France.[58]

The attitudes of the rank-and-file in the party and of the population generally cannot be ascertained. The impact of Ghana, the only colony that had become independent so far, was relatively limited because of the general paucity of communications between French- and English-speaking Africans,

[56] Speech of September 7, 1958.

[57] In the absence of published statements preceding the referendum, this account is based on opinions gathered during interviews afterwards. By the time these interviews took place, respondents already knew what France's reaction had been to the "no" vote in Guinea.

[58] This was an economically sound argument. Berg has indicated that although there was much to criticize in French developmental schemes in Africa, the factors of production nevertheless remained there and contributed to growth. (Berg, p. 396.)

except among Akan peoples on both sides of the border. But although clamors for independence were not as loud in 1958 as in later years, the word had already acquired its magic qualities. Students in Paris and in Dakar, together with their friends at home, openly announced their preference for a "no" vote. Many leaders and members of labor unions leaned toward Sékou Touré's views. What is more important than any appraisal of public opinion is the fact that the P.D.C.I. leaders *believed* that the sentiment for independence was widespread.[59] Therefore, they could not risk the consequences of a free expression of the people's choice.

Because he stood as the foremost champion of the Community, Houphouet-Boigny would not accept less than complete unanimity in the referendum. He also felt that a demonstration of overwhelming support was necessary to overcome any doubt concerning the country's political stability that remained from the interpretation of the low turnout in 1957 as a sign of "silent opposition." He ruled out abstentions as a sign of cowardice.[60] All party and government resources were mobilized to insure the desired result. Polling places were multiplied and registration procedures were facilitated. The government provided free transportation by railroad, trucks, and even dugout canoes to bring everyone to the polls. All African and European members of the Assembly were ordered into the hinterland to campaign for a "yes" vote.[61] Pressures were exerted on businessmen to help bear the financial burden of the campaign. But to these established

[59] Complaining about a racial incident during which a European had offended an African, Coffi Gadeau stated in the Assembly that such events made the task of the leaders very difficult because while they wanted the Community, most of the youth wanted independence. (Ivory Coast, Assemblée territoriale, "Debates," June 19, 1958.) This was also repeated in many interviews.

[60] Speech of September 7, 1958.

[61] The Assembly voted an order of mission, which made it possible to defray their campaign expenses from public funds. (*La Semaine en A.O.F.*, September 13, 1958.)

practices, new ones were added. Several individuals who were suspected of harboring the intention of voting "no" were temporarily detained until after September 28; others were exiled to neighboring countries. Houphouet-Boigny had indeed warned his opponents when he first returned to the Ivory Coast that anybody, "whether black or white, native to this country or not, man or woman," who threatened to undermine friendly ties between the Ivory Coast and France, would have less than twenty-four hours to leave the country.[62] This warning was repeated throughout the campaign.[63]

During the days preceding the referendum, endorsements flowed in from every quarter. They ranged from the nearly defunct Socialist Party to the president of the Association of Traditional Chiefs; from European and Africans veterans' associations to the local branches of the C.A.T.C. The Great Imam of the mosque at Bondoukou advocated a "yes" vote side-by-side with the Ivory Coast section of the Radical-Socialist party. Even spokesmen for the provisional executive of the Ivory Coast section of U.G.T.A.N. endorsed the leader's affirmative stand.[64] According to official results, the Ivory Coast led the entire Community in participation and in the proportion of affirmative votes. Over 99 per cent of the registered voters had gone to the polls; less than 1 out of

[62] Speech of September 7, 1958. The use of coercion during the referendum was an open secret in the Ivory Coast in 1959. Instances were cited by party leaders, who were often frank about such things, and from dissenters who had been subjected to them. Two French research workers who were in the Ivory Coast at the time and who wanted to vote "no" for reasons related to domestic politics in the metropole were asked not to do so. Since abstentions were not allowable either, it was finally agreed to remove their name from the electoral register altogether. Camille Assi Adam, the opposition candidate in Agboville, was reported to have advocated a "yes" vote (*Abidjan-Matin*, September 15, 1958); he was absent on the day of the referendum, on a visit to Ghana, but was arrested when he returned and enjoined to leave the country on October 1. (*Afrique Nouvelle*, October 24, 1958.)

[63] *Le Monde*, September 28-29, 1958.

[64] These examples are taken from daily issues of *Abidjan-Matin*, September 8 to 28, 1958.

every 5,000 violated Houphouet-Boigny's instructions.[65] On December 4, 1958, by a unanimous vote of its Territorial Assembly, the Ivory Coast decided to become a republic—a member of the Community.[66]

The referendum did not resolve the issue of federation in Africa. According to the constitution, territories were free to regroup before joining the Community. The fate of French West Africa was now completely in the hands of the 7 territories that had voted "yes." But since the federation would automatically break up at the end of a transitional period unless action were taken to preserve it, the constitution actually played into the hands of the antifederalists. The Ivory Coast remained firmly opposed to the creation of a primary federation with an executive which would only be a "screen between Africa and France."[67] Houphouet-Boigny prevailed upon the bureau of the Coordination Committee of the R.D.A., where Guinea was no longer represented since it had left the Community, to recommend that the territories enter individually into the Community. He announced that member states might later endorse "an entirely new and daring formula," an association of states comprising a customs union. These states would coordinate development plans, public services, and other common matters, but would have no political control over one another. There would be a solidarity fund to which each member would contribute one-tenth of its public income.[68]

[65] The results in the Ivory Coast were: registered, 1,646,624; valid votes, 1,613,143; "yes," 1,612,818; "no," 225. In French West Africa as a whole, not including Guinea, turnout was 66.2 per cent; 96.8 per cent of these voted "yes." In Guinea, turnout was 76.5 per cent, with only 4.6 per cent voting affirmatively. The only other territory with a substantial proportion of "no" votes was Niger. It is probable that only the active involvement of the French administration resulted in a majority of "yes" in that territory. The official results were published in *La Semaine en A.O.F.*, October 4 and 11, 1958.

[66] Ivory Coast, Assemblée territoriale (Constituante), "Debates," December 4, 1958.

[67] *La Semaine en A.O.F.*, October 15, 1958.

[68] This was first announced in an interview published in *Carrefour*,

This formula was unacceptable to the federalists. After the P.R.A. tried in vain to convene a round table of all African leaders to settle the issue once and for all, the president of the Grand Council, Gabriel d'Arboussier, invited all territories to send representatives to a constitutional convention in order to launch a new federation. Senegal, Sudan, Dahomey, and Upper Volta answered his call to meet at Bamako in December. After coordinating their views, they met in Dakar the following month to adopt a provisional constitution for the Federation of Mali. The new alignments overshadowed all previous political affiliations in French West Africa. Modibo Keita, a vice-president of the R.D.A., who was elected President of the Legislative Assembly of Mali, declared that "the struggle is now no longer between the P.R.A. and the R.D.A. but between federalists and antifederalists."[69] The Ivory Coast did not remain inactive. Houphouet-Boigny pursued his own scheme with the tacit support of France. By the time French West Africa ceased to exist, on April 1, 1959, the Federation of Mali was reduced to only Senegal and Sudan. One month later, two of its erstwhile members, Upper Volta and Dahomey, joined the Ivory Coast and Niger to launch the *Conseil de l'Entente* in Abidjan.

"Communauté, Non; Indépendance, Oui"

The decision to forego independence was soon reversed. It was superseded by another choice more in keeping with the prevailing trend in contemporary Africa and with the predispositions of the population of the Ivory Coast. The Community was stillborn. Independent Guinea, warmly ac-

---

October 15, 1958. Houphouet-Boigny indicated that in Europe, integration had to begin in the economic sphere; the political aspects could only come after a firm base had been established.

[69] *La Semaine en Afrique Occidentale*, February 21, 1959. For a useful summary of these realignments, see Thomas Hodgkin and Ruth Schachter, "French-Speaking West Africa in Transition," *International Conciliation*, No. 528 (May 1960), pp. 420-28.

claimed as a new nation—after having been deserted by France—became an irresistible pole of attraction for other French-speaking territories, for whom less than international status was intolerable. The administrative arrangements of the Community, more than its legal institutions, indicated that France had no intention of sharing sovereignty with the other members. Some African leaders wondered whether they had not lost a friend when their traditional foe, the Ministry of Overseas France, was dismantled and replaced by a maze of secretariats.[70] The Community did not fulfill its promise of accrued benefits to the members either. Less than a year after the referendum, the Ivory Coast, more devoted than any other member to the ideal of a Franco-African marriage, reminded the metropole that love was not enough. As the Baoulé maidens sing to their suitors, the Ivory Coast told France, "Friend, I gave myself to you; now it is up to you to keep me."[71]

When Madagascar and Mali requested the transfer of jurisdiction over common matters to their own governments, De Gaulle announced that they could remain in the Community even though they were independent.[72] The Ivory Coast announced soon afterwards that it would never be willing to play second fiddle to her fellow members.[73] In May 1960 a few

[70] This was expressed in an article entitled "Faut-il regretter la Rue Oudinot?" which appeared in *Afrique Nouvelle*, March 14, 1959.

[71] This was planted in the midst of a debate on agricultural cooperatives by Mamadou Coulibaly at the request of Houphouet-Boigny himself. (Ivory Coast, *Débats de l'assemblée législative*, No. 7 [1959], p. 87.) The theme was repeated also at a specially convened congress of the R.D.A. in September 1959. This cannot be seen as an interterritorial congress in the same way as the one held in Bamako in 1957. Neither the *Union Soudanaise* nor the *Parti Démocratique de Guinée*, both R.D.A. affiliates, sent delegates.

[72] In the course of a speech delivered during the Sixth Meeting of the Executive Council of the Community, Saint-Louis, Senegal, December 12, 1959. (*Le Monde*, December 14, 1959.) De Gaulle insisted on calling this "international sovereignty" rather than "independence."

[73] "Nous n'accepterons jamais une situation diminuée . . .," *Fraternité*, April 18, 1960.

days after Madagascar and Mali signed agreements providing for accession to full sovereignty, Article 86 of the French constitution was amended to accommodate independent states.[74] This Commonwealth-like *Communauté rénovée* was, two years late, the formula advocated by Sékou Touré; ironically, it also came close to a proposal sponsored by Ferhat Abbas in 1946.[75] The Ivory Coast, in an attempt to outbid its nationalist-minded neighbors, declared that this new scheme was unacceptable. Comparing itself to the bride who was left standing in front of the church, the country announced its intention of leaving the Community altogether.[76] On August 7, 1960, less than two years after having unanimously voted "yes," the Ivory Coast unanimously changed its mind.[77] Only after admission to the United Nations did it negotiate agreements of aid and cooperation with France. But the leaders remained adamant on their refusal to return to the fold.[78]

[74] According to Article 85 of the constitution, Title XII, devoted to the Community, could be amended by a simple vote of parliament and of the senate of the Community. The amendments added three paragraphs to Article 86, eliminating the need for a referendum to implement a decision of the legislative assembly of the member state under consideration; specifying that member states could become independent by means of negotiated agreements for the transfer of jurisdiction over common matters without automatically being cast out of the Community; and finally, that an independent state could enter into the Community without losing its sovereign status. (*Le Monde, Sélection hebdomadaire*, No. 617, August 11-17, 1960.)

[75] Professor Pinto pointed out that the guiding principle of the new Community was contained in Articles 107-110 of his proposal, rejected by the Second Constituent Assembly. (*Ibid.*)

[76] *Fraternité*, June 3, 1960.

[77] Agreements of transfer of jurisdiction over common matters were signed on July 11; they were approved by the French parliament on July 20, and unanimously by a standing ovation in the Ivory Coast Assembly at a solemn session on July 27, 1960. Independence was proclaimed at 0001 hours on August 7, 1960.

[78] The Ivory Coast was admitted to the United Nations in the fall of 1960, sponsored by France. Official circles there were much more tolerant of Houphouet-Boigny's *mouvement d'humeur* than they had been of Sékou Touré. Agreements of aid and cooperation were negotiated throughout the spring of 1961.

Internal Consequences

Although the Ivory Coast's choice of September 1958 signified a postponement rather than a rejection of independence, nevertheless, it revealed a lasting characteristic of the regime. For reasons previously stated, Houphouet-Boigny consciously relinquished the ideological tenets and the rhetoric of nationalism. The Ivory Coast Republic postponed choosing a flag for a whole year because it was thought investors would flock more readily toward the tricolor.[79] Writing in the party newspaper in 1959, Philippe Yacé, then acting general secretary of the P.D.C.I., reasserted that "we refuse to offer the present generation as a holocaust to future generations in the name of any ideology whatsoever."[80] One French observer, writing for a leftist public, described the political vocabulary he heard in the Ivory Coast as "borrowed from the radical-socialist jargon."[81] This mood has prevailed even after independence and has meant that the regime sees enemies on the left rather than on the right, if these terms may be adapted to the African context. The Ivory Coast's foes are not the "colonialist powers" or the "neo-colonialist infiltrators" but rather the nations that call themselves "revolutionary" and those who advocate rapid and radical change inside and outside the country.

The fact that the regime was on the defensive had a profound effect on the political climate while the country was framing its constitution in the months that followed the referendum. After Guinea became independent, the Ivory Coast

[79] This justification was given by A. Denise in February 1959. (Ivory Coast, Assemblée constituante, "Procès-Verbaux de la commission spéciale" [Abidjan, 1959], p. 25.)

[80] *Fraternité*, December 25, 1959.

[81] J. Carta, "Côte d'Ivoire: La bourgeoisie noire s'installe," *France-Observateur*, September 3, 1959. This issue of the French non-communist left-wing weekly was seized by the Ivory Coast government. Although the article cited contains many factual mistakes, it reflects fairly accurately the political mood of the country at the time.

leaders were more acutely aware than they had been during the campaign of the alienation of important segments of the population. The founding fathers were disturbed by the malaise that pervaded the entire country, a mood which even a newly arrived observer could perceive. The legitimacy of their rule was based on mass support, but they knew that the support they had elicited for their policies had been artificially engineered. There was a widespread loss of faith. Uncertainty prevailed, but the cost of obtaining information by means of free elections or by open discussion among the leadership increased as popular impatience grew. This led to further substitution of coercion for information and to continued uncertainty.

The decision to enter into the Community was partly motivated by concern over national integration; Ivory Coast leaders also sometimes justified their antifederation stand by arguing that it was necessary to create unity first within each territory. It is possible, however, that the choices they made in 1958 exacerbated ethnic conflicts and created further obstacles to national integration. Less than a month after the referendum, the Ivory Coast underwent the most intense disturbances in recent history. Incited by the *Ligue des Originaires de Côte d'Ivoire* (L.O.C.I.), an association composed mainly of low-level white-collar workers, the population of Abidjan turned against foreign Africans and especially against Dahomeyan and Togolese residents. The government was unable to bring the situation under control. After three days of rioting, from October 24 through 26, 1958, there were at least 6 dead and several score wounded. More than 500 houses were damaged or destroyed. An estimated 20,000 foreign Africans had found temporary refuge in the old Abidjan harbor, where they were given police protection. Related events occurred throughout the country. By the end of the year, over 25,000 Africans had left the Ivory Coast.[82]

[82] It was reported that the Minister of the Interior, J.-B. Mockey,

This phenomenon was only one manifestation, perhaps somewhat more dramatic than others, of the latent antagonisms between natives and foreigners noted throughout this study. Tribes of the interior, whose homeland was "invaded" by immigrants, and tribes of the Abidjan lagoon, swamped by the rapid growth of the city, seem to have played a major part in the Dahomeyan events. The fact that aggression was directed against people from the Benin Gulf in particular was due to their special position in the Ivory Coast occupational structure. Throughout the preceding decade, territorial representatives complained that these immigrants had cornered the market for white-collar jobs.[83] Competition among employees was

---

allegedly had been told well in advance of these events that the L.O.C.I. was planning to take some sort of drastic action, but that the government did nothing. The first clash occurred when L.O.C.I. members attacked a Togolese on October 19. They were questioned by the police. Sensing trouble, Mockey broadcast an appeal to order on October 22 directed to the *foreigners*, reassuring them that the rumors circulated by the *Association des Travailleurs de la Côte d'Ivoire*—another name for the L.O.C.I.—about the forthcoming expulsion of foreigners were unfounded. He added that the Africans expelled during the campaign and after the referendum had been involved in subversive activities. On the next day, the P.D.C.I. issued a statement condemning the L.O.C.I. but apparently felt that they had enough support to warrant negotiations. A meeting of all youth organizations was called for October 25. On the preceding day, however, leaflets called upon the population to take direct action against all foreigners. The L.O.C.I. leaders were arrested. This precipitated an all-out attack on Dahomeyan and Togolese residences which began that afternoon. This account is based on reports in *Afrique Nouvelle*, *La Semaine en A.O.F.* (A.F.P. dispatches), *Abidjan-Matin*, and *Le Monde*. For a narrative account and interpretation, see also Gwendolen Carter, *Independence for Africa* (New York: Praeger, 1960), Chapter X, "The Ivory Coast Expels Stranger Africans," pp. 106-18.

[83] Dahomeyans and Togolese had been recruited to work in the Ivory Coast before that territory began to produce a white-collar stratum of its own. By the 1950's, they had become firmly entrenched in private and public bureaucracies and naturally sought to facilitate recruitment of their own compatriots. Ivoiriens began to object to the continued stream of candidates from other countries who took examinations for service in that territory. In 1954 the government acknowledged that about one-third of those recruited that year as *commis* in the governmental sector were *non-originaires*. (Ivory Coast, Assemblée territoriale, "Debates," December 17, 1954.) This was also the case in the private

particularly keen in 1958 because the boom that began around 1952 had tapered off, leaving pockets of unemployment in its wake. In addition, the complex of circumstances of 1958 helped bring existing tensions to the point of explosion. By promoting Ivory Coast isolationism, the leadership not only responded to popular pressures but also indirectly condoned overt manifestations of antiforeign sentiments at home. The death in September 1958 of Ouezzin Coulibaly, who had been the keystone of the coalition of natives and foreigners that had insured the success of the P.D.C.I. during its formative years, deprived the party of its most skilled negotiator in this type of conflict.[84] Finally, there is no doubt that the level of frustration among civil servants and youth groups ran high after the referendum because they had not been allowed to vent freely their anti-European and anticolonial feelings. It is possible that foreign Africans constituted a convenient object for displaced aggressions.

The Ivory Coast government not only denied that these incidents were an expression of Ivory Coast *racisme* but asserted that they were the result of a concerted attempt to embarrass the regime. The government maintained that they were engineered by foreigners, who had recently been expelled from the country, working hand-in-hand with pro-communist

---

sector, where Dahomeyans and Togolese were thought to show more initiative and desire for self-improvement than Ivoiriens. (Ivory Coast, Chambre de Commerce, *Bulletin Mensuel*, No. 11-12 [November-December 1957], p. 81.) Tensions were so great in 1955 that the leaders of the *Solidarité Daho-Togo* in Abidjan requested control over the further immigration of their compatriots "lest the immigrants come to a bad end." (*Abidjan-Matin*, March 3, 1955.) To the resentment stemming from economic sources may be added a less easily identifiable factor. Dahomeyans, in the eyes of Ivoiriens, are very skilled wielders of black magic. The author was assured by high-level Ivory Coast officials that they practiced human sacrifices, for which their historical kingdom had been famous, in their neighborhood in Abidjan as well. No Ivoirien would wander there after dark. As is often the case, economic resentment and other fears complement each other.

[84] I am particularly grateful to Dr. Ruth Schachter Morgenthau of Boston University for bringing this point to my attention.

labor leaders, who sought to destroy the Community.[85] Public explanations aside, the regime was deeply disturbed. The events of October demonstrated the government's ineffectiveness, its lack of authority over the population, its inability to face a crisis. Civil disorder of this magnitude jeopardized all plans for economic development, contingent on the promotion abroad of an attractive image of the Ivory Coast as a peaceful, prosperous, industrious, and politically stable country in the midst of the tide of African nationalism. Houphouet-Boigny's prestige at the superterritorial level was diminished at the very time he was involved in a struggle for influence over other territories of French West Africa, including, among others, Dahomey. The events also indicated that the gap between the regime and some of the elements whose support was needed for rapid development, the civil servants and the workers, had continued to grow. If the government was unable to control them when they directed their resentment against foreigners, would it be able to withstand the next onslaught of discontent, perhaps directed at the regime itself?

These preoccupations, foremost in the minds of the leaders at the beginning of 1959, were somewhat offset by the beneficial economic consequences of the 1958 decisions. Community membership helped maintain prosperity by temporarily solving the coffee crisis, which had grown in acuity during the last two years, through continued market protection and indirect subsidies.[86] Dissolution of the federation

[85] See the Minister of the Interior's statement in *Abidjan-Matin*, November 3, 1958, and Houphouet-Boigny's assertions in an interview published in *Afrique Nouvelle*, December 12, 1958.

[86] At the time of the referendum, the price paid for Ivory Coast coffee in Le Havre was about 20 per cent higher than in the world market. In 1958 the average price per kg. was 77.5 cents in New York, 92 cents in Le Havre; in 1959, for the first six months, 65 cents and 71 cents respectively. (Communauté Economique Européenne, *Etude* . . ., p. 12.) In 1960, when coffee dropped to 15 cents per lb. in New York, i.e. 1.62 NF per kg., it brought 3.40 in France. (*Marchés Tropicaux*, March 11, 1961, p. 611.)

of French West Africa was reflected in further budgetary growth in the Ivory Coast. When the country began to receive the import taxes hitherto collected by Dakar, overnight, its public revenue increased by more than half.[87] Such a windfall enabled the government to substitute increased expenditures on tangible items such as schools, roads, and hospitals, for nationalist satisfactions. The regime was able to announce on January 1, 1960, that the *impôt de capitation*, the hated head-tax, which symbolized the last remnant of colonialism, was eliminated forever.[88] This was new fuel for the machine. But as P.D.C.I. leaders faced their new tasks, they realized that their organization was inadequate. Major modifications were needed in the party in order to overcome the problem of national integration and to give the government an unfailing instrument with which to control the country. While the rulers of the Ivory Coast attempted to control growing discontent among those who shared the African dream of independence, they knew that the Community relationship was untenable for very long. The need to prepare the country to face independence added to the sense of urgency.

[87] To the estimated income of 11,786,223,000 C.F.A. frs. for 1958, import taxes (customs and excise) added an estimated 6,173,000,000. This and gains from natural increases and better collection methods brought the estimated revenue for 1959 to 21,723,000,000, almost a doubling in one year. Revenue estimates for 1960 and 1961 were 25 and 27 billion respectively. (Annual estimates contained in Ivory Coast, *Budget pour 1958* [Abidjan: Imprimerie du Gouvernement, 1957]; *ibid.* for following years.)

[88] Ivory Coast, *Journal Officiel*, January 1, 1960 and *Fraternité*, January 5, 1960.

CHAPTER VIII

THE INSTRUMENTS OF RULE

FRANCE, otherwise loath to relinquish sovereignty to her dependencies, gave members of the Community complete control over the process of constitution making When work began on a basic law for the Ivory Coast after the referendum, most opposition leaders were either in exile or had rejoined the P.D.C.I.-sponsored coalition.[1] There were no organs of public opinion in which the projects might be discussed.[2] The constitution of 1959 was therefore framed by a government and an assembly dominated by a single party, itself controlled by one man. The decision-making process itself reveals that Houphouet-Boigny and his lieutenants, accountable only to one another, were unusually free to institutionalize their own political preferences. A local consultative committee composed of high-ranking party

[1] Pascal Krasso Gnahore, general secretary of the Ivory Coast section of the P.R.A., resigned to join the P.D.C.I. in October. (*La Semaine en A.O.F.*, October 4, 1958.) Digna Bailly, after having challenged the P.D.C.I. in 1957, hesitated but eventually joined in December 1958. (*Abidjan-Matin*, January 3, 1959.) Camille Assi Adam was in Guinea. The former opposition deputy, Sékou Sanogo, who had joined the party in May 1956, died in Bouaké on September 26, 1958. Houphouet-Boigny's sheer survival helps account for his political dominance. He was the oldest of the four Africans who had held office as Ivory Coast representatives in the National Assembly since 1945, but he alone survived in 1958. This fact also helps explain his great concern over his health, reflected in recurrent trips to Switzerland to rest.

[2] The only daily newspaper, *Abidjan-Matin*, is part of a French-owned chain and does not comment on political events. There was not even a party newspaper until *Fraternité* was launched in April 1959. *La Concorde* had disappeared. Other occasional publications were *Kô-moë*, published by Ivory Coast students in Paris, and "Action Démocratique," a mimeographed sheet published by a Catholic-minded group led by A. Niava. Outside papers have a very limited circulation. The only one concerned with Africa is the outstanding publication launched by the White Fathers in Dakar, *Afrique Nouvelle*. The Ivory Coast government occasionally seized individual issues of outside newspapers that contained information it found objectionable. The local radio station is part of S.O.R.A.F.O.M., a government-controlled corporation.

leaders and a few Africans and Europeans with legal training was formed shortly before the referendum to study a project drafted by the Ivory Coast government. Their proposals were discussed in Paris after the referendum by the coordinating committee of the R.D.A. in order to harmonize the constitutions of R.D.A.-dominant states. The project was then returned to the Ivory Coast at the end of 1958 and transformed into a modified government draft. This was submitted to a committee of 24 members of the Assembly, which included all the members of the committee on legislation, the presidents of the other committees, and whatever high-ranking party members were not included in the first two categories. This group was due to meet in January. When disagreements arose between some of its members and the government, a mission was sent to Houphouet-Boigny in Paris in order to secure his arbitration. The committee finally examined the draft from February 12 to February 21, for a total of 23 hours.[3] So far, none of these proceedings had been made public. The revised draft was returned to the government, which finally submitted the ultimate version to the Assembly. The constitution was not subjected to further examination but was approved with almost no debate in the Assembly on March 26, 1959.[4]

A similar situation prevailed the following year when a new constitution was drafted after independence. The process was even simpler. A law passed on July 27, 1960, made it unnecessary to resort to referendum for constitutional change if the proposed revision received a majority of four-fifths of the members of the Assembly. The chiefs of state of the *Conseil de l'Entente* met from August 8 to 11, 1960, to discuss common constitutions. Afterwards, a draft was adopted by the Ivory Coast Council of Government on October 14 and submitted on October 18 to a special committee of the As-

[3] Ivory Coast, Assemblée constituante, "Avant-Projet constitutionnel. Procès-verbaux des travaux de la commission spéciale." (mimeographed).
[4] Ivory Coast, Assemblée constituante, "Debates," March 26, 1959.

sembly that included all members. After a much shorter session, in which no modifications were made, the draft was returned to the government. When it was submitted to the Assembly on October 31 it was approved unanimously without debate.[5]

In keeping with the characteristics of the regime, the founding fathers did not derive guidance from one of the major ideologies available in the contemporary world but sought instead to implement a set of *ad hoc* political principles derived from their own political experience and from their appraisal of the country's needs.

The Ivory Coast Constitution

Political Thought

The Ivory Coast wants to be modern. As Shils has suggested, modernity entails democracy because a regime of civilian rule, through representative institutions founded on public liberties, is "the predominant, visible model, the model which commands assent by its actual achievement and by the prestige of the power and ascendancy of its earthly embodiments."[6] Only democracy can provide legitimacy for a modern regime. In the constitution of 1959, the founding fathers duly proclaimed their adherence to the principles of 1789 and to the Universal Declaration of Human Rights; defined the Ivory Coast as a democratic and social republic, erected on the principle of government of the people, by the people, and for the people; and declared for good measure that sovereignty belongs to the people and that no section of the people nor any individual may attribute to themselves the exercise thereof.[7] These pledges were renewed the following year.[8]

[5] Ivory Coast, *Débats de l'assemblée nationale*, No. 13 (1960), pp. 137-49 and No. 16 (1960), pp. 177-84.

[6] Shils, p. 380.

[7] Preamble, Articles 3 and 4, "Constitution de la République de Côte d'Ivoire" (Loi No. 59-1 of March 26, 1959; Ivory Coast, *Journal*

However, their concern with effectiveness has led them to qualify these assertions. As early as the campaign for the referendum, Houphouet-Boigny had stated: "Although I am against violence, although I am a democrat . . . although I hope that democracy will be triumphant, I want it to be known here . . . as well as beyond our near and distant borders . . . that here, in the Ivory Coast, we shall not accept license in place of freedom or of democracy."[9] He reminded his audience on this occasion of the limits imposed on democracy in other countries. In a well-established, stable democracy such as the United States, he explained, the government claimed that it was necessary to erect a protective barrier around a measly one-hundred-odd communists. Similarly, in the Soviet Union, although some dissent was tolerated within the party, the government would never accept penetration by bourgeois elements. "If so, then what about us in the Ivory Coast . . .? We are barely born to political life. We must seek help from the metropole or from other sources to make fruitful the wealth on which the lives of our brothers are dependent. Should we allow, because of our immoderate love of freedom or of democracy, an irresponsible minority to endanger the regime which we have freely chosen? Do not count on me to make such an error."[10]

In the same vein, the president of the constitutional committee of the Territorial Assembly warned one of his colleagues, who had advocated the use of the referendum in constitutional revision, against putting too much trust in the people.[11] Later, he amplified his statement as follows: "Democracy is a system of government for virtuous people. It seldom works

---

Officiel [Abidjan: Imprimerie du Gouvernement, March 28, 1959].)

[8] Preamble, Articles 2 and 3, "Constitution de la République de Côte d'Ivoire" (Ivory Coast, *Journal Officiel*. [Abidjan: Imprimerie du Gouvernement, November 4, 1960].)

[9] Speech of September 6, 1958.

[10] *Ibid.*

[11] Ivory Coast, "Avant-projet . . .," p. 23.

even in very mature countries. Why should we expect it to work here? We must be realistic. Our people are ignorant of the problems we face. They cannot be left to choose the solutions to our overwhelming problems but must approve the alternatives debated by an elite."[12] Similarly, the secretary-general of the P.D.C.I. saw the potential consequences of democracy as incompatible with the tasks at hand: "We don't want democracy to be a source of cleavages, of childish struggles in the course of which the better part of our energies would be wasted. We want . . . to pursue in peace and in union the work of national construction."[13]

It is on the basis of the complexity of this task that the leadership has justified their choice of institutions. In 1959 Prime Minister Denise reminded the constitutional committee that national construction required civic education, the elimination of tribalism, the development of educational and health facilities, "and above all, . . . foreign investments." Because of the Dahomeyan riots, many potential investors were hesitant. He concluded that "if we want to achieve our ultimate goals, which are to raise the standard of living of the Ivory Coast, to eradicate misery in all its forms, we must continue our policy of investments and in order to do this we need a stable government."[14] The goals were defined even more broadly after independence. P. Yacé outlined them for all the entente states as follows:

"a. The social and economic revolution of our States.
b. Restructuration of our traditional society in order to bring about evolution in harmony and without jolts.
c. Affirmation of authority, hitherto exercised by the colonial power for its own benefit and therefore not accepted by the Africans.

[12] Interview with Me. Camille Alliali, 1959.
[13] In a speech to an assembly of government employees. (*Fraternité*, February 12, 1960.)
[14] Ivory Coast, "Avant-projet . . .," pp. 114-16.

d. Institutionalization of a civic conscience (struggle against the ambitious and the greedy).
e. Construction of national unity (feelings still diffuse and hampered by a multiplicity of ethnic groups and racial boundaries)."[15]

These immense tasks, he concluded, legitimize a power that is authoritarian and strong. Because of this need for strong power the political system under which the Ivory Coast was nurtured—the parliamentary regime of the Fourth Republic—stood as a negative model to be avoided at any price. Prime Minister Denise reminded his colleagues of the consequences of such an ineffective constitutional framework in Europe after World War II:

"While small countries such as Belgium and Eastern Germany [*sic*] . . . were able to rebuild themselves rapidly by means of a healthy economy, France, because of her parliamentary regime, has only recently healed her wounds. . . . The ultimate result . . . was nearly to lead her to the abyss. . . . If . . . France did not perish, it is because she is an old country which was always able to rely on a two-thousand year old Administration.

"Therefore, if a country such as France, with a solid Administrative base managed with superlative skill, nearly sank because of a deficient parliamentary regime, I believe that the danger is even greater for a young country such as our own, because we have a great deal left to create."[16]

The Constitution of 1959

Although many would have preferred a presidential system outright, this solution was avoided in 1959 because of Houphouet-Boigny's desire to reinforce the significance of De Gaulle's role as head of state of the entire Community. The new system elaborated by the metropole for its own use

[15] Ivory Coast, *Débats de l'assemblée nationale*, No. 13 (1960), p. 138.
[16] Ivory Coast, "Avant-projet . . .," pp. 114-15.

and embodied in the constitution of the Fifth Republic, a parliamentary system modified to insure preeminence of the executive, provided a convenient model for new "intermediate" institutions in the Ivory Coast.[17] As in France, the Assembly's legislative powers were restricted by means of a limitative definition of the proper domain of the law, as contrasted with the *domaine règlementaire* in which the executive decides by means of its rule-making power. Furthermore, within its own domain, there were areas in which the Assembly could only set forth general principles, leaving specific proposals to the government.[18] The executive was given further control by the stipulation, once again as in the Fifth Republic, that members of the Assembly could not propose bills and amendments that would decrease public revenue or increase public expenditure without providing equivalent compensation. The cabinet's bills were given priority on the legislative calendar; when a government bill was reported out, the Assembly was to discuss it rather than any counterproject of its own.[19] Finally, since the government received the authority to execute

[17] *Ibid.*, p. 53. For a discussion of these devices in the Fifth Republic, see Stanley H. Hoffman, "The French Constitution of 1958: I. The Final Text and Its Prospects," *The American Political Science Review*, LIII, No. 2 (June 1959), 338-39.

[18] According to Article 37 of the constitution of 1959, rules are established by law in the following areas: civic rights and fundamental liberties, marriage and inheritance, and harmonization of local custom with constitutional principles, criminal procedure, definition of crimes and their punishment, organization of tribunals, determination and allocation of all taxes, electoral rules, creation of public institutions, rules concerning civil service, general organization of the administration, state of emergency. The law sets forth general principles in the areas of: administration of units of local government, education, property rights, labor legislation, control over the property of the state, cooperation, prisons, transport. Article 39 states that what is not in the legislative domain is in the domain of executive rule making; the latter is thus the residual category.

[19] Articles 42, 43, and 44. As in the case of France, the fact that the constitution specified the procedure to follow in examining bills subjected the Assembly to specific limits within which it could make its own internal rules. (For France, see Hoffman, *The American Political Science Review*, LIII, 338-39.)

the budget by simple ordinance if it was not voted in time by the Assembly, the legislative branch was thoroughly emasculated.[20]

By far the most important guarantee of executive dominance was contained in the definition of the political responsibility of the prime minister. Articles 48 to 52, which dealt with this question, took up about one-fourth of the total amount of time devoted to discussion of the constitution in the Assembly and gave rise to heated controversy within the party.[21] The government proposed three possibilities. First, the prime minister can request a vote of confidence on his general program and, if defeated by an absolute majority of the membership of the Assembly, his government must resign.[22] Secondly, the prime minister can request a vote of confidence on a specific text; the item is considered to have been adopted unless a motion of censure is tabled within 24 hours and approved by an absolute majority of the membership of the Assembly,[23] in which case also the government must resign. Thirdly, the Assembly can initiate procedures leading to the government's downfall if two-thirds of its members approve a motion of censure 24 hours after it has been tabled. In the last instance, resignation of the government brings about dissolution of the Assembly as well.[24] The very high price the Assembly must pay for any attempt to control the government gave rise to much protest among high-level party leaders who were not members of the executive. They agreed that stability was necessary but, as Coffi Gadeau put it, some

[20] Article 46. Similar provisions had governed the Territorial Assembly when it was first created in 1946.

[21] These articles took up 6 of the 23 hours spent by the committee in debate, an average of 72 minutes per article compared with an average of 16 minutes for the remaining 66 articles of the constitution. (Computed from Ivory Coast, "Avant-projet . . .") There were also informal meetings of party leaders on this issue some of which the author was allowed to attend.

[22] Article 48 of the government draft.

[23] Article 51 of the government draft.

[24] Articles 49 and 50 of the government draft.

control was needed because there was no guarantee anywhere that the government would effectively carry out the program for which the Assembly will have granted its confidence.[25] One of the members of the younger generation, recruited to the Assembly in 1957, added that there was danger also that too much stability might lead to *immobilisme*.[26] Debate was so animated that the entire issue was withdrawn from committee to be ironed out in the inner circle of the party.[27] Notwithstanding many attempts to substitute new articles for the old, the government was adamant, and its proposals, in slightly modified form, were adopted by the committee in a second reading.

When the constitution finally reached the floor of the Assembly, it had been modified even further to benefit the executive. Now, the government could wield great pressure to obtain support for its policies because its defeat under *any* conditions automatically brought about dissolution of the Assembly as well. A concession was made to the Assembly by specifying that the government could request a vote of confidence only on a statement of general policy, or on a proposal directly related to the implementation of such a statement.[28] Significantly, those who had dissented in committee now supported a constitution weighted even more heavily in favor of the executive than the original draft had been. Asked to explain why he changed his mind, one of the dissenters interviewed said that Houphouet-Boigny had personally convinced him of the paramount need for stability. Nevertheless, because there was still much uneasiness about this issue, Houphouet-Boigny interrupted the proceedings of the Assembly on March 26, 1959, and spoke from his deputy's

[25] Ivory Coast, "Avant-projet . . .," pp. 116-17. [26] *Ibid.*, p. 123.

[27] Coffi Gadeau, organizational secretary of the P.D.C.I., even threatened to resign unless the Assembly's powers were restored to some extent. He did not carry out his threat, however, and became Minister of the Interior.

[28] Articles 48 to 51, constitution of 1959.

desk to justify the system. In order to fulfill the promises they had made to the people, he stated, complete separation of powers was necessary. The Assembly must legislate and the executive must govern. When the Assembly approves the government's general program, it becomes obligated to give the executive the means needed to carry it out. If this pact is broken, he continued, then both Assembly and government must go to the people. The Assembly was by no means a rubber stamp, he concluded, because it had the last word in the sphere of legislation, properly speaking, when the legislation was not related to the government's program. After this explanation, Articles 48 to 52 were approved unanimously along with the remainder of the constitution.[29]

The Constitution of 1960

Yet, even this was deemed insufficient to insure an effective and stable government. After independence, the search for appropriate institutions began anew. Unhampered this time by any obligation toward the Community, the constitution-makers broadened their scope to include a wide range of contemporary institutions. The president of the constitutional committee reported to the Assembly: "A prior critical analysis of the contemporary constitutional experiments was necessary because, nurtured on the political philosophy of the 'social contract' and imbued with the old tradition of French parliamentarianism, we often found, in the course of these discussions—there is no shame in admitting it—that it was necessary to repress a kind of schoolboyish sentimentality."[30] The parliamentary model was rejected altogether because the greater effectiveness of other types seemed to be confirmed everywhere:

[29] The only change was an amendment by Houphouet-Boigny to add to the proposed institutions an economic and social council, inadvertently left out of the final draft. (Ivory Coast, Assemblée constituante, "Debates," March 26, 1959.)

[30] Ivory Coast, *Débats de l'assemblée nationale,* No. 13 (1960), p. 138.

"Carrying our observations to other experiences, one generalization was obvious from the very beginning: in the contemporary world, the States whose institutions reflect political health, including the United States, the U.S.S.R., Great Britain, Federal Germany, among others, have in common the same characteristic. They leave only a very unimportant place to parliamentary tradition.

"We came to the further conclusion that certain states of modest importance, modestly endowed by nature and by geography, are nevertheless managed in a healthy and wise fashion because they were able, from their birth onward, to avoid the mazes and the siren's song of the parliamentary regime or of government by Assembly. Tunisia is today the best illustration of this."[31]

Having completed their comparative analysis, the members of the committee agreed on a type of regime that combined legitimacy based on democratic principles with maximum effectiveness: "We have chosen a presidential regime because it offers, in our opinion and in the present circumstances, the best possibility of reconciling respect for democratic principles, of which Montesquieu said that they find no greater guarantee than in the separation of powers, with the existence of a strong and stable government."[32] The new institutions are visibly inspired from those that are thought to exist in the United States.[33] Executive power is wielded

[31] *Ibid.* The inclusion of Great Britain and West Germany in the category of non-parliamentary, stable political systems, is an interesting indication of the way in which African leaders rise above standard classifications and see what they want to perceive. Parliamentary system, to a French-speaking African, can by definition be only of the Fourth Republic type, and hence by definition unstable. Houphouet-Boigny and his lieutenants expressed their admiration for the British system in 1959 but selected those aspects which have prompted some British critics to decry executive dictatorship.

[32] *Ibid.* Although P. Yacé did not have any training in political science, he chose as his personal adviser the very able student of a distinguished French political scientist.

[33] The text of the constitution was published in *Journal Officiel de la Côte d'Ivoire,* November 4, 1960.

by a president, elected for five years by direct universal suffrage.[34] There is a one-house legislature, the National Assembly, also elected for a five-year period.[35] Finally, there is an independent judiciary and a supreme court, whose composition, membership, and functions are left to be defined by law.[36] But other constitutional provisions negate the separation of powers. The president can request a second reading of the law, in which case a two-thirds vote of the membership of the Assembly is required to override his veto, as in the American case;[37] but the president can also bypass the Assembly altogether and submit any proposal directly to the people to obtain its approval by referendum.[38] Finally, the narrow definition of the domain of the law, as well as the restrictions on the Assembly's power of the purse discussed in connection with the constitution of 1959 were retained in its successor.[39]

Institutionalization of the One-Party System

Political leaders had too much first-hand experience of French constitutional history to trust formal provisions alone to insure stability and strength. Competition between political parties for control of the government could only lead to disunity, they thought, because national unity was viewed as being synonymous with unanimous support for the P.D.C.I. Here appears the greatest gap between the democratic principles written into the constitution and political practice. In 1959 Houphouet-Boigny defined the limits within which he would tolerate the existence of an opposition:

"For the time being—and I am sure you know why I hope that this will last—the Ivory Coast is fortunate enough to have a movement that has gained a large majority throughout the country.

"As far as I am concerned, I am not against *any* opposition.

[34] Articles 8-12, 15-26.
[35] Articles 27-39.
[36] Articles 57-62.
[37] Article 13.
[38] Article 14.
[39] Articles 41, 47, 51.

I have defined the framework within which it could operate. Within the framework of the Community, which we have freely chosen, there is room for a policy of opposition, but not outside it. As long as the masses trust us, we will stand for no opposition or no party that questions the regime which we have freely chosen. This being stated, I repeat that there is room for opposition."[40]

Accordingly, Article 7 of the constitution guaranteed freedom of organization and expression to all parties and groups that respected democratic principles, those of the Community and of the Republic. Since these principles were not further defined, this meant in practice that the activities of almost any opponent of the regime could be restricted.[41]

Furthermore, because it felt that the penal code did not afford sufficient protection against dangers to the new institutions, the government demanded and obtained additional weapons to wield against dissenters.[42] A law "to reinforce the protection of the public order" provided, among other things, severe sanctions against persons who were guilty of actions and maneuvers that might discredit political institutions or their functioning or who received gifts or even promises of gifts in exchange for a commitment to undertake such actions.[43] It also modified the penal code to punish persons who published, diffused, divulged, or reproduced false news or documents if these actions, *whether they are performed in good or in bad faith*, lead to disobedience of the laws of the land, undermine the morale of the population, or discredit political institutions or their functioning. The same penalties would be incurred if the actions under consideration

[40] Ivory Coast, Assemblée constituante, "Debates," March 26, 1959.

[41] According to constitutional logic, the P.D.C.I. should not have been allowed to exist after it decided to leave the Community.

[42] The motives were explained by the Minister of Justice when the government tabled the law in the Assembly. (Ivory Coast, *Débats de l'assemblée législative*, No. 8 [1959], p. 103.)

[43] Law 59-118, *Journal Officiel*, September 1, 1959, Articles 1 and 2.

might have had such consequences.[44] These measures left little room for legitimate criticism and hence effectively discouraged any form of political competition or of public debate.

Within these narrow limits opposition might theoretically be tolerated. It was not viewed as a potential alternative government, however, but rather as a useful adjunct to the regime. Members of the Bureau Politique of the P.D.C.I. indicated, in response to questions during interviews, that they favored the existence of an opposition because it would give the masses something to fight against, as had been the case in the past. Without one, they found it very difficult to stir up enthusiasm among the rank-and-file. This doctrine was enunciated publicly by the Minister of Justice who told the Assembly that ". . . we are not trying to create a dictatorial political system. . . . An opposition may be necessary for a party, if only because it acts as a stimulus."[45] Several leaders admitted frankly that they had in mind for this purpose an opposition that was clearly ineffective. When Houphouet-Boigny told the Assembly that "if tomorrow our friend Niava organized a solid opposition to benefit from our weaknesses . . . well, I would invite all my friends to respect this opposition as England has so well respected Her Majesty's opposition,"[46] he knew very well, as did his entire audience, that Niava had no mass support and that he was neither willing nor able to compete with the P.D.C.I. even in a local election.[47]

[44] *Ibid.*, Article 4. The law also punished associations that deviated from their goals as stated in their registration on file with the government.

[45] Ivory Coast, *Débats de l'assemblée législative*, No. 8 (1959), p. 108.

[46] Ivory Coast, Assemblée constituante, "Debates," March 26, 1959.

[47] Albert Niava had organized a small Catholic-minded party, *Action Démocratique*, in 1957. Its major activity was the publication of a monthly mimeographed bulletin. It had some support among C.A.T.C. circles. But in 1959, when Houphouet-Boigny issued his invitation, Niava had given up all political activities and had even ceased publication of his bulletin. Houphouet-Boigny stated in an interview that Niava had come to ask him for a spot on the P.D.C.I.-sponsored ticket but that he had turned down his request in order to allow him to oppose more freely. Niava did not engage in further political activity.

Although the one-party system is not an article of faith in the Ivory Coast, many members of the ruling group, and even some dissenters, genuinely believe that in a country of this type only a single-party system is desirable. Some justified this argument on the basis of a Marxist notion of a correspondence between party and class. Since there were as yet no class distinctions in the Ivory Coast, there could be only one movement for the entire country. Sometimes it was argued in reverse that since parties were a manifestation of class cleavages, it was imperative to prevent the appearance of another one in order to avoid the development of a class struggle.[48] A similar argument was based on the imperative of national unity. Before independence, it was said that political competition interfered with the achievement of unity. On the very day of independence, the general secretary of the P.D.C.I. asserted that now, when the country could no longer count on any outsiders to insure progress, sterile struggles were unjustified; the work of national construction required the total union of all live forces in the nation.[49] A year later, the Minister of the Interior asserted that *because* unity had been achieved, it would be inconceivable to have more than one party competing in future elections.[50]

Electoral procedures were modified to discourage competition without necessitating a law to forbid it altogether. In 1959 the country's 19 constituencies were collapsed into 4

[48] It is interesting to note that this way of thinking was retained by many of the older leaders of the P.D.C.I. who had otherwise relinquished all Marxist ideological commitments in 1951. For a theoretical justification of the one-party system by an individual reared in a similar political tradition, see Madeira Keita, "Le Parti Unique en Afrique Noire," *Présence Africaine*, xxx (February-March 1960), 3-24.

[49] P. Yacé, president of the National Assembly, in a speech before that body during the solemn session devoted to the declaration of independence. (Ivory Coast, *Débats de l'assemblée nationale*, No. 9 [1960], pp. 74-75.)

[50] In answer to a question in a press conference, *Fraternité*, June 9, 1961.

larger ones, with from 22 to 29 members each. Within each constituency, members were elected on a list basis through a simple majority, single-ballot system, with no preferential vote and no *panachage*. Only a complete ticket could be entered in each constituency.[51] This was modified the following year by the new constitution which provided for the National Assembly's election on the basis of a complete national list elected by a simple majority on a single ballot.[52] Thus, even if several slates competed in the election, the law made sure that the Assembly would be monolithic *after* the elections.

Neither in 1959 nor in 1960 did any slates except the one sponsored by the P.D.C.I. appear on the ballot. In practice, competition had become impossible. Caucusing for nominations on the party ticket continued until a few minutes before the deadline for filing. Before the list of candidates was published, no one was willing to announce his candidacy on some other slate since such a move might jeopardize his chances of selection by the P.D.C.I. By the time nominees were known, disappointed candidates had no time to regroup —with the more than 20 other non-party candidates in 1959 or with 69 others in 1960—to get their name on the ballot.[53] As for the presidential elections, it was made clear in advance that there was only one possible candidate for that office.[54] Thus, in 1960, the party newspaper announced that "on November 27 next, the Ivory Coast people will unanimously elect M. Félix Houphouet-Boigny President of the Republic

[51] Law 59-2, March 27, 1959. *Journal Officiel*, March 28, 1959.

[52] Article 29 of the constitution and Law 60-358 of November 7, 1960. *Journal Officiel*, November 10, 1960.

[53] The requirement of a $100 deposit also hampered potential opponents since an entire list of 1960 would have had to wage $7,000 even to get its name on the ballot.

[54] *Fraternité*, November 18, 1960. The president is elected directly, by an absolute majority on the first ballot or by a relative majority on a second ballot held two weeks later, if necesary. (Articles 9 and 10, constitution of 1960.)

and the seventy candidates of the P.D.C.I. deputies to the National Assembly."[55] The people did.

Neither a regime in which the executive was dominant, nor even a system from which political competition was eliminated, was deemed sufficient to insure modernization of the Ivory Coast. Until 1959, as was indicated earlier, Houphouet-Boigny ruled through persons interposed and kept apart from the day-to-day affairs of government. This may have enhanced his indispensability but at least it gave the appearance of shared responsibility. After the referendum, all pretense was dropped. First the youth group of the party, then the P.D.C.I. itself requested that Houphouet-Boigny personally assume leadership of the government. After much suspense, during which P. Yacé, president of the National Assembly, "engaged in the usual consultations" to tap potential prime ministers, it was announced that Houphouet-Boigny had accepted the position of president of the Council of Government.[56] One-man rule was openly institutionalized afterwards. Yacé told a meeting of the government employees that "the P.D.C.I. is now the governmental party in the Ivory Coast. Government, Assembly, and party therefore share the same single goal. This is why you find at the head of the government a chief, Houphouet-Boigny; at the head of the elected bodies a leader, Houphouet-Boigny; at the head of the party a President, Houphouet-Boigny."[57]

Like the restrictions imposed on the Assembly and on political competition, this too was justified because of the immense tasks of national construction: "You will agree that this objective can be attained only under the authority of a chief. Every undertaking requires a taskmaster. . . . Our road is a long one and it is full of obstacles. Because the country's future, the people's happiness, is at stake, the chief,

[55] *Fraternité*, November 18, 1960. The elections are discussed below.

[56] The progress he made was announced in all seriousness in daily news broadcasts during three days of consultations.

[57] *Fraternité*, February 26, 1960.

like a father, has the right, and even the duty, to be severe, to be demanding of his sons, who sometimes let themselves be led astray and whose faith is unsteady. . . ."[58] Furthermore, one-man rule was legitimate because it was freely chosen. "The authority of a chief is not incompatible with democracy. We have freely chosen a chief who gathers around himself all the live forces of the country. . . ."[59] Because this chief was like a father, his authority could only be benevolent: "The authority of the father is not that of a tyrant who imposes his will to power. Our own chief has given repeated proof of this. . . . What greater guarantee can be given of democracy?"[60] Although Ivoiriens freely admit that in the West there is need for strict constitutional checks upon a leader because power corrupts, there is a widespread faith that in Africa this is not needed because there are more subtle ways to maintain his accountability to the people: "There is something unique in African tradition that you cannot understand. Wherever you find a chief, he is never an autocrat: the chief always has a council made up of elders, leaders of clans, young men, etc. . . . Even Samory, whom many called a tyrant, consulted his lieutenants. Orders are always carried out and this makes you think of dictatorship. But there has always been prior discussion which insures that the orders will be carried out with the approval of all concerned."[61] In the final analysis, however, it is not a concern with effectiveness but rather with legitimacy that justifies one-man rule. The constitution, to be valid, must be tailored to the stature of the hero:

"We must also admit that if any Constitution is designed for the future, it must also be designed for the present.

"The political situation of the Ivory Coast, where there exists nearly nation-wide unanimity around one man, his ideas,

[58] *Ibid.*, February 12, 1960. [59] *Ibid.* [60] *Ibid.*
[61] Interview with Me. Camille Alliali, 1959.

his program, around one party whose leader assures the rule of the State and from whom the entire Assembly owes its existence, naturally calls forth, after independence, for a regime which gives to the Chief of State, who draws support from the national will, preeminence over all other institutions.

"Institutions that would not take this political fact into account would not obtain a hearing in public opinion and would assuredly not secure the popular support of our fellow-citizens."[62]

However, in order to fully understand the Ivory Coast constitution, it is necessary to look beyond its formal provisions and to examine the functioning of some of the new institutions.

The Regime at Work

Elections

Under a one-party system concerned with bolstering its legitimacy by means of mass support, elections remain important but have functions other than their primary one as a mechanism for choosing representatives or rulers. In the absence of overt opposition, abstentions are viewed in the Ivory Coast as a negative attitude. A major concern of the leadership has therefore been to secure a very high turnout. In 1959 Jean-Baptiste Mockey, then general secretary of the P.D.C.I. and Minister of the Interior, warned his radio audience that the government would interpret abstentions as an expression of a lack of interest in the future of the nation.[63] This theme was repeated daily in the only newspaper: "To abstain is to vote against"; "To vote is an act of faith"; "Voting is a civic duty which no one should avoid"; and finally, on the eve of the elections, "those who abstain tomorrow will be taking a stand against the Community." Within the Ivory Coast context, this made participation in the election manda-

[62] *Fraternité*, February 12, 1960.
[63] In a broadcast, April 9, 1959.

tory.[64] A similar concern prevailed after independence as well.

Shortly before the elections of November 1960, the party newspaper stated that although the outcome was of course known in advance, "... it would be an error to believe that the President of the R.D.A. and with him the deputies ... can do without the votes cast by the citizenry." The article continued:

"The approval of all must be manifest because implicit support alone would be synonymous with a lukewarm attitude. Such an attitude is perhaps the greatest danger that threatens a young nation which must move resolutely forward in order to acquire a choice spot on the world stage and to insure the happiness of all on the internal front.

"This is why on November 27 next, the President of the Republic will have to be assured not only of the approval of the immense majority of those who have validly cast their votes but of the total support of all eligible voters who, without exception, will consider voting as a sacred duty.

"The candidates to the office of *député*, designated by the Party upon the advice of the general secretaries of the *sous-sections*, with the support of the militants of the party, the approval of the Honorary President of the P.D.C.I. and of the highest instances of the party, will have to be assured of the same massive support throughout the country.

"In this manner the Ivory Coast will reinforce her unity and present to the face of the world a bloc without cleavages, capable of weathering any storm whatsoever."[65]

Deploring the mood of "friendly apathy," which he had found during his latest tour of the country, Yacé explained in a press conference that after independence it was more necessary than ever for the citizens to participate actively in the task

[64] These slogans were gathered from various issues of *Abidjan-Matin* during March and April 1959.

[65] *Fraternité*, November 11, 1960.

of national construction. Colonialism had resulted in a *laisser-aller* attitude which was intolerable in a new nation. The electoral compaign, he concluded, was an excellent occasion to overcome this deficiency.[66]

A campaign is in effect waged at public expense, much as was the case in a referendum. Crucial groups in the society are urged to announce their support of the ticket. Among them, in 1959, were the Guinean residents of the Ivory Coast,[67] as well as some Europeans who had been heard to mumble their dissatisfactions with Community policies.[68] In 1960 there was a particular concern with publicizing the support stemming from foreign residents in general.[69] Although party-government teams are sent everywhere, Houphouet-Boigny does not usually participate in the campaign except to visit areas where advance teams have found a very serious political problem to exist, as was the case in Daloa in 1960. The plebiscitary character of the elections appeared clearly when, in 1960, it was announced that anyone in Abidjan could vote in any polling place whatsoever, regardless of where he had been registered in past elections and even if he had not previously been registered.[70] All efforts are mobilized to insure a high turnout, but it is quite obvious that not all those who are recorded as having voted actually came to the polls. Since the electoral count is supervised by representatives of the various lists—in this case, the P.D.C.I.'s alone—this presents no difficulties whatsoever. Many Ivoiriens boasted during and after the 1959 elections that they had demonstrated their enthusiastic support for Houphouet-Boigny and for the P.D.C.I. by voting early and often.

[66] *Abidjan-Matin*, November 16, 1960.
[67] *Ibid.*, March 31, 1959.
[68] *Ibid.*, April 10, 1959.
[69] Endorsements were signed by A. Diop for the Senegalese community (*ibid.*, November 15, 1960) and by incumbent French members of the Legislative Assembly who were not about to be reelected. (*Ibid.*, November 26, 1960.)
[70] *Ibid.*, November 26, 1960.

The results of the three national elections held since the founding of the Republic are summarized in Table 19. Only

TABLE 19

One Party Elections in the Ivory Coast

Election	*Registered* (1)	*Votes Cast* (2)	*Valid* (3)	*Per Cent* (3) of (1)
Assembly, 1959[a]	1,609,345	1,523,580	1,522,324	94.5
Assembly, 1960[b]	1,661,833	1,593,135	1,586,518	95.7
Presidency, 1960[b]	1,661,833	1,641,542	1,641,352	98.7

[a] Four recently created *conseils généraux* were elected at the same time; results were very similar. *Abidjan-Matin*, April 15, 1959.
[b] Results were published in *Fraternité*, December 9, 1960.

a handful of *subdivisions* fell below 90 per cent participation in either 1959 or 1960. The most outstanding exception to the general rule of unanimity was Aboisso *subdivision* of Aboisso *cercle*, where only 23 per cent of the eligible voters turned out in 1959 and 73 per cent in 1960.[71] Dissent there could not be hidden, for in 1959, the Agni of Sanwi State who inhabit the region had taken the precaution of informing the French press and even General de Gaulle that they would abstain.[72]

Elections in a mass one-party system are, first of all, a form of self-imposed discipline for the party leaders, who feel that their concentration on administrative duties carries the danger of a loss of contact with the masses. Electoral cam-

[71] The results for Aboisso were as follows: *1959:* registered, 13,441; votes cast: 3,262; valid votes, 3,085. *1960:* (Assembly): registered, 14,222; votes cast, 10,396; valid votes, 10,396. *1960:* (Presidency): registered, 14,222; votes cast, 10,422; valid votes, 10,422. (In all cases, valid votes were all for the P.D.C.I. candidates.)

[72] Because of this, French newspaper correspondents happened to be in the region on the day before the election when the population refused to allow ballot boxes to be installed there, having been warned by their leaders that if these boxes were allowed to stay, they would become mysteriously filled overnight. The case of Aboisso will be discussed in the next chapter.

paigns are a regular occasion to test their continued mastery of the techniques of persuasion and leadership that made the party successful in the past. The reward for the leaders is renewed self-confidence. Secondly, elections are a way of obtaining information. Campaigns give the leaders an occasion to find out which of their decisions need explaining to the rank-and-file and then to supply the proper explanation. At the same time, they provide an occasion for inspection of the party structure at the local level. Thirdly, since the leaders are genuinely concerned with legitimacy, elections offer a dramatic occasion for a campaign of agitation and propaganda in favor of the party and its policies. As one party official put it, it is not sufficient to have people vote a certain way; they must know why they must do so and, preferably, genuinely want to do so. Fourthly, it is important to demonstrate to the outside world, whether to France or to other African countries with which the Ivory Coast negotiates or competes, that the regime has widespread support. In this sense, electoral results are used to prove the absence of silent opposition.[73] Finally, elections retain their manifest function of choosing representatives or at least of endowing the party's choice with legitimacy.

Representation and Recruitment

Although electoral competition has been eliminated, in the realm of recruitment of representatives competition still exists in the Ivory Coast. This has insured that the system remains responsive to the demands of various groups in the population and that by doing so, it widens its base of popular support.

[73] Although this was never made explicit in the Ivory Coast, except indirectly in the article in *Fraternité*, the leaders of Sudan explained to the militants of their party that high turnout in the one-party election was necessary in order to add to the leaders' bargaining strength while negotiating with France. (*L'Essor*, March 25, 1960.) The functions suggested are generally similar to the ones attributed to Soviet elections by Fainsod. (*How Russia Is Ruled* [Cambridge: Harvard University Press, 1953], pp. 323-24.)

With only one party, nomination is tantamount to election. This process of selection within the party is not public. In theory, candidates are chosen by the general secretaries of the P.D.C.I. and by other major groups that participate in the coalition at the time of the election under consideration, then submitted to the *Bureau Politique* for final approval. In practice, the inner circle retains control over the entire process. Local party units are informed in advance of the number of places their region will have on the ticket and are then told to draw up a list of candidates for these places in order of preference. Most of the time, because of the large number of hopefuls, they submit many more names than they will be allowed to nominate. Although the actual number of candidates is never exactly known, it was estimated in 1959 that there were between 800 and 1,000 men competing for 100 seats in the Legislative Assembly.[74] Since this number includes almost everyone in the Ivory Coast who might possibly hope to be a candidate, the *Bureau Politique* seldom needs to look elsewhere for the candidates it wants.

Shortly before the final choice of nominees was made in 1959, Houphouet-Boigny told the nominating caucus that paramount political considerations required that some seats in the Assembly be allocated to non-Ivoiriens, including Europeans and foreign Africans, in addition to a few reserved for non-party groups. It was suggested that the party be allowed to nominate candidates for only 70 of the 100 seats; the other 30 would be retained by *la direction*, Houphouet-Boigny and his lieutenants, and allocated according to need.

Satisfaction of increasing demands for representation formulated by a variety of groups was facilitated by multiplying the number of offices available for distribution. The Assembly

[74] The lower figure was suggested by a correspondent for *Le Monde*. The higher one was obtained by projecting figures for known cases of specific *sous-sections* obtained in interviews with local party leaders to the entire country.

was enlarged from 60 members in 1957 to 100 in 1959. In addition, the Ivory Coast was divided into 4 departments and a *conseil général* of 40 members was created in each. In this manner, between 1957 and 1959 the total number of seats grew from 60 to 260. Those who could not be made *député* could at least be consoled with the title of *conseiller*.[75] This was the fate of many traditional chiefs and general secretaries of *sous-sections* who did not meet the educational qualifications the ruling group considered sufficient for members of a truly legislative assembly. In 1960 the Assembly was reduced to 70 members. Since members of the government were no longer issued from its ranks and there were new job openings in the diplomatic corps, this did not signify a reduction in the number of offices available for allocation to Ivoiriens. Houphouet-Boigny appeared to have even greater control over the nominating process than before. The general secretaries of the party, assembled in Abidjan as usual to prepare the lists, heard his recommendations and then approved a motion to give him and the *Bureau Politique* full authority to draw up the slate.[76]

The results of the process of selection are reflected in the characteristics of officeholders, summarized in Tables 20 to 23. In 1959 the Assembly and the government retained the coalition-like composition discussed in Chapter VII. The inclusion of Europeans and of foreign Africans (Table 21) was dictated by policy needs, particularly by the desire to attract private investments and to offset accusations of isolationism and racism. However, this entailed some political cost to the regime in the form of dissatisfaction among Ivoiriens. These

[75] These councils were patterned after those of French departments. They are not discussed because as of mid-1961 they had not yet met—two years after they had been created and their membership had been elected. Although they will eventually begin to operate, they do not indicate in any significant way a trend toward decentralization of authority.

[76] *Abidjan-Matin*, November 2, 3, and 5, 1960.

TABLE 20

Characteristics of Ivory Coast Officeholders, 1957-1960[a]
(in percentage of the total)

Attribute	*1957*	*1959*	*1960*
Age:			
Born before 1906	9	7	4
1906-1915	35	32	27
1916-1925	39	37	43
Born after 1925	17	24	27
	(N=54)	(N=84)	(N=83)
Education:			
Primary or less	17	11	12
Upper primary	26	20	20
"Brevêt" level	43	43	40
"Baccalauréat" and higher	15	26	28
	(N=54)	(N=84)	(N=83)
Ethnic Group[b]:			
Atlantic East: Baoulé	16	22	20
Other Akan	22	14	19
"Lagunaire"	12	12	11
Voltaic (Sénoufo and others)	8	9	11
Upper Niger (Malinké etc.)	16	17	14
Atlantic West: Kru	24	22	19
Peripheral Mande	2	5	5
	(N=50)	(N=78)	(N=83)
Occupation:			
By economic sectors:			
Public	63	67	66
Private (Salaried)	2	5	5
Private (Self-employed)	35	29	29
	(N=54)	(N=84)	(N=83)
By status category:			
Manual, small farmer	2	1	0
Clerk, teaching assistant, petty trader	40	21	25
Teacher, middle-rank civil servant, African doctor	33	43	39
University-trained professional, big business	24	35	36
	(N=54)	(N=84)	(N=83)
By specialization:			
Clerical	22	19	16
Educational	24	24	24
Health	11	13	18
Technical	6	8	12
Legal[c]	9	8	7
Agriculture, trading[d]	19	19	16
Managerial	9	8	7
	(N=54)	(N=84)	(N=83)

[a] Africans only are included. The totals (N) in each column include all members of the Assembly and the government and are not the same as the total number of offices, since some individuals held office in both the government and the Assembly simultaneously in 1957 and in 1959. Data were obtained from biographical summaries supplied by the officeholders themselves, on file in the office of the general secretary of the Ivory Coast National Assembly, and used with permission. They were supplemented by interviews with members whenever information was inadequate or not otherwise available.

[b] The classification follows that of Table 1.

[c] "Legal" includes attorney, *huissier* (bailiff), *commissaire-priseur* (legal auctioneer).

[d] Many persons report their occupation as *planteur-transporteur*, *planteur-commerçant*, or some other variation of the same categories. These are closely related occupations and many individuals move from one to the other depending upon their temporary economic fortunes. It may be noted that many people in the Ivory Coast would readily fall into more than one occupational category, since teachers or clerks often derive income from a family commercial farm, etc. Others have relinquished all occupations other than their political one since 1957. I have selected *one* occupation per person, usually the one in which the individual was classified at the time of his election.

TABLE 21

National Origins of Ivory Coast Officeholders
(in percentage of the total)

	1957		*1959*		*1960*	
Origin	*Assembly*	*Government*	*Assembly*	*Government*	*Assembly*	*Government*
Ivory Coast	73	83	77	80	100	93
Other African	7	0	5	5	0	0
French[a]	20	17	18	15	0	7
	(N=60)	(N=12)	(N=100)	(N=22)	(N=70)	(N=15)

[a] Includes West Indians, namely one in the 1957 and 1959 Assembly and one in government throughout. Sources are the same as in the preceding table.

two categories were completely eliminated in 1960. Among the new deputies recruited after independence, two had been outstanding for their participation in antiforeign agitation in 1957 and in 1958. In a different respect, the coalition quality persisted since representation was not restricted to

TABLE 22

Party Offices of African Officeholders in the Ivory Coast

Position	*1959*		*1960*	
	Assembly	*Government*	*Assembly*	*Government*
P.D.C.I.				
Bureau Politique[a]	6	9	4	7
Comite Directeur	14	3	11	5
J.R.D.A.C.I.[b]				
Executive Committee	5	6	6	4
Total high-level party	23	14	18	12
Other African members	44	3	51	2

[a] Includes Houphouet-Boigny, although he does not hold formal office in this group.

[b] J.R.D.A.C.I., the youth branch of the P.D.C.I., was created in 1959. The total "high-level party" is smaller than that of P.D.C.I. and J.R.D.A.C.I. because some members of the J.R.D.A.C.I. executive are included in the organs of government of the P.D.C.I. ex officio.

persons primarily identified with the P.D.C.I. Members of the national executive of the party dominated the government in 1959 and in 1960, but the P.D.C.I. officials constituted only a minority of the membership of the Assembly in both cases (Table 22). Although it is clear that the party shares representation in the Assembly with other groups, it is difficult to identify these groups. An examination of the organizational affiliations of individual officeholders and their own declarations in interviews suggest that representation on the basis of geographical and ethnic orgins, important in earlier years, continues to prevail. Tables 20 and 23 indicate that major ethnic groups have retained approximately the same proportion of the membership in the Assembly and in the government, notwithstanding all the changes that have occurred since 1957. Although almost every tribe is included, the Atlantic East civilization continues to be somewhat dominant, and northerners still fall short of their fair share, if the composition of the total population of the Ivory Coast is used as a standard.[77] Table 23 indicates that the absence of a northerner from the

TABLE 23
Ethnic Origins of the Ivory Coast Members of the Government

Origin[a]	*1957*	*1959*	*1960*
Atlantic East: Baoulé	2	6	4
Other Akan	5	2	3
"Lagunaire"	1	3	2
Voltaic	—	1[b]	1[b]
Upper Niger (Malinké)	—	1	1
Atlantic West	2	3	3
Total	10	16	14

[a] Ethnic classification follows that of Table 1.
[b] The representative of the Voltaic culture circle is the son of a Fulani father and of a Sénoufo mother, not generally accepted by the Sénoufo as a "proper" Sénoufo representative.

government in 1957, a source of Malinké complaints, was remedied later on.

Representation extends not only to the party and to ethnic or regional groups but also increasingly to corporate bodies. This is particularly obvious in the 1960 Assembly. It has three labor leaders: the leader of the U.T.C.I., the national trade-union federation;[78] the general secretary of the Railroad Workers' Union; and the president of the C.N.T.C., the direct-line descendent of the Christian Trade Unions. For the first time, representation was granted to African business groups, including the two most outstanding ones, the *Syndicat des Transporteurs* and the *Syndicat des Commerçants.* As had always been the case in the past, the S.A.A. is also represented through two of its national officers.

[77] Northerners have about 34 per cent of the total population but only 25 per cent of the officeholders. The Sénoufo, as numerous as the Baoulé, have only half as many representatives. (Compare Tables 20 and 23 with population data by ethnic group in Table 1.)
[78] Issued from the Ivory Coast section of U.G.T.A.N.

Flexibility is maintained by changing individuals within each of the categories represented. One person can be replaced by another from the same group, if the former appears to have lost the support of the group he represents. Daloa, a *cercle* that formed a two-member constituency in 1957, was represented in the Assembly by a Bété, ethnic champion for the rural native population, and by a Dioula, spokesman for the urban immigrant community. In 1959 the incumbent Bété was replaced by another Bété who had made a very good showing as an opposition candidate in 1957.[79] But the Bété population still objected to the presence of the Dioula; partisans of the former Bété representative were also dissatisfied with this change. In 1960 a further adjustment was sought by dropping both incumbents and replacing them with two Bété students who had recently returned from France and were relatively less involved in past community controversies. Houphouet-Boigny consecrated their role by traveling to Daloa during the campaign. Finally, one of them was elected a vice-president of the Legislative Assembly to enhance his position and to further pacify his region.[80] Similarly, when the general secretary of the Railroad Workers' Union, Gaston Fiankan, lost his bid for reelection to that office, after having incurred the wrath of his members through his antilabor activities while Minister of Labor and Social Affairs, he was replaced in the Assembly by the man who beat him in the union elections. Further change is reflected in the age, the occupation, and the educational level of representatives.

[79] He had obtained 31 per cent of the votes cast in the entire *cercle* and a majority in the *subdivision* of Daloa proper. It is important to note that although constituencies were enlarged in 1959 and eventually reduced to a single one in 1960, everyone knows who represents a particular region on the national slate.

[80] Similar cases occurred elsewhere as well: in Bouaké, Djibo Sounkalo, the object of Baoulé complaints in 1956, was replaced in 1960 by Gabriel Tiacoh, one of the founders of the M.U.T.A.C.I. and an unsuccessful opposition candidate in 1957. In Abidjan, Paulin Koutouan, representative of the Ebrié native population, was replaced by another Ebrié, Pierre Gadjé, in 1959.

Recruitment is no longer exclusively limited to those who fought the battles of the P.D.C.I. during its formative years—individuals characterized by an upper primary or Ponty education (*brevêt*-level in Table 20) and usually born around World War I. The post-1925 age group has grown in importance since 1957. The appearance of this new generation on the political stage is also reflected in the *doubling* of the proportion of members with a baccalaureate degree or some higher education between 1957 and 1960 and in the substantial increase in the proportion of professionals (*Occupation* by status category, Table 20).

The Assembly

Considering that the domain of the law, as contrasted with that of executive rule making, is fairly limited; that within it the Legislative Assembly's authority has been curtailed very severely; and that the members of the Assembly all belong to the same political party, it is difficult to appreciate the functions of parliament in the Ivory Coast. A legislative assembly could nevertheless continue to operate as a public forum if different points of view within the party or among the non-party groups in the coalition were freely expressed. This is not the case. During the 20 months of the life of the Assembly elected in 1959 unanimity prevailed. Seldom was there any debate on the floor. At no time were more than 3 votes cast against a government proposal.[81] Some members

[81] The Assembly held 39 meetings during this period. All but 5 of the 83 items that came to a vote were introduced by the government. Out of the total, 64 were recorded as unanimous, with no abstentions; 5 had some abstentions but no negative votes; in the other 14, from 1 to 3 negative votes were cast. Only once did the government risk defeat. This was not a case on record, however. It concerned an amendment from the floor to make the dissemination of false news punishable in case of bad faith only. The government threw in its own votes to defeat the amendment. Afterwards, nearly everyone supported the law, with only 2 abstentions and 1 vote against it. (This analysis is based on the published debates of the Assembly supplemented by personal observation of most meetings held in 1959 and by interviews with participants during the same period.)

claim that the appearance of unanimity is misleading because most directives from the executive are discussed in caucus before being launched through the public part of the legislative process. One account of this procedure was as follows: "Usually, when a bill is first proposed, we all forget more or less about party discipline. Dissent is voiced fairly openly at first. Then, after suggestions have been made, if there is any trouble, the item goes back inside and the party irons out the problem and makes compromises. Then the item comes out again with the party decision. Usually the deputies are called together before discussion begins the second time and are given additional explanations for the party's decision on this particular matter. This means that the deputies have had a chance to express their views and that the party takes them into account." When asked to verify this statement, others suggested that this is the way things *ought* to be but that in reality they were not so. In every case investigated, the executive treated the Assembly in a high-handed fashion. For example, in the case of the constitution of 1959, the modifications made by the Assembly in the area of the political responsibility of the prime minister were ignored by the government. Although the constitution required the government to submit its budget at the beginning of the October session of the legislative year, in order to give the Assembly sufficient time to consider it before the December 31 deadline—after which the budget can be implemented by executive action—it was not presented to the Assembly until December 21, 1959. The members grumbled. But when the Prime Minister appeared in person on December 31, the Assembly agreed to forego all debate and unanimously adopted the budget as submitted by the executive.[82]

[82] When it was first submitted on December 21 with a request that the Assembly hurry up, one old militant of the P.D.C.I. wondered out loud whether "they were making fun of us." Others stood up to point out that the procedure was unconstitutional. Actually, according to Article 46 of the constitution, the government can ask for emergency

Valuable clues concerning the functions of the Assembly were obtained from the members' own conceptions of their role. Comparing himself with a French *député*, one member thought that his French equivalent was essentially a legislator, concerned with matters of general policy and questions of broad principle. In the Ivory Coast, in addition to this parliamentary function, the *député* had a social function as well, he explained. Because he was usually better educated than his constituents and better informed than they were concerning what was necessary to modernize the country, he must lead them by advising them on what they should do in order to improve their lot. Many others expressed similar views. Some added that in a one-party state, the *Bureau Politique* of the party, which includes most of the government and the officers of the Assembly, properly makes decisions. Individual deputies have no business trying to discuss them in the Assembly because rhetoric is a waste of time and could even be harmful, since it is often misleading. Instead, members should concentrate on the "civic education" of the masses by coordinating action at the local level. This was worded by one *député* as follows: "I must advise my constituents in the search for an improvement of their way of life, especially in the field of agriculture. Our methods and our spirit are primitive. People waste their resources and their energy. A *député*, in coordination with the various services of the government, must advise his people on how to improve themselves and must suggest the development of new sources of revenue in agriculture. Of course, the *député* is also a legislator, but that kind of work is usually taken care of by a few comrades in committee." Because this concept of the role of the representative appeared to be remarkably similar to that of the *commandant* during the last phase of welfare colonialism, a

---

authorization to collect revenue if the financial bill could not have been submitted in time. (Ivory Coast, *Débats de l'assemblée législative*, No. 15 [1959], pp. 194-204.)

député was asked to compare the two roles. He explained that "the *député* is actually the *patron* of his region. He initiates and coordinates all programs. This is similar to what the *commandant* did in the old days, but there is also an important difference. The *commandant* did it by force, while the *député* does it by persuasion in the name of the party."

Representatives are also important links in a system of two-way communication between the decision makers at the uppermost levels of the party and the population at large. In an illiterate country, where written communications are rare and relatively ineffective, where broadcasting has only recently been put to use as a channel of communication for government directives, information concerning policies must be transmitted orally. It is probable also that it must be transmitted *personally* because the effectiveness of a message seems to depend as much on the status of the carrier as on that of the sender and on its contents.[83] The *députés* perform this task admirably. They are identified with specific constituencies, and are not tied down to administrative duties as are government officials, or kept busy by day-to-day party affairs as are the local party general secretaries. They are equally valuable when they report to Abidjan on the state of affairs at home. Viewing themselves as ambassadors of their region and of their ethnic group to the center, or as the spokesmen for the organization to which they belong, the *députés* are concerned mainly with gaining access to the ministers in order to secure tangible benefits for their constituents. Regardless of his specific duties as a member of the executive, each minister is also a kind of superrepresentative who keeps in touch with the country through his clientele of deputies. At the uppermost level, as

[83] This is based on personal observation. For example, a member of the executive committee of the J.R.D.A.C.I., who bore tidings of a decision affecting the population of Séguéla, was asked by spokesmen for the people of the *cercle* how the decision could possibly be important if such an unimportant man as himself had been delegated to announce it.

suggested in an earlier chapter, tensions within the ruling group enhance Houphouet-Boigny's position.

In this manner the regime combines effective control over the country without sacrificing a high flow of information. Although they do not effectively participate in decision making, representatives of the many groups that make up the Ivory Coast are a crucial link in the process that may lead to the emergence of a new nation. With the instruments of rule discussed in this chapter, the founding fathers of the Republic have undertaken to accelerate this process.

CHAPTER IX

MODERNIZATION AND CONTROL

THE institutionalization of a stable one-party government, centered around one man, is justified by the rulers of the Ivory Coast on the grounds that it is necessary to achieve modernity. The means of achieving modernity discussed in the preceding chapter are not thought to be sufficient, however. Until 1959, the party leaders were concerned mainly with eliminating their opponents and with gaining electoral control. More recently, they have tried to use the instruments they have forged to construct a new society. As we have already seen, the founding fathers did not build the Ivory Coast Republic according to precepts drawn from a very elaborate political theory. Similarly, their efforts to guide social change are in the nature of reactions to specific events that have occurred in the traditional and the modern sector of society rather than procedures derived from a finely drawn blueprint of the future. Although the time perspective from which we shall view some of them in this chapter is very short, the direction of transformation can already be detected.

THE MODERNIZATION OF SOCIETY

Although social scientists have suggested that racial and tribal pluralism are not incompatible with national integration, and that the greater the number of tribes in a state and the smaller their size, the better the chances for effective amalgamation,[1] few members of the Ivory Coast political elite would accept the validity of such hypotheses. They view the survival of primordial tribal attachments among the rural population as an indication of backwardness. The reappearance of ethnic

[1] Coleman, "Sub-Saharan Africa" in Almond and Coleman, p. 368. See also the hypothesis advanced by Wallerstein and my own suggestions discussed in Chapter V of this study.

affiliations in different form in the growing towns is noted with dismay. During the constitutional debates of 1959, Prime Minister Denise revealed his concern in these terms: "We are not a territory fortunate enough to have but a limited number of ethnic groups. We have more than 62 tribes and, during the 10 or 13 years since the Ivory Coast was born to political life, we have had as our ambition in the midst of a party all of you know well and in which the majority of us are militants, we thought that we might arrive at a fusion of these tribes, in order that little by little a sort of single race might emerge. Instead of this, we see the opposite and there is a proliferation of societies that do nothing but separate the population into ethnic and tribal compartments."[2] Therefore, as we saw earlier, restructuration of traditional society and elimination of ethnic boundaries have a high priority among the stated goals of the regime.

Under these circumstances, it may appear surprising that although the Ivory Coast government obtained jurisdiction over the chiefs under the *Loi-Cadre*, little official action has been taken so far to define their status in the Republic. In reality, this is not an omission. Direct rule and past political action had already undermined traditional structures of authority almost everywhere. More recently, there has been an unspectacular but nevertheless steady effort to accelerate this process. As early as 1956, *La Concorde* stated under the headline "*Le crépuscule des dieux*" (*Götterdämmerung*) that in the eyes of the population the chiefs were necessary figureheads, nothing more.[3] A few officeholders look upon the chiefs as the colonial administration had done in the past and think that they are still useful, since in exchange for a few favors and a guarantee that they will keep their job, most chiefs are usually willing to follow suggestions and to use their influence

[2] Ivory Coast, "Avant-projet . . .," p. 20.

[3] *La Concorde*, April 5, 1956. Note that this newspaper was then the closest thing to an official party publication.

to persuade their subjects to do what must be done. Others feel that all chiefs constitute an unnecessary obstacle to modernization and that they wrongfully corner scarce financial resources. One government official who shared this view said that "the chiefs are the survivors from a dead past, whose death sentence has already been passed by history."[4] The government's doctrine has been that although the chiefs are now useless, there is no need to act brutally toward them lest they regain support among the backward part of the population. The institution of the *chefferie* has lost its necessary character. By voting as they had done in the past, the population had implicitly given to their rulers a mandate to replace the old institution of the *chefferie* with modern ones. Therefore, the politically desirable approach is to give these institutions "just enough life to prepare them for an honorable death."[5]

A sharp distinction is usually made between village chiefs and the *chefs de canton*. In the villages, the chiefs are thought to have a useful function because the government is not directly represented there by bureaucratic officials. In practice, secular criteria were introduced long ago in the selection of village chiefs. In many cases, the same person is chief and party secretary. Elsewhere, the *Bureau Politique* has often told party officials not to attempt to supplant the chiefs but only to supervise them politically. The *chefs de canton*, on the other hand, find few defenders. One *député* asserted that "they were colonial creatures and they must die with their creators."[6] The chiefs' own behavior has made them extremely vulnerable to political pressures. At the end of World War II, most of them joined a secular organization founded by Houphouet-Boigny, the *Association des Chefs Coutumiers*

[4] Because the government has avoided meeting this problem, there are few documents stating official policy. Unless otherwise indicated, this account is based on interviews and on personal observation of the situation in various localities.

[5] Unpublished memorandum, Ministry of the Interior, Office of Political Affairs, 1958. (Typescript.)

[6] Interview with M. Yapo Komet, 1959.

et de Canton. Afterwards, this body supported the colonial administration against the R.D.A. One of its spokesmen, Kwame Adingra, paramount chief (*chef supérieur*) of the Abron (Brong) was elected by the anti-P.D.C.I. *Union Française* to the Assembly in 1952. When the party regained its influence after its reconciliation with the French, there were purges everywhere of chiefs who had been appointed by Governor Péchoux during the time of troubles. By 1956, Kwame Adingra had joined the U.D.E.C.I., and he was elected the following year as a P.D.C.I. candidate. At the same time, the *Association* was transformed into a *Syndicat*, a trade-union, with Houphouet-Boigny as its honorary president. In 1961 this organization was one of many unions that participated in a round-table conference to unify the labor movement.

The *Syndicat des Chefs*, as it is usually called, has been the major vehicle for the expression of the chiefs' grievances, which relate mostly to the bureaucratic aspects of their role. They have demanded in recent years better salary scales, more favorable conditions of recruitment and promotion, additional clerical help, and guarantees of tenure of office and of retirement pay.[7] This has facilitated the regime's task because the chiefs can be treated like any other voluntary association. They received a 10 per cent raise in 1958. The following year they lost their lone representative in the Assembly because the *Bureau Politique* of the P.D.C.I. felt that the chiefs had no role to play at the national level. Instead, a few chiefs were elected to the *conseils généraux* in the various regions.

Although the traditional rulers are concerned over their future, they are afraid to press for a clarification of their status lest they be eliminated altogether. In 1957, Houphouet-Boigny told them that ". . . we are witnessing today an evolutionary current against which you can do nothing. You will remain chiefs until it is time for a change."[8] After he

[7] Amon d'Aby, *Le problème des chefferies . . .*, pp. 38-45.
[8] Quoted in *ibid.*, p. 43.

became prime minister, he called the chiefs to Abidjan and reassured them that his own government would not take any measures to abolish the *chefferie*, although there were probably good reasons why this had been done in Guinea and in Sudan.[9] He warned them, however, that he would never hesitate to take rigorous sanctions against any chief who attempted to hamper progress. Shortly afterwards, the president of the Legislative Assembly reiterated this warning. "We don't want to eliminate the soul of tradition and be left with a modern society without a soul," he wrote in an editorial. But this must not interfere with the emancipation of the masses. The people will tolerate chiefs only if they are on the side of progress. If they oppose reforms, they will be subject "to popular condemnation without right of appeal, so great is the thirst for emancipation and for progress throughout the country."[10]

On the whole, this approach seemed successful. It is evident, however, that traditional structures of authority retain the allegiance of the population in some parts of the country, particularly among the Agni, where resistance to secularization took the form of an attempt to secede from the Ivory Coast. This has led to a clarification of the status of the chiefs and of the place of traditional political systems in a modern secular state.

At the beginning of 1959, acting with the approval of the traditional ruler of Sanwi State in Aboisso *cercle*, a group of Agni sent a delegation to Paris to demand the autonomy of Sanwi State as a French protectorate under a treaty signed in 1843.[11] These ambassadors also announced to the press that

[9] The meeting was held in the Legislative Assembly on May 17, 1959. The "good reasons" to which he alluded were that in the two territories mentioned, highly structured traditional systems were more prevalent and had been a source of active resistance to the R.D.A. in the past. (*Fraternité*, June 5, 1959.)

[10] *Ibid.*

[11] The State of Sanwi, which coincides with the geographical extent of the central *subdivision* of Aboisso *cercle*, has a population of about 40,000 distributed among 119 villages. Its area is 5,800 square kilo-

the entire region would abstain in the forthcoming elections because participation might be construed as an acknowledgment of the authority of the Ivory Coast Republic over their kingdom. Amon N'Douffou III, paramount chief of the traditional unit and *chef supérieur* of Aboisso, used his authority to enforce this decision. Aboisso, as noted earlier, was the only area which deviated from the rest of the country in 1959. After their plea was rejected in France, the Agni sought support elsewhere and eventually established a government-in-exile in nearby Ghana at the beginning of May.[12]

The survival of Sanwi State as a political entity was due to the policies of the French administration.[13] It is in this region that the French bridgehead into the Ivory Coast was established in the nineteenth century. The integrity of the

---

meters. (Ivory Coast, Ministère du Plan, *Inventaire* . . ., p. 20.) It was formed through the reconstitution into a centralized organization of several Akan groups that moved westward from Ashanti during the eighteenth century. The Brafe tribe, which led the exodus, retained the paramount (usually called "royal") stool; other stools were transmitted to the descendants of military wing commanders, as is traditional among the Akan. (Rougerie, *Les pays agni* . . ., pp. 59-64.)

The incidents of the spring of 1959 were not reported in the Ivory Coast press until much later, but the presence of the Sanwi ambassadors in Paris and their grievances were reported in *Le Monde* (March 28, 1959). Unless otherwise indicated, this case is based on interviews with informants involved in both sides of the controversy.

[12] Its prime minister was the *chef de canton* of Aby, who was also leader of one of the wings in the Agni military system. He was a school director in secular life. The Ghana government denied being involved in the case. (*Ibid.*, June 3, 1959.) Later, however, President Nkrumah supported Agni claims.

[13] Because the Sanwi case is examined here from the point of view of its relevance to Ivory Coast politics, I have emphasized aspects that are particular to the situation of that country. It may be noted, however, that Sanwi State, as an Akan political system, has much in common with Ashanti. It is a "consummatory-pyramidal" system, of which Apter has said that they are "highly resistant to all forms of innovation . . ." and in which conflict between traditional and modern secular authority tends to be very great. (David E. Apter, "The Role of Traditionalism in the Political Modernization of Ghana and Uganda," *World Politics*, XIII [October 1960], 49-68.) I do not have sufficient information on the traditional system of Sanwi to verify Apter's hypothesis.

state was guaranteed in a protectorate agreement negotiated in 1843.[14] Although in 1900 traditional rulers lost all legal authority except that which they wielded as members of the French administrative hierarchy, the office of king of Sanwi, with some of its perquisites, continued to be recognized by the colonial government.[15] When some Agni migrated to the Gold Coast during World War I because they felt that manpower levies were a violation of the treaty and demanded incorporation into the British colony, the state was officially dismembered.[16] Under the leadership of their educated, well-to-do planters, who constituted the first modern elite group in the Ivory Coast, the Agni fought without letup to obtain the revival of the state. This was done in 1943. Since that time, there has been a *chefferie supérieure* in Aboisso, and the office of chief at that level has been occupied by whoever was at the time ruler of Sanwi State. Although his secular powers were only those of a *chef de canton,* he was usually considered by the *commandant* to be *primus inter pares.* In this manner, Sanwi State retained its political integrity notwithstanding the prevalent system of direct rule.

Recent discontent among the Agni stemmed from several sources. Antagonism between the Agni and the Baoulé had grown because of Agni failure to lead a country-wide political movement after World War II and Baoulé success in a similar undertaking. The Agni either supported the *Parti Progressiste* or abstained in most postwar elections. Resentment of the Baoulé was exacerbated by continued immigration of Baoulé and other savanna dwellers into the area. Between 1941 and

[14] The treaty is reprinted in Amon d'Aby, *La Côte d'Ivoire . . .*, pp. 169-72.

[15] The history of the region is detailed in Henri Mouezy, *Assinie et le royaume de Krinjabo, histoire et coutumes* (Paris: Larose, 1954). It is interesting to speculate on the fact that Sanwi State, called also the Kingdom of Krinjabo, is the only area of the Ivory Coast that has been the object of fairly detailed historical study by both Africans and Europeans. The fact that its history has been written may help the unit maintain its identity in the face of change.

[16] *Ibid.*, p. 210.

1953 the proportion of strangers in the total population of the *cercle* grew from 17 to 31 per cent.[17] The population was becoming less and less Agni; land passed into foreign hands; hence, the very existence of Sanwi State was threatened. Around 1957, the Agni organized a mutual defense association to withstand claims pressed by immigrants over land they had earlier leased but which they now wished to buy outright. A second source of Agni complaint has been economic renascence among the Ehotilé, whom they consider a vassal people. Earlier, the Ehotilé had been content to fish in the southern lagoons, leaving control of the land to the Agni overlords. Because of this "symbiotic relationship," as Rougerie put it, a modus vivendi was worked out between the two groups.[18] More recently, when the Ehotilé began to grow cocoa and coffee, many latent controversies were revived between the two groups, centering mainly on the attribution of forests suitable for clearing which were located at the boundary between Agni and Ehotilé villages.[19] Attempts by the Abidjan government to arbitrate only aroused Agni suspicions.

A specific controversy between the Agni and the Ehotilé of the Aby lagoon area over a contested forest was the proximate cause of the Sanwi secessionist attempt. When an Ehotilé disappeared in January 1959, after having wandered into that forest, his tribesmen accused the Agni of murder and sought reparation. The Agni mobilized their young men to fight back. Warfare broke out between villages. Abidjan sent a police detachment to restore the peace and tried to settle

[17] These figures are drawn from an unpublished study of land and migration problems in Aboisso by Miss M. Dupire, researcher for O.R.S.T.O.M. I am grateful to Miss Dupire for this and other information useful for the background of the Sanwi case.

[18] Rougerie, "Lagunaires et terriens de la Côte d'Ivoire," *Cahiers d'Outre-Mer*, No. 8 (October-December 1950), p. 12.

[19] Earlier disputes had led to an all-out war (1887) and to prolonged court action in 1931. (Mouezy, pp. 130, 215.) For the Ehotilé revival under the leadership of their energetic *chef de canton*, Léon Amon, see Rougerie, "Les Pays Agni . . .," p. 118.

the dispute by negotiation, but the Agni seized the opportunity to revive more generalized issues, including acknowledgment of their feudal rights over the Ehotilé, dismissal of the Ehotilé *chef de canton*, and recognition of Sanwi State as an autonomous political entity within the Ivory Coast Republic. It was at that time that the Agni ethnic association in Abidjan, *Mutualité Amicale du Sanwi*, dispatched the aforementioned delegation to Paris. The establishment of a "government-in-exile" supplied sufficient legal ground for the arrest of the Sanwi representatives in Paris and their extradition to the Ivory Coast, as well as for the arrest of the king and some of his followers.[20] A total of 29 persons were indicted for violating Article 80 of the French Penal Code by having jeopardized the external security of the state.[21] When brought to trial in the spring of 1960, all the accused were found guilty. The king was sentenced to ten years' imprisonment, twenty years' banishment, and loss of civic rights.[22] The *chefferie supérieure* of Aboisso was discontinued. All *chefs de canton* who had supported the king were replaced by politically reliable appointees.[23]

The Sanwi case indicates that the Ivory Coast government will not hesitate to use coercion to ward off threats to national unity. Houphouet-Boigny told the Assembly in 1959:

"It is at this very moment, at a time when we abandon the

[20] *Abidjan-Matin*, May 28, 1959; *Le Monde*, June 3, 1959.

[21] President Nkrumah's statements while the accused were awaiting trial helped establish the case for the prosecution. He said in a foreign policy speech that recent developments indicated the Agni's desire to join Ghana and that justice demanded that full opportunity be afforded to them to rejoin their brothers and sisters. (*West Africa*, December 26, 1959, p. 1126.) Later, in a visit to the border region, he hinted that Ghana had legitimate territorial claims over the Sanwi area. Houphouet-Boigny warned Ghana against pursuing an irridentist policy and spoke disparagingly of "neo-colonial conquerors." (Broadcast over Radio-Abidjan, February 8, 1960.)

[22] The account of the trial and of the appeal proceedings is found in *Abidjan-Matin*, February 17, March 2, April 9, 26, May 10, 1960.

[23] Ivory Coast, *Journal Officiel*, December 24, 1960. The appropriate decision is Order 2982, I, CAB, AG, of December 14, 1960.

status of subjects for that of citizens, that this man, the King of Krinjabo, this guilty King, this stupid King, asks for a certain degree of autonomy. France, by her silence, had indicated her pity for such aberrations. Today, it is I who say 'no' to the autonomy they seek, because Aboisso is part of the Ivory Coast Republic.

"Let these men know that all those who would question the unity of this country will henceforth have to cope with our Constitution, which is unambiguous on the subject, and with the laws of the Ivory Coast Republic, which will severely punish any attempt to question the unity of our country."[24]

But the implications of the incident extend to the entire problem of the conflict between traditional and secular authority. The decision of the court of appeal to uphold the sentences of the lower court was interpreted by the government to mean that the treaties negotiated between traditional rulers and France during the nineteenth century were no longer valid and that the title of "king" as well as the designation "kingdom" were devoid of legal significance and constituted a usurpation of authority. Most important of all, the government announced that traditional chiefs were without recognized powers other than those generally exercised within the framework of local administrative regulations.[25] Once the *chefferie* had been secularized, criteria of political loyalty had to prevail as they did in every other aspect of Ivory Coast public life.

In addition to the survival of traditional structures of authority, tradition manifests itself also in the persistence of primordial ties among people who live beyond the confines of traditional communities. This is usually designated as *racisme* by political leaders. In 1959 the government asked and obtained the inclusion of a statement condemning all manifestations of racism in the preamble to the constitution.

[24] Ivory Coast, *Débats de l'assemblée législative,* No. 1 (1959), p. 9.
[25] *Abidjan-Matin,* May 11, 1960.

On the strength of the recent Dahomeyan events, however, President Denise argued that it was imperative to give the government authority to punish "any particularistic propaganda of ethnic or racial character, all manifestations of racial discrimination."[26] This was incorporated into the constitution of 1959 and repeated in its successor.

Under cover of modernization, however, it is obvious that the ruling group is concerned with extending its control over all aspects of Ivory Coast life. Over and above their functions from the point of view of national integration, ethnic groups and tribes can also be considered as secondary groups that mediate between the individual and society and hamper the development of a mass society, the prelude to totalitarianism. Coleman, writing on political integration in Africa, concludes that racial and tribal pluralism contribute to the development of a competitive society and that "it could be argued that such a rich pluralism makes dictatorship less likely by providing countervailing power centers which cannot be coerced into a single authoritarian system."[27] Although Ivory Coast leaders would probably agree with the validity of this observation, they would draw radically different conclusions from it, as they have actually done. As politicians, they are concerned primarily with the maintenance of the P.D.C.I.'s monopolistic position. National unity, in effect, means party unity. Some aspects of tradition, it is argued, constitute obstacles to modernization; but behind this concern looms the distrust of any area that escapes political control. In answer to a question raised by a European member of the constitutional committee,

[26] Article 6. This would also give the government authority to take measures against Europeans who, even in the Ivory Coast Republic of 1959, sometimes discriminated against Africans. Except at the uppermost political and business levels, relations between French and Africans seldom appear in any form but the master-servant relationship of yesterday. On the day of the proclamation of the Ivory Coast Republic, December 4, 1958, the French inhabitants of Korhogo (about 50 altogether) held a ball to which no Africans were invited.

[27] Coleman, *The Politics of the Developing Areas*, p. 368.

A. Denise explained that the government would soon table a proposal to abolish "all these ethnic associations that only aggravate the racial problem."[28] In the face of some objections on the part of the members, he explained that there would be little harm in the continued existence of tribal societies if not for the fact that "all these little associations are engaged in a constant struggle for different political views, even though they claim to be absolutely apolitical."[29] It is therefore *because* tradition is a source of pluralism that it must be combated.

Controls in the Modern Sector

Next to the nationalist movement itself, voluntary associations have been the most important transmitters of modern values in the Ivory Coast.[30] As such, they constitute an extremely useful auxiliary to the government in bringing about the desired transformation of society. From the point of view of the rulers of a one-party state, however, their modernizing functions are offset by their potential functions as secondary groups. Free voluntary associations in the modern sector of society are an even greater danger than tribes and neotraditional associations. The regime has sought to replace existing voluntary associations with associations of its own and to amalgamate them into the party. This process emerges clearly in the case of youth and labor.

Labor

Freedom of action of the labor movement has been curtailed

[28] Ivory Coast, "Avant-projet . . .," p. 20.

[29] *Ibid.*, p. 30.

[30] Concerning this question, see the study by Immanuel Wallerstein of the functions of voluntary associations in the Ivory Coast and in Ghana. Wallerstein raises the question of the functions of voluntary associations in a one-party system, which was emerging in the Ivory Coast while he studied the country, but does not attempt to answer it. (Immanuel Wallerstein, "The Emergence of Two New Nations: The Ivory Coast and Ghana" [unpublished Ph.D. dissertation, Department of Sociology, Columbia University].)

since 1957, when the executive committee of the *Union des Travailleurs de Côte d'Ivoire* (U.T.C.I.), territorial section of U.G.T.A.N., agreed to enter into the coalition. The Ivory Coast section was increasingly isolated from its parent body when the latter took a pro-federation and anti-Community stand in 1958.[31] Some individual unions, especially among government employees, however, remained oriented toward the federal organization and shared its ideological preferences. Continued adherence of labor to an interterritorial movement was perceived by the Ivory Coast government as a serious threat. Philippe Yacé stated at the P.D.C.I. congress that although interterritorial unions had been necessary in the past, since colonialism itself knew no boundaries, it was now dangerous for Ivory Coast unions to receive directives from abroad because central organs might not take into account the peculiar social and economic context of the country. Therefore, he announced, a new Ivory Coast *centrale*, regrouping most territorial unions, would soon be created.[32]

The P.D.C.I. congress also defined the proper role of unions

[31] A split occurred in U.G.T.A.N. at the December 1958 meeting of its provisional executive in Dakar. It was consummated the following month when the movement held its first congress in Conakry, beyond the pale of the Community. Territorial sections were split not only in the Ivory Coast but in Senegal and in Niger as well. Since both sides claimed to be U.G.T.A.N., a distinction was made between U.G.T.A.N.-*unitaire* (Conakry-oriented) and U.G.T.A.N.-*autonome*. The circumstances of the split were reported by the provisional executive of the U.T.C.I. at a congress held in Abidjan, July 1959. See also *Afrique Nouvelle*, January 30, 1959, and the earlier discussion of labor in this study. Although Ivory Coast unions are organized bureaucratically, they are in fact bands gathered around one or more leaders rather than highly structured bodies. Unfortunately, there is no adequate study of their growth and characteristics.

[32] P. Yacé, "Rapport sur le Syndicalisme" (Proceedings of the Territorial Congress of the P.D.C.I., Abidjan, 1959 [Mimeographed].) Similar action was taken in other member states of the Community at approximately the same time. In the spring of 1959, U.G.T.A.N.-*autonome* called for a meeting of all the territorial sections that had broken with Conakry. Before it was held, however, there was a further split between pro- and anti-Mali sections. (*Le Monde*, April 9 and May 3, 1959.)

in the Republic. President Denise stated that although trade-unionism must exist in a free country, it is necessary to "rethink" its role. During the anticolonial struggle, he explained, all means to destroy the administration apparatus of oppression had been legitimate. Once government responsibility was transferred to the nationalist movement, however, the ruthless use of the power of labor would weaken the nation and would lead to its destruction. This was particularly true in the Ivory Coast, he argued, because the unions were dominated by government workers: "Labor must understand that . . . the *fonctionnaires*, who constitute almost the entire intellectual cadre of our nation, have a privileged status which reveals an enormous gap with that of other strata of the country. It would be dangerous to aggravate this. Therefore, I ask each of the unions to set aside their particular interests for the general interests of the nation. I ask them not to wield a power of which they might no longer remain the masters and which can jeopardize the objectives they wish to reach."[33] This theme was further developed in an editorial in *Fraternité*, which argued that unlike in Europe, there was no necessary antagonism between labor and the wielders of political or economic power because ". . . the fundamental goal of the Ivory Coast government is economic and social construction. Hence, a unity of views, a civic consensus, is necessary at all levels of the nation. Hence, the workers are increasingly associated with the government's efforts. . . . But their political participation does not imply the abandonment of bargaining functions, still the most essential aspect of trade-unionism. If a government action is contrary to the interests of the workers, their representatives will publicize their position. They can protest against such measures but they should always seek with the government the most adequate national solution."[34]

[33] A. Denise, "Rapport Moral" (Proceedings of the P.D.C.I. 1959), pp. 12-13.

[34] *Fraternité*, May 29, 1959.

Although it is true that government employees constitute the most privileged group among wage earners, they are also the most dissatisfied. They have had more contact than any other stratum with European officials, whose standard of living is very high. They also compare their own *standing* (a word in common usage in French-speaking countries to denote status) with that of their former colleagues who now occupy high posts in the government or in the Assembly. Until 1957, their grievances had been directed to the Dakar authorities, which controlled their conditions of employment. After the *Loi-Cadre* shifted this authority to the territorial government, grievances followed as well. The demands of government employees concern material improvement, including higher pay, higher per diem, and better housing facilities.[35] Furthermore, civil servants disagree for obvious reasons with the regime's conservative policies on *africanisation des cadres.*[36] There was much concern over the nature of the forthcoming basic law specifying conditions for the recruitment, promotion, and disciplining of government employees, as well as their freedom to bargain and right to strike. Although the government began drafting a *Statut de la fonction publique* in consultation with trade-unions in 1957, there were many postponements because of the changing institutional framework. Final consideration was still pending at the time of the July 1959 congress of U.T.C.I.[37] Expectations among civil servants

[35] For a sample of demands, see Ivory Coast, Assemblée territoriale, "Debates," May 15, 1957. It was estimated at the time that budgetary cost would increase by about 10 per cent if they were met.

[36] Houphouet-Boigny repeatedly emphasized in interviews and in public statements that he would continue to use expatriate officials for reasons of efficiency until Africans were properly trained. He and his lieutenants answered all critiques of this policy by pointing out that genuine africanization had already been effected since political authority was in African hands. (See, among others, *Fraternité*, June 16, 1961.) Needless to say, this argument carried little weight among the government employees, especially after the sudden departure of Europeans from Guinea in 1958 assured extremely rapid promotions there.

[37] For the history of this statute, see *Abidjan-Matin*, June 17, 1957;

were high, but there were rumors that the statute would not fulfill them. When some of its employees walked out at the end of 1957, the Ivory Coast government broke the strike by suspending them without pay. In mid-1958 the government declared that field duty was normal duty and would no longer warrant extra pay. All civil servants whose work involved traveling in the hinterland, including medical nurses, epidemic control teams, water and forestry services, went on strike from September 1958 to June 1959, bringing these vital services to a halt.[38] By the time of the U.T.C.I. congress, it was apparent that some of the civil servants' unions were resisting pressures to sever Conakry ties and to play the role assigned to trade-unions in the Ivory Coast system. They even refused to attend the congress.[39] It is impossible to determine the respective strength of the two factions among government workers. Actually, this was one of the major questions in the controversy. U.T.C.I. claimed at the congress that it controlled about 90 per cent of the civil servants' unions; the dissenting group objected. Since the leaders constantly shifted their allegiance and since there was never any showdown by a vote of the members, these claims could not be settled empirically. This is, of course, one of the important characteristics of the types of political conflict that arise in the Ivory Coast and of the consequences of the lack of communication and information. With no standard of measurement of support, claims by all sides tend to be more extreme and compromise becomes more difficult to achieve.

The provisional executive of the U.T.C.I. acknowledged the need to redefine the functions of labor. Amon Tanoh, its general secretary, maintained that labor as a whole could not take a permanent doctrinal stand against the government

---

Ivory Coast, Assemblée territoriale, "Debates," September 15, 1957, and June 19, 1958.

[38] *Ibid.*, December 23, 1958; *Abidjan-Matin*, June 13, 1959.

[39] *Abidjan-Matin*, July 11, 1959.

and for "revolution," as Conakry-oriented groups would have it, because the government sometimes agreed with the workers' demands. Rejecting the concept of the class struggle as being irrelevant to Africa, he asserted that the projected *Union Nationale des Travailleurs de Côte d'Ivoire* (U.N.T.C.I.), as U.T.C.I. would be called after the congress, would be neither "revolutionary" nor "reformist." The movement must use all means to achieve its goals: negotiation and compromise first, the strike if all else failed. In conclusion, he emphasized that the role of the unions was more difficult than ever before because they were no longer concerned with destruction but with the construction of a nation.[40] Standing on this platform, Amon Tanoh and his running mates were elected to the national executive of U.N.T.C.I. by an overwhelming majority of the congress.[41]

The government-approved *centrale* now included most of the U.G.T.A.N.-*autonome* unions. U.G.T.A.N.-*unitaire*, C.A.T.C., and some independents were left out. After the congress, the contest over the allegiance of government workers' unions continued. Seven out of nine members of the executive committee of the *Intersyndicat des Travailleurs de la Fonction Publique* had pulled out of this committee by August 3. Four of them reappeared as officers of U.N.T.C.I. Under the leadership of Blaise Yao N'Go, general secretary of the Water and Forestry Service, the *Intersyndicat* was reconstituted. A strange alliance was reached between this Conakry-oriented group and the C.A.T.C., whose federal president had himself been exiled from Guinea because of his resistance to governmentalization of unions there a few months

[40] This is based on personal notes taken at the congress.

[41] The final vote was 208 delegates for Amon Tanoh's slate and 82 against. The opposition within the congress was not ideological, since the partisans of U.G.T.A.N.-*unitaire* had stayed away. It was headed by Mamery Cherif, a *député* from the north. Interviews with principals suggest that the struggle was a north-south one, as is often the case in voluntary associations in the Ivory Coast.

earlier. By mid-August, the *Intersyndicat* claimed that although most of its erstwhile leaders had defected, it retained the support of the rank-and-file in 24 out of the 29 government workers' unions.[42] When the U.N.T.C.I. next sponsored a meeting of all the unions of the Entente States that had broken with Conakry, the *Intersyndicat* retaliated by convening an assembly of those that had not.[43]

The *Statut de la fonction publique*, which became law on August 28, 1959, after a meeting of the *Conseil de l'Entente* had coordinated projects for the four member-states, fell far below the expectations of even the U.N.T.C.I.-affiliated unions. The powers of representative councils were much more restricted than those of France, which had served as a model for the aspirations of Ivory Coast civil servants.[44] The right to strike was limited by a provision enabling the government to requisition employees needed to perform vital services. Freedom of opinion was guaranteed within the range defined by the Community and by the constitution of the Ivory Coast. Vacation time was cut from three months every two years to one

[42] Claims and counterclaims were exchanged in *Abidjan-Matin*, August 6 and 12, 1959. The strange presence of the C.A.T.C. in this camp was due to its doctrinal stand against government-controlled trade-union movements in general and to the desire of its leaders to exploit this opportunity to gain a reputation as fighters, which they had formerly been unable to acquire.

[43] The meeting of the Entente unions was held on August 15-16, 1959. It was attended only by Ivory Coast and Niger unions. (*Abidjan-Matin*, August 20, 1959.) The *Intersyndicat* meeting included Ivory Coast and Upper Volta government workers.

[44] The *Statut* became Law No. 59-135, September 3, 1959 (Ivory Coast, *Journal Officiel*, September 12, 1959, p. 838). For the French model, see Herman Finer, *The Theory and Practice of Modern Government* (rev. ed.; New York: Henry Holt and Company, 1950), p. 910. The unions had demanded *commissions paritaires*, joint boards with equal representation of government and employees, mandatorily consulted for promotions, assignments, and disciplinary measures, with a higher body, the *conseil supérieur de la fonction publique*, to act as a sort of appellate board. (Earlier texts and union proposals were obtained from the personal files of union officials.) In the final version, the *commissions* had much more limited functions and the *conseil supérieur* was reduced to a *comité consultatif* with no specified attributes of authority (Article 5).

month every year, and family allocations, formerly granted to an unrestricted number of children, were now limited to a maximum of six.

The reactions of union officials differed significantly. Amon Tanoh, who had overcome the dilemma stemming from his roles as labor leader, member of the national executive of the P.D.C.I., and *député* by being absent on the day of the final vote in the Assembly, nevertheless agreed to work within the framework established by the *Statut* in the hope of bargaining for improvements later on.[45] When the U.N.T.C.I. attempted to explain its stand to the rank-and-file, however, the *Intersyndicat*, unhampered by any other responsibilities, accused the organization of collaborating with a government "worse than any form of colonialism."[46] All meetings had to be cut short because of mounting tensions. Houphouet-Boigny warned the *Intersyndicat* that any union which maintained relations with a hostile country would be outlawed.[47] On October 7, after repeated private admonitions, he ordered that Blaise Yao N'Go be arrested and deported to the Guinean border. His followers called a strike the following day. About one-fourth of the government workers in Abidjan walked out.[48]

This was the first major disturbance since Houphouet-Boigny had assumed personal command of the Ivory Coast government. He declared the strike illegal because of its political rather than economic character and requisitioned all govern-

[45] Interview with Amon Tanoh, 1959. He became Minister of Education in 1963.

[46] From personal notes taken during a public meeting. The first meeting was called by the U.N.T.C.I. on September 10, the second, a week later. More than a thousand people were crowded each time into the Bourse du Travail (Union Hall) in Treichville. Heated insults were exchanged between leaders; heckling prevented U.N.T.C.I. leaders from speaking. Insults were hurled at Houphouet-Boigny and at the Community. None of this was reported in the press.

[47] *Fraternité*, September 25, 1959.

[48] Yao N'Go admitted in several interviews that Houphouet-Boigny had pleaded personally with him. All information on the strike is based on personal observation during this period.

ment employees.[49] During the course of a protest march from Treichville to the Plateau, the strikers retaliated by tearing down from the new bridge the plaque bearing his name. They were prevented from reaching the Prime Minister's house by armed forces.[50] During the next three days, the city was under a state of siege. *Gendarmerie* and police occupied strategic locations, a curfew was imposed on Treichville, and a barrage established at the bridge. A dozen union leaders were arrested; more than 200 government employees were dismissed; over 300 were suspended for varying periods without pay.[51] They were easily replaced and within a week, services functioned normally. The U.N.T.C.I. expressed its sympathy with the "innocent victims" but acknowledged that the government's action had been necessary and correct. A spokesman for some of the dismissed employees appealed to the humanitarian sentiments of the government for forgiveness on the grounds that they had been misled by their own leaders.[52]

Although by these actions the immediate threat to the regime was averted, the long-run problem remained. Its solution required a further extension of control. *Fraternité* explained that a government employee is entitled to make legitimate demands, ". . . but as soon as he wishes to rebel against the public authority which employs him . . . the only freedom to which he is decently entitled is to resign quietly. . . . The restoration of psychological health in the public service is therefore a national imperative, without which all that can be expected in the near or distant future is chaos and anarchy."[53]

[49] Decrees 59-186 and 59-187 of October 8, 1959. (Ivory Coast, *Journal Officiel*, October 8, 1959.)

[50] *France-Observateur*, October 15, 1959, reported that there had been some bloodshed. This was officially denied in *Fraternité* (October 30, 1959). Although it is known that tear gas was used, verification of the other allegations was impossible.

[51] *Arreté* 96 and 97 PM. FP. of October 10, 1959; *Journal Officiel*, October 13, 1959. See also *Abidjan-Matin*, October 19, 1959.

[52] *Abidjan-Matin*, October 17, 20, 24, and 26, 1959.

[53] *Fraternité*, October 30, 1959.

Furthermore, because the government worker participates in the management of the state, he must be dedicated to serve it with enthusiasm. The party reminded the civil servants and at the same time the entire nation that they had failed to support the nationalist movement in its hour of need ten years earlier. Then, as now, they stood aloof. "The country sees this reticence as a kind of class selfishness and believes that this behavior reveals a desire to reap the benefits of a struggle in which they did not participate," Yacé asserted. He concluded that "we cannot tolerate . . . that a part of the Nation remain a foreign particle within the whole."[54]

In order to implement this doctrine, the party announced the creation of special committees in its midst for civil servants. Yacé, inviting them to join, said: "Let all the government workers . . . help us. In our midst you will find the support, the aid, the moral comfort you seek. . . . In our midst you will find an explanation for the problems that face us, a mystique without which any action is futile and depressing."[55] He asserted that the organizational drive in their ranks would assuredly succeed, but that in any case it would clearly reveal where the friends of the people really were. These new party branches were created throughout the country during 1960. In the smaller towns, a single committee includes all civil servants assigned there. In Abidjan, all government workers are organized on the basis of the service in which they work. Although it was never stated explicitly, this meant in practice that the party committees replaced the trade-unions.[56]

[54] *Ibid.*, February 12, 1960.

[55] *Ibid.*, February 12, 1960.

[56] *Abidjan-Matin*, February 22 and 25; March 2, 11, 31; May 6 and 8, 1960. There were also indications of renewed efforts to bring hitherto unaffiliated unions, including even the *Syndicat des Chefs Coutumiers*, into the nationalized U.N.T.C.I. (*Ibid.*, March 7, 9, and 22, 1961.) It is important to note that the regime does not operate by coercion alone. The union leaders jailed in October 1959 were released a few months later without ever having been brought to trial. One of them, the president of the C.A.T.C., was elected to the National Assembly in October 1960. Labor representation in that body went from 2 in 1959

Youth

Although the Bamako Congress of 1957 had advocated the creation of youth branches affiliated to territorial sections of the R.D.A. wherever they did not yet exist, P.D.C.I. leaders answered all requests for greater participation formulated by spokesmen for the younger and better educated generation by telling them to join the party individually and work their way up through the P.D.C.I. hierarchy, beginning at the level of the ethnic subcommittees.[57] The grant of some representation in the Assembly and the government extended to the youth in 1957 did not signify access to decision-making authority. It was not until mid-1958 that Houphouet-Boigny finally authorized the creation of a youth branch of the party. Negotiations took place between various youth leaders and members of the P.D.C.I. executive to work out an acceptable formula. The *Jeunesse R.D.A. de Côte d'Ivoire* (J.R.D.A.C.I.) was finally launched shortly before the referendum.[58] Its provisional executive consisted mainly of former leaders of Ivory Coast student associations in France, who had come home and were willing to work within the framework of the Community.[59]

---

to 4 in 1960. In addition, labor retains the Ministry of Labor and Social Affairs and was granted one ambassadorial post in 1961. With independence, africanization of the civil service was accelerated somewhat. Many European field administrators were replaced by Africans, and a school to train high-level civil servants was created. (*Ibid.*, February 7 and December 8, 1960; January 18, 1961; *Fraternité*, March 11 and December 16, 1960.) Nevertheless, in mid-1961 Houphouet-Boigny repeated that he did not want any "cut-rate africanization" and would retain expatriates as long as possible. (*Ibid.*, June 16, 1961.)

[57] See for example the exchange between members of the *Comité Directeur* and M. Boni Aka in *Abidjan-Matin*, October 22, 1957. The similarity between the P.D.C.I. and American machines is apparent in this connection as well as in the ones already discussed. It has proved very difficult in the United States to integrate within the old-fashioned Democratic Party, for example, the newer generation of middle-class intellectuals. Only recently have new political groupings emerged to accommodate them.

[58] *Ibid.*, September 12, 1958.

[59] Most of the information on youth was obtained in interviews with participants during 1959 and on personal observation of members of

After the Dahomeyan incidents, Houphouet-Boigny ordered the provisional executive to make room for L.O.C.I. leaders, most of whom were not students. As one member of the organization put it, unless they obeyed the orders, they would not have obtained money and transportation facilities needed to launch the organization. Branches sprang up everywhere, even though youth organizers encountered much hostility among the secretaries of the P.D.C.I. *sous-sections*, who were loath to share their authority with newcomers. The first congress, scheduled for January 1959, finally opened in March.

It had been hoped that the J.R.D.A.C.I. would draw support from Ivory Coast students who were still abroad. The ideological gap between them and the regime had grown too wide, however. The *Association des Etudiants de Côte d'Ivoire en France* (A.E.C.I.F.), affiliated through the *Fédération des Etudiants d'Afrique Noire en France* (F.E.A.N.F.) with the communist-dominated International Union of Students took a stand against the Community and objected to the regime's policies on Algeria. They considered the willingness of their former leaders to work within the existing framework in the Ivory Coast as a betrayal of their ideological principles. At its annual congress held in Paris in December 1958, the A.E.C.I.F. pledged itself to work during the forthcoming year to reverse the "yes" vote of the Ivory Coast population. They condemned the J.R.D.A.C.I. as a government-sponsored association, as its suspiciously rapid growth indicated. They also endorsed the decision of their outgoing president, Memel Fote Harris, to teach at the Conakry Lycée rather than in Abidjan.[60] Considering the restrictions imposed by the founding fathers on legitimate dissent, A.E.C.I.F. can be viewed as a subversive organization. It sent representatives to the J.R.D.A.C.I. con-

---

the executive committee at work during a tour of the Ivory Coast devoted to launching the organization.

[60] *Kô-Moë* (the organ of the A.E.C.I.F.), No. 7, February 1959.

gress but did not hide its fundamental disagreement with the leaders' orientation.

A tense atmosphere prevailed at the opening of the congress, held in Treichville from March 14 to 16, 1959.[61] The P.D.C.I. leaders who came to deliver the opening speeches were greeted coldly. In contrast, student representatives were received with great enthusiasm by the rank-and-file. The major issue that emerged, in addition to the election of an executive committee, was the definition of the structure of the group and its relationship to the P.D.C.I. From the very beginning, its status was ambiguous. Before the congress, former opposition sympathizers began to join many of the J.R.D.A.C.I. branches created throughout the country in order to belong to the party yet avoid being under the thumb of P.D.C.I. general secretaries. It was reported also that some of the units had begun to draw up their own electoral slates and political programs.[62] It was imperative to determine, therefore, whether the J.R.D.A.C.I. would simply be an ancillary organization of the senior party or whether it would have some autonomy as a sort of parallel organization, a party within a party, which might provide some party democracy. The youth, of course, hoped for the latter. As one member of the organizing committee explained it to the congressional delegates, a single-party system signified dictatorship. (This was greeted with much applause.) To overcome it, a sincere and effective opposition was needed. Since there were good reasons for avoiding an opposition in the country at this time, dictatorship could be overcome only by having an opposition, or at least an *aile marchante*, within the party. In order to play this role, the youth group demanded its own autonomous constitution. This was unacceptable to the P.D.C.I. because it would signify complete autonomy. The compromise solution was to give

[61] This account is based on personal notes of speeches and proceedings, unless otherwise indicated.

[62] *Abidjan-Matin*, February 26, 1959.

the J.R.D.A.C.I. its own *règlement intérieur* but not a separate charter.

Compromise pervades the entire structure of the organization. The J.R.D.A.C.I. is based on *sous-comités* (at the level of the P.D.C.I. *comités de base*) which elect a *comité* that is affiliated with the *sous-section* of the P.D.C.I. in each *subdivision.* These committees elect a national executive annually. At each level, including the national, a delegation of the J.R.D.A.C.I. participates in the activities of the senior party. In return, the P.D.C.I. has the right to be represented at all levels of the J.R.D.A.C.I. and to send observers to all meetings. A further compromise was reached on the question of membership and dues. In order to emphasize its distinctiveness, the J.R.D.A.C.I. demanded to be allowed to sell its own membership cards. The P.D.C.I. objected to the symbolism this would have as well as to the financial loss the party might incur if younger adults (for the time being, up to 40 years of age, but later on up to 30 years of age) paid dues to the youth branch rather than to the senior party. It was finally decided that the J.R.D.A.C.I. would issue its own membership cards but that 30 per cent of the amount collected would be turned over to the senior party. Ultimately, however, the P.D.C.I. retained the right to dissolve the youth branch.[63]

The election of the 19-member executive committee was hotly contested but eventually the field was narrowed down to 2 slates. The losing one was composed of the leaders of L.O.C.I. and of the spokesman for U.G.T.A.N.-*unitaire*, Yao N'Go, together with some of their lieutenants; it included neither northerners nor foreigners. The victorious slate, headed by Dr. Mamadou Kone, a Malinké and a former president of A.E.C.I.F., obtained 90 of the 113 votes cast by the delegates. Half of the new officers were former student leaders; the others were associated with U.G.T.A.N.-*autonome* (including

[63] J.R.D.A.C.I., "Règlement Intérieur." (Mimeographed proceedings of the 1959 congress, Abidjan.) See also *Fraternité*, May 22, 1959.

Amon Tanoh) and with other voluntary associations. They also represented an ethnically balanced group.[64] The spoils of victory were extremely valuable. Of the 19 members, 9 were elected afterwards to the P.D.C.I. national executive. In 1959 and again in 1960 all but 3 of the 19 found their way to high-level public office.[65]

The stated policy objectives of the J.R.D.A.C.I. included reorganization of the P.D.C.I. along democratic lines and promotion of free discussion within the party. Furthermore, they stated they would seek to persuade Houphouet-Boigny to take personal command of the state.[66] In a statement of the role of the organization, its second-in-command, Ahoussou Koffi, rejected accusations that the J.R.D.A.C.I. had failed to carry out the revolutionary mission of youth. He wrote in an editorial in *Fraternité* that "it is possible to be young and realistic. This is undoubtedly what differentiates us from many other youths." Because the preoccupations of the masses are economic rather than political, youth feels that it is necessary to follow the advice of President Houphouet-Boigny, who believes that at this stage of the country's evolution economic considerations have primacy over political ones. "We are practical people who do not like to carry the burden of overly abstract theories."[67] Privately, several members of the executive disagreed with the long-term feasibility and desirability of the Community policy. They felt nevertheless that it was perhaps necessary to postpone independence for two or three

[64] It included 2 foreigners (one from Upper Volta and one Senegalese). The 17 Ivoiriens included 3 Malinké-Dioula, 3 Baoulé, 5 Akan from the southeast, 3 Sénoufo, and 3 from various southwestern groups.

[65] In 1959, 10 became *députés*; 5 of these, along with 1 other, were appointed to the government as ministers or secretaries of state (junior ministers). Three were elected to the *conseils généraux*. Another 3 became *attaché* or *chef de cabinet*, essentially patronage appointments to cabinet staff. In 1960 this same group included 6 *députés*, 4 ministers, 2 ambassadors, 2 members of the *conseils généraux*, and 3 staff officials.

[66] J.R.D.A.C.I., "Résolution finale de politique générale" (Proceedings of the Treichville Congress, 1959). (Mimeographed.)

[67] *Fraternité*, October 9, 1959.

years in order to reorganize the country. The current policies of the regime were appropriate because of this need to buy time. "We are opportunists and we may as well admit it," one of them said. He added that two or three years did not count for much in the life of a nation and that what mattered was the long-term task of national construction. Several shared the view that the old leadership could not be challenged openly and that it was therefore necessary to work from within prescribed limits. They hoped in this manner to act as the left wing of the party, as a kind of permanent internal opposition.

A few months after the congress, however, these same individuals expressed their disappointment and their feeling of paralysis. Those who participated in government found that all decisions stemmed from one man only. Furthermore, the relative autonomy of the J.R.D.A.C.I. was reduced in 1960, when it was no longer authorized to sell its own membership cards.[68] The general secretaries of the P.D.C.I. were given the right to veto all activities of the youth committees in their region if they thought they jeopardized unity.[69] The movement was thus made more clearly an ancillary of the senior party. Viewed by the general secretary of the P.D.C.I., it was to be much less an *aile marchante* than a junior branch, a training ground for a new crop of leaders who would emerge in the remote future. Philippe Yacé reassured a meeting of officials of the P.D.C.I. that they had nothing to fear from the youth: "Do you know a family whose head, the patriarch, does not prepare his succession . . .? There are not two R.D.A.'s. There is only one. But you all know that it is difficult to improvise in politics. . . . We want to train our youth, prepare them so that twenty or thirty years from now, when we will have disappeared from this world, we shall be sure that the task we have undertaken will be properly carried on."[70]

[68] *Ibid.*, February 26, 1960.
[69] *Abidjan-Matin*, October 5, 1960.
[70] *Fraternité*, February 5, 1960.

The students remained beyond the pale. J.R.D.A.C.I. negotiators went to Paris in the late spring of 1959 but later reported that they had failed to reach an understanding.[71] Although the organ of the student association admitted that the J.R.D.A.C.I. was "a light shining in the darkness" and that it gave the P.D.C.I. the semblance of a real party, the students said they could not agree with the capitalistic and bourgeois ideology of the P.D.C.I. Only a revolutionary solution could bring about progress for the Ivory Coast.[72] During the following summer vacation, usually a time of great activity among student organizations, a crisis was reached. Memel Fote Harris was arrested when he stopped in Abidjan on his way from Guinea to Ghana.[73] Members of the J.R.D.A.C.I. executive traveled throughout the country to warn the population against what the returning students might say or do. The *Union Générale des Etudiants de Côte d'Ivoire* (U.G.E.C.I.), an association which counted among its members students in France, in Dakar, and in the Ivory Coast, was not allowed to hold its annual summer congress in Abidjan. Its leaders were questioned by the police and put under surveillance. When the annual congress of F.E.A.N.F. at the end of 1959 approved a strongly worded resolution attacking the Ivory Coast regime,[74] the government announced that all students active in A.E.C.I.F. would lose their scholarships. The organization lost control over the management of student hostels and welfare funds. Students were urged to join a new organization, the *Union Nationale des Etudiants et Elèves de Côte d'Ivoire* (U.N.E.E.C.I.), launched with the help of a govern-

[71] *Ibid.*, May 8, 1959.

[72] *Kô-Moë*, April 1959.

[73] The arrest of Memel Fote Harris was not publicized until Houphouet-Boigny answered questions during a press conference in Paris. He said that there had been evidence of the prisoner's involvement in an anti-Ivory Coast plot. (*Fraternité*, June 19, 1959.) See also statements by spokesmen for the youth association in *L'Essor* (organ of the Sudanese Union, section of the R.D.A.), August 7, 1959, and February 12, 1960.

[74] *L'Etudiant d'Afrique Noire*, No. 28, January-February 1960.

ment subsidy in January 1960. The government rewarded the students willing to lead it with the gift of a station wagon. Fresh fruit was shipped from the Ivory Coast when the new association held its first ball in Paris in April. By the end of that month, U.N.E.E.C.I. claimed a membership of 1,100 out of the 1,700 students pursuing a secondary or higher education in Senegal or in France.[75]

The governmentalization of labor and youth associations in 1959 and 1960 was due principally to conflict over a single issue—the Community. Resolution of this controversy came about when the Ivory Coast became independent. However, the regime did not relinquish control over associations in the modern sector. Shortly after independence, the government secured new mechanisms of control. The rationale behind a new law governing associations was expressed unequivocally by the Minister of Justice, who stated that "the action of the government must not be hampered by the proliferation of organizations which, under an innocuous exterior, might work to undermine the policies we must follow."[76] Among other provisions, the law requires that two months in advance of its first meeting, an association must file a declaration of purpose. The minister remarked that since an association could be any permanent group, such as amateur jazz musicians who met weekly at someone's home, theoretically all such groups must obey the law. Many will not do so and it will be impossible to enforce the law. Nevertheless, the legal requirement "leaves in the hands of the government a powerful weapon in case its attention is drawn to the suspicious activities of one of these organizations."[77] No evidence is yet

[75] It was reported that the dissenting students "sabotaged" the ball and later slashed the station wagon's tires. (*Fraternité*, February 26; March 4; April 1, 8, 22, and 29; May 27, 1960.) A new attempt at reconciliation was undertaken after independence. In 1961 Memel Fote Harris was teaching at the Abidjan Lycée. Three more students, including one of the former leaders of U.G.E.C.I., were recruited to the Assembly in 1960.

[76] Ivory Coast, *Débats de l'assemblée nationale*, No. 12 (1960), p. 130.

[77] *Ibid.*

available of the consequences of this law, but there is no doubt that the trend is toward an extension of official control over all aspects of associational life and a transformation of some of the most important organizations in the modern sector into ancillary bodies of the P.D.C.I.

The Party

Although Ivoiriens admit that democracy of the Western type has been restricted because it is undesirable at this stage of the country's development, the outside observer is told to look for a substitute form of democracy inside the party. Spokesmen for the regime maintain that there he will find genuine responsiveness on the part of the leadership, extensive consultation, and mass participation in decision making. This version of reality, however, conflicts with available evidence.

It has been shown throughout this study that the gap between the theory of "democratic centralism" on which the party was founded and the practice of machine control by a small self-appointed ruling group grew with the party itself. When the first P.D.C.I. congress held in ten years finally met in Treichville, from March 19 to 24, 1959, Coffi Gadeau, organizational secretary since 1947, publicly acknowledged in his autocritique that the *Comité Directeur* had failed to keep in touch with the masses and to maintain lively participation in the party.[78] On the following day, a spokesman for the general secretaries asserted that the leadership had weakened, that the *Comité Directeur* lacked cohesion, and that it had not consulted the country on a single important issue in recent years. The lack of accountability of the leadership to the

[78] "Rapport d'Organisation" (Proceedings of the P.D.C.I. Congress of 1959, Treichville, March 19-24, 1959). The congress had first been scheduled for 1957 (*La Concorde*, January 10, 1957) but was repeatedly postponed. This account is based on published proceedings and on personal observation supplemented by interviews with participants. There were 81 *sous-sections* represented at the congress. The total crowd, including observers and unofficial delegations, was estimated at 3,000.

organs of party government was discussed throughout the congress. Although there was evidence during the congress that several factions were vying for power inside the party, a process which might have provided some internal democracy,[79] the aftermath showed that decisions of the congress were not binding upon the uppermost level of the hierarchy.

Pressures to open the upper ranks to new elements, desire to exert some control over the inner circle, and the growing realization that the party was inadequate in the face of its task of national construction, resulted in demands for thorough reorganization. D. Coffi Bile, general secretary of the Grand Bassam *sous-section*, speaking in the name of the other *sous-section* leaders, asked that the *Comité Directeur* of 30 members be enlarged to 60 in order to make room for representatives from the hinterland and that the 5-member secretariat be widened to 15. After this proposal was finally adopted, over the objections of the incumbent members of the party executive, the struggle over nomination and election of new officials was so intense that it prolonged the congress two additional days. Controversy began over the composition of the nominating committee, which was finally made up of members of the outgoing *Comité Directeur* and of general secretaries, a concession to the latter. Half of the members of this caucus were Baoulé, with the remainder distributed among various other groups. At least three slates were proposed to the congress and rejected. Although little is known of the internal proceedings,[80] the final outcome revealed some important changes in the composition of the party leadership. Besides the

[79] Houphouet-Boigny stated in an interview shortly before the congress that factions in the party made for free discussion, a process which he considered to be very healthy. His own function, he explained, was to act as referee and to reconcile the disputants afterwards.

[80] Several informants reported that Houphouet-Boigny told the representatives of local *sous-sections* that they were entitled to nominate about half of the members from their own ranks, while he and the outgoing executive would select the remainder according to their own preferences and political obligations. The results suggest that this is a valid account.

18 members of the outgoing *Comité Directeur*, the new committee of 60 included 25 general secretaries, 9 members of the J.R.D.A.C.I., 5 leaders of voluntary associations such as the U.N.T.C.I., and 3 former opposition leaders.

There were even more significant changes in the make-up of the highest party stratum. The *Bureau Politique*, which replaced in importance the old *Comité Directeur*, included only 8 members of the outgoing executive.[81] The newcomers were: 3 J.R.D.A.C.I. officials, 3 voluntary association leaders, and Coffi Bile, the spokesman for the general secretaries at the congress. Auguste Denise, who had been general secretary of the P.D.C.I. since the beginning of the party's existence, was replaced by Jean-Baptiste Mockey, another of Houphouet-Boigny's foremost lieutenants. Denise was a Baoulé while Mockey was not;[82] furthermore, the new general secretary was known to be less wholeheartedly committed to the Community than Denise had been. There was little doubt that Mockey was not Houphouet-Boigny's choice. This and other changes mentioned marked a genuine coming of age of new elements of the party, supplementing the founders who had ruled without much accountability to the membership for over ten years. It appeared at first that Houphouet-Boigny would bow to the wishes of the congress. Almost all the members of the *Comité Directeur* were elected or appointed to public office in the elections that followed shortly afterwards.[83] Furthermore, as we saw in Table 22 on p. 277, the party hierarchy clearly dominated the Ivory Coast government in 1959 and in 1960, as well as the important offices in the Assembly.

[81] This meant that the other 10 who remained on the new *Comité Directeur* but who were not on the *Bureau Politique* were actually demoted.

[82] He is an Nzima, the tribe to which Kwame Nkrumah also belongs. The Baoulé were well represented on the *Bureau Politique*, however, with 5 out of 15 members.

[83] Eleven were in the cabinet, 29 in the Assembly, and 32 in the *conseils généraux*; some individuals cumulated several of these roles. Only 9 of the 60 held no office above the municipal level.

Mockey, who had been Minister of the Interior since 1957, retained that post and became in addition vice-president of the Council of Government. During Houphouet-Boigny's numerous absences, he was Acting Prime Minister.

It was announced suddenly on September 8, 1959, that Mockey had resigned from the Government "in order to devote himself more fully to the task of reorganizing the party," and that the Prime Minister personally assumed responsibility for the Ministry of the Interior.[84] Two months later, on November 5, a communique stated that he had resigned his office as general secretary of the P.D.C.I. as well as his membership in the *Bureau Politique*.[85] Afterwards, the municipal council of Grand Bassam, of which he was President, was dissolved by executive order.[86] Whatever the reasons for these actions, it is clear that an act of the party congress could be reversed by a personal decision of Houphouet-Boigny.[87] Although the

[84] The Political Bureau issued a terse communique stating that Comrade Mockey had requested that the Bureau ask the Prime Minister to allow him to resign. The cabinet then met and accepted this resignation. The Prime Minister extended his congratulations. (*Abidjan-Matin*, September 9, 1959.) It is curious that although the P.D.C.I. abandoned the tenets of communist ideology in 1950, the style has been retained.

The important position of Minister of the Interior, which carries full control of the coercive apparatus of the state, was formally taken over by Houphouet-Boigny but actually entrusted to a Frenchman who was made "General Secretary for the Interior," a staff position in the office of the Prime Minister. There was a thorough purge in this ministry; the Director of the Security Police (*sureté*) appointed by Mockey, also a Frenchman, was replaced. In 1960 the job of Minister of the Interior was entrusted to G. Coffi Gadeau, organizational secretary of the P.D.C.I., a Baoulé.

[85] All members of the *Comité Directeur* were called to Yamoussoukro, Houphouet-Boigny's birthplace and place of retreat, on a few hours' notice to attend a meeting on October 29, 1959. At that time they were told of Mockey's alleged resignation. The *Comité Directeur* then met formally in Abidjan on November 4 and issued a communique in which it acknowledged the request and approved of it. (*Abidjan-Matin*, November 5, 1959.) The Yamoussoukro meeting, reported by a local French correspondent, resulted in his being called in and reprimanded for reporting "unofficial news."

[86] *Fraternité*, January 15, 1960.

[87] Among the possible explanations was that Mockey had repeatedly

party came out of the congress as a more representative body than what it had been, it was by no means more democratic than in the past.

The most important accomplishment of the congress was to make explicit what had already been visible for some time, namely that the party was now the most important instrument of government control, an *auxiliaire d'autorité*. Performance of this role, however, required reorganization and reactivation. During the months that followed, the party press, virtually extinct since 1952, was revived.[88] Flying teams, invested with the authority to make whatever changes were necessary in the bureau of the *sous-sections*, traveled everywhere in the fall of 1959 and again in the spring of 1960. They explained to rallies held in every *subdivision* that now that the P.D.C.I. was a governmental party, the task of local units was to help execute directives transmitted from Abidjan to the administration in the field.[89] Renewed efforts were made to collect party

---

expressed his disagreement with the Community policy. There was also a sheer struggle for political prominence and control of the party apparatus, probably between Baoulé and non-Baoulé elements in the party. It was also reported and widely circulated that Mockey and others, including several Dioulas and foreigners, had been hatching a plot against Houphouet-Boigny's life, using magic to attain their goal. (This was carried in *Le Canard Enchainé*, October 7, 1959.) It must be added that so far, such purges in the Ivory Coast were far from bloody. In 1960 Mockey was named Ivory Coast Ambassador to Israel; in 1963 he became Minister of Agriculture.

[88] The original R.D.A. newspaper, *Réveil*, published in Dakar, had been replaced by *Afrique Noire* in 1952. This was short lived. In the Ivory Coast the party had a mimeographed bulletin, "Le Démocrate," published fairly regularly during the agitational phase, but only during electoral campaigns later on. In 1956 several party officials including A. Denise launched, with the aid of some Europeans, *La Concorde*. This was a commercial newspaper which reflected the general party position on most issues. It too was short lived. The P.D.C.I. finally published *Fraternité*, a tabloid-size weekly, beginning in April 1959. It is an extremely attractive publication which carries party and government news, sports information, general educational features (health, cooking, etc.). As late as 1963 it was still printed in France and flown to the Ivory Coast for distribution.

[89] *Fraternité*, February 5, 1960.

dues, after the head-tax payable to the government was eliminated in January 1960.[90] As an electoral machine, the P.D.C.I. had been content to obtain financial support from the various sources discussed in Chapter VII; as a government party, it continued to have access to them. Payment of dues was emphasized not so much for the financial income the money would bring as for the symbolic value—an act of allegiance to the party—it would have. When the party became the major instrument of rule wielded by a government concerned with the transformation of the Ivory Coast into a modern nation, personal commitment was required once again, as it had been during the militant years.

Yet, although the effectiveness of party control over most aspects of Ivory Coast life seems clear, its contribution to modernization is more ambiguous. It has already been indicated in Chapter V that during the militant phase, the P.D.C.I.'s structure contributed to the maintenance and even the reinforcement of affiliations based on ethnic ties. Nothing was done to alter this afterwards. A similar situation existed in some other R.D.A. sections as well; at the Bamako Congress of 1957, Modibo Keita stated that ethnic committees, "having a sentimental base, must gradually disappear in order to avoid future difficulties due to the crystallization of militants on positions based on ethnic affiliations."[91] The P.D.C.I. discussed plans to implement this directive during all of 1958 but did not act, lest the party be weakened during the period of transition from the old to the new form of organization. The J.R.D.A.C.I. provisional executive attempted to organize the youth movement on the basis of neighborhood committees in Abidjan but reverted to the ethnic form because of great difficulties in communicating with the members and in obtaining attendance at meetings.[92]

[90] *Ibid.*, March 4, 1960.

[91] "Rapport d'Organisation," *Comptes-rendus du troisième congrès interterritorial du R.D.A.* (Bamako, 1957.) (Mimeographed.)

[92] Interview with a member of the provisional executive of the J.R.D.A.C.I., 1959.

In his report to the P.D.C.I. congress, A. Denise stated again that by maintaining an archaic structure based on ethnic ties, the party did not contribute sufficiently to the transformation of society.[93] It was therefore resolved to replace ethnic subcommittees by ward units. In June 1959 the *Bureau Politique* announced that a pilot project would be launched in Treichville.[94] But the committee appointed to implement this decision reported a few months later that it had been unable to carry out its assignment because "there were no natural neighborhoods in Treichville."[95] They had encountered serious resistance among the subcommittee leaders who form the backbone of the party. In 1960 it was announced once again that ward committees would soon be created. But these turned out to be special units for civil servants, who already live in government housing areas and who, for the most part, had not been previously involved in the party.[96] Moreover, notwithstanding party resolutions, new ethnic subcommittees continue to appear. The Bakoué, a small ethnic group from the western part of the country, complained that they had been lost among the Bété, the Yacouba, and other subcommittees; in September 1960 they called a meeting of all the residents of Treichville who considered themselves Bakoué. The general secretary of the P.D.C.I. *sous-section* attended this gathering and warmly welcomed the new ethnic unit into the party fold.[97] The hope of restructuring the party and thus accelerating the transformation of the Ivory Coast into "*une nation moderne et modèle*," as Houphouet-Boigny is fond of saying, has by no means been abandoned. But for the time being, the party remains essentially a political machine, capable of neutralizing many threats to its maintenance, capable of absorbing change, but not yet capable of constructing a new society.

[93] "Rapport Moral," p. 8. [94] *Abidjan-Matin*, June 18, 1959.
[95] Interview with a member of the *Bureau Politique*, 1959.
[96] *Abidjan-Matin*, February 25, March 11, 1960.
[97] *Ibid.*, October 3, 1960.

CHAPTER X

THE DIRECTION OF CHANGE

THE pattern of political development discernible in this study is far from unique. Like many other Asian and African countries the Ivory Coast has evolved in recent years from dependent to independent status through a series of constitutional steps taken by colonial rulers in response to pressures exerted by local leaders within the context of a secular trend toward self-determination. Decolonization is intrinsically important from a historical point of view. Moreover, the appearance of many new actors has deeply altered the nature of the international political system. From the point of view of the student of political change, however, this juridical evolution is significant mainly because it has provided the institutional mold in which the transformation of an agglomerate of traditional communities into a modern nation began to occur.

This study confirms generalizations proposed by social scientists who have observed the transitional process elsewhere or who have deduced such generalizations from theoretical constructs. In the society as a whole, normative patterns of social behavior that were predominantly ascriptive, diffuse, and particularistic, tend to be supplemented or replaced by more modern ones which emphasize achievement, specificity, and universalism.[1] Political structures have been affected by this transformation and have contributed to it as well. From another point of view, but still at a high level of generalization,

[1] This general pattern of change has been discussed by a variety of social scientists. The concepts involved, developed by Talcott Parsons in *The Social System* and by Marion Levy, Jr., in *The Structure of Society* have been applied to social and political change in emerging nations by F. X. Sutton, in "The Social Basis of New States in Africa" (Unpublished paper, 1959), and in slightly different form by Fred W. Riggs in "Agraria and Industria: Toward a Typology of Comparative Administration," in *Toward the Comparative Study of Public Administration* (Bloomington: Indiana University Press, 1957), pp. 23-116.

political change can be seen as a process of institutional transfer. Localized structures of authority based on tradition are being replaced by secular centralized structures patterned after the model provided by the colonizer. The colonial administration, African political organizations, and individual leaders all contribute to this transformation.[2] Eventually, institutions are modified to suit local needs, as defined by successful nationalist leaders according to their own perceptions.

The analysis presented here attempts to generalize at a lower level. More specifically, the Ivory Coast exemplifies the growth of a regime in which a single mass party is clearly dominant. As suggested in the introduction, this political form is a common one throughout the modern world. Because it is not as well known as others that cluster around the two polar types of liberal democracy and totalitarianism, much exploration is necessary. Comparative analysis, a prelude to greater understanding of single-party systems, has begun only recently.[3] The detailed study of particular cases such as this one will make further work of this type possible.

I have distinguished three major phases of development, which correspond to successive stages of constitutional evolution but which I have analyzed in terms of the structure, the strategies, and the goals of the dominant political organization. In spite of differences in timing, in style of rhetoric or action, and in institutional arrangements, similar phases characterize the political growth of many other former British and French dependencies.[4] The *Parti Démocratique de Côte d'Ivoire* began its career as a protest movement within a framework that afforded but limited opportunities for political participation

[2] This conceptualization is fully developed by Apter in *The Gold Coast in Transition.*

[3] See for example the article by Ruth Schachter in *The American Political Science Review*, LV, No. 2 (June 1961), 294-307.

[4] They have been singled out by Thomas Hodgkin in *Nationalism in Colonial Africa* and in *African Political Parties* (London: Penguin Books, 1961). See also Immanuel Wallerstein, *Africa: The Politics of Independence* (New York: Vintage Books, 1961).

by Africans (1946-1951); it was transformed into a political party during the period of terminal colonialism (1952-1958); and it became synonymous with government when the Ivory Coast Republic was founded (1959-   ).

The movement began as an agglomerate of affiliated associations, a "congress,"[5] but was soon to become more formally structured through the efforts of its leaders and with the help of European sympathizers. Its objectives were both highly specific, in that they constituted the sum of the particular grievances of the various component groups, and highly general, in that they had as their common denominator resentment against alien rule. A desire for some form of autonomy, if not outright independence, was shared by members of the elite and communicated to their followers. Common discontent, together with a reorientation of individuals away from traditional authority, provided the cement for organizational solidarity. These processes were precipitated by one man who embodied the new aspirations, possessed the skills needed for leadership, and thus acted as the catalyst.

Like Nkrumah in Ghana, Houphouet-Boigny is a charismatic leader. Apter's analysis of the role of such leaders is applicable: "The efficiency of charisma lies in the fact that it satisfied the same functional requisites of leadership as did traditional leadership in the past. Nkrumah's charismatic authority has replaced the chief's traditional authority by meeting the same functional requirements, but by introducing new types of structures for their satisfaction."[6] The functional requirements involved are: serving as a source of norms, which become a standard for followers; serving as a symbol, which helps disparate groups in the territorial society acquire a sense of identity with one another; serving as a focus for political integration, by appearing as the central figure of authority within the new institutional framework; and finally, serving

[5] Hodgkin, *Nationalism in Colonial Africa*, pp. 143-48.
[6] Apter, 304.

as a living symbol of the new territorial community, encouraging individuals to transcend traditional ethnic group affiliations.[7] Although during this protest period the nationalist movement opposes the colonial government, the resulting conflict helps promote the goal of the colonial authorities: the institutionalization of a centralized secular political structure.

Incentives for leaders and followers during this period are not material. It is the era of the true believer; those who are frustrated and dissatisfied are willing to make sacrifices for a cause which has, at the time, little tangible prospect of success, because "things which are not are indeed mightier than things that are."[8] It is a period of myth making, of selflessness, during which schoolteachers and junior civil servants, often recent graduates, are presented with an opportunity to become immortal historical actors. There is little need to compromise, little doubt, few pressures to dampen enthusiasm with political realism. Frustrations, grievances, maladjustments stemming from the colonial situation, serve to reinforce the movement. Although one leader overshadows all others, he is not remote, for there has been little time to fully differentiate roles. Fraternal fervor prevails.

Since the colonial framework provides *some* opportunities for political participation by means of elections, nationalist strategy usually involves electoral pursuits. Hence, the movement exhibits from the very beginning some of the features of a vote-getting organization. Nevertheless, since suffrage is limited and elected representatives do not wield much authority, it can be argued that results are not a significant index of support and that elections are not the sole legitimate avenue to political power. The movement demonstrates its strength by engaging in agitational activities, probably easier to promote than any other form of political action. The upheaval that accompanies social change is thus useful to organizations

[7] *Ibid.*, 305-06.

[8] Eric Hoffer, *The True Believer* (New York: Mentor Books, 1958), pp. 70-73.

based on protest and which have no responsibility for government.

After a relatively brief period of suppression, sufficient however to create an enduring mythology relating the struggle for national emancipation, the colonial government becomes more accommodating. The foremost nationalist leader is acknowledged to be an *interlocuteur valable.* Institutions are modified, either by means of a new constitution or less formally by a more liberal interpretation of existing rules, to broaden popular participation and to give modern elites a greater role in the structure of decision making. This is the period of dyarchy or terminal colonialism, during which nationalist movements become political parties. Although ultimate responsibility for government still belongs to colonial officials, who can be blamed for inadequacies of the system and for other ills that befall the country, the party can take credit for the greater emphasis on social welfare and economic development reflected in an expansion of government personnel and in the allocation of a larger share of the budget to tangible items such as new roads, educational and health facilities, or urban construction. Since its leaders participate in government, the party has some control over the allocation of offices, goods, and services. Its distributive capacity is vastly increased.

Earlier, support was often spontaneous. Now, the faithful have grown middle-aged physically and emotionally. They seek rewards more tangible than the knowledge that they are in the mainstream of history. The organization becomes more dependent upon material incentives, not only to satisfy its own members but also to secure the support of former enemies. Because the party's goals can be attained through institutionalized channels, regular demonstration of strength by means of electoral turnout takes priority over agitational tactics. The good party bureaucrat, who can be relied upon to bring out the vote, rather than the firebrand, who can arouse the market crowds, is needed and prized. Differentiations between leaders and followers become more pronounced as the former gain access to a new style of life that is associated with the high positions in the institutional structure they now occupy. The leaders not only derive status from these positions but also endow the institutions of which they are the pinnacle with renewed legitimacy in the eyes of their followers.

Although the party towers over other organizations and is politically secure, there is, during this period, increasing concern with the achievement of a political monopoly. This is justified on the ground that national unity is the primordial goal; since the nationalist movement represents all the people, national unity is defined as being synonymous with political unity. What is sought, the leaders maintain, is not a "unitary" party, but rather a "unified" party. The emphasis is not on exclusiveness but on inclusiveness: opponents are not to be eliminated; they are to be amalgamated. That this was accomplished earlier in the Ivory Coast than in other West African countries, or indeed that it was accomplished at all, remains a source of puzzlement. Disagreement among leaders over policies, together with the existence of consistent cleavages, would lead one to expect that several parties, rather than a single all-encompassing organization, would emerge and sustain themselves. Why did this not occur? No single factor can provide an adequate explanation. The first political body that moves into an organizational vacuum gains a considerable advantage over all competitors. Later, it is easier to hold this position than to conquer it.

The dominant organization also benefits from a bandwagon effect, observed not only in the Ivory Coast but in many other countries as well. During the period of terminal colonialism, opponents find that it is increasingly costly to pass up immediate opportunities in exchange for the uncertainty of future electoral success. More generally, the bandwagon effect can be ascribed to the widespread belief among members of the political elite that there is room for only one nationalist movement, that only one organization can speak validly for an entire country when dealing with alien rulers, that political competition jeopardizes national unity, and, as Ouezzin Coulibaly stated in 1956, that the primacy of a single political party is a prerequisite for the achievement of political maturity and territorial self-government. This belief becomes a social fact which in turn helps transform the belief into political reality. It is a case of self-fulfilling prophecy, an illustration of W. I. Thomas' basic theorem, "if men define situations as real, they are real in their consequences."[9]

Once political supremacy has been achieved, it becomes difficult to maintain it in the face of centrifugal forces at work in the society. Where few natural factors provide unity, it must be authoritatively enforced. Thus, after the party has achieved its monopoly, its character begins to change. This coincides approximately with the attainment of self-government or independence, when the party assumes full responsibility for government. There is a basic change in the logic of the political situation. From the vantage point of the seat of authority, the elite perceive prospects and problems much in the same way as their predecessors did.

Having risen to power as spokesmen who channeled grievances to the center, nationalist leaders now assume a new task: to exert leverage upon the public in order to modernize the country. The functions of the executive are normally complex, strange, and unsettling. Common problems, such as lack of information concerning the consequences of choice and difficulties encountered in translating policies into programs of action, are intensified because of the inadequacy of the political structures. In the face of discrepancies between what must be done and the tools available for the job, frustration and impatience grow. This is translated into an attempt to free government from the pressures of accountability.

[9] Quoted by Robert K. Merton in a discussion of the self-fulfilling prophecy in *Social Theory and Social Structure* (Glencoe: The Free Press, 1949), p. 179.

Certain characteristics of the party, hitherto functional to its maintenance and the achievement of its goals, are now viewed as obstacles to the realization of governmental objectives. This is particularly true of the multiple commitments the party contracted earlier. For example, politically loyal supporters who expect the rewards of office seldom possess relevant administrative skills. Certain patterns of political behavior developed during the period of militancy, such as the expression of grievances by means of civil disturbances, jeopardize vital economic programs by frightening off potential investors. Ultimately, the very success of the organization in promoting institutional transfer creates new difficulties: it has led to the centralization not only of political support but of political demands as well.[10]

The burdens of government are intrinsically very heavy. We have seen how the leaders discovered to their dismay that the balance sheet of national integration at the time of self-government was not entirely favorable, however much progress had been accomplished. Unity must be achieved at any price. But how is this to be done? Moreover, the new nation must summon its energies to tackle its most dreaded foe, economic backwardness. The magnitude of this task is not easily appreciated. Nearly self-sufficient in terms of food and with some valuable export commodities, the Ivory Coast is fortunate in comparison with other underdeveloped countries, where the primary problem is sheer survival in the face of huge population growth and the constant danger of famine, or where no easily exploitable natural resource exists to make the transition from take-off to sustained growth possible.[11] But relative affluence

[10] These concepts are related to an input-output type of political model developed by David Easton in "An Approach to the Analysis of Political Systems," *World Politics*, IX, No. 3 (April 1957), 383-400.

[11] W. W. Rostow argues that the general requirement of this transition "is to apply quick-yielding changes in productivity to the most accessible and natural productive resources." Capital imports can help, of course, but in the end, loans must be serviced. In most cases, this transformation has to take place in the realm of agriculture, which must not only feed an

brings problems, for the gap between material aspirations promoted by increasing social communications and the system's economic capability grows larger. Ivory Coast leaders are fully aware of this process and of its dangers.

Underdeveloped countries which are left to their own devices or still living in a purely colonial economic state, they argue, run only the risk of continued stagnation. But a country in which some development has already occurred cannot afford to undergo regression, "a phenomenon worse than stagnation and the generator of bitterness which leads more easily to explosions."[12] The achievement of independence temporarily assuages this thirst for material improvement but in the long run it exacerbates the problem. Speaking before the First Committee of the United Nations, the Ivory Coast delegate echoed the concern of many of his compatriots and probably of leaders in many other new nations as well: "We must find a rapid solution to our economic problems because the people, whose standard of living is very low, expect independence to bring about an improvement in their condition. Their impatience jeopardizes the social peace that is a necessary prerequisite of economic expansion."[13] We do not know how these factors will affect the political development of new nations. Even if we consider the Ivory Coast case alone, it is difficult to extrapolate present trends in order to obtain an outline of the future. Nevertheless, the efforts of the founding fathers have already resulted in the elaboration of a type of regime that appears to recur, *mutatis mutandis*, in many other developing areas.

During the period of terminal colonialism, the transfer of

---

expanding population, but do so while at the same time liberating manpower for work in new sectors and providing a foreign exchange surplus to import capital equipment. (W. W. Rostow, *The Stages of Economic Growth: A Non-Communist Manifesto* [Cambridge: Cambridge University Press, 1960], pp. 21-23).

[12] *Fraternité*, October 9, 1959.

[13] *Ibid.*, April 21, 1961.

conciliar and democratic institutions inspired from the metropolitan model is completed. After independence, the framework of government is modified to suit local needs and to reflect more faithfully political realities. Provisions are made to insure the dominance of the executive over the legislature. Parliamentary bodies are reduced to the status of deliberative or consultative assemblies. Paradoxically, this step can be thought of as a return to an earlier state of affairs, following Napoleonic precepts such as the ones that guided colonial decision makers. Although universal suffrage is maintained, elections become plebiscitary in tone rather than competitive. Institutional devices may even be introduced to buttress the political monopoly of the government party. Even where the constitution proclaims separation of powers in keeping with liberal prescriptions, one-man rule becomes official. The man who led the movement for national emancipation now becomes the paramount executive, legislator, and judge. In case he is made vulnerable to criticism, as the result of his personal involvement in day-to-day government, his heroic stature is bolstered by mechanical devices of public glorification. Tradition is also invoked to reinforce the legitimacy of his role, either through the public bestowal of formal titles or by more subtle means.

In the course of meeting various contingencies, the rulers extend their control to new spheres. In some countries this is done in accordance with the directives of an ideological blueprint which prescribes total control as the essential strategy for rapid modernization. Although the Ivory Coast has explicitly rejected commitment to such an ideology, its leaders have in fact followed a similar path on an *ad hoc* basis. Their actions are visible in both the traditional and the modern sector. Because the survival of primordial ties is thought to be incompatible with modernity, the government seizes every available opportunity to accelerate the deterioration of the fabric of traditional society. Here, the strategy is a Fabian one; elsewhere, where statesmen have embraced a more militant style, a frontal assault may be preferred. Turning to the modern sector, the rulers view the growth of autonomous voluntary associations with much suspicion. They remember from their own beginnings that such groups can easily become politicized and that they can serve as stepping stones for political entrepreneurs. Two approaches are used simultaneously to meet this threat: on the one hand, secondary associations are transformed into ancillary organizations, subservient to the party; on the other hand, legal controls over associational life and over communications, inherited from the colonial regime, are revived or reinforced.

The lesser importance of parliamentary organs has already been noted. Although the national assembly remains the principal representative body, there is a growing dissatisfaction with the geographical basis of representation. Electoral districts tend to be identified as the home of particular ethnic groups. For this reason, as well as to facilitate control over recruitment of officeholders, the Ivory Coast began to enlarge constituencies until they disappeared altogether. An increasing number of representatives are designated as the spokesmen for occupational groups, "estates," or sectors of the population defined on some other non-geographical basis: they represent government employees, workers in the private sector, women, youth, small or large farmers, coffee or banana growers, foreigners. At the same time, after voluntary associations have been transformed into semi-official organs, they are granted a consultative role in policy making. These developments suggest a possible trend toward corporatism. This has not yet been formally institutionalized, except through the creation of advisory social and economic councils, perhaps because there is little familiarity with European models and because the corporate state has been associated in continental Europe with the right rather than with the left. Here is perhaps the nucleus of a trend more fully visible in the *P.R.I.* of Mexico.

Many of these changes have repercussions inside the party as well. Having merged with the government, the party becomes the coordinator of administration. It must disseminate information and directives from the center to the local level as well as supervise their execution. Its major task is to engineer consent among the population: it must induce consumer demands that are compatible with the product government wants to sell. Since the party is an important component of the bureaucratic apparatus, it must perform its new functions efficiently. Competition within the organization, factionalism, and open debate, all of which had maintained an atmosphere of freedom and had contributed to inner cohesion by providing opportunities for the expression of conflict, must be eliminated because they are thought to endanger the effectiveness of government. There is much ado concerning the revival of party life and of internal democracy. In order to combat apathy, there is renewed emphasis on political pageantry as well. But the good party man, or in a mass-party state, the good citizen, is defined as one who follows directives without questioning the wisdom of his leaders.

The use of coercion to engender support and enforce adherence to the regime grows considerably. Techniques include warning and threats, backed by restriction upon freedom of movement, jailing, banishment, and exile. Although much publicity has been given to such events in African states, several things must be noted: first, that coercion is used *after* other tactics have failed; secondly, that these sanctions, however severe, are usually temporary; and thirdly, that coercion is not used methodically to induce a climate of terror. Relationships between rulers and dissenters retain the air of a family quarrel, followed by grand reconciliations when the crisis is over. This may be attributed in part to the intimate nature of politics in countries that have a small elite bound by a network of personal relationships. Almost anyone of sufficient consequence to be jailed is bound to be a member of at least the extended family of someone high in the ruling hierarchy. Furthermore, it is possible that prescriptions governing the use of coercion have been inspired from their experience under colonial rule. In almost every country of French- and English-speaking Africa, the colonial government eventually recognized that today's troublemakers benefited from popular support, that they had to be coopted in order to secure the consent of the governed, and that they might well become tomorrow's legitimate representatives of the people. The expression of grievances through agitation against the government and retaliatory sanctions may thus be viewed as complementary parts of an intricate process of institutionalized bargaining.

During the period of alien rule, the physical presence of European officials, traders, or colonists, as well as the colonial situation in general, contributes to the maintenance of internal cohesion by providing an external enemy against whom common energies can be directed. Although these objects are removed after independence, others are substituted. Particular choices reflect the more or less militant style of the regime. In some cases, the leadership will emphasize the threat of neocolonialism, the desirability of liberating hitherto unfree African countries, and the need to create a powerful, unified pan-African whole, capable of intervening positively in world affairs. In other cases, among which the Ivory Coast may be included, the threats are identified somewhat differently. They have included other African countries suspected of having designs on Ivory Coast wealth; nations of the more militant type to which irridentist propensities can be attributed; and more recently, there have been occasional references to the dangers of Chinese communism. The choice of objects used to externalize inner tensions helps explain the different stand African countries with similar regimes have taken on international issues. Finally, it is not unusual to find that some group within the country inherits the unfortunate role of scapegoat. Immigrant African communities are particularly vulnerable in this respect.

Reliance on coercion to obtain support, the use of external threats to strengthen cohesion, the appearance of a scapegoat mechanism, must not be allowed to overshadow the fact that the priority assigned to these tactics remains lower than that which is attributed to others in the regime's panoply. Cooptation, distribution of tangible rewards, and persuasion remain significant. Similarly, the gap between constitutional theory and political practice, the growth of executive dominance and of personal rule, must not be allowed to hide the responsiveness of the regime, its concern with goals shared by most of the people, and the constant practice of formal and informal consultation. The rulers continue to benefit from a vast store of trust and consent. The most important source of support continues to stem from the ties thinner than air but stronger than steel that bind the people to the national hero. Although corrosion has attacked these bonds as the result of new political difficulties, they have not yet been destroyed. The people continue to believe in the benevolent intentions of their leader, in his wisdom in choosing policies, and in his power to overcome obstacles as long as he continues to fulfill the mission for which he assumed responsibility long ago: yesterday, to terminate alien rule; today and tomorrow, to secure rapid improvement of economic and social conditions at the least possible cost to his people.

To affix a label upon regimes such as the one we have analyzed is a most delicate task because of the inadequacy of the classificatory terminology and the emotional response evoked by such unavoidable terms as "democracy," "oligarchy," and "totalitarian." Professor Shils has refined the taxonomy of new states by qualifying the above terms by means of adjectives which refer partly to the *intentions* of the ruling elite: thus we obtain a larger number of categories including "political" and "tutelary" democracies, as well as "modernizing," "traditional," and "totalitarian" oligarchies.[14] Some writers have rejected the use of a non-structural dimension, such as the intention of the rulers, because of its fickle character.[15] Yet this objection ignores the nature of many of the new states in which the very structural fact that authority is concentrated in the hands of a ruling group relatively free from accountability enhances the relevance of their intentions.

Whether the intentions of ruling elites can seriously affect the growth of political structures is one of the most basic questions of political science and can be answered only after careful empirical investigation. This study has suggested that the political outlook of the leadership in the Ivory Coast has had important consequences for the regime and that it will probably influence the direction of future transformation as well.

The Ivory Coast is not a political democracy in the sense usually attributed to this concept in the West. There is no institutionalized competition between two or more political parties to determine who will govern. Although in a one-party system it is possible for internal contests to serve as a substitute, this does not occur in the P.D.C.I. Furthermore, civil liberties, which never flourished under French tutelage, have been severely curtailed by the new rulers. While in external appearance it is a government of laws rather than of men, these laws, including the constitution itself, have been tailored to suit a specific set of governors and can easily be altered at their discretion.

It is not difficult to argue, however, that the regime is more democratic than its traditional or colonial predecessors. The Ivory Coast and other new nations that are governed by a modern elite, ruling through a mass party which has a broad

[14] Edward Shils, "Political Development in the New States," *Comparative Studies in Society and History*, II, 379-411.

[15] For a discussion of this subject, see Ernest B. Haas, "System and Process in the International Labor Organization," *World Politics*, XIV, No. 2 (January 1962), 324-25.

popular base, which is inclusive rather than exclusive, and which is genuinely representative of most strata in the population, have passed a point of no return on the road toward political modernization. Further development may be arrested; oligarchical tendencies may become more pronounced; controls may be greatly extended; but whatever else political change may bring, never again will rulers base their legitimacy solely on traditional claims, on the right of conquest, or on racial superiority. Today's rulers must proclaim their adherence to democratic values even when they depart from them. That they should do so must be seen less as a sign of hyprocrisy than as the mark of a bad conscience. Ivory Coast leaders acknowledge the desirability of democracy but justify undemocratic practices on the basis of expediency. They view the regime they have helped to create as a tutelary democracy. As Shils has indicated, there is something instinctive about this: "Tutelary democracy is a variant of political democracy which recommends itself to the elites of the new states. It does so because it is more authoritative than political democracy, and also because the institutions of public opinion and the civil order do not seem qualified to carry the burden which political democracy would impose on them. It is not the object of a theory in the way in which political democracy and totalitarian oligarchy have become theories; it is the 'natural theory' of men brought up to believe in themselves as democrats, who have, for various reasons, considerable attachment to democratic institutions and who have, for good or poor reasons, little confidence in their people's present capacity to operate democratic institutions effectively amidst the tasks of the new states."[16]

This type of regime is characterized by an adaptation of the institutions of political democracy in the direction of executive dominance. There tends to be a merger of party and government, with emphasis on discipline. Although freedom of ex-

[16] Shils, pp. 389-90.

pression, of assembly, and of association may be impaired, the rule of law must be maintained: "When it goes, then tutelary democracy turns more determinedly toward oligarchy."[17] The regime must truly attempt to reinstate the institutions of political democracy whenever feasible. Furthermore, the incumbents must tolerate some criticism and accept at least in principle the idea of an opposition. The opposition, on its side, must overcome the twin dangers of self-destruction in the face of great odds and transformation into a subversive organization.[18]

The distinction between a tutelary democracy and a modernizing oligarchy is a subtle one. Similar aspirations among the elite underlie both types. The oligarchy, whether it is manned by a military or a civilian elite, is characterized by the elimination of parliament or by a drastic reduction in its role. There is greater interference with the rule of law than in the tutelary democracy. Opposition is definitely not tolerated. It is important to note, however, that the term encompasses regimes that are representative, responsive, and concerned with eliciting consent among the governed. Tutelary democracies and modernizing oligarchies can be thought of as being part of a continuum, with the latter being more distant from the pole of political democracy than the former. If we use the actions of the Ivory Coast rulers rather than their stated intentions as classificatory criteria, then we must consider the country as a modernizing oligarchy. It is ruled by a set of benevolent managers. Like that of its colonial predecessor, its mood is one of paternalism.

Evolution toward democracy in the near future is unlikely but not impossible. However, there is little desire to bring this about. Also, the achievement of unanimity between 1958 and 1960 makes it very difficult to return to a competitive system or even to hold free one-party elections without damning

[17] *Ibid.*
[18] *Ibid.*, p. 391.

the regime's own past or appearing to lose support. If only 60 or 80 per cent, rather than nearly 100 per cent of the eligible voters turned out to vote, or if *some* opposition were tolerated, the leaders would have to admit either that they had caused dissatisfactions among their supporters or that the results of earlier elections were not genuine. In either case, the legitimacy of the regime would be endangered. It is unlikely, therefore, that the incumbent leadership, having curtailed democracy, would reinstate it. Furthermore, we have found little differentiation in the attitudes and the political values of the contemporary political generation. Hence it is unlikely that a change in government within the framework of the regime would modify the existing situation to any significant extent. Looking at potential successors among the younger generation, there is probably even less attachment to democratic values and greater devotion to non-democratic ideologies that hold the promise of rapid modernization.

Is it not possible, however, that the social and economic development, which the modernizing oligarchy might bring about, will foster a new environment more conducive to the growth of democracy? Should the prospect of more education, increases in individual and collective wealth, urbanization, industrialization, exposure to mass media, foster long-run hopes? These factors are thought to be prerequisites of democracy.[19] They might transform society by creating a new web of group relationships that will overcome the consistent cleavages which exist today while preserving differentiations. Ultimately, a favorable conjunction of consensus and cleavage might be reached, and the seed of democracy would fall on fertile soil. Although this possibility should be entertained, we must note that these prerequisites are not conditions sufficient to bring democracy about. They are at least equaled in importance by the requirement that there be an elite devoted to the philosophic ideal itself. From what sources will the

[19] Lipset, "Some Social Requisites of Democracy . . .," pp. 75-85.

elites of today and tomorrow derive greater respect for democratic values than they now exhibit? Certainly not, unfortunately, from the political model to which the Ivory Coast continues to be most exposed, contemporary France.

The prospect of accelerated social and economic change suggests yet another possibility. Although in the process of becoming modern, societies acquire some of the structural characteristics that are associated with democracy, the breakup of traditional society can also result in the growth of a mass society that is associated with the development of totalitarianism.[20] If social conditions accompanying the early stages of economic development resemble their European antecedents, then the growth of *anomie* is not unlikely. Traditional affiliations can be replaced by more modern ones, such as voluntary associations, that mediate between the individual and the state, if they are free, but which can be used to attain total control by an oligarchy skilled in the use of the organizational weapon, motivated by a sense of urgency, and inspired by an ideology that holds great promise. Indeed, communism, like other forms of totalitarianism, can be viewed as "a disease of the transition."[21] Finally, it is also possible that the regime will become more firmly institutionalized: "It is . . . reasonable to believe that oligarchical regimes are capable of persistence; even though the particular group of persons who rule in an oligarchy might change by cooptation or forcible displacement, the oligarchical regime has a toughness which makes it resistant to efforts to replace it by another type of regime. The question, however, is whether modernizing oligarchical elites can succeed in their efforts to modernize their societies, to rule with stability and effectiveness and to mobilize the enthusiastic support of a politically impotent populace."[22]

[20] There is a vast literature on this subject. See among others Emil Lederer, *The State of the Masses* (New York: W. W. Norton, 1940) and Hannah Arendt, *The Origins of Totalitarianism* (New York: Harcourt, Brace, 1951).

[21] Rostow, pp. 162-64.

[22] Shils, p. 398.

Although systems of this type can adjust to changing circumstances, their very nature makes for some rigidity. Even when they are revolutionary in style, oligarchic leaders tend to be truly conservative since they are loath to depart from the policies they have initiated and which they believe to be correct. From their point of view, modernity can be achieved only through the rational pursuit of specified goals. In the political realm, the equivalent of planning is efficient management of demands and support. Hence, the rulers of a modernizing oligarchy view discontent as a source of interference with rationality which must be eliminated. As the founders of a new state, these leaders have become immortal actors who see themselves as indispensable. To relinquish control or to share it with others therefore implies the abandonment of a historical responsibility.

In the absence of effective and legitimate channels for the articulation of grievances, however, some pressures are allowed to build up until they reach the point of explosion. New political generations, often more educated than their elders, aspire to participate in decision making at the highest levels, but are told to wait indefinitely. Their frustrations engender despair and lead them to espouse millennial hopes. In order to secure a political foothold, these and other opponents of the regime may revive primordial loyalties; in order to hasten the departure of the incumbents, they may resort to violence.

I have tried to resolve the apparent paradox of the emergence of a one-party system in a very heterogeneous country by referring to the legacy of nationalism, the perceptions of leading political actors, and the ease with which they were able to impose their solution to the lack of national unity in the face of weak resistance. But enforced political unanimity is a mere palliative, not to be confused with the achievement of national integration and the growth of a mature polity. In the Ivory Coast, as in other African societies, it is unlikely that such a deeply imbedded feature of the social structure as the consistent cleavages which prevailed during the period of political take-off can be erased by political fiat. Now as in the past, almost any issue can provide the spark needed to revive the latent conflicts which, unhampered by cross-pressures, rapidly reach the level of the political community. Hence, political change tends to be discontinuous. The persistence of the one-party system or of the modernizing oligarchy may be expressed not by the political longevity of a specific set of rulers, but by its recurrence as an institutional form after periods of adjustment through political conflict.

The direction of change remains undetermined. If we are to understand the variables that affect political growth more clearly than we do today, we must explore the relationships between political structures and the tasks that governments are called upon to perform in developing societies. This study stops short of the analysis of these questions. Further investigations should observe the manner in which different regimes approach problems common to them all, such as modernization of agriculture, national integration, creation of a reliable bureaucracy, as well as the way in which they adjust to the difficulties they encounter. Are there limits to the burdens that regimes can shoulder without undergoing profound transformation? Does the nature of the burdens inexorably determine the nature of the new states? Attempts to answer these and similar questions can lead to difficult but rewarding undertakings in the study of politics.

APPENDIX

THE FIRST DECADE

IN Chapter VIII, "The Instruments of Rule," and Chapter IX, "Modernization and Control," an attempt was made to provide some understanding of the political processes characteristic of a new nation by examining the choices made by rulers in designing suitable political institutions and by analyzing the manner in which they undertook major tasks and responded to challenges. The present appendix extends these chapters to the close of the first decade of political autonomy which began with the establishment of an indigenous regime following the referendum of 1958. From mid-1962 to mid-1964 political life in the Ivory Coast was dominated by a serious crisis stemming from the involvement of high-level persons in one or more plots to overthrow the regime. The crisis provides an opportunity to refine our understanding of the tensions which characterize Ivory Coast society and of the relationships between that society and the regime. The regime responded to the threats to its maintenance by a series of short-term, mainly repressive, actions; but at the same time it initiated longer-term projects designed primarily to anticipate difficulties by institutionalizing more adequate structures of political control, communications, and participation and by speeding of the modernization of society itself.[1]

The Crisis Years

In the last days of 1962 President Houphouet-Boigny convoked party leaders, elected officials, and ranking administrators to a meeting in his home town of Yamoussoukro to be held on January 3, 1963; but the meeting was repeatedly postponed and finally was held on January 14. During the inter-

[1] Unless otherwise specified, the materials in this appendix are based on interviews and direct observation during two brief visits in the Ivory Coast in 1963 and in 1964, and on regular reading of the weekly party newspaper, *Fraternité Hebdomadaire*. Some of the data and analyses were used in my comparative study, *Creating Political Order: The Party-States of West Africa* (Chicago: Rand McNally & Co., 1966).

vening period, rumors spread that many people had been arrested; the President recalled all Ivory Coast ambassadors from abroad; there was a wave of consultations at the Presidential palace in Abidjan; the government obtained approval by the National Assembly of a proposal for the creation of a special court of state security empowered to deal with criminal acts directed against external and internal security; and the Assembly modified the Constitution to place members of the government within this court's jurisdiction. On January 12 Philippe Yacé, President of the National Assembly and Secretary-General of the *P.D.C.I.*, denied rumors that there had been an attempt to assassinate the President, but stressed that the Ivory Coast would not tolerate any subversive acts inspired by Communists.

After the Yamoussoukro conference was over, Yacé reminded the country that the Communist Party was outlawed and announced that an investigation was under way to ascertain who was responsible for subversive propaganda. He also said that the new court would try those against whom sufficient charges could be proffered, that the party would launch a purge in all sectors of national life, and that the Party Congress, scheduled for March 28, would be postponed until July. Shortly afterwards, the government announced that three cabinet ministers had been dismissed by the President and were under arrest; the National Assembly lifted the parliamentary immunity of eight of its members; the President of the Supreme Court resigned. The wave of arrests reached into the administration, including several recently appointed *préfets* and *sous-préfets*, as well as the head of the national information service. Eventually it was learned that between 120 and 200 persons had been arrested, many of them while attending the Yamoussoukro conference, and that they were being held incommunicado in the President's compound there. During the months that followed, 126 individuals were formally investigated; 40 were cleared and the remainder were tried behind closed doors in Yamoussoukro from April 5 to 9, 1963. Of the 86 brought to trial, 22 were acquitted; 44 were sentenced to hard labor for periods ranging from 5 to 20 years; 7 to hard labor for life; and 13 received the death penalty. Soon after these sentences were made public, however, party officials asserted privately that the death sentences would not be carried out.

Official accounts eventually specified that it had been learned in mid-1962 that a conspiracy was afoot to seize power toward the end of the year, probably by surrounding Yamoussoukro while President Houphouet-Boigny and other officials were gathered there in council. This information enabled the government itself to set a trap in Yamoussoukro in January. Official comments further referred to the Communist-inspired activities of "Young Turks" who had retained a leftist orientation since their student days in Paris. Using the *J.R.D.A.C.I.* as a cover, they had recruited conspirators at all levels of society, exploiting latent divisions along tribal or regional lines. Indeed, the examination of the 64 individuals condemned in April shows that they included 6 of the 19 members of the executive committee of the *J.R.D.A.C.I.*, as well as others known to be local *J.R.D.A.C.I.* officials and former student leaders. Furthermore, many of those tried bore names recognizably associated with ethnic groups which had opposed Baoulé dominance in national political life since shortly after World War II, such as Dioula and Sénoufo in the North, Bété in the West, and Agni of Sanwi in the Southeast.

Before and after the trial, the regime took a series of decisions designed to bolster its authority which included: the passage of a "law for the utilization of persons," enabling the government to mobilize idle men into a labor corps; the reassignment of numerous civil servants; the creation of party committees inside each ministry and at the level of every major administrative district; the negotiation of agreements with generally like-minded African countries to help fight domestic subversion; the retention of a larger number of university-level students at home by reducing the number of scholarship awards; and the requirement of demonstrations of political loyalty as a prerequisite for these awards. In June a spokesman for the President admitted publicly that the senior party leaders who opposed the creation of the *J.R.D.A.C.I.* on the grounds that it would become a party within a party had been correct; hence, the organization was formally dissolved and its local committees were brought under the direct authority of local party officials. The long-awaited Party Congress, at which plans for a thorough reorganization of its structures would be discussed, was postponed until the end of the year.

President Houphouet-Boigny had left the country on April 19, shortly after the Yamoussoukro trial, in order to attend the summit meeting of the Organization for African Unity in Addis-Ababa scheduled for May. He went on to visit the Malagasy Republic, Egypt, and reached Europe in mid-summer for his annual rest. Meanwhile, the wave of disturbances throughout French-speaking Africa, which had begun with the Senghor-Mamadou Dia showdown in Senegal the previous fall, and had engulfed Togo, now reached Brazzaville. The President returned to Abidjan on August 28 amid a climate of renewed tension. The popular celebrations usually held upon his return were cancelled. Instead, he sped to his palace under full armed guard and began a new series of consultations. It was announced in rapid succession that the government intended to create a party militia composed of able-bodied young men and army veterans; that the Party Congress was postponed once again in order to permit the thorough renewal of party branches; and that government employees, whose salaries had been frozen for several years, would receive a substantial raise.

Once again, arrests were not publicized at the time, but it can be estimated in retrospect that they had numbered over a hundred. From information made public later, it became evident that the individuals implicated were of generally higher political stature than those allegedly involved in the earlier plot and that opposition to the regime had reached the highest levels of the party and of the government. The most prominent names included five party founders who were members of the *Bureau Politique* and of the Security Court created at the beginning of the year; the three most outstanding leaders of regional movements who had been coopted into the Houphouet-Boigny coalition during the previous decade; and additional representatives of the university-trained second generation. Six of these men were also cabinet members, including the Minister of the Interior and the Minister of Defense; four were members of the National Assembly; and one had recently been President of the Supreme Court. Several long-time French residents of the Ivory Coast were expelled from the country as well.

At his press conference on September 9 the President hinted that the new plot had been "ideological" in character, and asserted that while Socialism was appropriate for other countries there was no reason to establish it in the Ivory Coast. A few weeks later Yacé offered a more elaborate interpretation. Tracing the sources of the crisis to 1950-51, when the *R.D.A.* severed its links with the French Communist Party, he said that some senior party leaders had stayed in touch with the Communists and had slowly organized a subversive network linking them with ex-opposition politicians, some Frenchmen, and politicians of neighboring African countries. Together, and with the anticipated support of the Army, they plotted to establish a tribal federation within the Ivory Coast, which would itself be linked to a socialist-minded multinational union of West African states. The reference here was clearly to the then existing union of Ghana, Guinea, and Mali. However, no explanation was given then or later as to how known antagonists within the *Bureau Politique* had suddenly become reconciled, how *P.D.C.I.* stalwarts had become the allies of the party's oldest enemies, how party leaders who had opposed the formation of the *J.R.D.A.C.I.* had come to plot with youth leaders, or how any of these alleged leftists had become involved with a conservative Frenchman who had defended to the very end the maintenance of a two-college system in the old *Conseil Général*, except that they were all Freemasons, using their lodge activities as a cover for subversion.

Preparations began immediately for a giant rally in support of President Houphouet-Boigny, to be held in Abidjan on September 28, the 5th anniversary of the referendum. The Army was disarmed, while order was maintained throughout the city by the armed party militia (described by some observers as "Baoulé warriors"), brought in from the President's home region. The President assumed personal responsibility for all the areas covered by the ministers who had been arrested; in addition to foreign affairs, which he already directed, this included interior, defense, information, agriculture, animal husbandry, and housing. He then withdrew to Yamoussoukro and slowly returned to Abidjan in a triumphal march through loyal villages. All activity stopped throughout the country as huge crowds, reported by the government to number about a million, poured into the capital city for the expected rally.

In their major speeches before the crowd gathered in and around the Abidjan stadium, President Houphouet-Boigny and Secretary-General Yacé repeated many of the announcements of previous weeks, including the decisions to reorganize the Army and launch the party militia, punish subversives, and renovate party structures. In addition, the President stressed his desire to satisfy the people's legitimate needs; since farmers suffered from the consequences of depressed world market prices, he was taking over agriculture personally to seek adequate solutions. The government would launch compensatory regional development programs in order to reduce disparities; civil servants would get better salaries; there would be greater freedom for trade unions so long as they did not engage in political strikes; distribution circuits would be improved to the benefit of African traders; foreign Africans living and working in the Ivory Coast would be granted double nationality; greater control would be exerted over students. He also warned that corruption and favoritism must be eliminated from all sectors of Ivory Coast life.

A number of these measures and related actions were implemented in the months that followed. The Security Court was reorganized in preparation for the new trial; in addition to the party militia, the government announced the creation of a presidential guard distinct from the regular army; and all students were ordered to join the government-sponsored student union (*U.N.E.C.I.*) lest their scholarships be withdrawn. The Party Congress was again postponed, while ad hoc measures for internal reorganization were taken, including the stabilization of ethnic group representation in the Abidjan branches, the renewal of a number of other sections and the creation of additional ones to bring the party in line with territorial administration, and the creation of a "political committee" distinct from the *Bureau Politique* whose ranks had been depleted as the result of the crisis.

In the early months of 1964 the atmosphere appeared to have relaxed somewhat as the regime regained confidence. The President prepared a long-awaited family reunion of *R.D.A.* leaders, including Presidents Modibo Keita of Mali and Sékou Touré of Guinea, at Bouaké on April 9 to discuss common problems of internal security. But the mood changed suddenly on April 6 when it was announced that Ernest Boka, a student leader who had served as Minister of Education, Minister of Public Service, and President of the Supreme Court, had committed suicide while detained in the President's compound in Yamoussoukro. Rumors that he had been assassinated or died of ill treatment immediately spread both in the Ivory Coast and abroad. After a number of hasty emergency party meetings, President Houphouet-Boigny convoked an ad hoc national council to which foreign diplomats, religious authorities, and businessmen were invited as well. Claiming that Boka had been neither beaten nor tortured, he devoted the major part of his address to the reading of a confession allegedly written by Boka before his death, and to his own commentaries on it.[2]

In this document Boka admits that he had repeatedly engaged in financial manipulations while holding public office, that he had remained sympathetic to the French Communist Party since he joined its ranks while a university student at Grenoble in 1951-52 and had used his influence to place Communists in key administrative posts, and that he had plotted throughout to eliminate those who stood in the way of his self-appointed status as the President's political heir. But the document also contains strange statements concerning Boka's constant reliance on diviners and wielders of occult power to realize his political ambitions. In a final peroration, he repeats his confession of guilt, asks forgiveness for his family, and demands to be immediately executed as an unworthy monster, hinting that he had been in contact with someone who was in a position to poison the President, while also employing an individual "to work on the President's photograph." And he concludes: "It is as if I had assassinated him. May God forgive me!"

After this reading, President Houphouet-Boigny severely condemned "fetishist practices." He said that, having been initiated to their use, he knew that fetishes themselves can do no evil, but that evil stems only from the use that can be made of them; fetishes do not kill, only the poison that is behind them. He also explained that the Ivory Coast was suffering from the consequences of the abandonment of traditional religious controls over the use of fetishes, while indi-

[2] The transcripts were published in *Abidjan-Matin*, April 16, 1964; and in *Fraternité*, "Supplément," April 17, 1964.

viduals retained their belief in the power of the fetishes themselves. "Atheism," especially among the educated young, is therefore a great threat which can be overcome only by the serious practice of Christianity and Islam. Finally, the President displayed as evidence two suitcases allegedly seized from members of Boka's family and others containing magic philters, a variety of fetishes, and small coffins holding his own corpse in effigy.

Additional information concerning the crisis was published about a year later, following a new trial by the Security Court. This time, its verdicts included 6 death sentences, 2 life sentences, 19 jail terms, 19 acquittals, and 18 "absolutions." The latter were granted to a number of old party militants who had been found guilty, but whose previous services warranted forgiveness. These absolutions were conditional upon public confessions before assemblies in Abidjan and throughout the country. In the course of the confessions it was revealed that there had been a second plot to arrest President Houphouet-Boigny when he disembarked in August; the capital would then have been invaded by tribesmen from the North, the West, and the Southeast, who would help bring to power an ethnic federation. Its head was to have been Jean-Baptiste Mockey, the man who had been elected Secretary-General of the *P.D.C.I.* in 1959 against President Houphouet-Boigny's wishes but who had been ousted shortly afterward amid rumors that he leaned toward a "socialist" orientation and had resorted to witchcraft to plot against the President (see pp. 316-18, including notes 85-87, above). After a short period of enforced retirement, Mockey had been appointed Ambassador to Israel; he was brought back to head the Security Court in January 1963, and appointed Minister of Agriculture to implement cooperative methods he had studied while in Israel. At about the same time, the Ivory Coast charged that the Ghanaian ambassador had participated in the conspiracy on behalf of his government.

Many aspects of the Ivory Coast crisis of 1962-64 remain obscure. We cannot ascertain whether the various elements involved in one or more attempts to overthrow the existing regime relied on internal resources alone or whether they benefited from external support, as the Ivory Coast government claimed they did, any more than we can verify the proposition that at least one of these attempts would have succeeded if the regime had not itself benefited from French military support. From the point of view of this study, however, even the incomplete account available is useful, because it confirms that the origins of the crisis lay in the persistence of old patterns of conflict characteristic not only of the Ivory Coast, but of other new African nations as well. One major source of strain stems from the cleavages between ethnic groups discussed throughout this book. From this point of view, the crisis confirms my hypothesis that in the short run, at least, processes of social, economic, and political modernization increase rather than reduce the likelihood of severe conflict. The other major source of strain stems from the deep cleavage between the founding generation of nationalist leaders and the generation of potential successors, who view themselves as better qualified to rule on the basis of their higher education. In the case of the Ivory Coast, President Houphouet-Boigny's persistent avoidance of militancy in the fields of foreign affairs and economic development insures that these oppositions speak in the name of the left; but the experience of similar sources of opposition in other African regimes which themselves identify with the left suggests that ideology as such is not a determining factor.

The allusions to magic and witchcraft which emerged in the course of the crisis were, so far as I know, the first public references by the Ivory Coast regime to processes that are often hinted at by Ivorians discussing politics privately. Are these references to be dismissed as trumped up accusations in this particular case, and as irrelevant lurid gossip generally?

What matters is not whether or not a specific individual resorted to such means but rather whether actors involved in important social and political processes *believe* that such means are used and that they can be effective, as is indeed the case in the Ivory Coast. At the most manifest level, these beliefs contribute to the generation of a climate of great suspicion, especially among individuals who are closely associated with one another; and this climate itself contributes to the fulfillment of the prophecy. But at a less manifest level, these beliefs are associated with a sense that the equilibrium which prevailed in traditional society between the use of occult powers and controls over the circumstances and consequences of this use has been lost. How can it be restored?—Only by creating a new reliable order of society. Initially, for many Africans, this order was sought in the political realm. But as recurrent disturbances demonstrated the failure of this strategy, or as the costs of political fervor came to be viewed as overly high, one could expect the emergence of alternatives. Viewed in this light, President Houphouet-Boigny's appeal for participation in Christian and Muslim religious activities and the subsequent implementation of this appeal by means of specific efforts, must be taken as an important key to the understanding of the institutionalization of patterns of integration in the Ivory Coast.

Institutional Renovation

The experience of the crisis years revealed that existing party structures were faction-ridden, that they were inadequate instruments of control over the administration and over the population, and that they did not provide an effective network of political communication. Although party reconstruction began immediately, the record of the last 5 years suggests that the Ivory Coast regime has come to rely much more heavily on the development of an effective territorial state bureaucracy for the performance of critical tasks. Furthermore, although the Party, the National Assembly, and regular elections remain the formal nexus for popular participation in political life, in effect this nexus seems to have become merely one component of an incipient institution which can be called the Estates-General of the Ivory Coast.[3]

At the time of independence, the Ivory Coast was still divided territorially into *cercles* and *subdivisions* manned primarily by French colonial officials with some African aides. Below this, in the rural areas, the *canton* was still functioning as a unit headed by an appointed African chief. It is in this sphere that the most significant institutional innovations have taken place. By the end of 1965 the *cercles* and *cantons* had been eliminated and the country had been reorganized into six *départements*, each headed by a *préfet*, and further into approximately 100 *sous-préfectures*, each headed by a *sous-préfet*. More recently, this administrative network has been further extended by the creation of several *centres d'état-civil* below the *sous-préfecture* level. The organizational model is clearly that of contemporary France; but the spirit in which the organization operates appears to be closer to that of the French Second Empire in the mid-nineteenth century. The prefects are the President's personal representatives at the regional level, endowed with broad authority to implement his directives; several of them are also members of the *Bureau Politique*. The sub-prefects are usually products of the National School of Administration, but political criteria enter into their recruitment and assignment to specific posts.

The role of the sub-prefect in the Ivory Coast and of equivalent officials elsewhere is critical in the overall process whereby a modernizing center attempts to reach into those spheres of society least affected by social change. This is clear from the extent of the tasks entrusted to them: they are in charge of

[3] A most useful source of detailed information on recent Ivory Coast institutions is: Conférence Olivaint de Belgique, *La Côte d'Ivoire, Chances et risques* (mimeographed report, 1966; 71 Avenue de Cortenberg, Brussels 4).

the newly created civil registry services, whereby the most intimate aspects of social life become publicly regulated acts; they "animate" development policies and coordinate the activities of technical officials in their district; they report on political life in the area by keeping track of the activities of individuals and groups.[4] There are no assemblies with decision-making authority at this level in the Ivory Coast, but merely a *Conseil des Notables* of from 8 to 16 members who must be consulted by the sub-prefect at least once a year. The status of chiefs is ambiguous. Although the 1934 law concerning their recruitment and functions has never been abolished (see pp. 52-54, 101-102, and 286-94, above), the administrative chiefs have been stripped of their authority in the fields of tax-collection, judicial arbitration, and police. During their lifetime they are consulted by the sub-prefect, but the government has not been recruiting successors when the incumbents die.

From mid-1964 on, the *P.D.C.I.*'s territorial organization was modified to parallel the territorial state bureaucracy; approximately 40 new sections, corresponding to the new sub-prefectures, were created. As in the past, these sections are divided into village committees in the rural areas and into ward or ethnic subcommittees in the towns. In keeping with a long-standing suspicion of regional centers of power, there is no party organization corresponding to the departmental level. In preparation for the Party Congress of September 1965, national teams supervised the election of secretary-generals in the new sections and in old ones where officials had been dismissed during the crisis; unusual publicity was given in the Party press to the democratic character of the electoral process by citing actual results.

The Congress's main task was to replenish the membership of the Party's governing bodies, one-third of whom had been involved in opposition activities. The Congress maintained all

[4] See Robert Guidon Lavallée, *Le Manuel du Sous-Préfet* (Abidjan: Editions Africaines, n.d.).

10 remaining members of the *Bureau Politique* and selected 15 new members, for an enlarged total of 25. About two-thirds of the additions appeared to be "old companions," individuals who had been active at the local level in the late 1940's. The remainder were technocrats who had remained faithful to the President throughout the crisis, including some outstanding members of the university-trained second generation. Significantly, these men were selected as individuals rather than as representatives of organizational components of the party. The *Comité Directeur* was enlarged to 85 (including the 25 members of the *Bureau Politique*). Its membership consisted mainly of old and new secretary-generals, and the only visible innovation was the inclusion of 10 women.

The Congress was also concerned with finances and communications. In recent years the payment of party dues has become such a universal phenomenon that it may be assimilated to the payment of a head tax. Indeed, the secretary-general has become a tax farmer, since he retains approximately one-third of the proceeds gathered in his section, much as the *chef de canton* did in respect to the head tax before it was abolished. Furthermore, although the basic rate has been set at 200 C.F.A. francs a year (approximately 80 cents), a lower rate has been set for poorer areas. Besides the secretary-general's share, half of the proceeds are allocated to the national level, mostly for the construction of a national headquarters, leaving only approximately 15 per cent for the activities of the section and the local committees, including their building program. The party has increased the production of its weekly, *Fraternité Hebdomadaire*, to nearly 20,000 copies, but it can be guessed from recurrent complaints and appeals for subscriptions that actual readership is very much lower. Little imagination is used in party propaganda. In 1966, for example, *Fraternité* announced the forthcoming publication of a "History of the Party" in three volumes. But when details were given, this merely turned out to be a reprint of the 1950 *Rap-*

port Damas to the French National Assembly on the Ivory Coast disturbances of 1949 (see p. 111, note 13, above). At a cost of 10,000 C.F.A. francs ($40) a set, it is unlikely that many were sold; indeed, a year later *Fraternité* began to serialize the report verbatim.

Finally, the Congress of September 1965 formally nominated candidates to the National Assembly whose mandate expired in November. Its membership, which had been reduced from 100 to 70 in 1960, was increased to 85. Of the 70 members elected in 1960, only 48 were renominated. Of the remainder, approximately one-third had been appointed to other positions (ambassadors, heads of administrative agencies, etc.); about one-third had been arrested; and the others included some deaths and retirements. Official statements concerning the 37 new candidates stressed only that they included for the first time three women. The others appear to have been selected, as in the past, for their representative character according to ethnic criteria (including three foreign Africans), or to functional criteria (through their role in important associations); many of them were "old companions" as well. The elections for the National Assembly, the Presidency, and the General Councils at the departmental level—those elected in 1960 had never met—were held simultaneously in November 1965, following the pattern of 1959 and 1960. The new government which was formed in early 1966 signaled a deconcentration of the offices gathered under the Presidency during the crisis and the elimination of the last non-African from the cabinet. With two additions in later months, its total membership was brought to 18, excluding the President. Eight of the cabinet ministers are also members of the *Bureau Politique*; but this included several individuals who were coopted to the party's governing body because of their effective performance in government service. Several younger men with high professional qualifications were included as junior ministers and later promoted to full cabinet rank.

In other institutional spheres the regime remained consistent with its earlier approach, stressing the unification of major functional associations such as labor unions, businessmen's groups, women's organizations, and youth, under government and party sponsorship. It continued to experience difficulties in dealing with labor and particularly with university students. The *J.R.D.A.C.I.* was completely dismantled to avoid the formation of a party within the party; youths who wanted to participate in politics must do so as individual members of party sections and committees. After further manifestations of discontent among students, leading to 14 arrests, the government agreed to meet with them in January 1965.[5] In the course of a three-day confrontation the government agreed to release the students in exchange for a renewed pledge that Ivorians in France would abandon *U.G.E.C.I.* and join *U.N.E.C.I.*, as they had already promised to do in 1960 (see pp. 312-13, above). The government also accelerated the development of an adequate university in Abidjan in order to diminish the exodus to France. Although there were recurrent reports that the operation had been successful, new and more severe clashes occurred at the University of Abidjan in January 1967, and again following the Paris student uprising in 1968. This time, it was announced that *U.N.E.C.I.* itself was to be dissolved.

In spite of these occasional difficulties there was a general relaxation of the political atmosphere after 1965 and particularly after the fall of Kwame Nkrumah in early 1966 removed what the regime believed to be the main source of external support for internal opposition. In recent years there has been less reliance on coercive measures. A number of political prisoners were released to celebrate the 1965 elections, while others had their sentences reduced; the last seven, all of whom had initially received death sentences, were freed on the occa-

[5] Victory D. DuBois, "The Student-government conflict in the Ivory Coast," *American Universities Field Staff Reports Service*, West Africa Series, VIII, No. 1 (Ivory Coast), 1965.

sion of the state funeral for President Houphouet-Boigny's maternal aunt in May 1967. Sanwi exiles in Ghana were returned by the new Ghanaian government and forgiven after a public confession of their subversive activities. In 1966-67 the presence of President Nkrumah in Guinea was a new source of international tension, but there is no evidence that it affected internal political processes.

The general patterns of political control and of participation within the Ivory Coast version of the West African party-state appear to be fairly well institutionalized for the time being. Their major locus is not the party, nor the government, nor formal representative assemblies, but a national council convened by the President whenever important issues arise for a face-to-face encounter. The composition of this body varies, but most of the time it includes the *Bureau Politique*, the *Comité Directeur*, the remaining secretary-generals of hinterland sections, the secretary-generals of ethnic committees and of foreign African committees in Abidjan; the cabinet, heads of government services and agencies, prefects and sub-prefects; the National Assembly, members of the Economic and Social Council, and of the departmental General Councils; labor leaders, representatives of veterans and of women as well as student spokesmen; and finally "notables" not included in the above categories such as traditional chiefs who retain some influence and leaders of the Catholic, Protestant, Harrist, and Muslim religious communities. Since there is a lot of overlap among individuals in these various categories, the total probably ranges from 400 to 800 people. These estates-general function as a parliament with a limited but genuine role in decision-making, informing the President of the state of affairs in the country and disseminating his directives downward into every sphere of Ivory Coast society. They do not have the power to initiate decisions or to oppose Presidential initiatives, but rather to influence the extent of their implementation and to help establish priorities. Their negative response to the announcement of a new policy may even lead to the withdrawal of Presidential initiative, as seems to have been the case with the proposal to extend Ivory Coast citizenship to the foreign Africans who constituted about one-fourth of the country's total population in 1966-67.

At the top, all these institutional segments coalesce, but beneath, they remain distinct. The two key roles are probably those of the Party secretary-general and of the sub-prefect, who constitute the locus of interaction between local and national concerns. As we would expect, the relationships between the individuals who occupy these roles are tense. It is probably through an investigation of these relationships, however, that we can make further progress in understanding the process of political modernization in the Ivory Coast.

Modernization Policies

The study of political modernization, however, requires not merely an understanding of political institutions and processes, but also an understanding of the eventual political consequences of changes in the nonpolitical sectors of the society. These changes occur in part autonomously, from the point of view of the political system, but to a varying extent they are themselves the result of political decisions to pursue specific policies in such obviously important fields as education and economic development, as well as in less obvious ones which impinge on the character of social relationships, such as family law. Since this sphere requires basic research which is not yet available for the Ivory Coast, I shall merely sketch possible avenues of inquiry.

In Chapter V, I suggested that a key to the general policy orientation of the Ivory Coast could be found in the importance of economic considerations in the decision to sever ties between the *R.D.A.* and the French Communist Party in 1950-51. From then on, the achievement of maximum economic growth was given precedence over most other goals.

While most other underdeveloped countries also assign a high priority to this goal, the Ivory Coast regime is distinguished by its great consistency in this respect and by its willingness to sacrifice to it possible political satisfactions derived from militant nationalism. As elsewhere, economic policies are intimately connected with political policies, properly speaking; but while in some cases, such as Mali, economic decisions reflect a desire to achieve immediate regime needs, such as the creation of economic structures dominated by nationals and which provide the party-state with physical evidence of its reality, in the Ivory Coast these decisions reflect a belief that economic growth achieved by the most effective means, including dominance by foreign personnel and capital, will maximize the regime's capability for distributing material benefits to its population and hence foster support.[6]

The results of this orientation, whose details cannot be described here, have been that the Ivory Coast has experienced the most spectacular rate of economic growth in tropical Africa during the last decade. Even economists critical of the Ivory Coast's choices acknowledge a growth rate averaging 7.5 per cent a year from 1950 to 1960, and an increase in that rate to 11.5 per cent from 1960 to 1965.[7] Furthermore, there has been a relatively harmonious distribution of the increment among the regions and between economic sectors. Exceptionally, the government has not absorbed most of the increment; after the usual spurt around the time of independence, the growth of administrative expenditures has tapered off. Finally, in spite of the generally unfavorable terms of trade that prevail on the international markets for producers of tropical primary prod-

[6] For the contrast with Mali see my chapter, "The Political Use of Economic Planning in Mali," in Harry Johnson, ed., *Economic Nationalism in Old and New States* (Chicago: The University of Chicago Press, 1967), pp. 98-123.

[7] The most detailed study is Samir Amin, *Le Développement du Capitalisme en Côte d'Ivoire* (Paris: Les Editions de Minuit, 1967).

ucts, the Ivory Coast has achieved a favorable balance of payments.

Whether it is accurate to characterize the Ivory Coast pattern as "growth without development," as some have done, in the sense that its economic structures are unlikely to lead to take-off but rather to increased external dependence and internal blockages, is more properly an economic question. From a political point of view, there is little doubt that on balance economic policy choices have achieved the results desired by the regime at least in the short run. Demands continue to be voiced by workers, employees, and farmers for a greater share of material benefits, but it has been relatively easier to satisfy these demands than it would have been under conditions of economic stagnation. The political costs of avoiding socialism have been most obvious in the tense relationships between the political generations; but it is possible that these tensions are independent of ideology and in any case, they are somewhat balanced by the regime's ability to eventually coopt members of this generation by recruiting them to rewarding positions whose establishment is made possible by economic expansion itself. In the longer run, the regime is betting on the contributions that economic growth will make to the transformation of social relationships by fostering national transaction flows. That is a more problematic question, however, since political crises of great depth often occur precisely during periods of rapid economic growth as a result of the structural upheavals this growth generates in the society as a whole.[8]

The modernization of social relationships remains a subject of great concern not only for its own sake, but also because it is believed that it is a prerequisite to further economic development and that enemies of the regime can manipulate tra-

[8] Similar questions can be raised about the impact of educational development. See particularly, Rémi Clignet and Philip Foster, *The Fortunate Few: A Study of Secondary Schools and Students in the Ivory Coast* (Evanston. Northwestern University Press, 1966).

ditional relationships and beliefs to achieve their own political purposes, as revealed by the crisis of 1962-64. An investigation of policies designed to achieve this objective in the Ivory Coast and elsewhere is very much needed if we are to acquire a more balanced understanding of the politics of modernization. In the Ivory Coast itself, for example, the President's attack on fetishism and atheism during the Boka affair can be seen as the source of a campaign launched in early 1965 to raise funds for the building of Catholic, Protestant, Harrist, and Muslim religious edifices in Abidjan. This was an extra-governmental policy entrusted to the party and to specially created associations; but there is no doubt that it ranked in importance with major governmental decisions. Initially the President of the Republic, the President of the National Assembly, and the President of the Supreme Court each contributed approximately $1,000 to the fund; mandatory contributions were imposed on lower officials as well. A special assessment, to be collected by the party from each family in the country, with a lower rate in poorer areas of the North, was announced; the collection of this assessment constituted a major party activity during the rest of the year.

The primary strategy for modernizing social relationships has been the creation of a new national Civil Code pertaining especially to family law. Its purpose was stated clearly by President Yacé at the time of passage of the eight laws that compose it by the National Assembly in October 1964, when he said: "We believe, not without reason, that the social structures of the Republic have fallen behind the political and economic structures." The Code was radically innovative in that it deliberately avoided the codification of existing customary law and formally abolished three major social institutions: "bride price," i.e., dowry paid by men, in the West; "matriarchy," i.e., matrilineal inheritance from uncle to nephew, in the Akan culture area; and "polygamy" in the North as well as generally throughout the country. It was made clear from the outset, however, that the government had no intention of enforcing all the provisions of the Code everywhere and immediately. Presently, it stands as a major symbol of the orientation of the Ivory Coast toward modernity; it also provides a new legal framework toward which individuals already imbued with modern values can orient their behavior; and it serves as a model against which existing practices can be evaluated. The slow task of diffusing the norms the Code embodies is shared by the major political institutions: while the government has been investing resources in the creation of appropriate civil registry services at the local level, party officials and the party press function as educators.

But the main source of legitimacy for this and other major undertakings remains one individual, President Houphouet-Boigny. When he led the country in the celebration of a national funeral for his aunt at Yamoussoukro in 1967, he used the occasion for a sermon on the Ivory Coast's approach to modernization. Why, was he asked, did he celebrate a "pagan" funeral at great expense, when he had himself often urged the abolition of such practices? He explained that his aunt, who was in effect his mother since the death of the latter many years ago, had agreed to the abolition of "matriarchy," and specifically that she had foregone her son's right to inherit from the President, in exchange for the promise of a dignified funeral. Already, the President went on, he had knowingly violated his family traditions in order to modernize them: there were no human sacrifices at the funeral; the ceremonies were celebrated in broad daylight and in the presence of strangers; the burial was not carried out by family members but by a public undertaker. He deplored having to abide by the "anachronistic, non-economic" practice of displaying wealth which would then be withdrawn from commercial circuits, rather than invested, but concluded that deeply rooted traditions can be eliminated only gradually.

On this occasion the Party newspaper commented that the

Ivory Coast "was united as a single tribe and a single family." Although traditions remain important, the meeting at Yamoussoukro "proves that our country has not awaited the disappearance of tribal customs to achieve its unity." A nation is to be created not by revolution but by the growth of a common sentiment of belonging together. At Yamoussoukro, "all the races of the Ivory Coast" renewed their pledge of allegiance to Houphouet-Boigny, the cement that binds the nation.

The President of the Ivory Coast provides an interesting test of the heuristic value of the concept "charismatic leader" when used in a serious analytic sense to understand authority relationships in new nations. According to David Apter's recent restatement, "The true charismatic leader accepts his own mystique, his consciousness of his role in history, so that the public or a significant subgroup allows him to relate his personal political goals with a wider moral vision and thereby affect public action."[9] In the light of Houphouet-Boigny's effective role, as revealed by his repeated citation of personal beliefs and experiences to justify policies, as well as by the responses to these attempts on the part of much of the Ivory Coast public over a quarter of a century, I conclude that the concept does have some explanatory value in this case. But many others, including Apter, disagree.[10] Why? I think it is because in spite of efforts to dissociate the analytic use of charisma from its more popular usage, observers commonly seek evidence on the basis of their own subjective responses to a leader's presence. It is fairly obvious that an African leader who almost always dresses in elegant continental suits, who usually expresses himself, when speaking for foreign ears, in the vocabulary of the French Center-Left, and who has pursued "moderate" policies for nearly two decades, hardly evokes feelings of moral fervor among Western social scientists.

[9] David E. Apter, "Nkrumah, Charisma, and the Coup," *Daedalus*, 97, No. 3 (Summer 1968), p. 760.
[10] *Ibid.*, note 8, p. 789.

But our own feelings are a poor test of charisma in a new nation. For many Ivorians, the personal world of Houphouet-Boigny does provide a moral, future-oriented vision, on the basis of which they are willing to obey. Paradoxically, what makes it most difficult to perceive the charismatic aspects of Houphouet-Boigny's leadership is that the landscape has been filled out by an elaborate political machine. But does that not suggest that we may have before us a rare case of successful routinization of charisma?

✧ BIBLIOGRAPHY

BOOKS

Africanus. *L'Afrique Noire devant l'indépendance.* Paris: Plon, 1958.

Almond, Gabriel A., and Coleman, James S. (eds.). *The Politics of the Developing Areas.* Princeton: Princeton University Press, 1960.

Amon d'Aby, F. J. *La Côte d'Ivoire dans la cité africaine.* Paris: Larose, 1951.

———. *Le problème des chefferies traditionnelles en Côte d'Ivoire.* Abidjan: Privately printed, 1957.

Angoulvant, G. *Guide du commerce et de la colonisation à la Côte d'Ivoire.* Paris: Office Colonial, 1912.

———. *La pacification de la Côte d'Ivoire.* Paris: Larose, 1916.

Apter, David E. *The Gold Coast in Transition.* Princeton: Princeton University Press, 1955.

Avice, E. *La Côte d'Ivoire.* Paris: Société d'éditions géographiques, maritimes et coloniales, 1951.

Baumann, H., and Westermann, D. *Les peuples et les civilisations de l'Afrique.* Translated from the German by L. Homberger. ("Bibliothèque Scientifique.") Paris: Payot, 1957.

Blanchet, André. *L'itinéraire des partis africains depuis Bamako.* Paris: Plon, 1958.

Borkenau, Franz. *European Communism.* New York: Harper and Brothers, 1953.

Brogan, Dennis W. *The Development of Modern France.* London: Hamish Hamilton, 1940.

Bromberger, Merry, and Serge. *Les 13 complots du 13 mai.* Paris: Librairie Arthème Fayard, 1959.

Buell, Raymond Leslie. *The Native Problem in Africa.* Vol. I. New York: The Macmillan Company, 1928.

Capet, Marcel. *Traité d'économie tropicale: Les économies

d'A.O.F.? Paris: Librairie Générale de Droit et de Jurisprudence, 1958.

Carter, Gwendolen M. *Independence for Africa.* New York: Frederick A. Praeger, Inc., 1960.

Carter, Gwendolen M., and Brown, William O. (eds.). *Transition in Africa: Studies in Political Adaptation.* ("African Research Studies," No. 1, African Research and Studies Program, Boston University.) Boston: Boston University Press, 1958.

Chapman, Brian. *Introduction to French Local Government.* London: George Allen and Unwin Ltd., 1953.

Coleman, James Samuel. *Community Conflict.* (A publication of the Bureau of Applied Social Research, Columbia University.) Glencoe: The Free Press, 1957.

Coleman, James Smoot. *Nigeria: Background to Nationalism.* Los Angeles: University of California Press, 1958.

Coser, Lewis. *The Functions of Social Conflict.* Glencoe: The Free Press, 1956.

Cowan, L. Gray. *Local Government in West Africa.* New York: Columbia University Press, 1958.

Dadié, Bernard B. *Climbié.* Paris: Seghers, 1956.

De Gaulle, Charles. *The Call to Honor.* Vol. I of *The War Memoirs of General De Gaulle.* New York: The Viking Press, 1955.

Delafosse, Maurice. *Vocabulaire comparatif de soixante langues ou dialectes parlés en Côte d'Ivoire.* Paris: Leroux, 1904.

Delavignette, Robert. *Les paysans noirs.* Edition Nouvelle. Paris: Editions Stock, 1947.

———. *Service africain.* ("Problèmes et Documents.") Paris: Gallimard, 1946.

Deschamps, Hubert. *L'éveil politique africain.* ("Que sais-je?," No. 549.) Paris: Presses Universitaires de France, 1952.

Deutsch, Karl W. *Nationalism and Social Communication: An Inquiry into the Foundations of Nationality.* Jointly published. Cambridge, Mass.: The Technology Press of the

Massachusetts Institute of Technology, 1953; New York: John Wiley and Sons, Inc., 1953.

Devèze, Michel. *La France d'Outre-Mer.* Paris: Hachette, 1948.

Duverger, Maurice. *Political Parties: Their Organization and Activity in the Modern State.* Translated by Barbara and Robert North with a foreword by D. W. Brogan. New York: John Wiley and Sons, Inc., 1955.

Emerson, Rupert. *Empire to Nation: The Rise to Self-Assertion of Asian and African Peoples.* Cambridge, Mass.: Harvard University Press, 1960.

Fainsod, Merle. *How Russia Is Ruled.* Cambridge, Mass.: Harvard University Press, 1955.

Fauvet, Jacques. *La IVe République.* Paris: Librairie Arthème Fayard, 1959.

Finer, Herman. *The Major Governments of Modern Europe.* Evanston: Row-Peterson and Co., 1960.

———. *The Theory and Practice of Modern Government.* Rev. ed. New York: Henry Holt and Co., 1950.

Gouilly, Alphonse. *L'Islam dans l'Afrique Occidentale Française.* Paris: Larose, 1952.

Grivot, R. *Le Cercle de Lahou.* Paris: Larose, 1948.

Guernier, Eugène (ed.). *Afrique Occidentale Française.* ("L'Encyclopédie Coloniale et Maritime.") 2 vols. Paris: Encyclopédie Coloniale et Maritime, 1949.

Hardy, Georges. *Histoire sociale de la colonisation française.* Paris: Larose, 1953.

———. *Une conquête morale: l'enseignement en A.O.F.* Paris: Librairie Armand Colin, 1917.

Hodgkin, Thomas. *Nationalism in Colonial Africa.* ("Man and Society Series.") London: F. Muller, 1956.

Holas, B. *Les Sénoufo (y compris les Minianka)* ("Monographies Ethnologiques Africaines de l'Institut International Africain.") Paris: Presses Universitaires de France, 1957.

Hugnet, P. *Code du travail d'Outre-Mer: Texte et commentaires.* Paris: Recueil Sirey, 1953.

Joseph, Gaston. *La Côte d'Ivoire: le pays, les habitants.* Paris: Larose, 1917.

Kitchen, Helen (ed.). *The Educated African.* New York: Frederick A. Praeger, 1962.

Labouret, Henri. *Colonisation, colonialisme, décolonisation.* Paris: Larose, 1952.

———. *Paysans d'Afrique Occidentale.* ("Le Paysan et la Terre.") Paris: Gallimard, 1941.

Lecuyer, Roland. *La législation fiscale de Côte d'Ivoire.* Abidjan: Editions de la Côte d'Ivoire, 1955.

Luethy, Herbert. *France Against Herself.* New York: Frederick A. Praeger, Inc., 1955.

Mackenzie, W. J. M., and Robinson, Kenneth. *Five Elections in Africa.* Oxford: At the Clarendon Press, 1960.

Maguet, Edgard. *Concessions domaniales dans les colonies françaises.* Paris: Larose, 1930.

Mercier, René. *Le travail obligatoire dans les colonies africaines.* Paris: Larose, 1933.

Milcent, Ernest. *L'A.O.F. entre en scène.* Paris: Bibliothèque de l'Homme d'Action, 1958.

Mitterand, François. *Présence française et abandon.* ("Tribune Libre," No. 12.) Paris: Plon, 1957.

Mongo-Béti. *Le pauvre Christ de Bomba.* Paris: Robert Laffont, 1956.

Mouezy, Henri. *Assinie et le royaume de Krinjabo: Histoire et coutumes.* 2d ed. ("Les Origines de la Côte d'Ivoire [A.O.F.].") Paris: Larose, 1954.

Murdock, George Peter. *Africa: Its Peoples and Their Culture History.* New York: McGraw-Hill Book Company, Inc., 1959.

Neumann, Sigmund (ed.). *Modern Political Parties.* Chicago: The University of Chicago Press, 1956.

Padmore, George. *The Gold Coast Revolution.* London: Dennis Dobson Ltd., 1953.

Parsons, Talcott. *The Social System.* Glencoe: The Free Press, 1951.

Présentation de la Côte d'Ivoire. Abidjan: Editions du Centre I.F.A.N., 1953.

Raulin, Henri. *Mission d'étude des groupements immigrés en Côte d'Ivoire: problèmes fonciers dans les régions de Gagnoa et Daloa.* ("Documents du Conseil Supérieur des Recherches Sociologiques Outre-Mer," Fascicule 3.) Paris: Office de la Recherche Scientifique et Technique Outre-Mer, 1957.

Richard-Molard, Jacques. *Afrique Occidentale Française.* 3d ed. rev. Paris: Editions Berger-Levrault, 1956.

Rostow, W. W. *The Stages of Economic Growth: A Non-Communist Manifesto.* Cambridge: Cambridge University Press, 1960.

Roussier, Paul, *L'établissement d'Issiny, 1687-1702.* ("Publications du Comité d'Etudes Historiques et Scientifiques de l'Afrique Occidentale Française.") Paris: Larose, 1935.

Sarraut, Albert. *La mise en valeur des colonies françaises.* Paris: Payot et Cie., 1923.

Schumpeter, Joseph A. *Capitalism, Socialism and Democracy.* 3d ed. New York: Harper and Brothers Publishers, 1950.

Simmel, Georg. *Conflict.* Translated by Kurt H. Wolff. Glencoe: The Free Press, 1955.

Stillman, Calvin W. (ed.). *Africa in the Modern World.* Chicago: The University of Chicago Press, 1955.

Tauxier, Louis. *Nègres gouro et gagou.* Paris: Paul Geuthner, 1924.

———. *Le noir de Bondoukou: Koulangos, Dyoulas, etc.* ("Etudes Soudanaises.") Paris: E. Leroux, 1921.

———. *Le noir du Soudan: pays Mossi et Gourounsi.* ("Documents et Analyses.") Paris: Emile Larose, Librairie-Editeur, 1912.

Thompson, Virginia, and Adloff, Richard. *French West Africa.* Stanford: Stanford University Press, 1958.

Tournoux, J.-R. *Secrets d'état.* Paris: Plon, 1960.

Villamur, R. *Instructions aux administrateurs et chefs de poste de la Côte d'Ivoire sur leurs pouvoirs de répression en matière indigène, leurs fonctions d'officier de police judiciaire.* Paris: Lavauzelle, 1900.

Villamur, R., and Delafosse, M. *Les coutumes agni.* Paris: Challamel, 1904.

Villamur, R., and Richaud, L. *Notre colonie de Côte d'Ivoire.* Paris: Challamel, 1903.

Vincenti, M. J. *Coutumes attié.* Paris: Larose, 1914.

Williams, Philip. *Politics in Post-War France: Parties and Constitution in the Fourth Republic.* New York: Longmans, Green and Co., 1954.

Wilson, James Q. *Negro Politics: The Search for Leadership.* New York: The Free Press of Glencoe, 1960.

Wright, Gordon. *The Reshaping of French Democracy.* New York: Reynal and Hitchcock, 1948.

ARTICLES AND PERIODICALS

Abidjan-Matin, 1957-61.

Action Démocratique (Abidjan), 1958-59.

Afrique Nouvelle (Dakar), 1956-61.

Africa Special Report. Vols. I-IV. Washington: The African-American Institute, Inc., 1956-61.

Agence France Presse. *Bulletin Quotidien d'Information* (Abidjan), 1956-60.

Apter, David E. "The Role of Traditionalism in the Political Modernization of Ghana and Uganda," *World Politics*, XIII, No. 1 (October 1960), 45-68.

Apter, David E., and Lystad, Robert. "Bureaucracy, Party and Constitutional Democracy: An Examination of Political Role Systems in Ghana," *Transition in Africa: Studies in Political Adaptation.* Ed. by Gwendolyn M. Carter and William O. Brown. Boston: Boston University Press, 1958.

Apter, David E., and Rosberg, Carl G. "Nationalism and

Models of Political Change in Africa," *The Political Economy of Contemporary Africa.* Ed. by Donald P. Ray. ("Symposia Studies Series," No. 1) Washington, D.C.: The National Institute of Social and Behavioral Science, 1959, pp. 7-16.

Attoungblan (Abidjan), 1956, 1957.

Berg, Elliot J. "The Economic Basis of Political Choice in French West Africa," *The American Political Science Review,* LIV, No. 2 (June 1960), 391-405.

Bertho, Jacques. "La légende de la reine qui sacrifie son fils unique: comparaison entre la version des Baoulé de la Côte d'Ivoire et la version des Yorouba de la Nigéria," *Notes Africaines,* No. 31 (July 1946), p. 432. (Publication of I.F.A.N.)

Bingo: L'Illustré Africain (Dakar), No. 65, June 1958.

Boka, Ernest. "Côte d'Ivoire 1959. L'Education," *Marchés Tropicaux et Mediterranéens,* No. 701 (April 18, 1959), pp. 1025-36.

Bouscayrol, R. "Notes sur le peuple ébrié," *Bulletin I.F.A.N.*, XI, No. 3-4 (July-October 1949), 382-408.

Bulletin de l'Enseignement de l'A.O.F. (Gorée, Senegal), 1922-34.

Bulletin Mensuel de la Chambre de Commerce de la Côte d'Ivoire, 1957-60.

Le Canard Enchainé (Paris), 1959-60.

Carta, Jacques. "Côte d'Ivoire: la bourgeoisie noire s'installe," *France-Observateur,* September 3, 1959.

Chambre d'Agriculture et d'Industrie de la Côte d'Ivoire. Circulaire hebdomadaire d'Informations, 1957-61.

"Coffee," *Encyclopaedia Britannica.* 1956 ed. Vol. v.

Coleman, James Smoot. "Nationalism in Tropical Africa," *The American Political Science Review,* XLVIII, No. 2 (June 1954), 404-24.

La Concorde (Abidjan), 1956-57.

Corby, C. "Une assemblée locale dans l'Union Française, le

Grand Conseil de l'A.O.F.," *L'Afrique et l'Asie*, No. 22 (1953), pp. 122-51.

La Côte-d'Ivoire (Abidjan), 1945-52.

Le Démocrate (Abidjan), 1952-56.

Dresch, Jean. "Villes d'A.O.F.," *Cahiers d'Outre-Mer*, III, No. 11 (July-September 1950), 200-30.

Dunglas, S. "Coutumes et Moeurs des Bété," *Coutumiers Juridiques de l'A.O.F.*, III, 361-454.

Ebur (Abidjan), 1954.

L'Education Africaine (Gorée, Senegal), 1934-50.

"L'Enseignement en Côte d'Ivoire," *Chroniques d'Outre-Mer*, No. 7 (July-August 1953), pp. 37-38.

L'Essor (Bamako), 1959-61.

L'Etudiant d'Afrique Noire (Paris), No. 28, January-February 1960.

France-Afrique-Abidjan, 1953-55.

Fraternité (Abidjan), 1959-61.

Fréchou, Hubert. "Les plantations européennes en Côte d'Ivoire" (Reprint of Département de Géographie, No. 3), Dakar: Institut des Hautes Etudes. (First published in *Cahiers d'Outre-Mer*, No. 29 [January-March 1955].)

Gayet, Georges. "Les libanais et les syriens dans l'Ouest Africain," *Ethnic and Cultural Pluralism in Intertropical Countries.* Brussels: International Institute of Differing Civilizations, 1957, pp. 161-72.

Godin, M. "Côte d'Ivoire 1959. Problèmes démographiques," *Marchés Tropicaux et Méditerranéens*, No. 701 (April 18, 1959), pp. 1021-24.

Gonidec, P. F. "Les assemblées locales des Territoires d'Outre-Mer," *Revue Juridique et Politique de l'Union Française*, VI (1952), 327-38; VII (1953), 443-91.

———. "La Communauté." (Reprint Series No. 7.) London: University of London Institute of Commonwealth Studies, 1960. (First published in *Public Law*, Summer 1960.)

———. "L'évolution des Territoires d'Outre-Mer depuis 1946,"

Revue Juridique et Politique de l'Union Française, XII, No. 1 (January-March 1958), 43-92.

Grivot, R. "Agboville, esquisse d'une cité d'Afrique Noire," *Etudes Eburnéennes*, IV (1955), 84-107. (Publication of I.F.A.N.)

Guillemin, Philippe. "Les élus d'Afrique Noire à l'assemblée nationale sous la Quatrième République," *Revue Française de Science Politique*, VIII, No. 4 (December 1958), 861-77.

Hauser, A. "Les industries de transformation de la Côte d'Ivoire," *Etudes Eburnéennes*, IV (1955), 108-13. (Publication of I.F.A.N.)

Hodgkin, Thomas. "After Bamako," *Africa Special Report*, II (December 1957), 1-7.

Hodgkin, Thomas, and Schachter, Ruth. "French-Speaking West Africa in Transition," *International Conciliation*, No. 528 (May 1960), pp. 375-436.

Hoffman, Stanley H. "The French Constitution of 1958. I. The Final Text and Its Prospects," *The American Political Science Review*, LIII, No. 2 (June 1959), 332-57.

Holas, B. "Bref aperçu sur les principaux cultes syncrétiques de la Basse Côte d'Ivoire," *Africa*, XXIV, 55-61.

———. "Les peuplements de la Côte d'Ivoire," *Cahiers Charles de Foucauld*, VI (June 1954), 210-22.

Houphouet-Boigny, Félix. "Black Africa and the French Union," *Foreign Affairs*, XXXV, No. 34 (July 1957), 593-99.

———. "Réponse à d'Arboussier," *L'Afrique Noire*, No. 27, July 24, 1952.

"Industrialisation en Côte d'Ivoire." *Chambre de Commerce, Bulletin No. 8* (August 1958), pp. 14ff.

Joseph, Gaston. "Une atteinte à l'animisme chez les populations de la Côte d'Ivoire," *Bulletin du Comité d'Etudes Historiques et Scientifiques de l'A.O.F.* (1916), p. 344; (1917), p. 497.

Keita, Madeira. "Le Parti unique en Afrique," *Présence Africaine*, XXX (February-March 1960), 3-24.

Köbben, André. "Le planteur noir," *Etudes Eburnéennes*, v (1956), 7-190. (Publication of I.F.A.N.)

Kô-Moë: Organe des étudiants de la Côte d'Ivoire (Paris), 1958-59.

Lefèvre, Raymond. "Cacao et café, cultures révolutionnaires pour l'évolution des peuples de la forêt," *Revue Géographique, Humaine et Ethnologique*, No. 1 (October 1948-October 1949).

Lewis, W. Arthur. "The Economic Development of Africa," *Africa in the Modern World*. Ed. by Calvin W. Stillman. Chicago: University of Chicago Press, 1955.

Lipset, Seymour M. "Some Social Requirements of Democracy: Economic Development and Political Legitimacy," *The American Political Science Review*, LIII, No. 1 (March 1959), 69-105.

McCall, Daniel F. "Dynamics of Urbanization in Africa," *The Annals of the American Academy of Political and Social Science*, No. 298 (March 1955), pp. 151-60.

Mangeot (Colonel). "Manuel à l'usage des troupes opérants au Soudan français et plus particulièrement en zone saharienne," *Bulletin du Comité d'Etudes Historiques et Scientifiques de l'A.O.F.* (1922), pp. 590-607.

Marchés Coloniaux du Monde, 1945-56.

Marchés Tropicaux et Méditerranéens, 1956-61.

Mercier, Paul. "Political Life in the Urban Centers of Senegal: A Study of a Period of Transition," *Prod Translations*, III, No. 10 (June 1960), 3-20. (Originally appeared in *Cahiers Internationaux de Sociologie*, XXVII [July-December 1959], 55-84, under the title, "La vie politique dans les centres urbains du Sénégal." Translated by T. H. Stevenson.)

Merle, Marcel. "Les relations extérieures de la Côte d'Ivoire," *Revue Française de Science Politique*, LX, No. 3 (September 1959), 686-706.

Merton, Robert K., and Kitt, Alice S. "Contributions to the Theory of Reference Group Behavior," *Continuities in So-*

cial Research. Studies in the Scope and Method of "The American Soldier." Ed. by Robert K. Merton and Paul Lazarsfeld. Glencoe: The Free Press, 1950, pp. 40-105.

Miège, Jacques. "Les cultures vivrières en Afrique Occidentale. Etude de leur répartition géographique, particulièrement en Côte d'Ivoire," *Cahiers d'Etudes d'Outre-Mer*, VII, No. 25 (1954), 25-50.

Le Monde (Paris), 1946-61.

Le Monde Diplomatique, 1958-61.

Moynihan, Daniel P. "When the Irish Ran New York," *The Reporter*, June 8, 1961.

Pottier, R. "Les oeuvres missionaires," *Marchés Coloniaux*, April 28, 1951.

Présence Africaine, 1957-61.

Reubens, Edwin P. "Commodity Trade, Export Taxes and Economic Development," *Political Science Quarterly*, LXXI, No. 1 (March 1956), 42-70.

Robinson, Kenneth. "Constitutional Reform in French Tropical Africa." (Reprint Series No. 2.) London: University of London Institute of Commonwealth Studies, 1958. (First published in *Political Studies*, Vol. VI, No. 1.)

———. "Local Government Reform in French Tropical Africa," *Journal of African Administration*, VIII, No. 4 (October 1956), 179-85.

———. "Political Developments in French West Africa," *Africa in the Modern World.* Ed. by Calvin W. Stillman. Chicago: University of Chicago Press, 1955, pp. 140-81.

———. "The Public Law of Overseas France Since the War." (Reprint Series No. 1a.) Oxford: Oxford University Institute of Colonial Studies, 1954. (First published in *Journal of Comparative Legislation*, Vol. XXXII, 1950.)

Roche, J. "Aspects financiers de la loi-cadre," *Annales Africaines* (Published under the auspices of the Faculté de Droit et des Sciences Economiques of Dakar). Paris: Imprimerie Guillemot et de Lamothe, 1958.

Rouch, Jean. "Migrations au Ghana: Enquête 1953-55," *Journal de la Société des Africanistes*, Vol. XXXI, Nos. 1 and 2 (1956).

Rougerie, Gabriel. "Lagunaires et terriens de la Côte d'Ivoire," *Cahiers d'Outre-Mer*, III, No. 12 (October-December 1950), 370-77.

Rougerie, Gabriel. "Les pays agni du sud-est de la Côte d'Ivoire forestière," *Etudes Eburnéennes*, VI (1957), 7-213. (Publication of I.F.A.N.)

Schachter, Ruth. "Trade Unions Seek Autonomy," *West Africa*, January 19 and 26, 1957.

La Semaine en Afrique Occidentale Française, 1958-59.

Shils, Edward. "Political Development in the New States," *Comparative Studies in Society and History*, II, No. 3 (March 1960), 265-92; No. 4 (June 1960), 293-409.

"La situation de l'enseignement primaire en A.O.F.," *Afrique Française*, June 1923, p. 330.

"Soviet Views on Africa," *Soviet Survey*, April-June 1959, p. 40.

Tricart, Jean. "Les échanges entre la zone forestière de Côte d'Ivoire et les savanes soudaniennes," *Cahiers d'Outre-Mer*, IX, No. 35 (July-September 1956), 209-308.

L'Unité: Organe central du Bloc Populaire Sénégalais (Dakar), 1957-58.

Université de Dakar. *Annales Africaines* (Published under the auspices of the Faculté de Droit et des Sciences Economiques of Dakar). Paris: Imprimerie Guillemot et de Lamothe, 1958.

Vignaud, M. "Les élections du 2 janvier 1958 en Côte d'Ivoire," *Revue Française de Science Politique*, VI, No. 3 (July-September 1956), 570-82.

Wahl, Nicholas. "The French Constitution of 1958. II. The Initial Draft and Its Origins," *The American Political Science Review*, LIII, No. 2 (June 1959), 358-82.

Wallerstein, Immanuel. "Ethnicity and National Integration," *Cahiers d'Etudes Africaines*, II, No. 3 (1960), 132-39.

West Africa (London), 1952-61.

Wirth, Louis. "Urbanism as a Way of Life," *Reader in Urban*

Sociology. Ed. by Paul K. Hatt and Albert J. Reiss. Glencoe: The Free Press, 1951, pp. 32-48.

Zolberg, Aristide R. "Effets de la structure d'un parti politique sur l'intégration nationale," *Cahiers d'Etudes Africaines*, I, No. 3 (January 1961), 140-49.

———. "Politics in the Ivory Coast," *West Africa*, July 30, August 6, August 20, 1960.

GOVERNMENT DOCUMENTS

FRANCE

Ambassade de France. Service de Presse et d'Information. "*African Affairs*," Nos. 1-20. New York, 1953-58.

———. Service de Presse et d'Information. "*Speeches and Press Conferences*," Nos. 84 and 85. New York, 1957.

Annales de l'Assemblée Nationale Constituante élue le 21 octobre 1945. *Débats*, Vol. II-IV, 1946.

Assemblée Nationale. Annexe No. 11348 à la séance du 21 novembre 1950. *Rapport fait au nom de la Commission chargée d'enquêter sur les incidents survenus en Côte d'Ivoire par M. Damas, député.*

Débats parlementaires. *Assemblée Nationale.* 1946-58.

Débats parlementaires. *Conseil de la République.* 1946-58.

Ministère de la France d'Outre-Mer. *Ecole Nationale de la France d'Outre-Mer.* Paris: Librairie Vuibert, 1955.

———. *Reformes apportées dans les Territoires relevant du Ministère de la France d'Outre-Mer par la Loi No. 56,619 du 23 juin 1956, dite Loi-Cadre, et par les décrets pris pour son application.* August 1957. (Mimeographed)

———. Service des Statistiques. *Etude démographique du premier secteur agricole de la Côte d'Ivoire*, 1957-58.

———. Service des Statistiques. *Inventaire social et économique des Territoires d'Outre-Mer.* 1950-55. Paris: Imprimerie Nationale, 1957.

French West Africa

Gouvernement-Général de l'Afrique Occidentale Française. *Annuaire 1922.* Dakar: Imprimerie du Gouvernement, 1922.

———. "*Organisation municipale des communes de plein exercice en Afrique Occidentale Française. Recueil des Textes.*" n.d. (Mimeographed.)

Haut-Commissariat de la République en Afrique Occidentale Française. Direction Générale des Services Economiques et du Plan. *A.O.F. 1957: Tableaux économiques.* Dakar, 1957.

Haut-Commissariat de la République en Afrique Occidentale Française. Service de Coordination des Affaires Economiques et du Plan. *Les Salaires en A.O.F.: Salaires minima hiérarchisés au 28 février 1958.* Dakar, 1958.

Ivory Coast

Assemblée Constituante. "*Avant-projet constitutionnel. Procès-verbal des travaux de la Commission spéciale.*" Abidjan, 1959. (Mimeographed.)

———. "*Procès-verbaux des débats,*" December 1958-March 1959. (Mimeographed.)

Assemblée Législative. *Projet de Loi relatif au statut général de la fonction publique.* Deuxième Session Extraordinaire. 1959.

———. *Projet de statut général de la fonction publique territoriale: Exposé des motifs.* n.d.

Assemblée Territoriale. "*Création, formation et règlement intérieur.*" Abidjan, n.d. (Mimeographed.)

———. "*Procès-verbaux des débats,*" 1952-58. (Mimeographed and typewritten.)

Budget du service local. 1946-57. Abidjan: Imprimerie du Gouvernement, 1946-57.

Budget. 1958-59. Abidjan: Imprimerie du Gouvernement, 1958-59.

Conseil Général. "*Procès-verbaux des débats,*" 1946-52. (Mimeographed and typewritten.)

Journal Officiel de la Côte d'Ivoire, 1946-58.

Journal Officiel de la République de Côte d'Ivoire. *Débats de l'Assemblée Législative*, 1959-60.

Journal Officiel de la République de Côte d'Ivoire. *Débats de l'Assemblée Nationale*, 1960-61.

Ministère de l'Agriculture. *"Programme Agricole."* Abidjan, 1959. (Mimeographed.)

Ministère de l'Intérieur. Direction des Affaires Politiques. Electoral Returns, 1945-59.

———. Service de l'Information. *"La santé en Côte d'Ivoire."* Abidjan, 1956. (Mimeographed.)

Ministère du Plan. Service de la Statistique Générale et de la Mécanographie. *Bulletin statistique mensuel*, 1957-61.

———. Service de la Statistique. *Inventaire économique de la Côte d'Ivoire, 1947-56*. Abidjan: Imprimerie du Gouvernement, 1958.

———. Service de la Statistique. *Bulletin statistique mensuel.* Supplément trimestriel (Deuxième Trimestre), 1959. (Mimeographed.)

———. *Troisième plan quadriennal de développement économique et social, 1958-62*. Abidjan: Imprimerie du Gouvernement, 1958.

Programme d'action économique, politique et sociale. Abidjan: Imprimerie du Gouvernement, 1933.

Rapport au Conseil Général, 1951. Abidjan: Imprimerie Officielle, 1951.

Rapport au Conseil Général présenté à la session budgétaire 1952 de l'Assemblée Territoriale de la Côte d'Ivoire par M. le Gouverneur Bailly. Abidjan: Imprimerie du Gouvernement, 1952.

Rapport présenté à la session budgétaire 1953 de l'Assemblée Territoriale de la Côte d'Ivoire par M. le Gouverneur Bailly. Abidjan: Imprimerie Officielle, 1953.

Rapport présenté à la session budgétaire 1954 de l'Assemblée

Territoriale de la Côte d'Ivoire par M. le Gouverneur Messmer. Abidjan: Imprimerie du Gouvernement, 1954.

Rapport présenté à la session budgétaire 1955 de l'Assemblée Territoriale de la Côte d'Ivoire par M. le Gouverneur Messmer. Abidjan: Imprimerie du Gouvernement, 1955.

Rapport présenté à la session budgétaire 1956 de l'Assemblée Territoriale de la Côte d'Ivoire par M. le Gouverneur Lami. Abidjan: Imprimerie Officielle de la Côte d'Ivoire, 1956.

Rapport sur l'activité générale et sur la marche des services publics territoriaux pour l'année 1957 présenté à l'Assemblée Territoriale par M. le Vice-President du Conseil du Gouvernement. Abidjan: Imprimerie du Gouvernement, 1958.

Service de l'Agriculture. *Enquête agricole sur le premier secteur de la Côte d'Ivoire, juin 1956-janvier 1957.* Abidjan: Imprimerie du Gouvernement, 1958.

———. *Rapport Annuel.* Année 1938. (Typescript.)

Service de l'Information. *Discours prononcé par M. le Ministre d'Etat Houphouet-Boigny au Stade Géo-André à Abidjan le 7 septembre 1958.* Abidjan: Imprimerie du Gouvernement, 1958.

———. *Discours et allocutions de M. le Ministre Houphouet-Boigny.* Abidjan: Imprimerie du Gouvernement, 1956.

———. "*Les industries en Côte d'Ivoire,*" n.d. (Mimeographed.)

Service de la Statistique. Commune d'Abidjan. "*Recensement de la Commune d'Abidjan.*" Abidjan, October 1956. (Mimeographed.)

Service de la Statistique et de la Mécanographie. *Enquête nutrition-niveau de vie. Subdivision de Bongouanou, 1955-56.* Abidjan, 1958.

———. "*Recensement des centres urbains du Territoire, 1957.*" (Mimeographed.)

Other

Communauté Economique Européenne. Direction Générale des Pays et Territoires d'Outre-Mer. *Etude sur le marché du café*. Document de Travail VIII/D/112/c-f, January 1960.

Great Britain. Colonial Office. *Report on the Commission of Enquiry into Disturbances in the Gold Coast, 1948*. London: His Majesty's Stationery Office, 1948.

ORGANIZATIONAL REPORTS AND PROCEEDINGS

D'Arboussier, Gabriel. "Rapport au Comité de Coordination," May 1, 1949. (Mimeographed.)

Houphouet-Boigny, Félix. "Proclamation de foi," November 1946. (In the files of the Ministry of the Interior, Ivory Coast.)

———. Rapport du Président Houphouet-Boigny au Congrès Extraordinaire du Rassemblement Démocratique Africain. Abidjan: Imprimerie du Gouvernement, 1959.

Jeunesse RDA de Côte d'Ivoire, Proceedings of the founding Congress of the J.R.D.A.C.I. Held in Abidjan, March 1959. (Mimeographed.)

Parti Démocratique de Côte d'Ivoire. Proceedings of the Territorial Congress Held in Abidjan, March 1959. (Mimeographed.)

Rassemblement Démocratique Africain. Proceedings of the Second Interterritorial Congress Held in Abidjan, 1949. (Mimeographed.)

———. Proceedings of the Third Interterritorial Congress Held in Bamako, September 1957. (Mimeographed.)

Union des Travailleurs de Côte d'Ivoire. Proceedings of Congress Held in Abidjan, July 1959. (Mimeographed.)

UNPUBLISHED MATERIAL

Dupire, Marguerite. Unpublished study of land and migration problems in Aboisso, 1958. (Typescript.)

Dejaument, M. A. "Notes sur l'évolution politique du R.D.A." Paper presented at the round table of the Association Française de Science Politique on African political parties, March 1959.

Schachter, Ruth. "Political Parties in French West Africa." Unpublished Ph.D. dissertation, Oxford University, 1958.

S.E.R.E.S.A. "Rapport d'enquête dans le secteur agricole." Abidjan, 1959. (Mimeographed.)

Wallerstein, Immanuel. "The Emergence of Two West African Nations." Unpublished Ph.D. dissertation, Columbia University, 1959.

INDEX*

* This index does not have entries for material from the Introduction to Revised Edition or from the Appendix.

INDEX